S0-AAF-185

DEVILS' LINE 3

A Vertical Comics Edition

Translation: Jocelyne Allen
Production: Risa Cho
          Lorina Mapa

© 2016 Ryo Hanada. All rights reserved.
First published in Japan in 2014 by Kodansha, Ltd., Tokyo
Publication rights for this English edition arranged through Kodansha, Ltd., Tokyo
English language version produced by Vertical, Inc., New York

Translation provided by Vertical Comics, 2016
Published by Vertical, Inc., New York

Originally published in Japanese as *Debiruzurain 3* by Kodansha, Ltd., 2014
Debiruzurain first serialized in *Morning two*, Kodansha, Ltd., 2013.

This is a work of fiction.

ISBN: 978-1-942993-39-1

Manufactured in the United States of America

First Edition

Vertical, Inc.
451 Park Avenue South
7th Floor
New York, NY 10016
www.vertical-comics.com

Vertical books are distributed through Penguin-Random House Publisher Services.

OUR BOSS

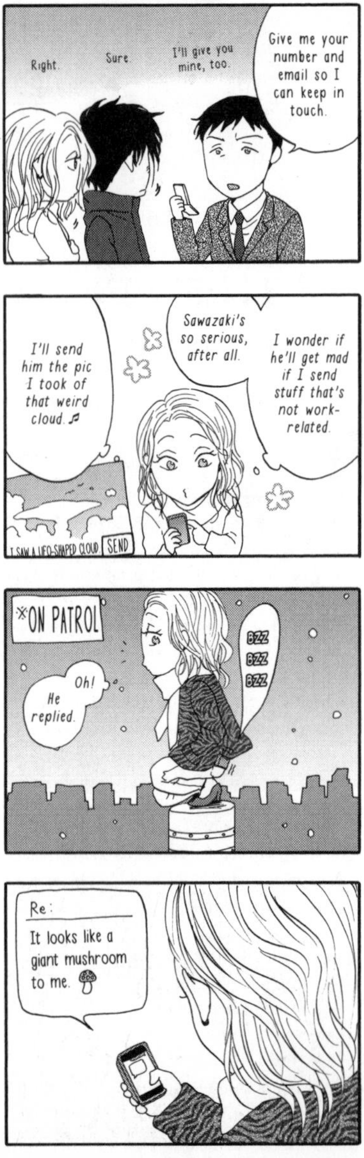

Give me your number and email so I can keep in touch.
I'll give you mine, too.
Sure.
Right.
I wonder if he'll get mad if I send stuff that's not work-related.
Sawazaki's so serious, after all.
I'll send him the pic I took of that weird cloud. ♬
I SAW A UFO-SHAPED CLOUD
SEND
BZZ BZZ BZZ
※ON PATROL
Oh!
He replied.
Re:
It looks like a giant mushroom to me.

NOT ANZAI'S EQUIPMENT

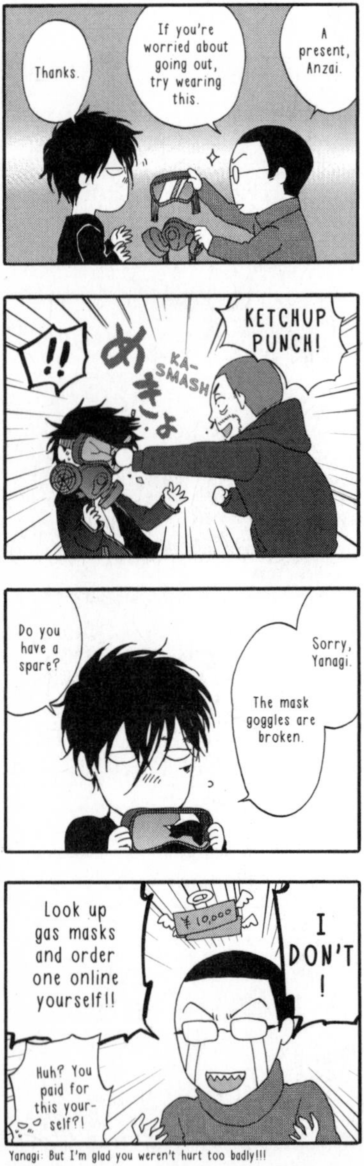

A present, Anzai.
If you're worried about going out, try wearing this.
Thanks.
KETCHUP PUNCH!
KA-SMASH
めきょ
!!
Sorry, Yanagi.
The mask goggles are broken.
Do you have a spare?
I DON'T!
¥10,000
Look up gas masks and order one online yourself!!
Huh? You paid for this your-self?!

Yanagi: But I'm glad you weren't hurt too badly!!!

ONLY ON DAYS LIKE THIS

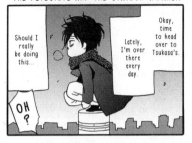

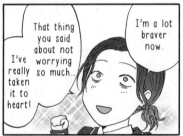

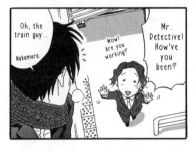

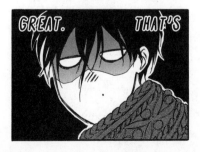

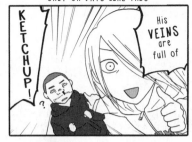

His VEINS are full of
KETCHUP!
You talk too much, KETCHUP!
KAPOW
YUKI KUN♡
HOT'N TOASTY
I wrote everyone's name on theirs! ♡
Yum!

THE DETECTIVE AND THE STATION WORKER

Okay, time to head over to Tsukasa's.
Lately, I'm over there every day.
Should I really be doing this...
OH?
Mr. Detective! How've you been?
Wow! Are you working?
Oh, the train guy...
Nakamura.
I'm a lot braver now.
That thing you said about not worrying so much...
I've really taken it to heart!
THAT'S
GREAT.

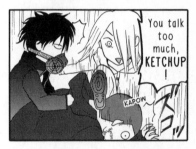

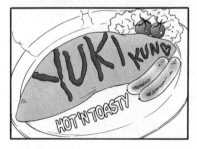

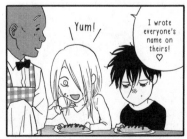

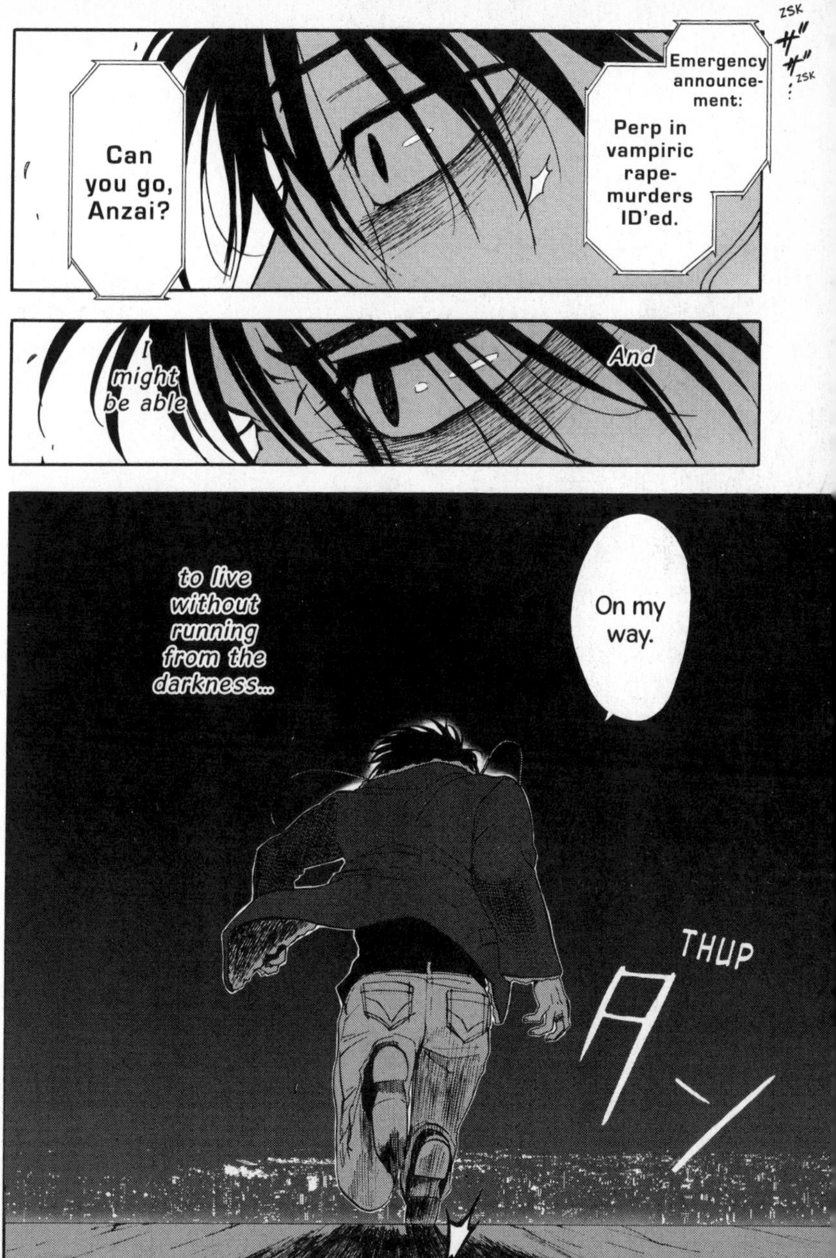
ZSK
ZSK
Emergency announcement:
Perp in vampiric rape-murders ID'ed.
Can you go, Anzai?
And
I might be able
On my way.
to live without running from the darkness...
THUP

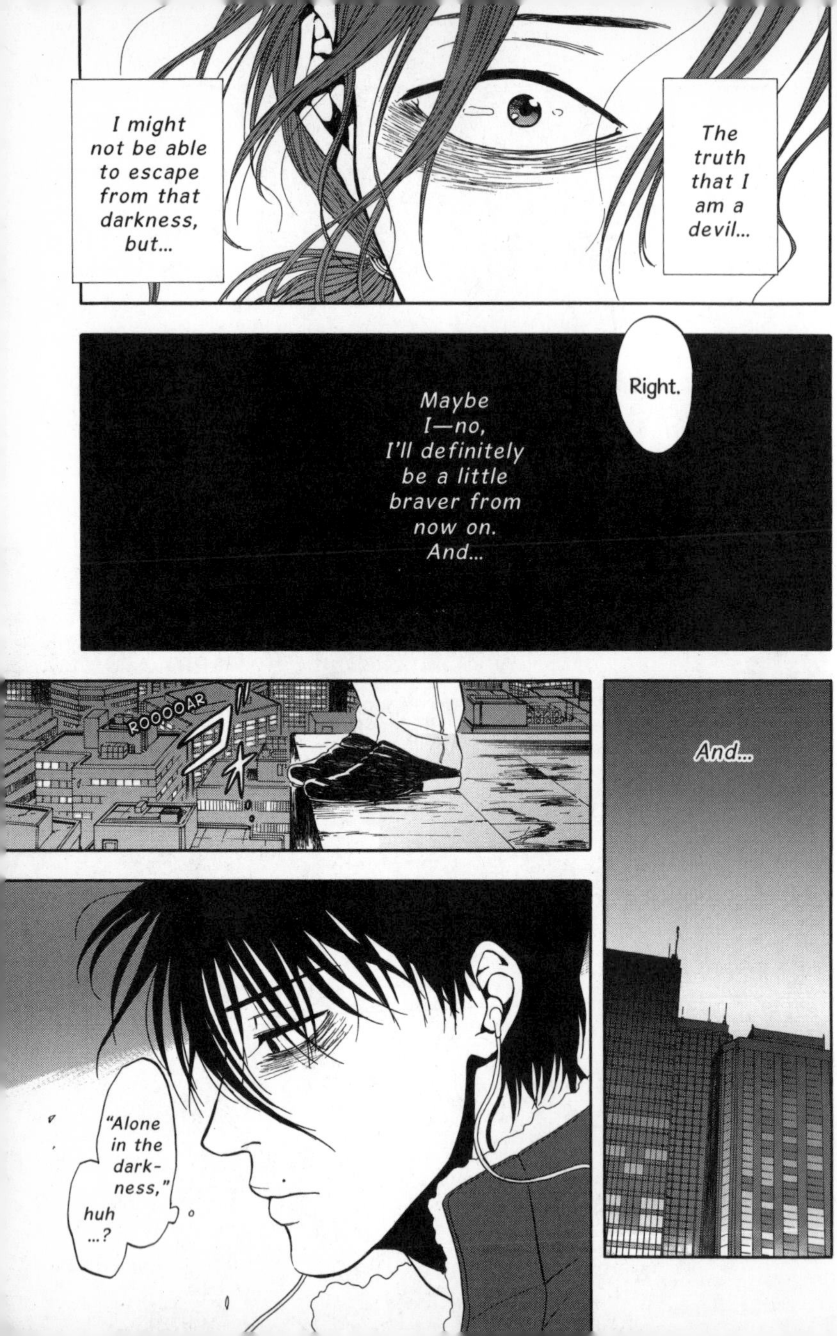
The truth that I am a devil...
I might not be able to escape from that darkness, but...
Right.
Maybe I—no, I'll definitely be a little braver from now on. And...
And...
ROOOOAR
"Alone in the dark-ness," huh ...?

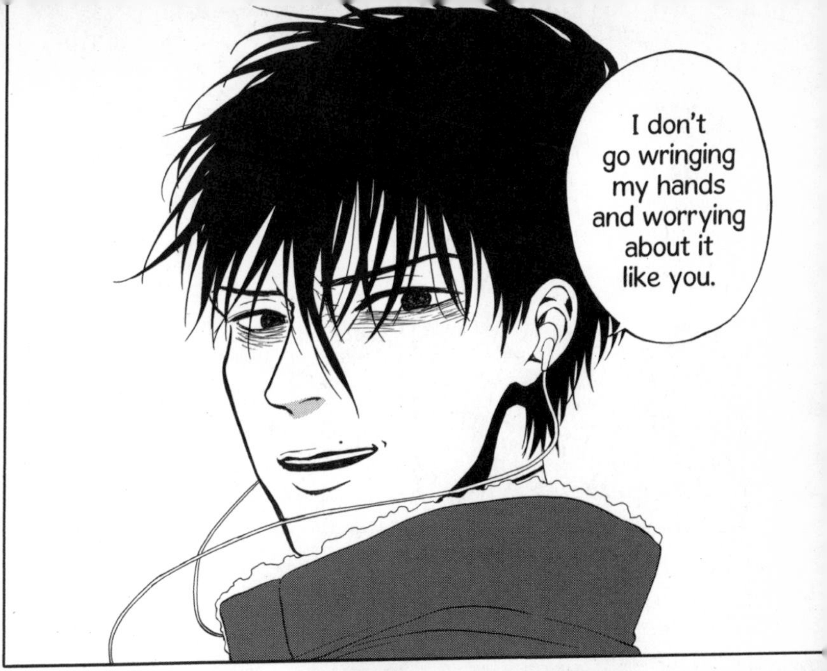
I don't go wringing my hands and worrying about it like you.

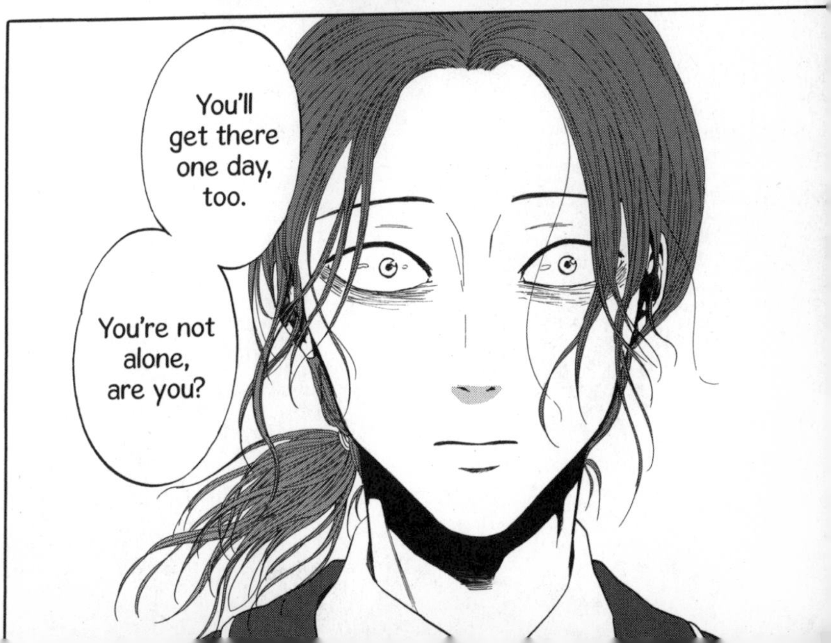
You'll get there one day, too.
You're not alone, are you?

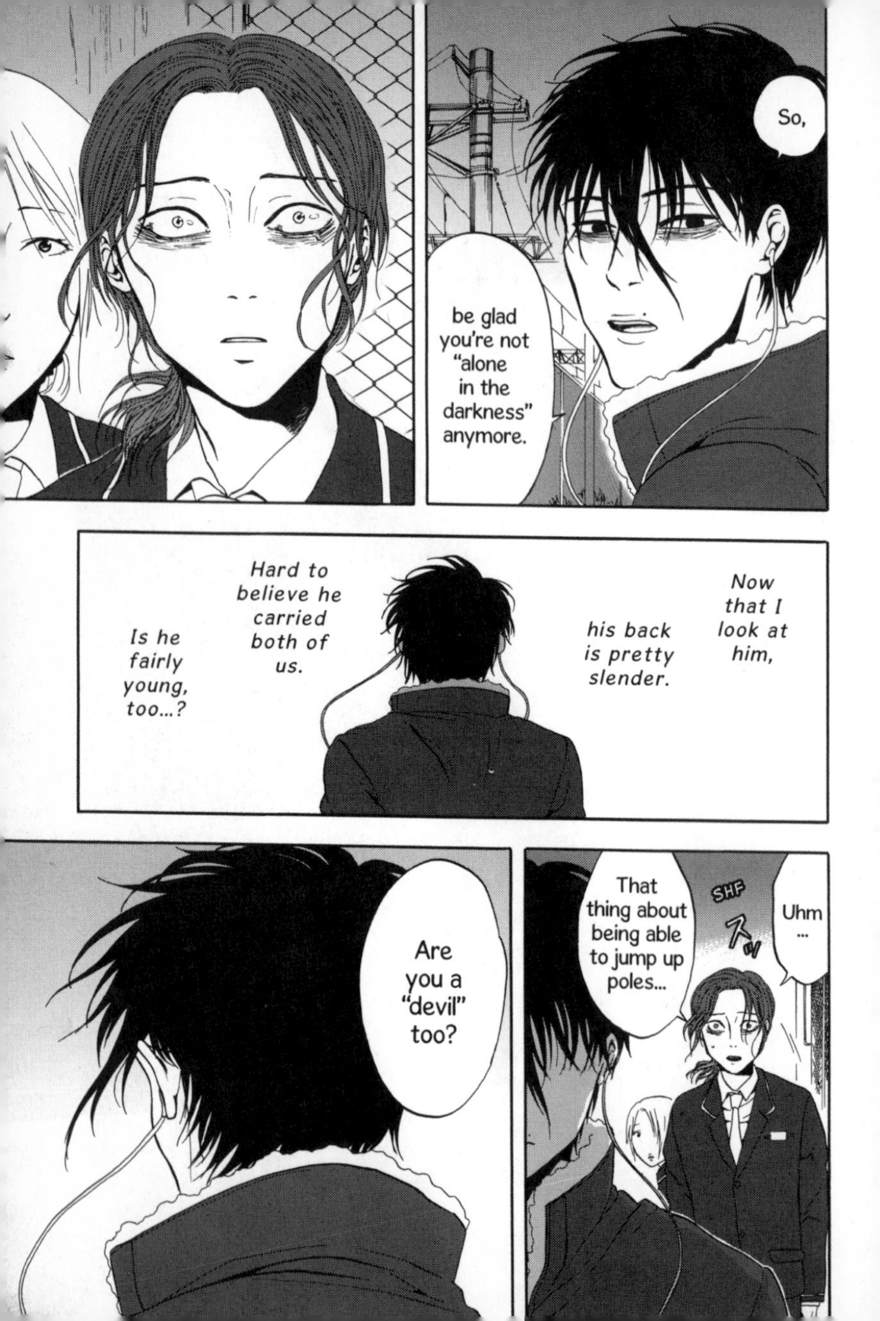
So,
be glad you're not "alone in the darkness" anymore.
Now that I look at him,
his back is pretty slender.
Hard to believe he carried both of us.
Is he fairly young, too...?
Uhm ...
SHF
スッ
That thing about being able to jump up poles...
Are you a "devil" too?

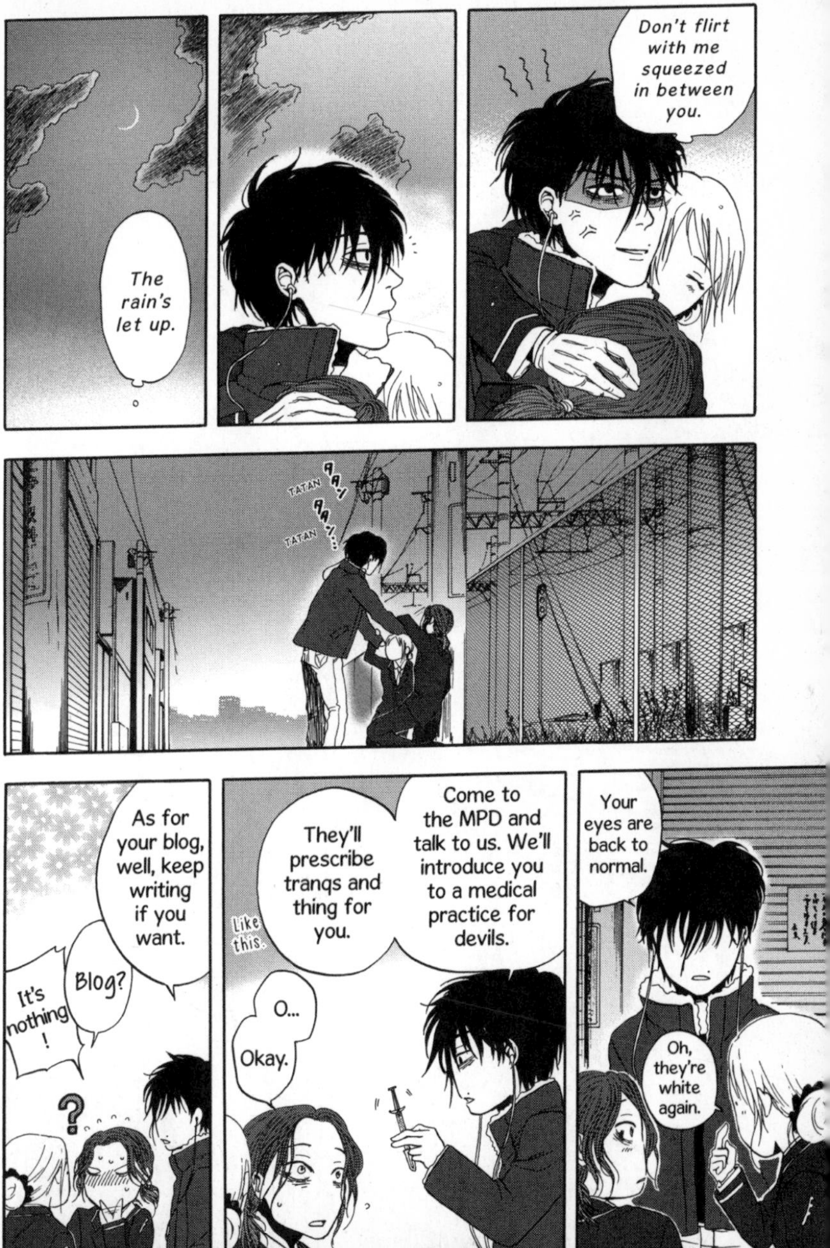
Don't flirt with me squeezed in between you.
The rain's let up.
TATAN
TATAN
Your eyes are back to normal.
Oh, they're white again.
Come to the MPD and talk to us. We'll introduce you to a medical practice for devils.
They'll prescribe tranqs and thing for you.
Like this.
O...
Okay.
As for your blog, well, keep writing if you want.
Blog?
It's nothing!

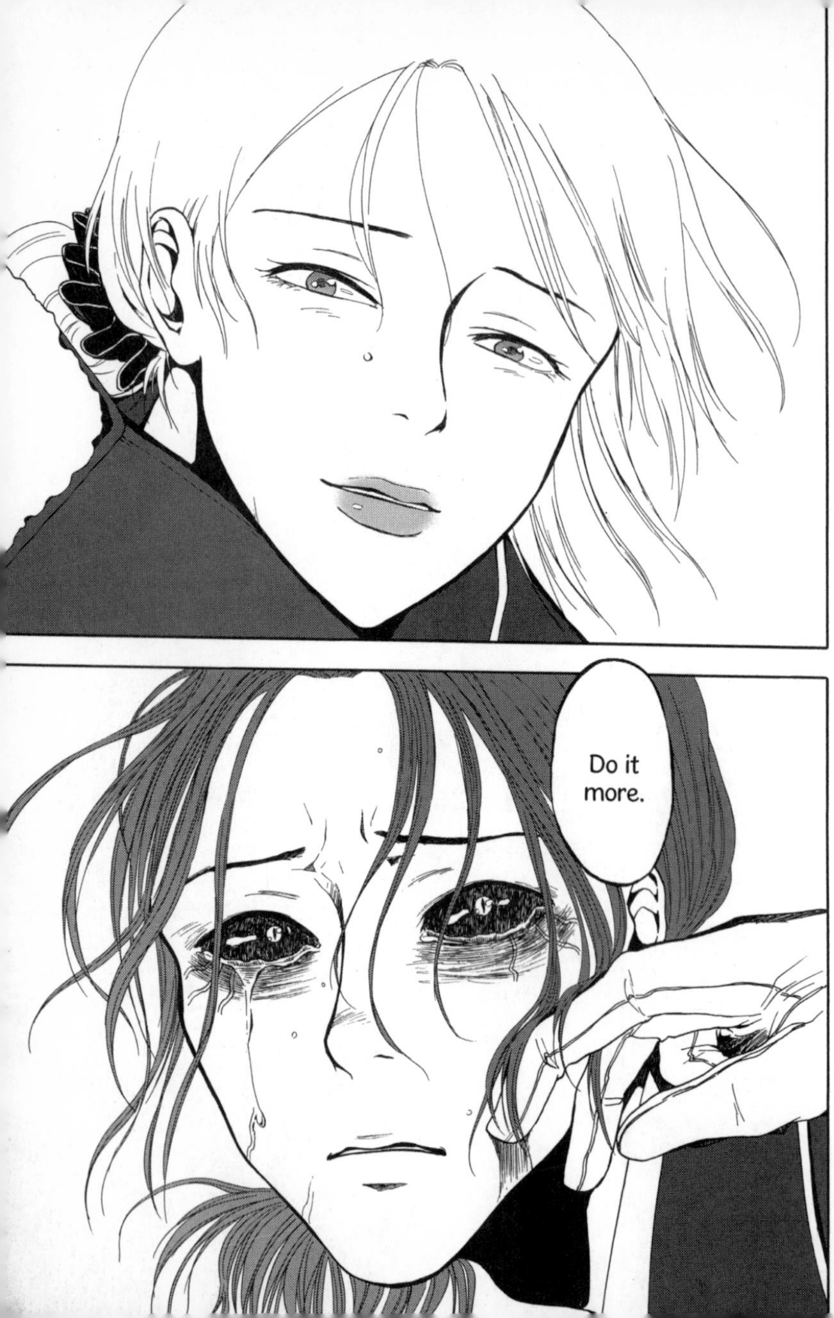
Do it more.

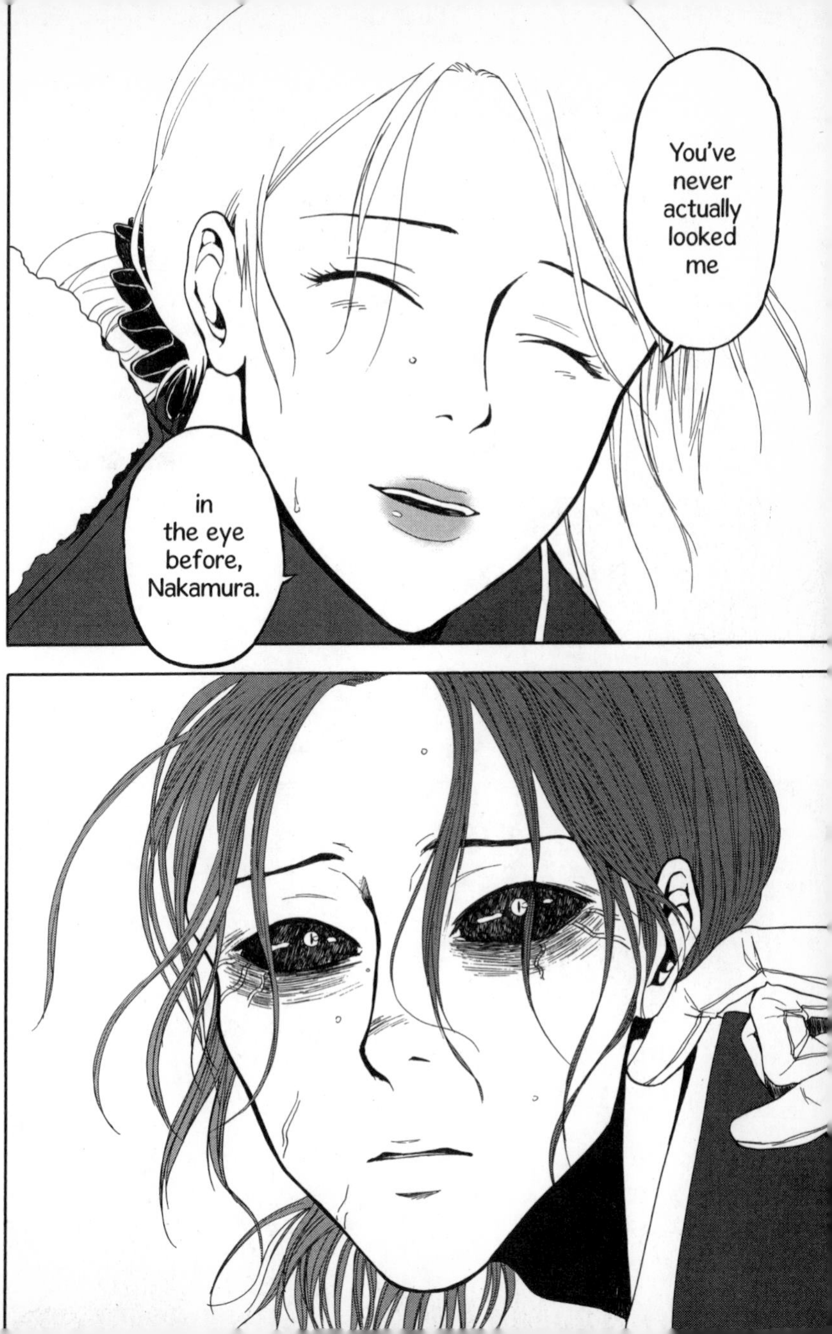
You've never actually looked me
in the eye before, Nakamura.

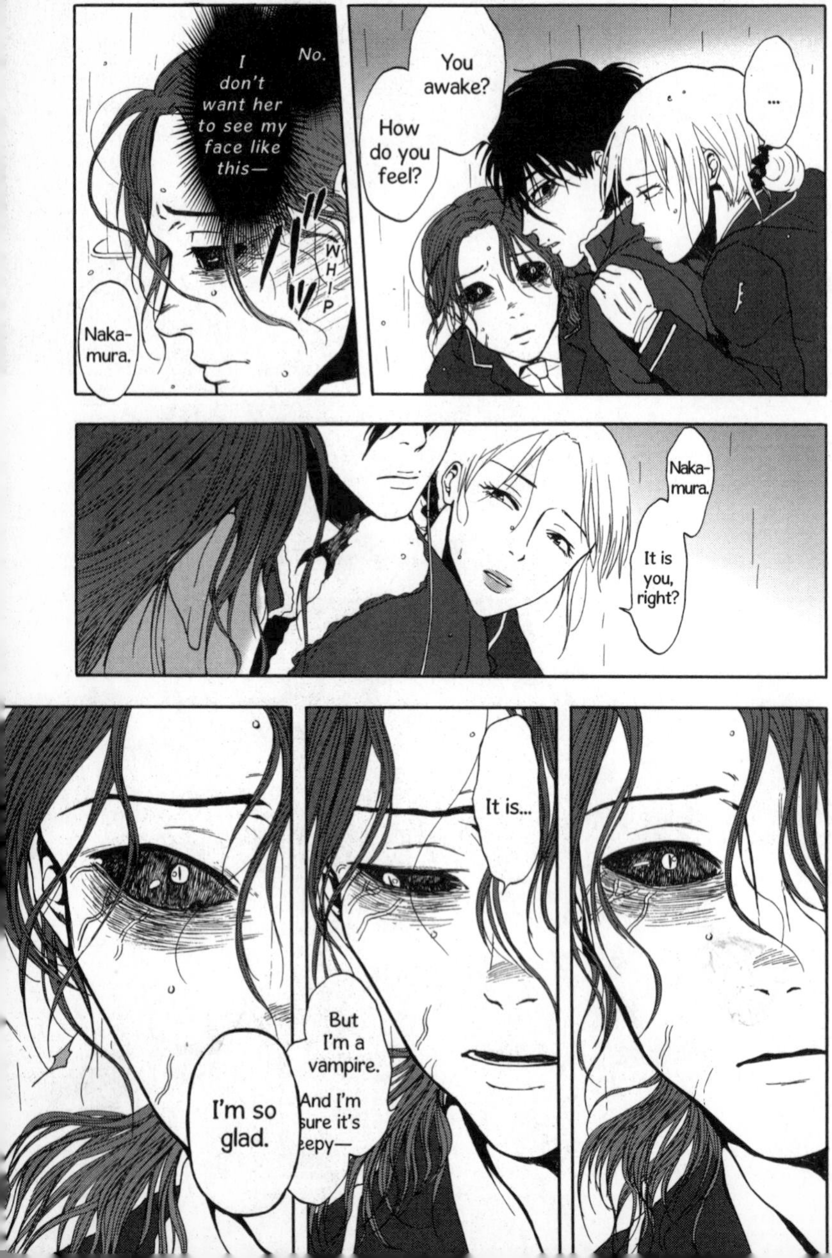
...
You awake?
How do you feel?
No.
I don't want her to see my face like this—
WHIP
Naka-mura.
Naka-mura.
It is you, right?
It is...
But I'm a vampire.
And I'm sure it's eepy—
I'm so glad.

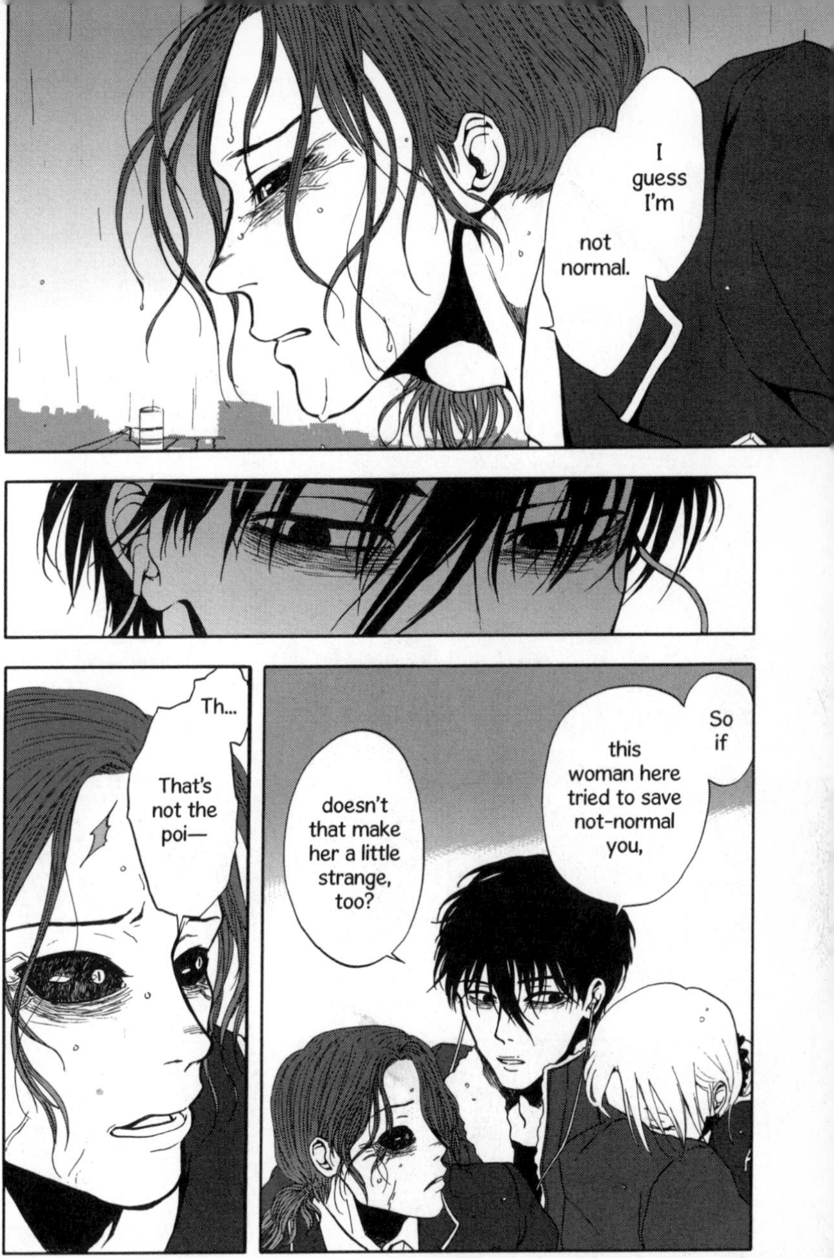
I guess I'm not normal.
So if this woman here tried to save not-normal you,
doesn't that make her a little strange, too?
Th...
That's not the poi—

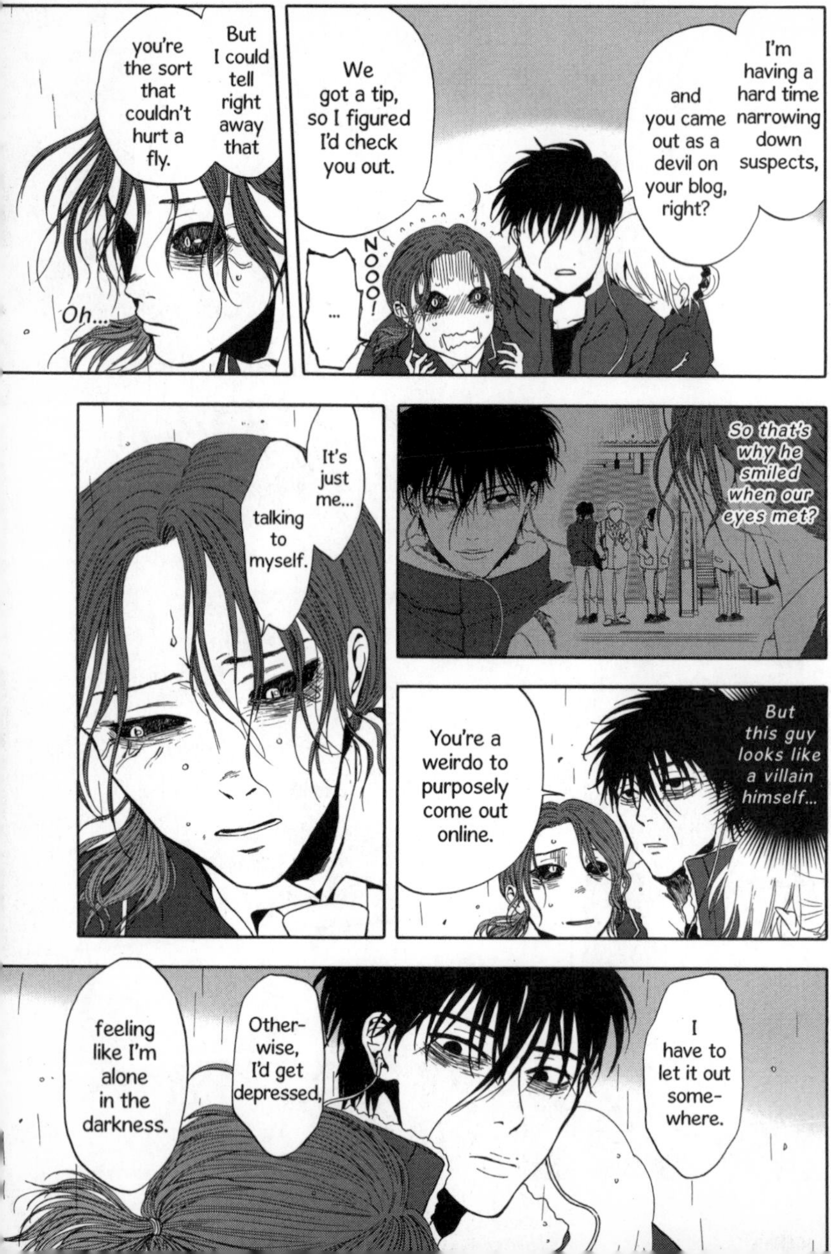
I'm having a hard time narrowing down suspects,
and you came out as a devil on your blog, right?
We got a tip, so I figured I'd check you out.
NOOOO!
...
But I could tell right away that
you're the sort that couldn't hurt a fly.
Oh...
So that's why he smiled when our eyes met?
But this guy looks like a villain himself...
You're a weirdo to purposely come out online.
It's just me...
talking to myself.
I have to let it out somewhere.
Otherwise, I'd get depressed,
feeling like I'm alone in the darkness.

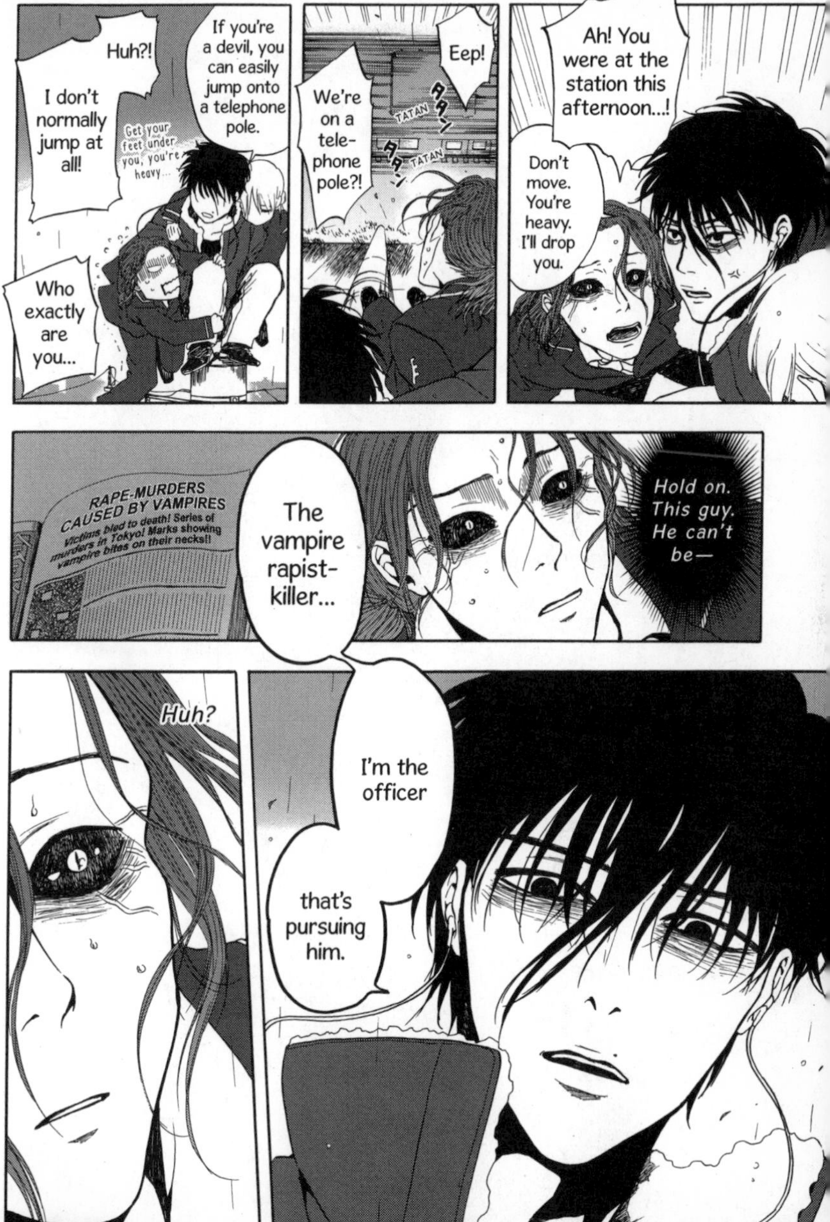
Ah! You were at the station this afternoon...!
Don't move. You're heavy. I'll drop you.
Eep!
We're on a telephone pole?!
TATAN
TATAN
If you're a devil, you can easily jump onto a telephone pole.
Huh?!
I don't normally jump at all!
Get your feet under you, you're heavy...
Who exactly are you...
Hold on. This guy. He can't be—
The vampire rapist-killer...
RAPE-MURDERS CAUSED BY VAMPIRES
Victims bled to death! Series of murders in Tokyo! Marks showing vampire bites on their necks!!
I'm the officer
that's pursuing him.
Huh?

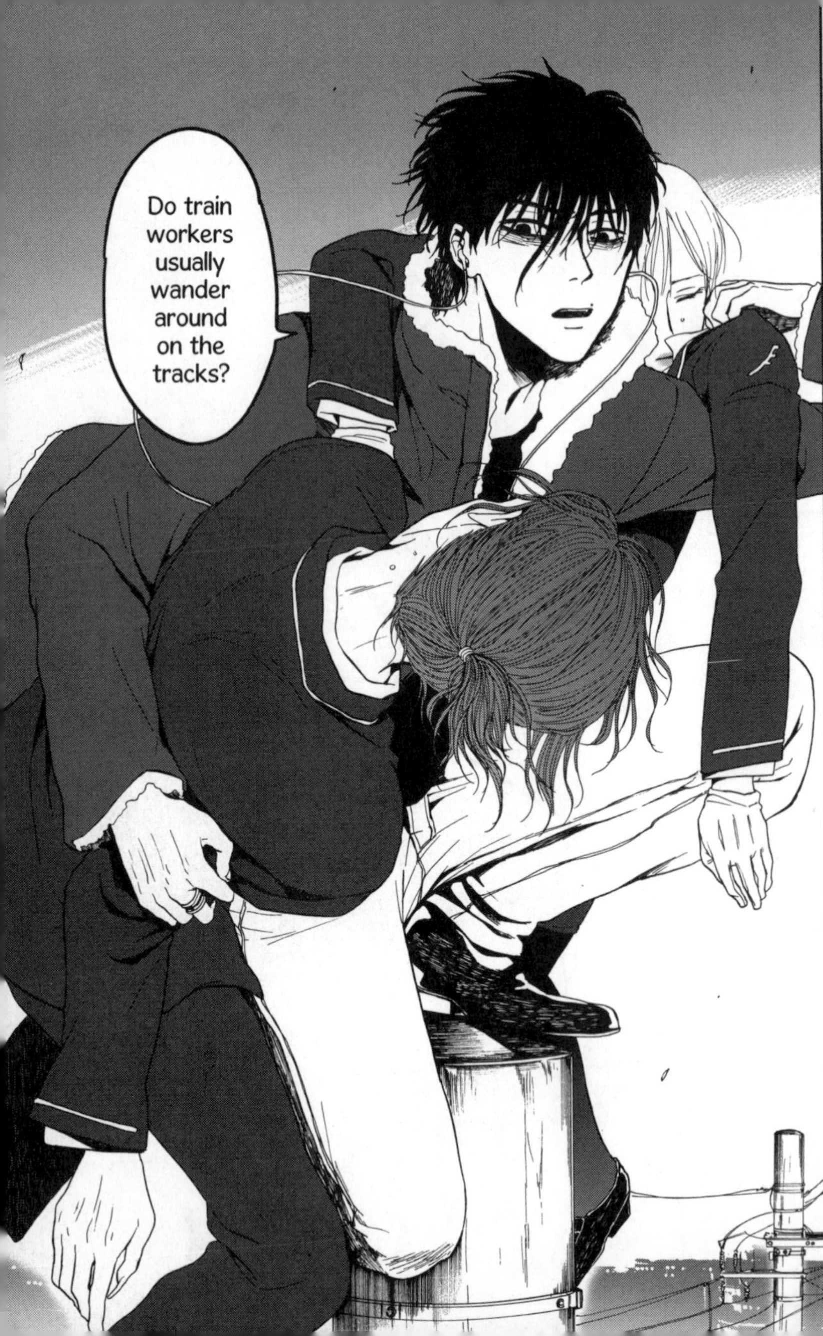
Do train workers usually wander around on the tracks?

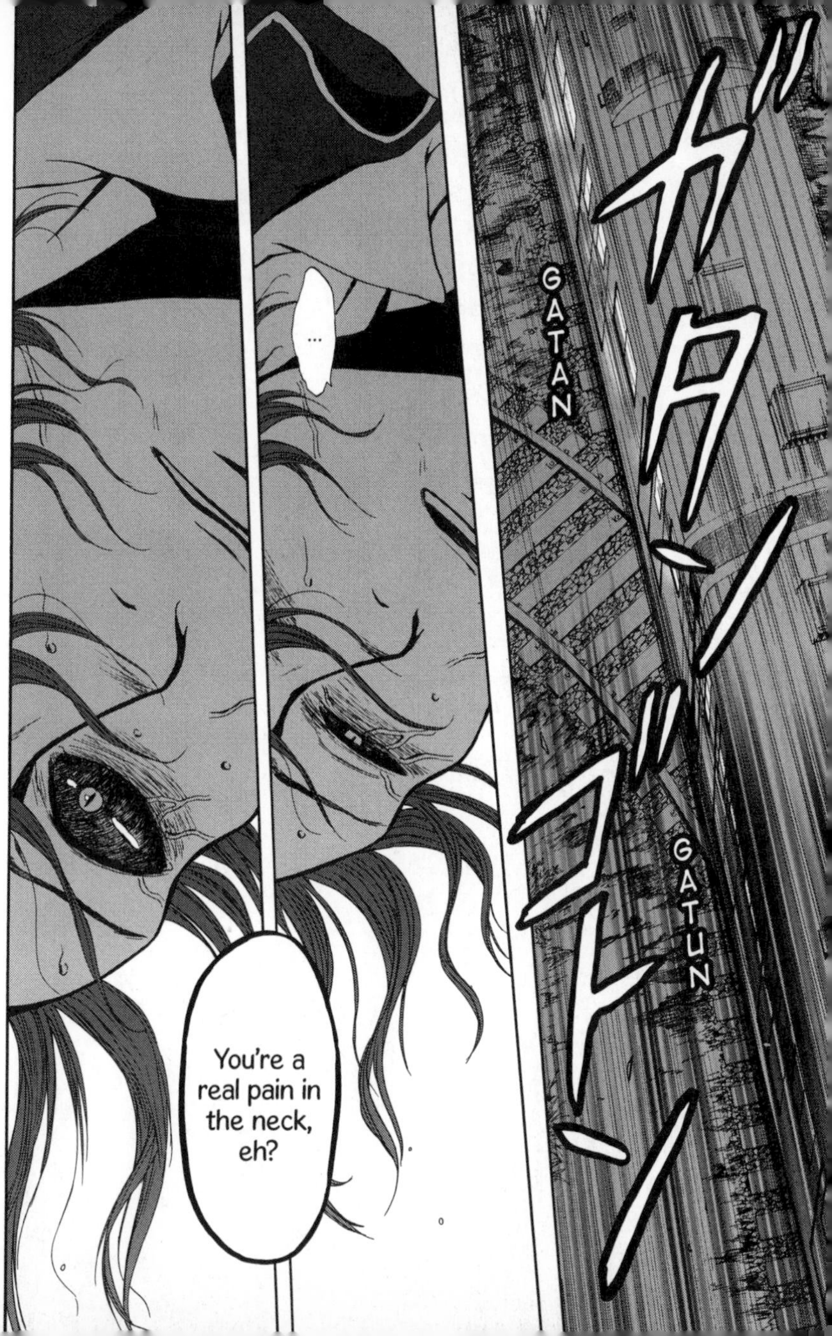
ガタンゴトン
GATAN
GATUN
...
You're a real pain in the neck, eh?

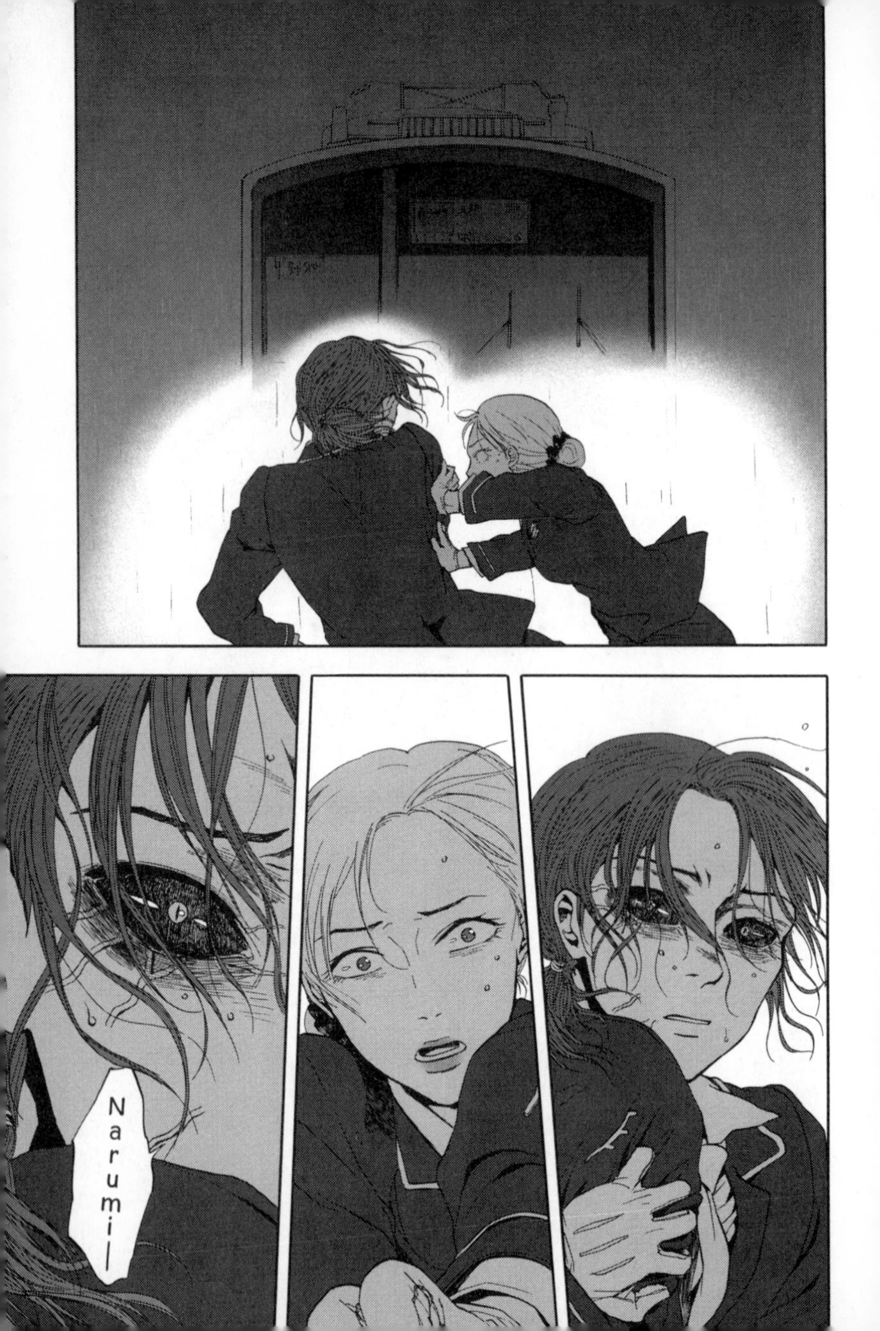
Narumi!

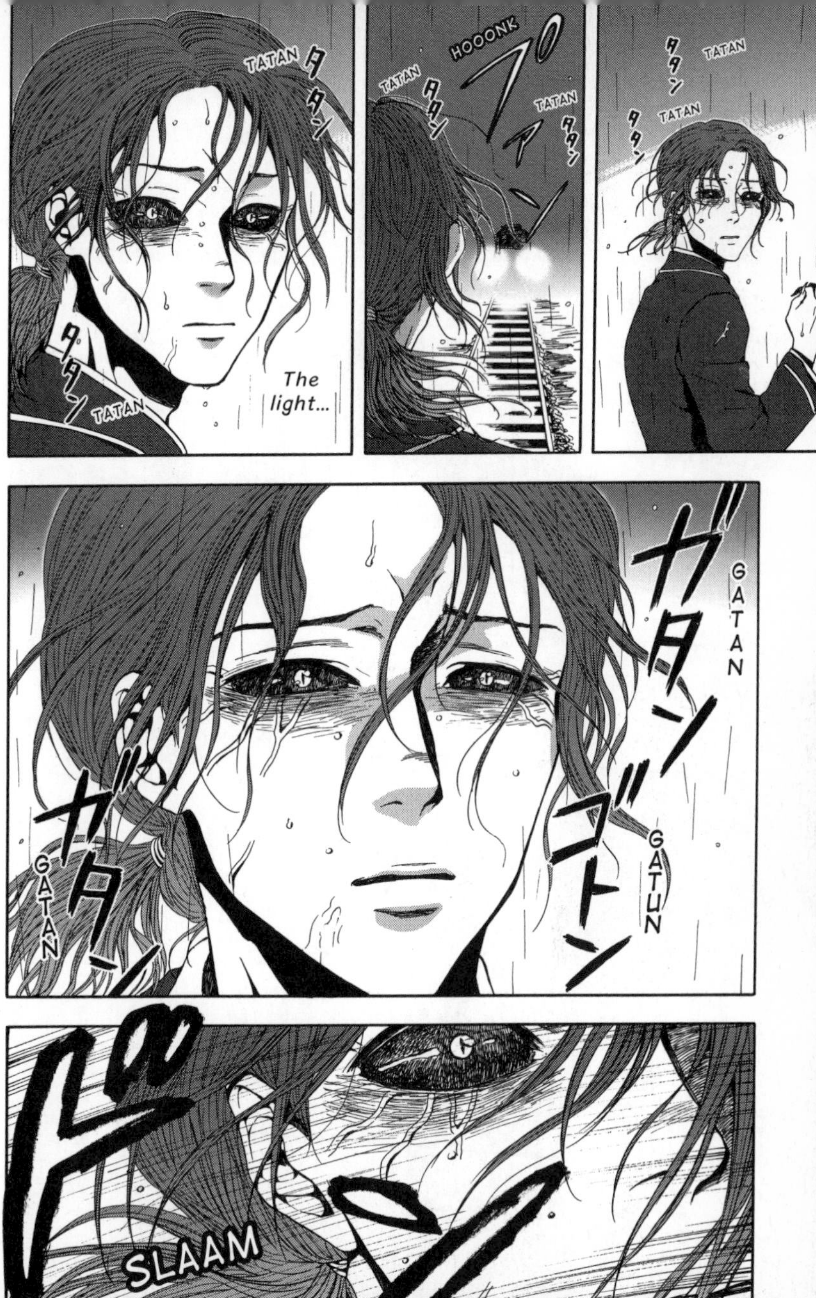

TATAN
タタン
TATAN
タタン
HOOONK
プァーン
TATAN
タタン
TATAN
タタン
TATAN
タタン
The light...
タタン
TATAN
ガタン
GATAN
ゴトン
GATUN
ガタン
GATAN
SLAAM

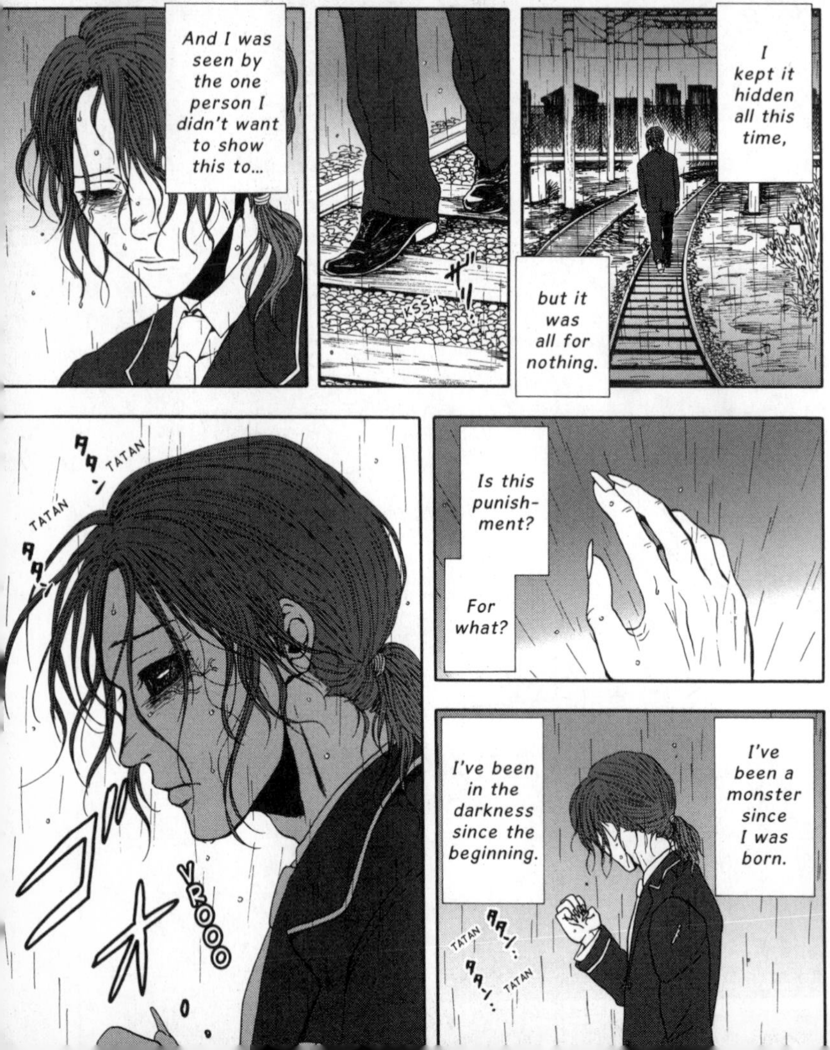
I kept it hidden all this time,
but it was all for nothing.
KSSH
And I was seen by the one person I didn't want to show this to...
Is this punishment?
For what?
I've been a monster since I was born.
I've been in the darkness since the beginning.
TATAN
TATAN
TATAN
TATAN
VROOO

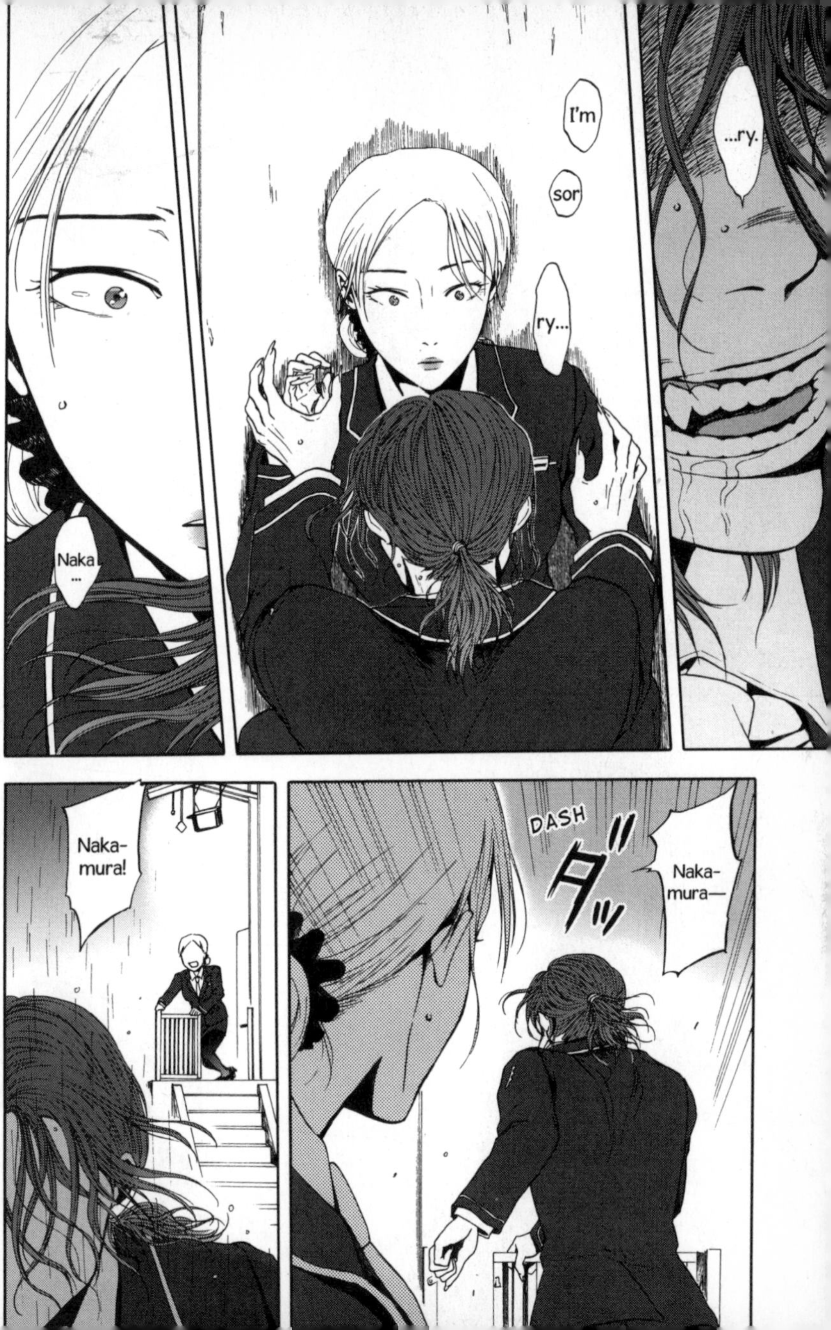
...ry.
I'm
sor
ry...
Naka ...
Naka-mura—
DASH
ダッ
Naka-mura!

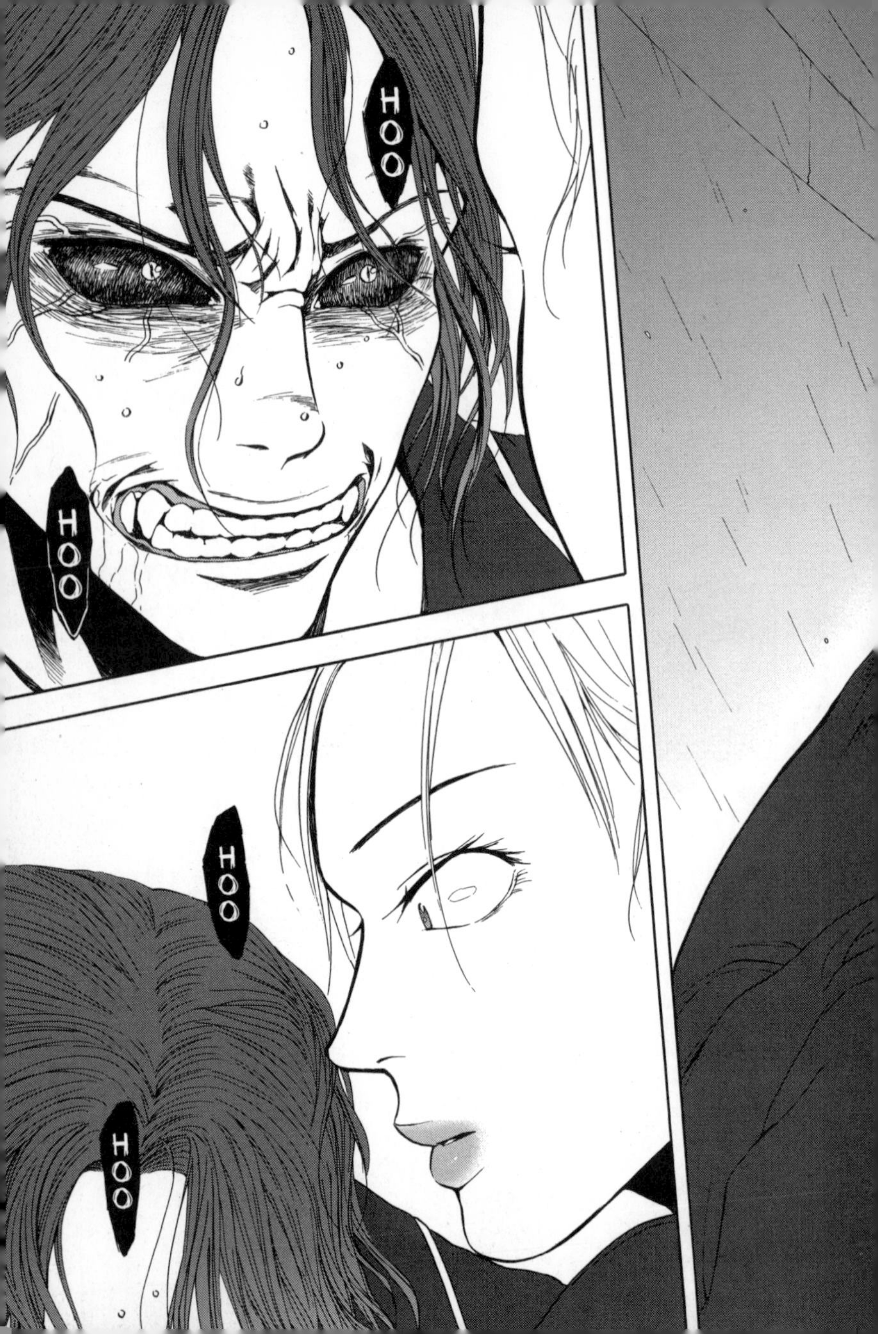
HOO
HOO
HOO
HOO

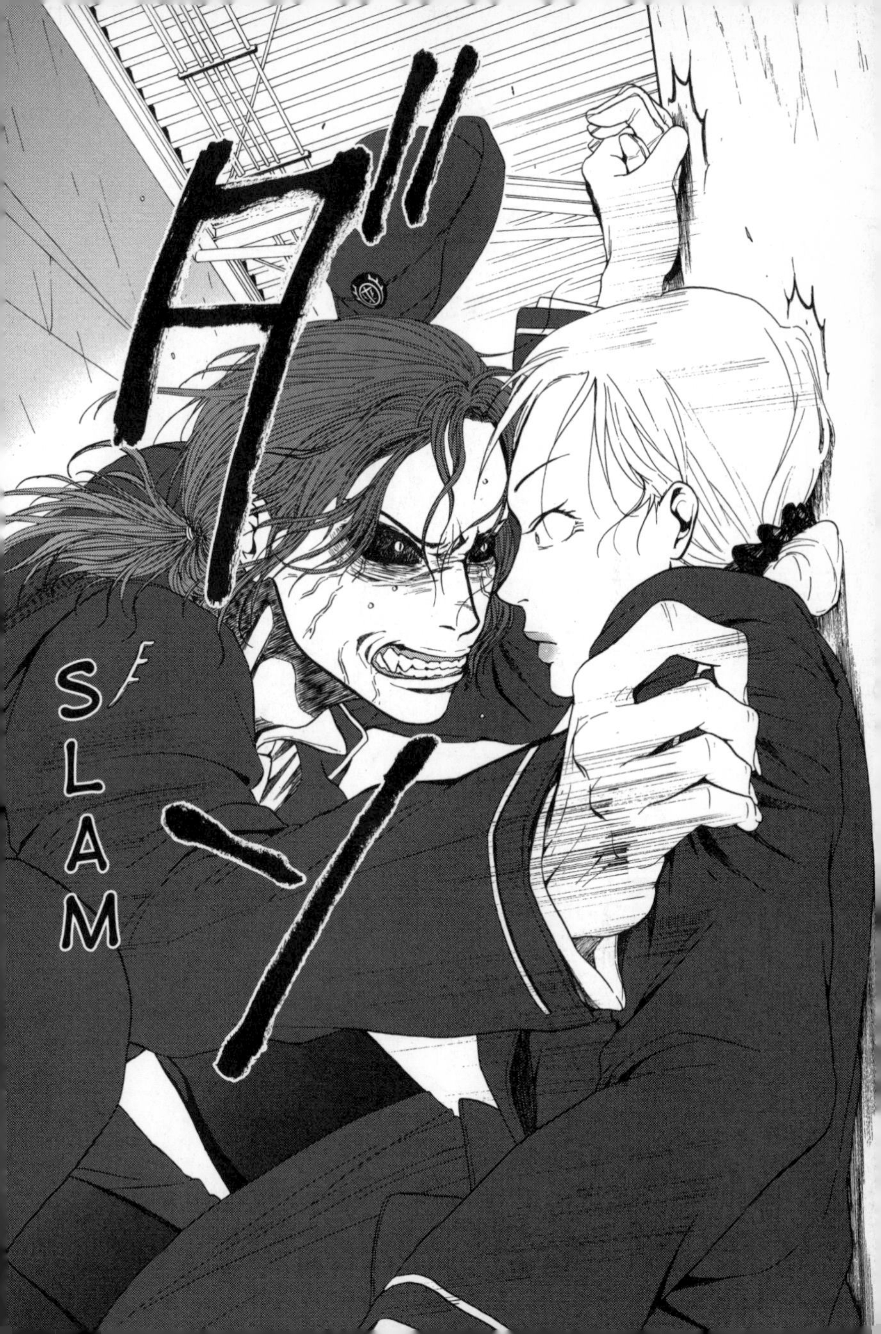
ガッ
SLAM

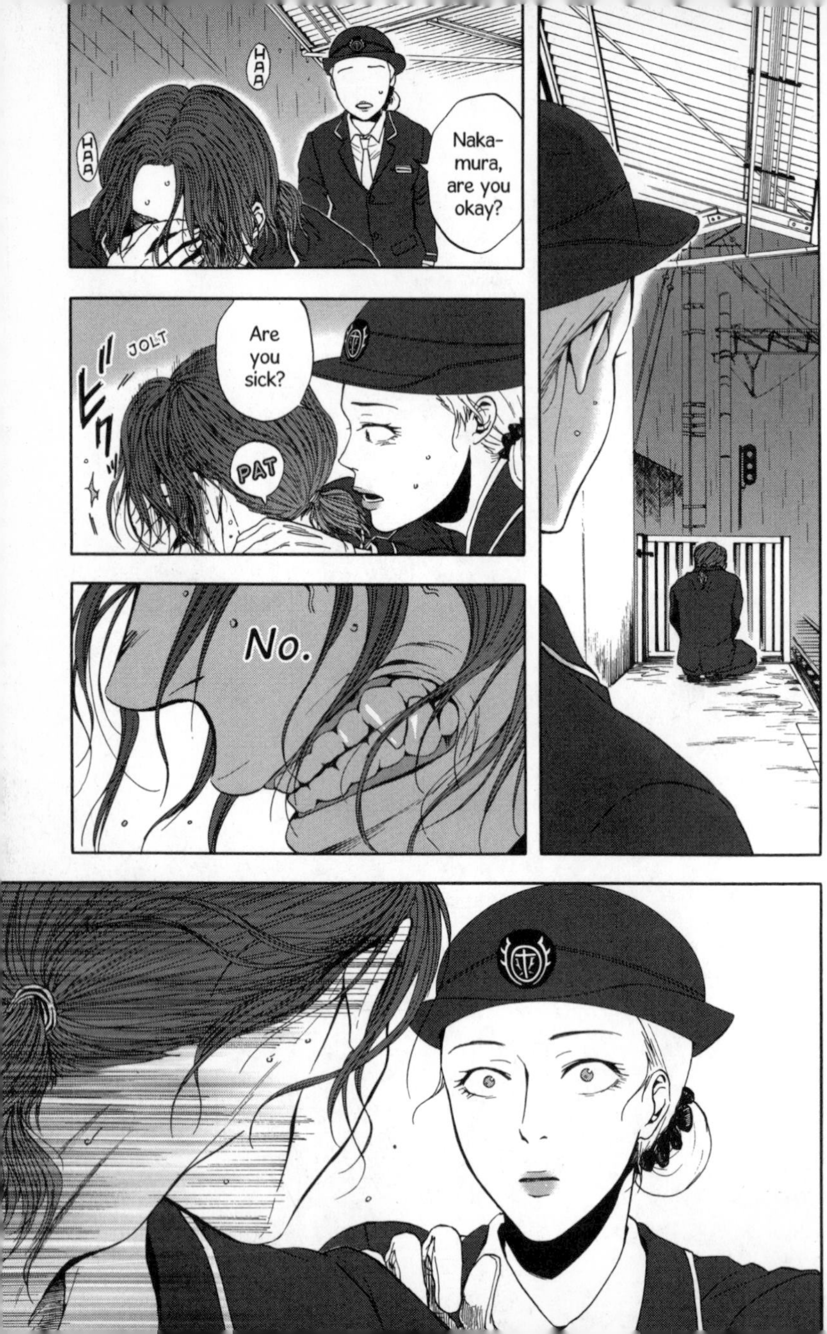
Nakamura, are you okay?
HAA
HAA
Are you sick?
JOLT
PAT
No.

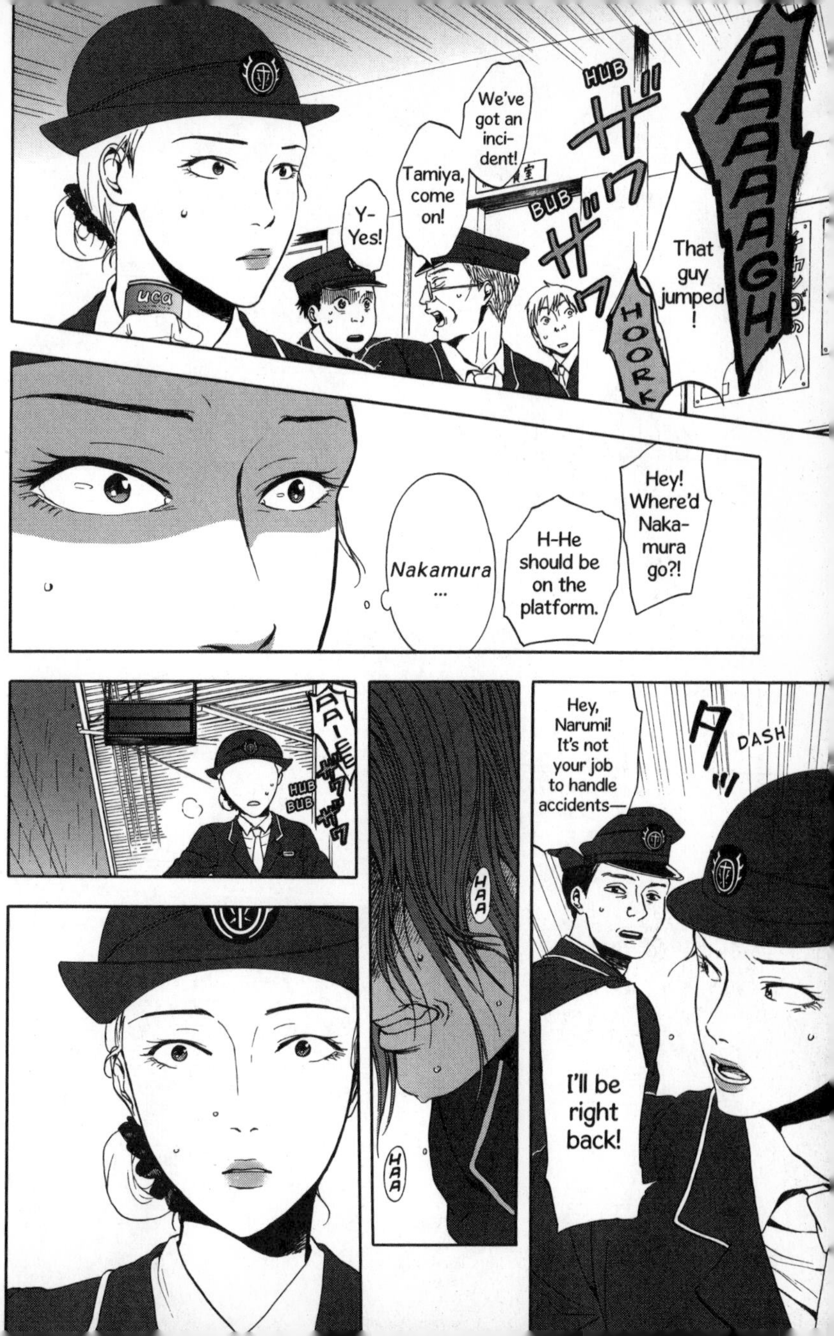
AAAAAAGH
That guy jumped!
HOORK
HUB ザワ
BUB ザワ
We've got an inci-dent!
Tamiya, come on!
Y-Yes!
Hey! Where'd Naka-mura go?!
H-He should be on the platform.
Nakamura ...
ダッ DASH
Hey, Narumi! It's not your job to handle accidents—
I'll be right back!
HAA
HAA
AAIEE
HUB BUB

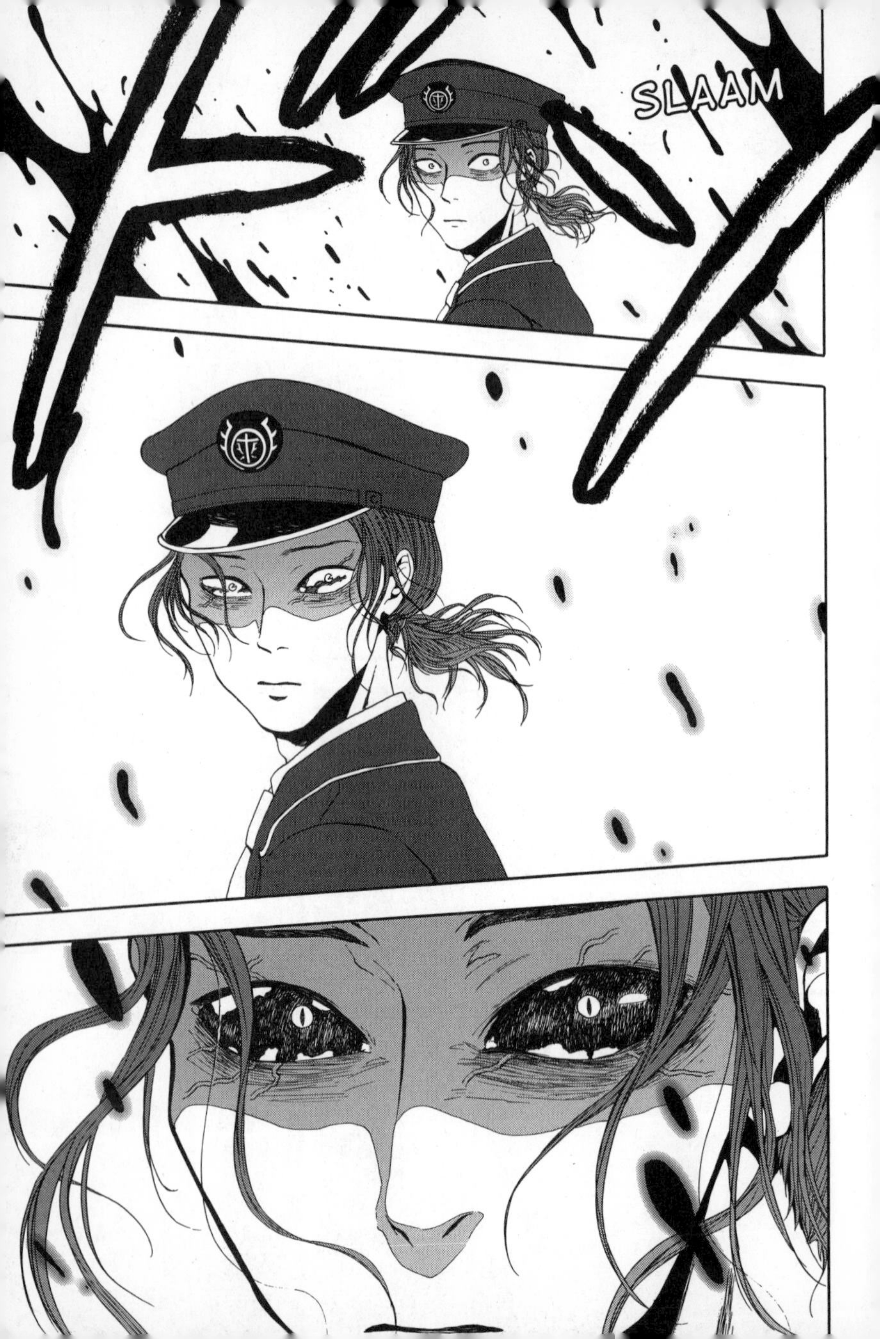
SLAAM

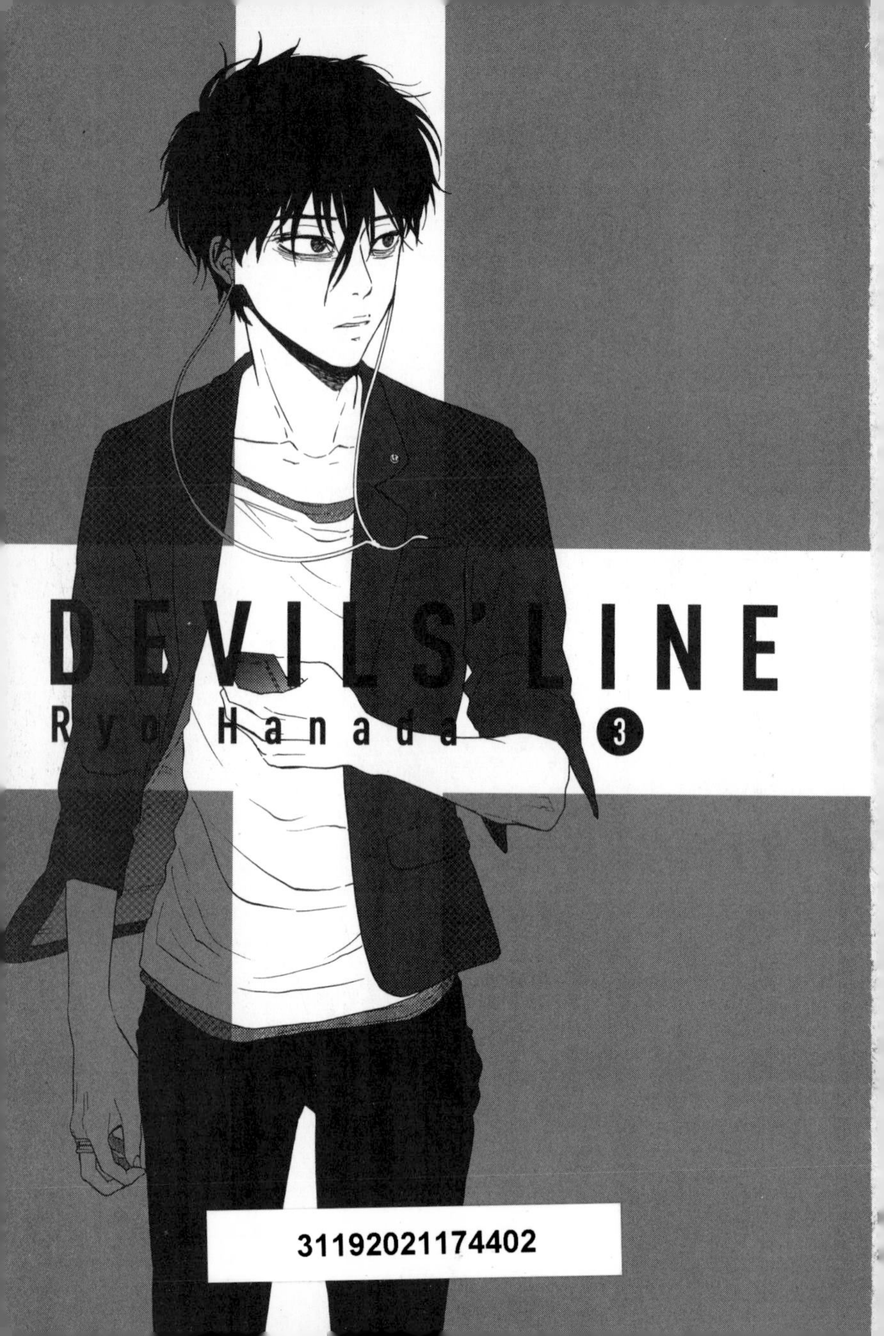
DEVILS'LINE
Ryo Hanada
3

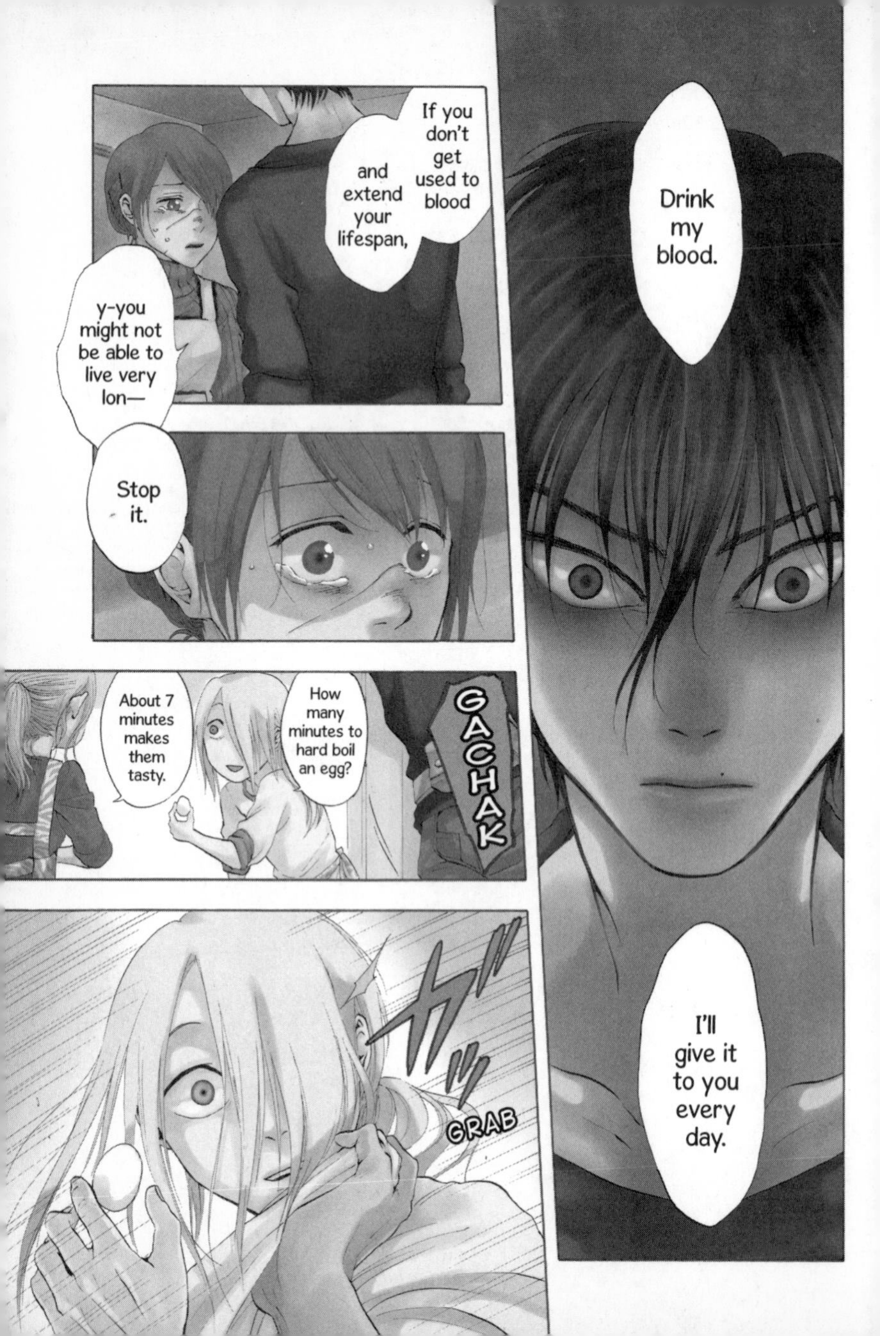
Drink my blood.
I'll give it to you every day.
If you don't get used to blood
and extend your lifespan,
y-you might not be able to live very lon—
Stop it.
GACHAK
How many minutes to hard boil an egg?
About 7 minutes makes them tasty.
GRAB

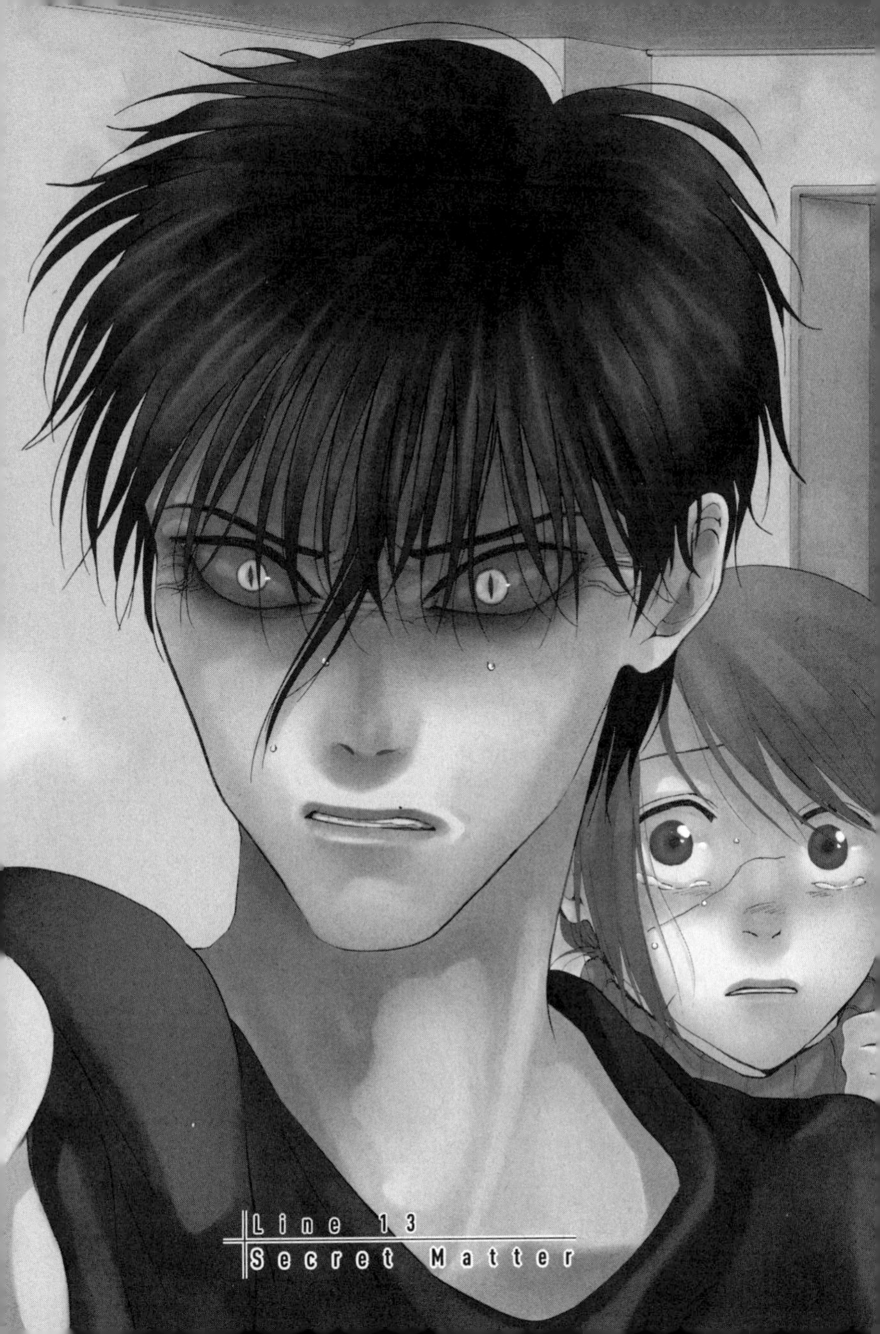
Line 13
Secret Matter

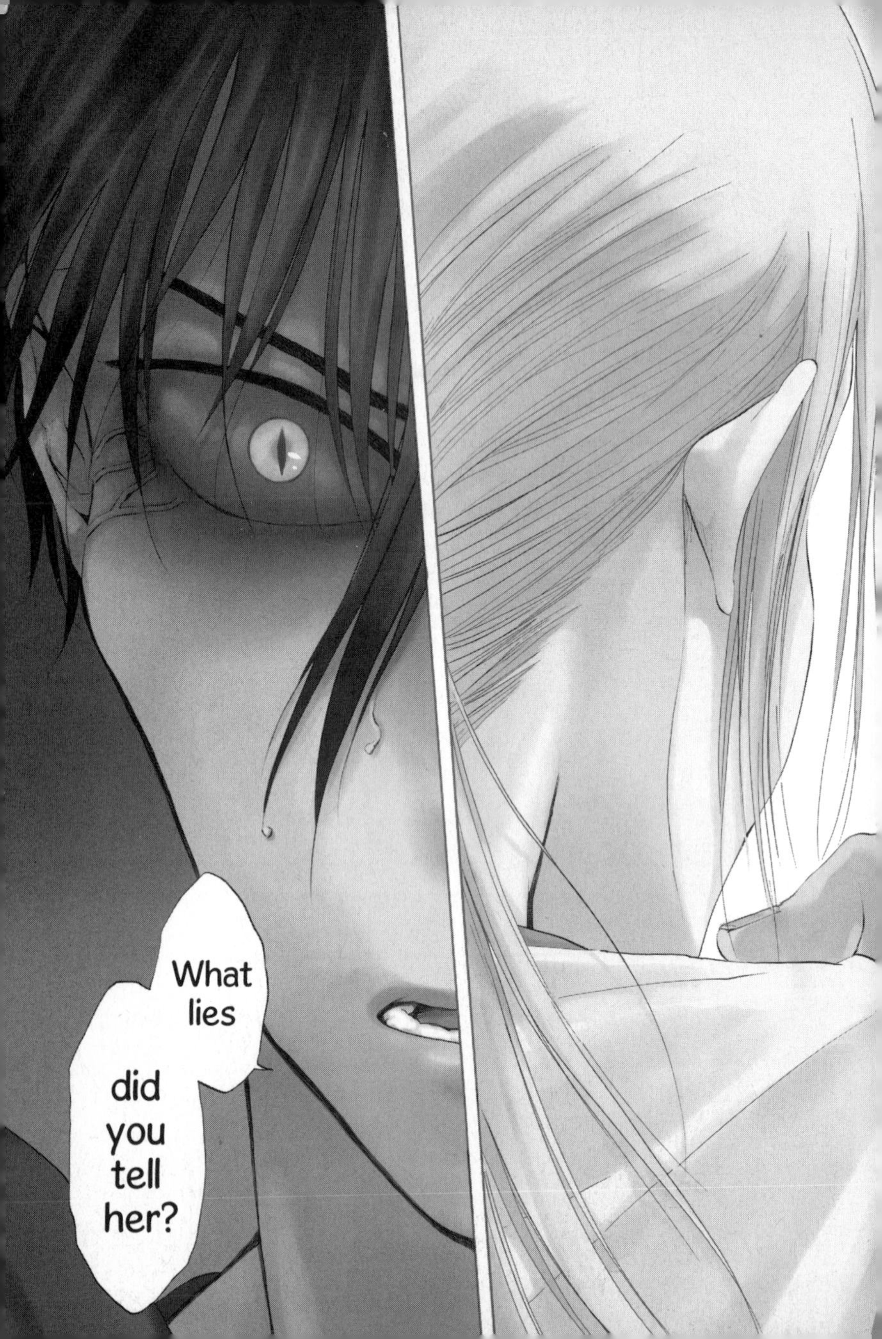
What lies did you tell her?

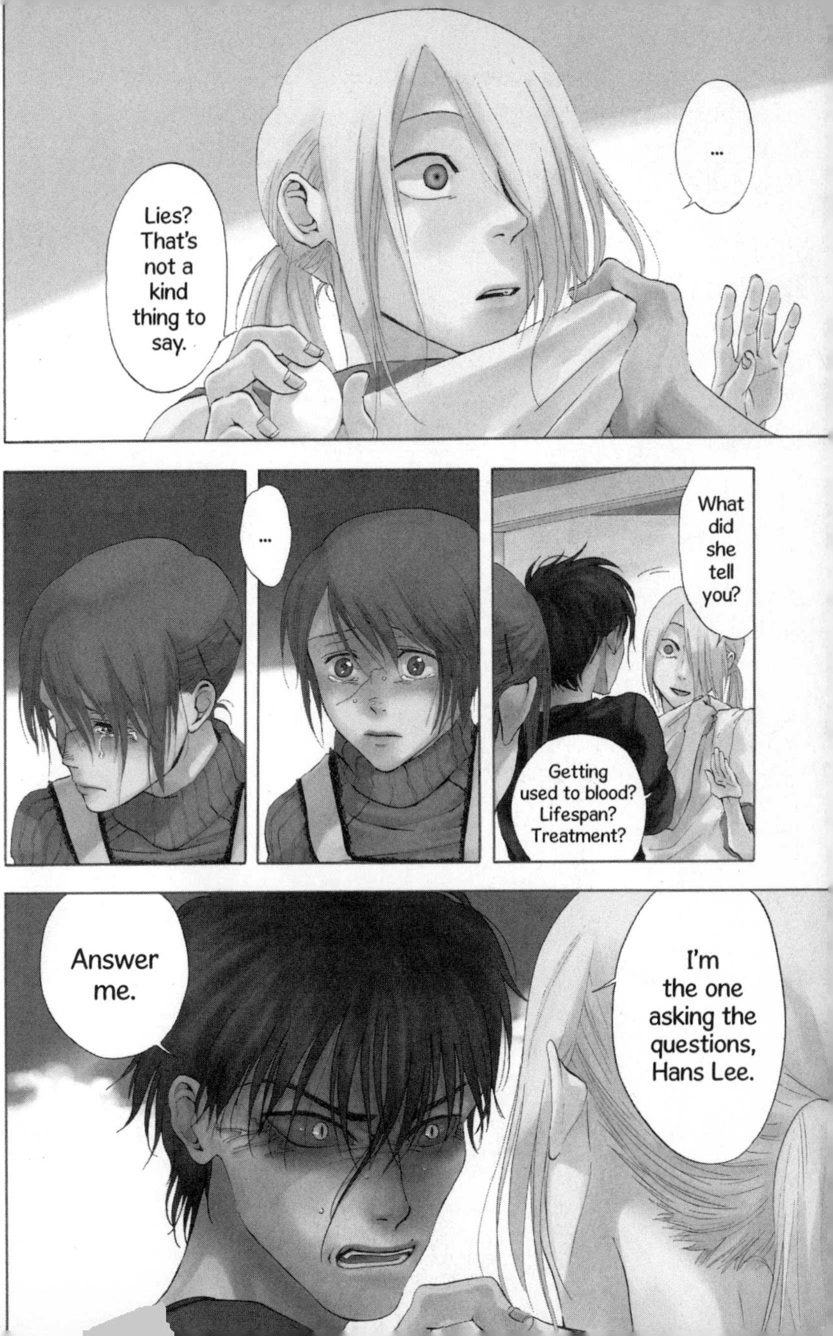
...
Lies? That's not a kind thing to say.
What did she tell you?
Getting used to blood? Lifespan? Treatment?
...
I'm the one asking the questions, Hans Lee.
Answer me.

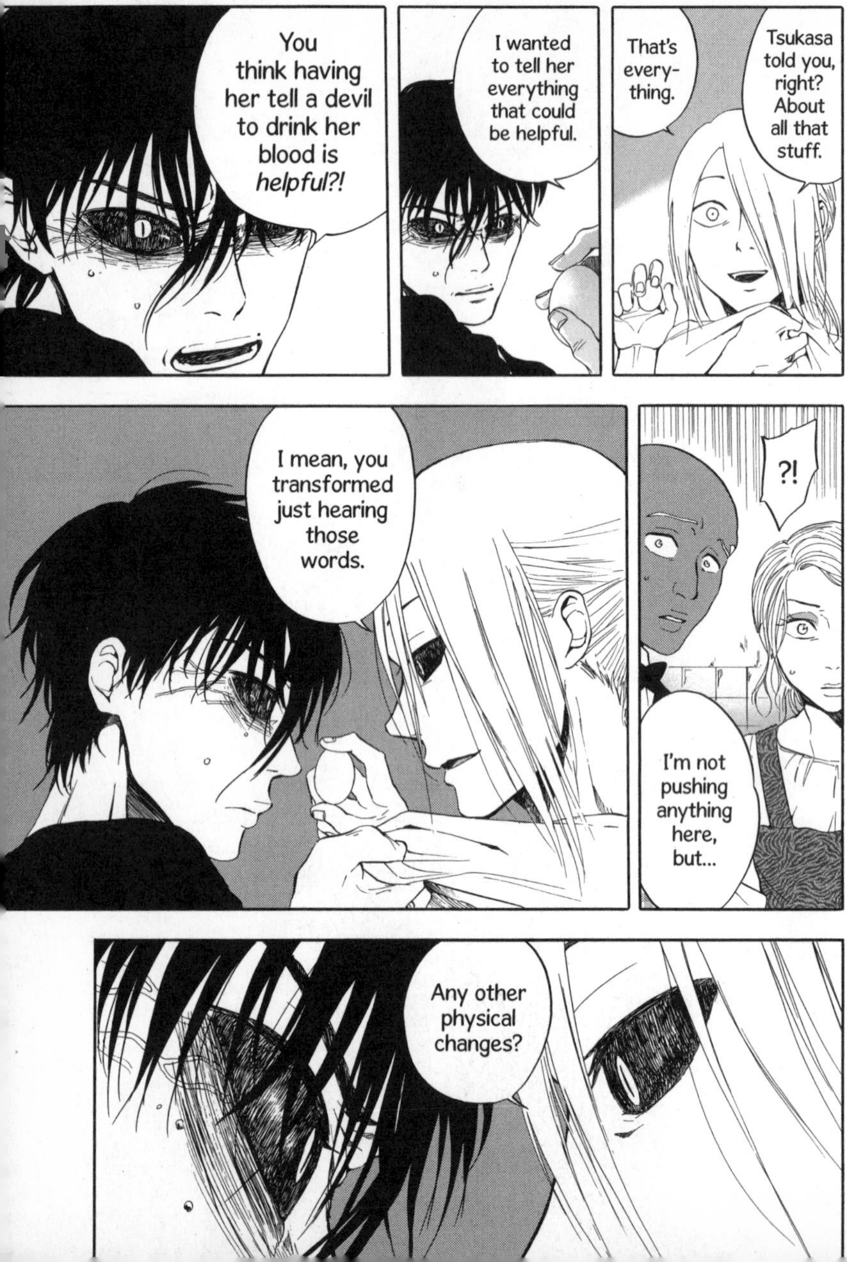
Tsukasa told you, right? About all that stuff.
That's every-thing.
I wanted to tell her everything that could be helpful.
You think having her tell a devil to drink her blood is *helpful*?!
?!
I'm not pushing anything here, but...
I mean, you transformed just hearing those words.
Any other physical changes?

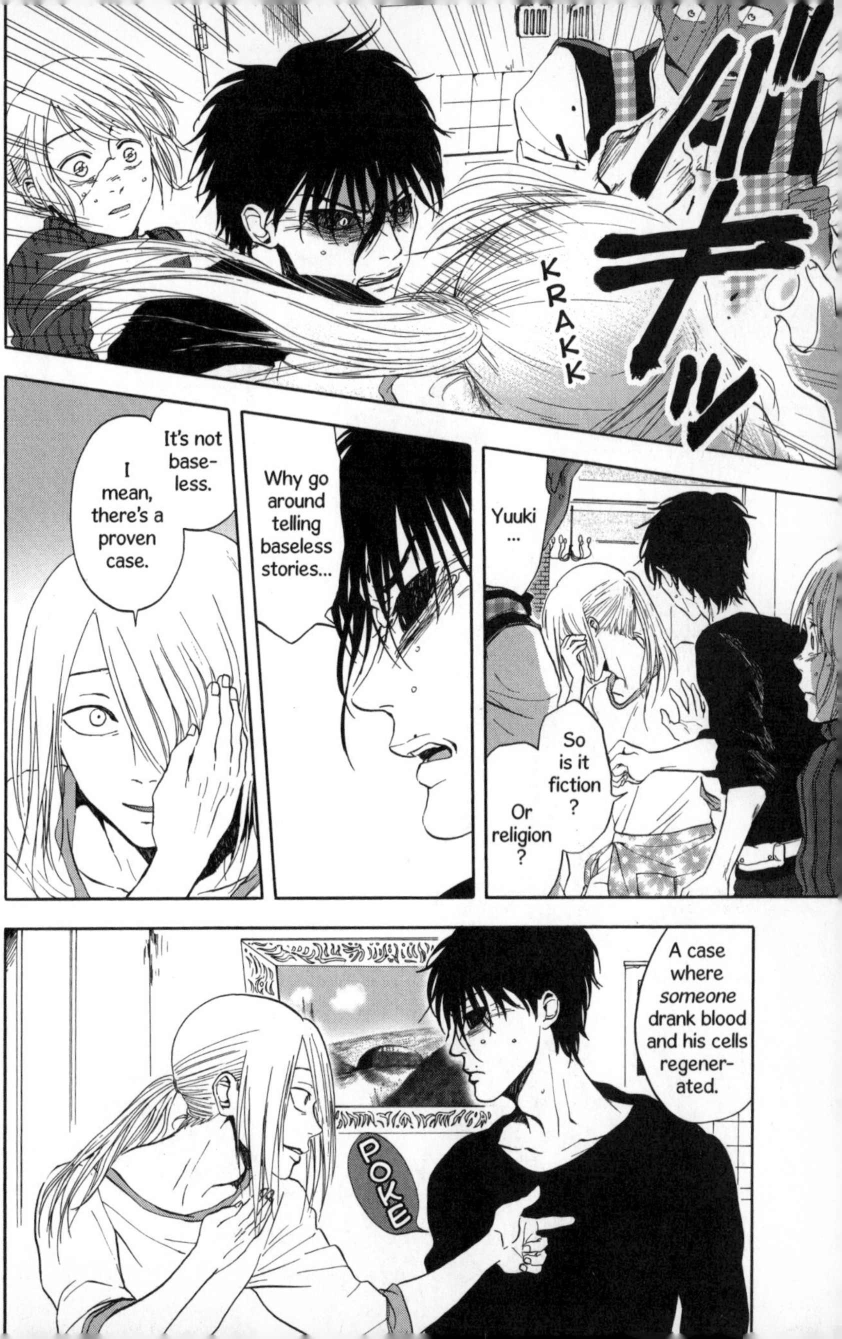
KRAKK
Yuuki ...
So is it fiction ?
Or religion ?
Why go around telling baseless stories...
It's not baseless.
I mean, there's a proven case.
A case where *someone* drank blood and his cells regenerated.
POKE

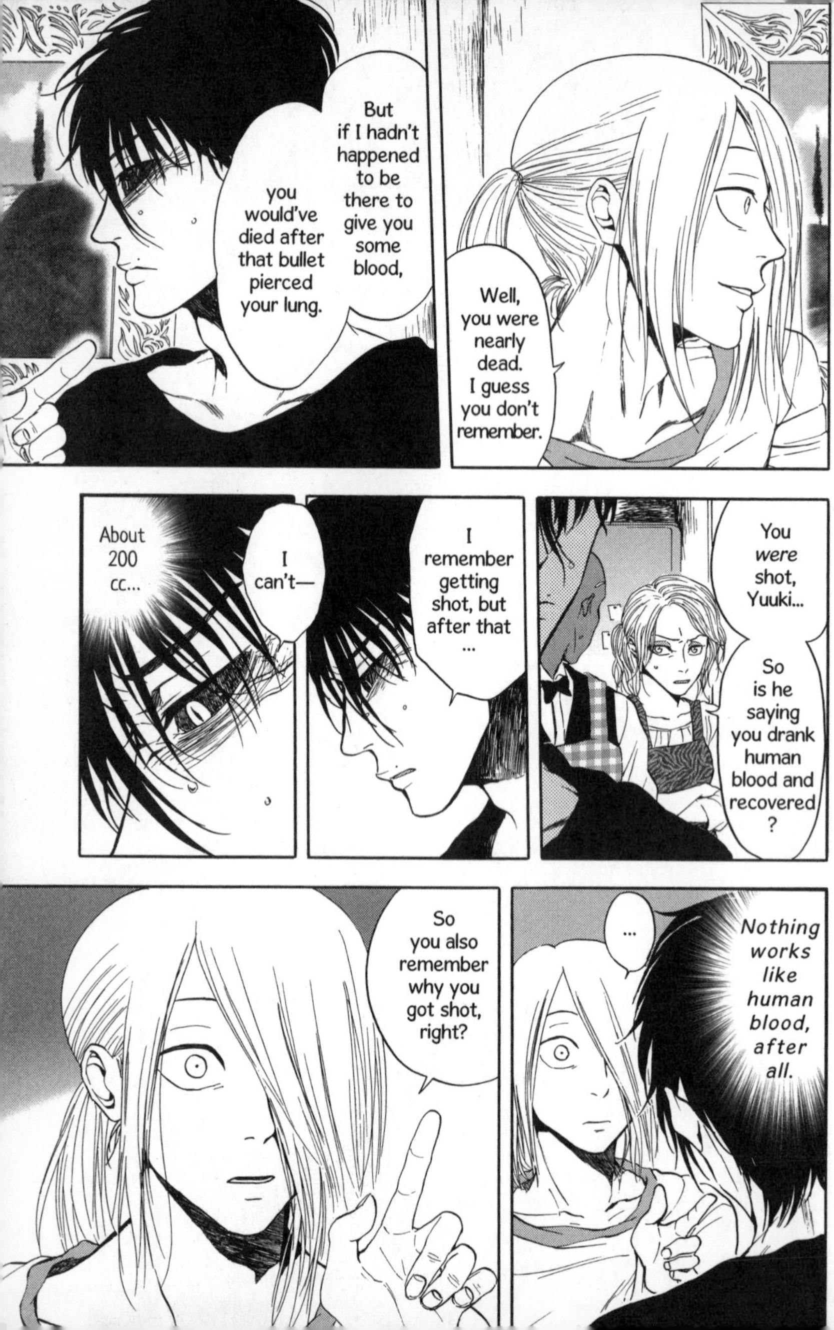
Well, you were nearly dead. I guess you don't remember.
But if I hadn't happened to be there to give you some blood,
you would've died after that bullet pierced your lung.
You *were* shot, Yuuki...
So is he saying you drank human blood and recovered?
I remember getting shot, but after that ...
I can't—
About 200 cc...
Nothing works like human blood, after all.
...
So you also remember why you got shot, right?

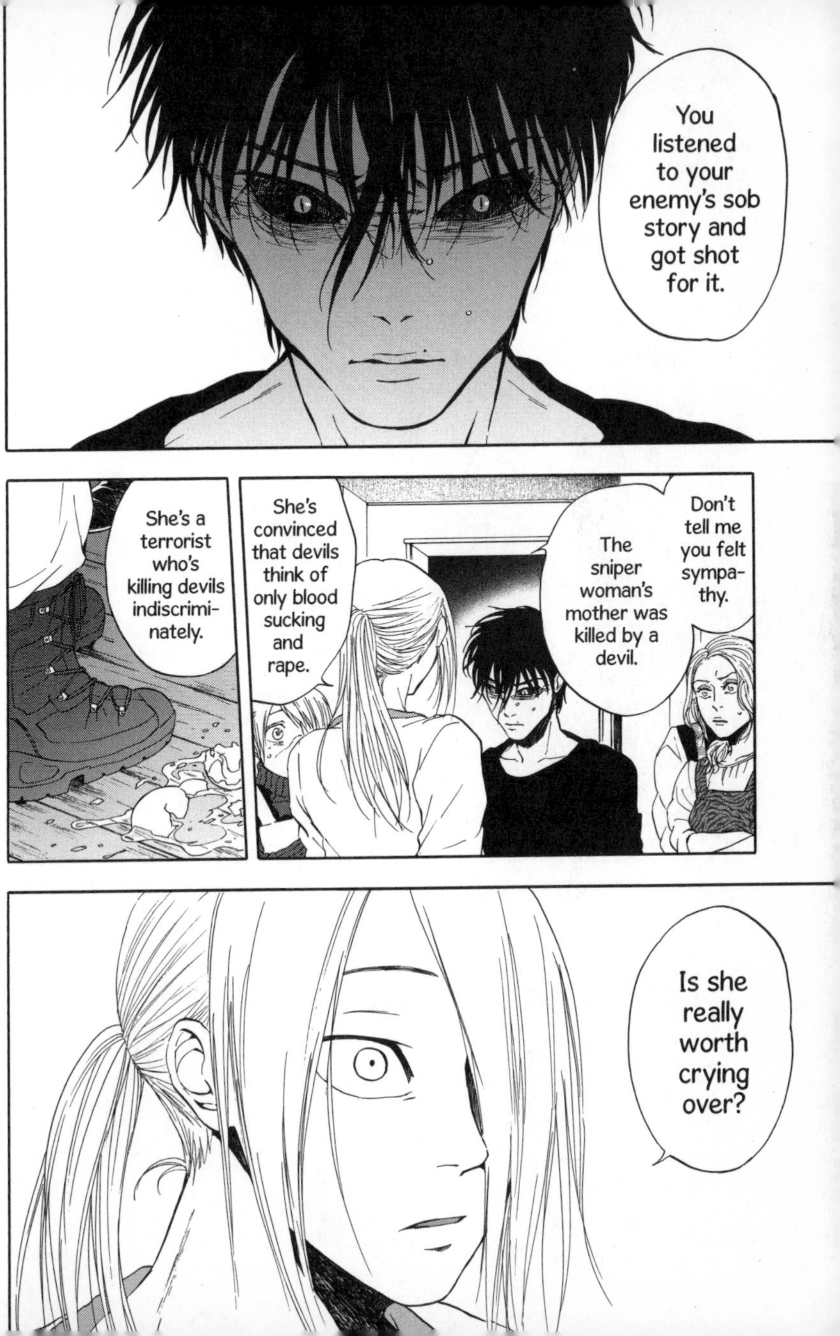
You listened to your enemy's sob story and got shot for it.
Don't tell me you felt sympa-thy.
The sniper woman's mother was killed by a devil.
She's convinced that devils think of only blood sucking and rape.
She's a terrorist who's killing devils indiscrimi-nately.
Is she really worth crying over?

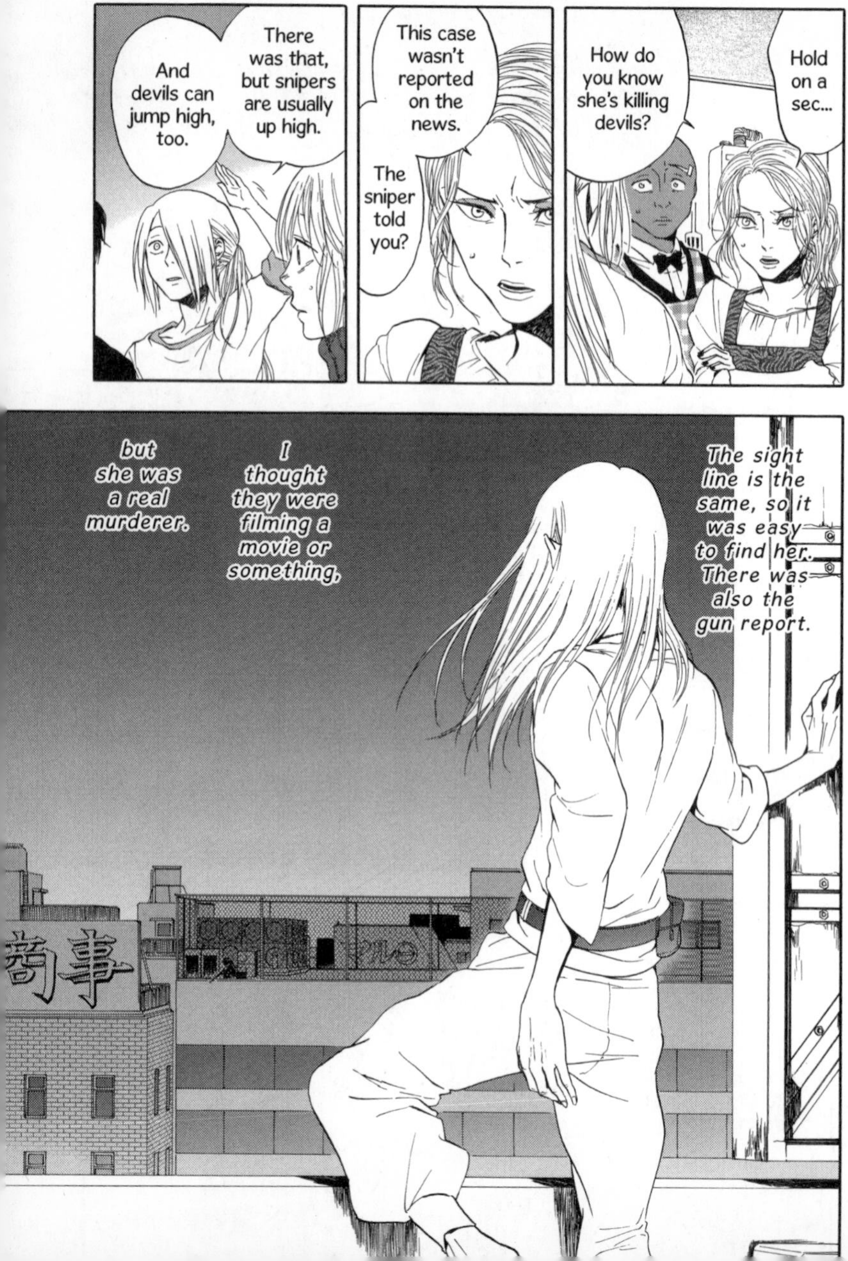
Hold on a sec...
How do you know she's killing devils?
This case wasn't reported on the news.
The sniper told you?
There was that, but snipers are usually up high.
And devils can jump high, too.
The sight line is the same, so it was easy to find her. There was also the gun report.
I thought they were filming a movie or something,
but she was a real murderer.

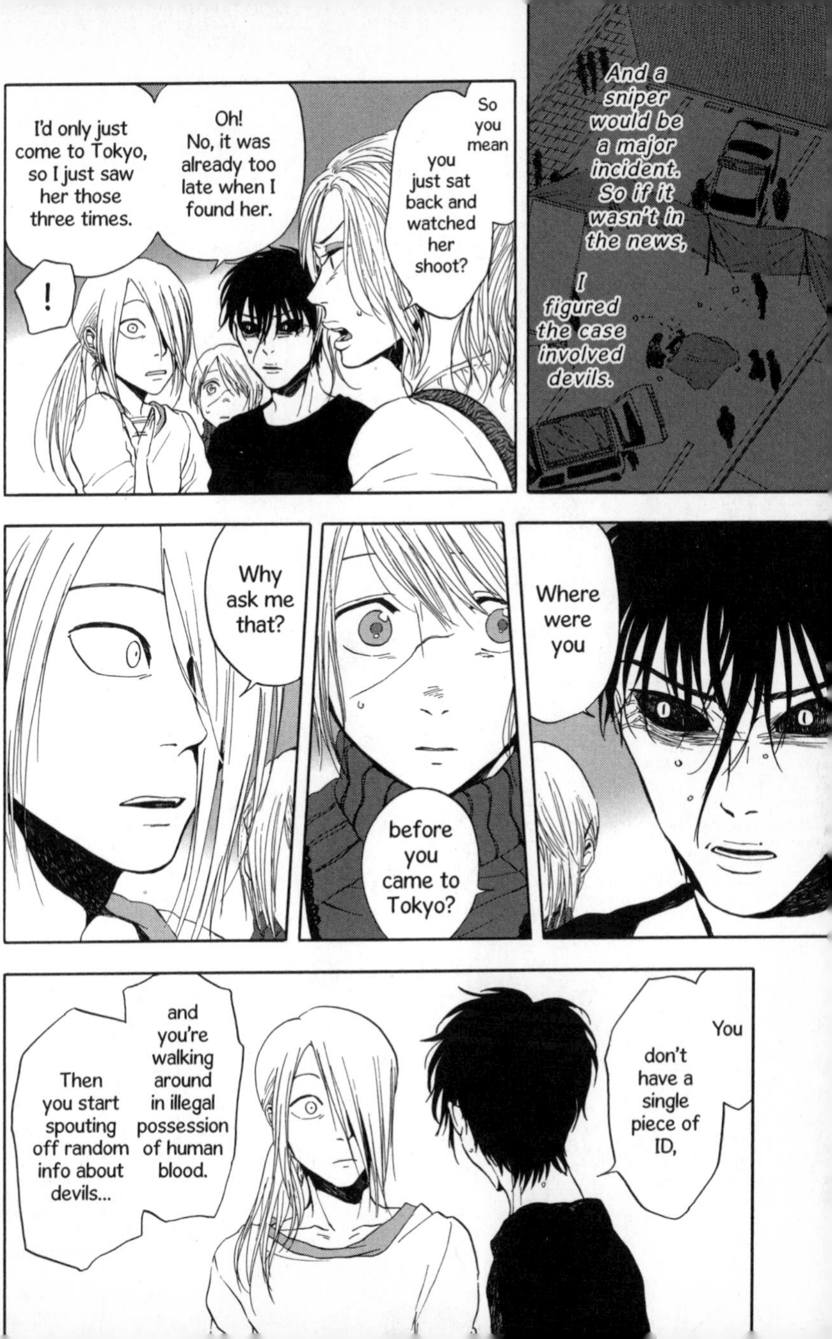
And a sniper would be a major incident. So if it wasn't in the news, I figured the case involved devils.
So you mean you just sat back and watched her shoot?
Oh! No, it was already too late when I found her.
I'd only just come to Tokyo, so I just saw her those three times.
!
Where were you
before you came to Tokyo?
Why ask me that?
You don't have a single piece of ID,
and you're walking around in illegal possession of human blood.
Then you start spouting off random info about devils...

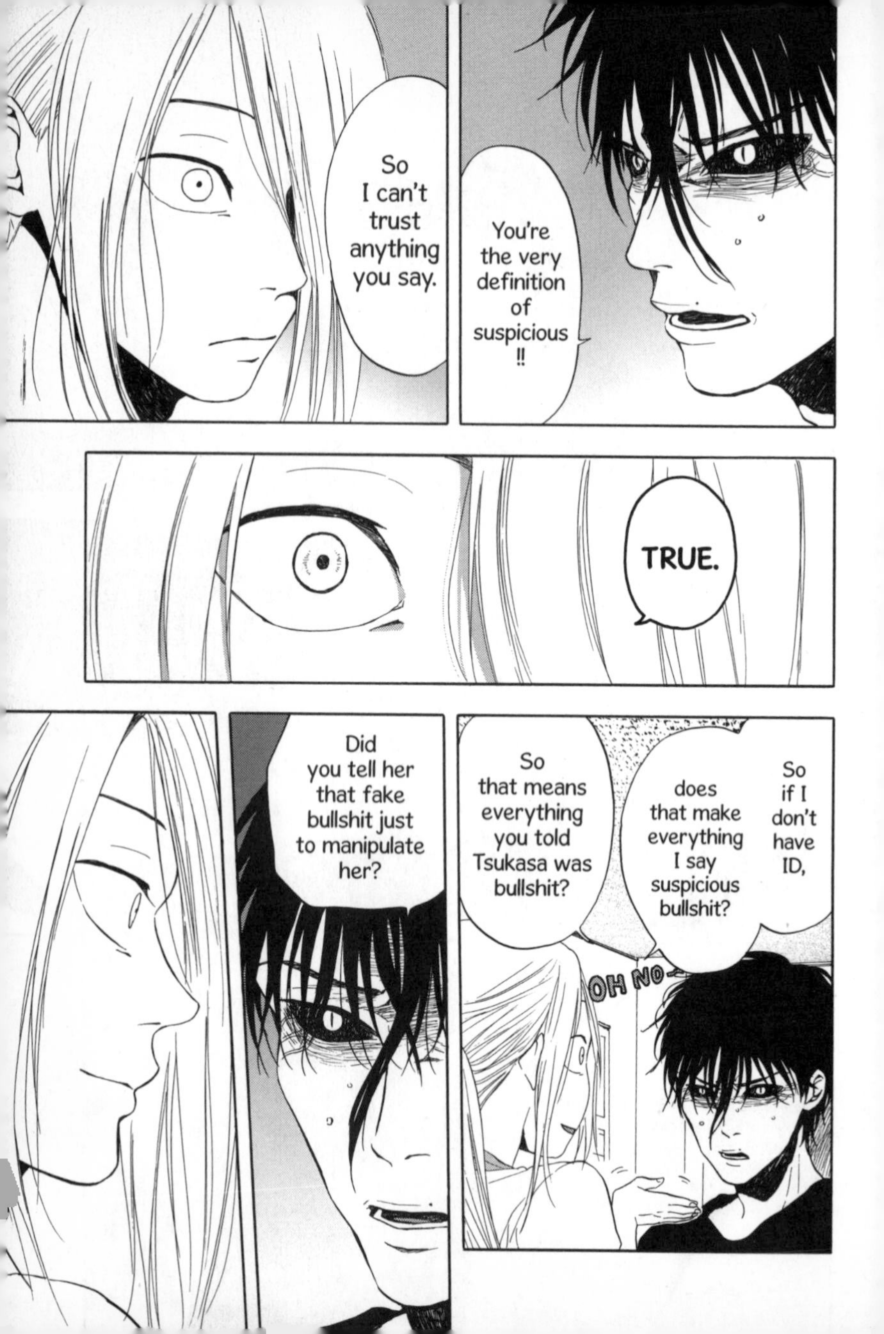
You're the very definition of suspicious!!
So I can't trust anything you say.
TRUE.
So if I don't have ID,
does that make everything I say suspicious bullshit?
So that means everything you told Tsukasa was bullshit?
OH NO-
Did you tell her that fake bullshit just to manipulate her?

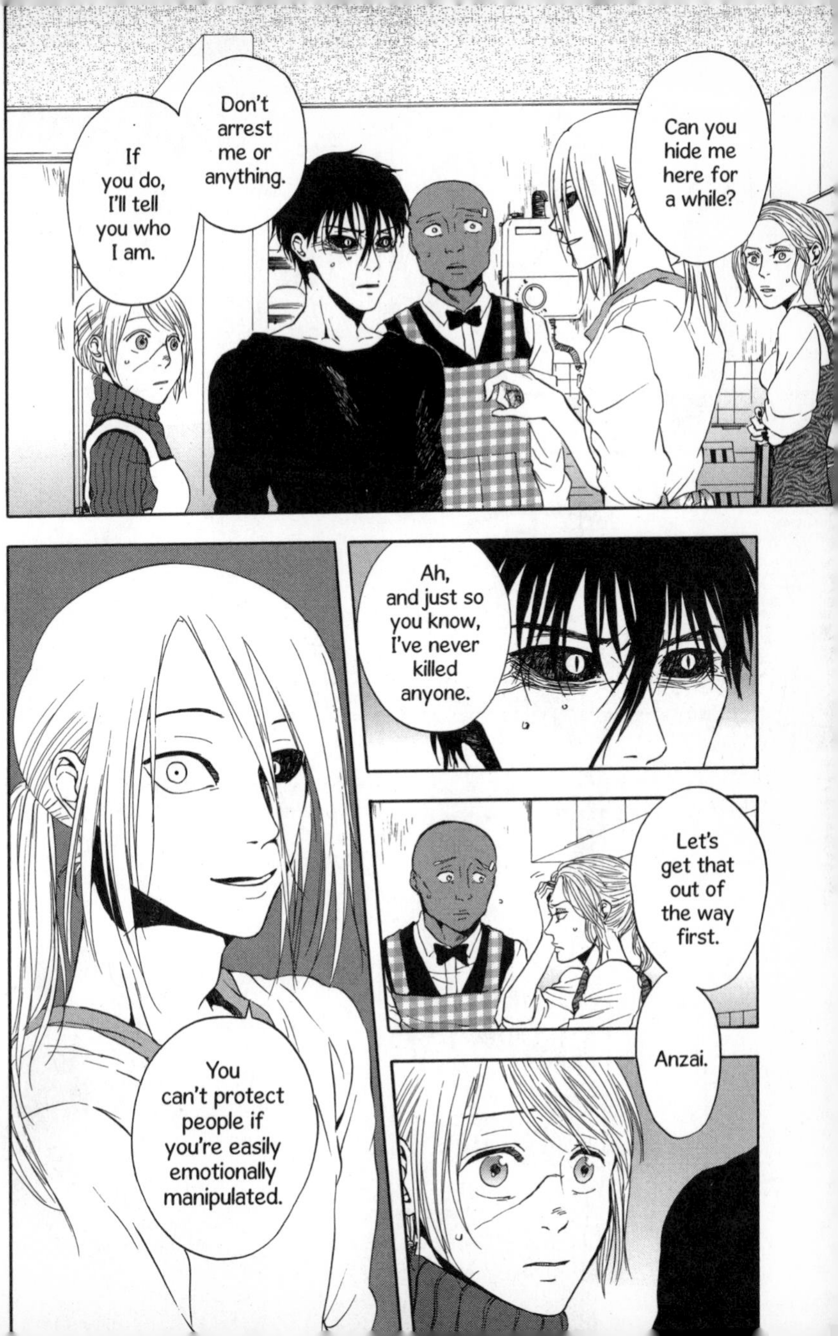
Can you hide me here for a while?
Don't arrest me or anything.
If you do, I'll tell you who I am.
Ah, and just so you know, I've never killed anyone.
Let's get that out of the way first.
Anzai.
You can't protect people if you're easily emotionally manipulated.

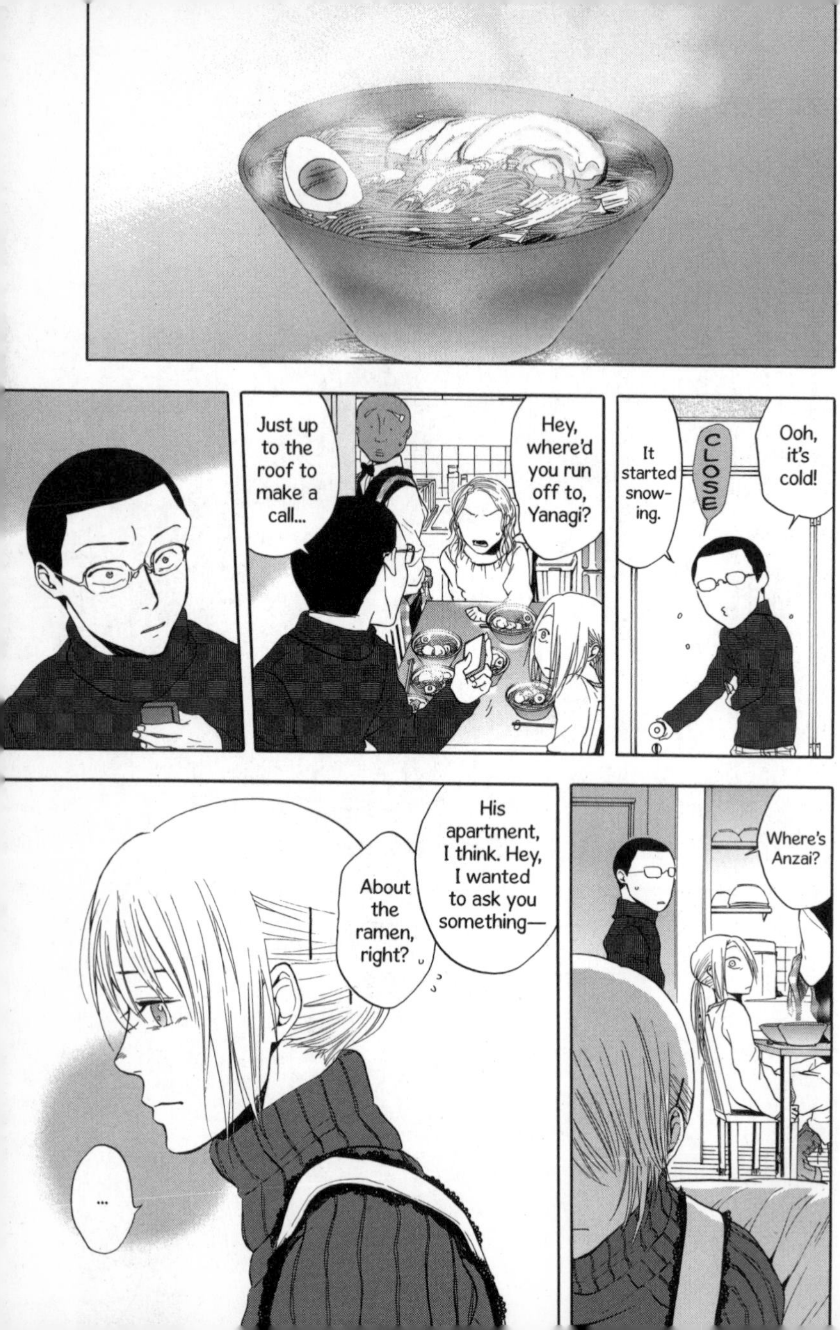
Ooh, it's cold!
CLOSE
It started snow-ing.
Hey, where'd you run off to, Yanagi?
Just up to the roof to make a call...
Where's Anzai?
His apartment, I think. Hey, I wanted to ask you something—
About the ramen, right?
...

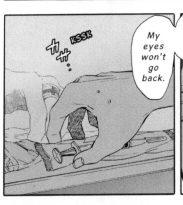

KSSK

My eyes won't go back.

So hot.

...

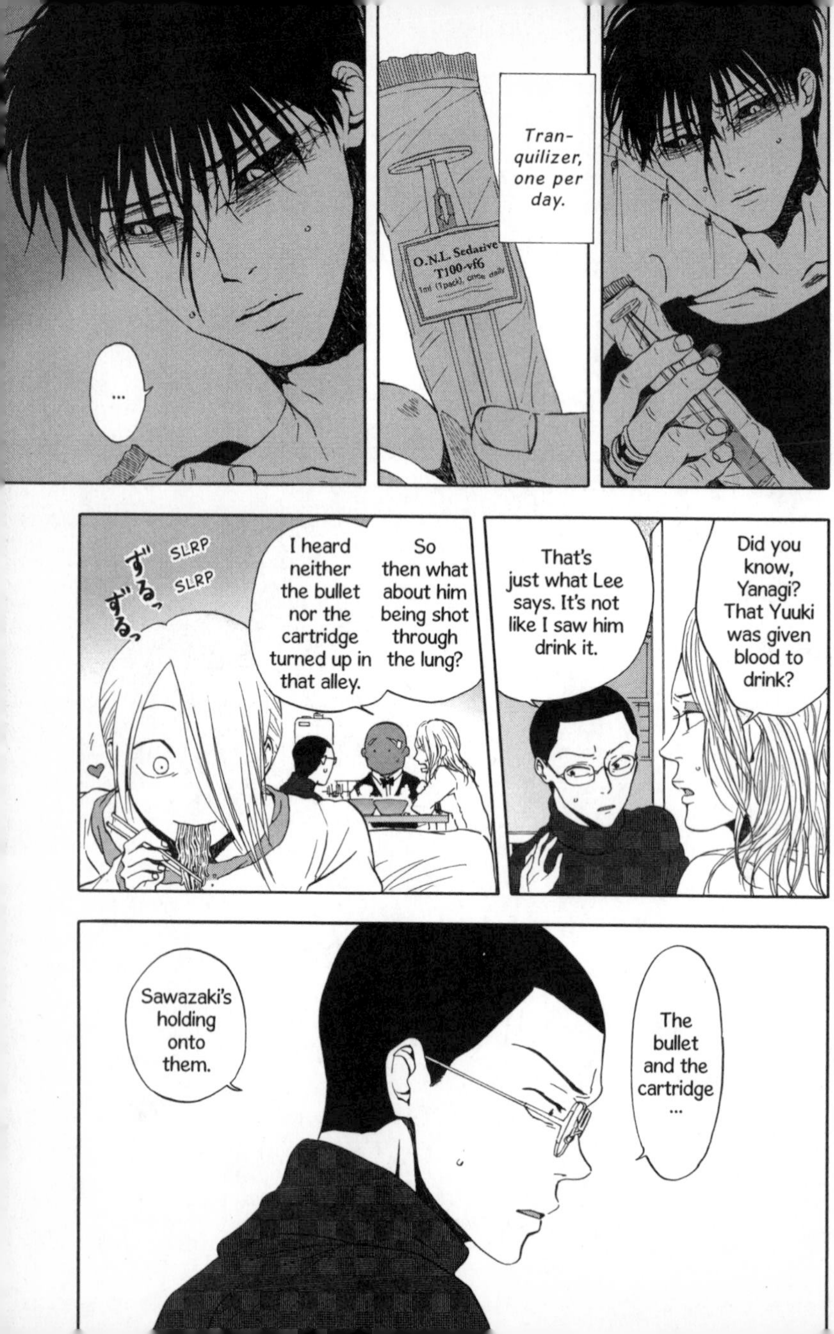
Tran-quilizer, one per day.
O.N.L. Sedative
T100-vf6
1ml (1pack), once daily
...
Did you know, Yanagi? That Yuuki was given blood to drink?
That's just what Lee says. It's not like I saw him drink it.
So then what about him being shot through the lung?
I heard neither the bullet nor the cartridge turned up in that alley.
ずるっ SLRP
ずるっ SLRP
The bullet and the cartridge ...
Sawazaki's holding onto them.

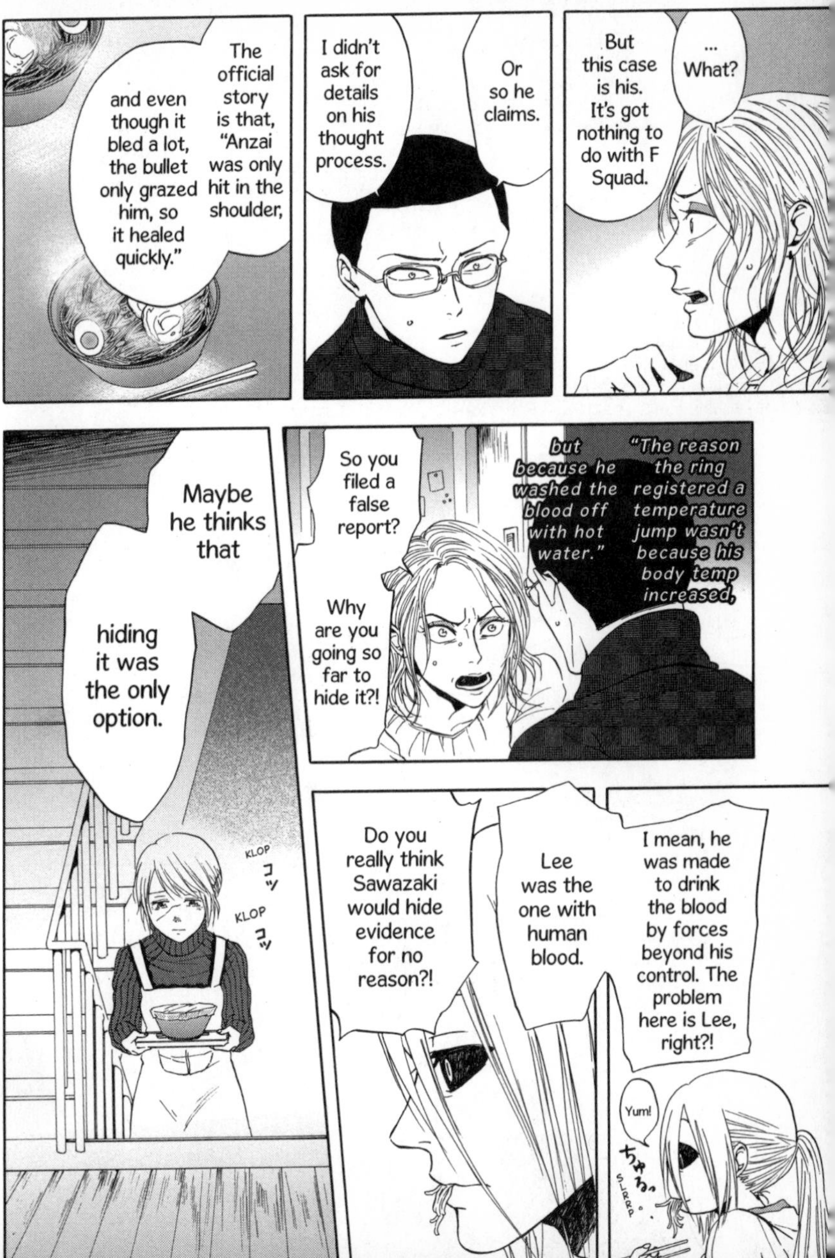
...
What?
But this case is his. It's got nothing to do with F Squad.
Or so he claims.
I didn't ask for details on his thought process.
The official story is that, "Anzai was only hit in the shoulder,
and even though it bled a lot, the bullet only grazed him, so it healed quickly."
"The reason the ring registered a temperature jump wasn't because his body temp increased,
but because he washed the blood off with hot water."
So you filed a false report?
Why are you going so far to hide it?!
I mean, he was made to drink the blood by forces beyond his control. The problem here is Lee, right?!
Yum!
ちゅるっ
SLRRP
Lee was the one with human blood.
Do you really think Sawazaki would hide evidence for no reason?!
Maybe he thinks that
hiding it was the only option.
KLOP
コッ
KLOP
コッ

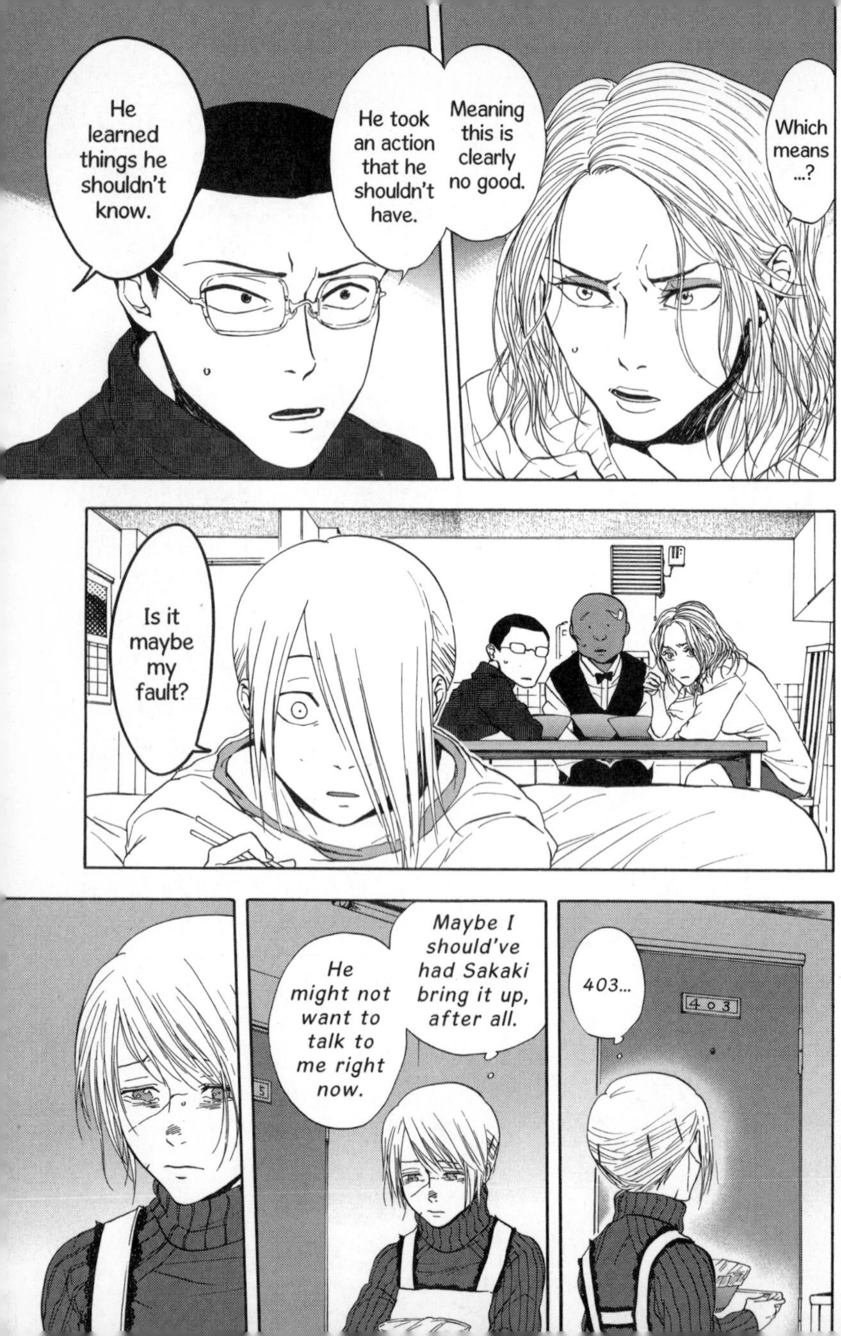
Which means ...?
Meaning this is clearly no good.
He took an action that he shouldn't have.
He learned things he shouldn't know.
Is it maybe my fault?
403...
403
Maybe I should've had Sakaki bring it up, after all.
He might not want to talk to me right now.

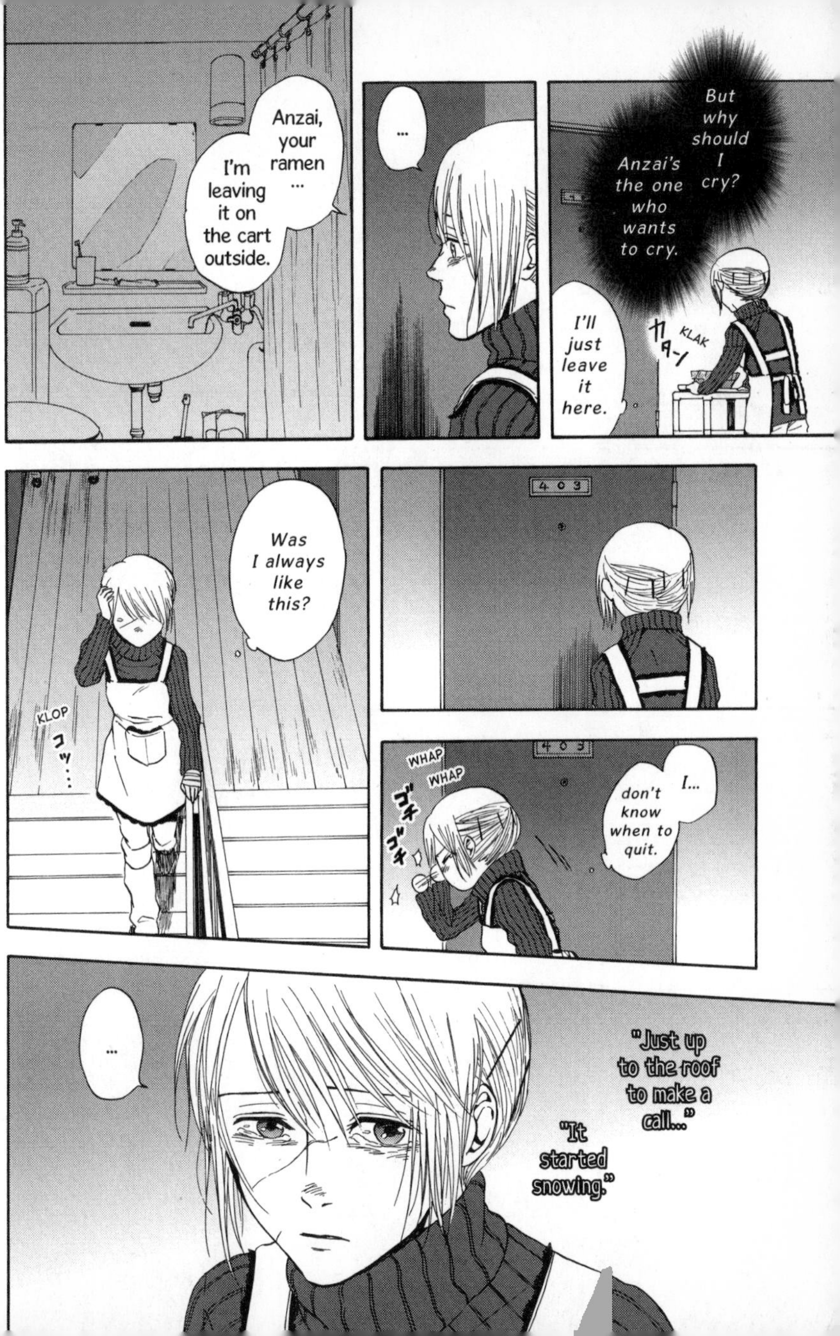
But why should I cry?
Anzai's the one who wants to cry.
I'll just leave it here.
KLAK
カターン
...
Anzai, your ramen ...
I'm leaving it on the cart outside.
WHAP WHAP
ゴチゴチ
I...
don't know when to quit.
Was I always like this?
KLOP
コッ...
"Just up to the roof to make a call..."
"It started snowing."
...

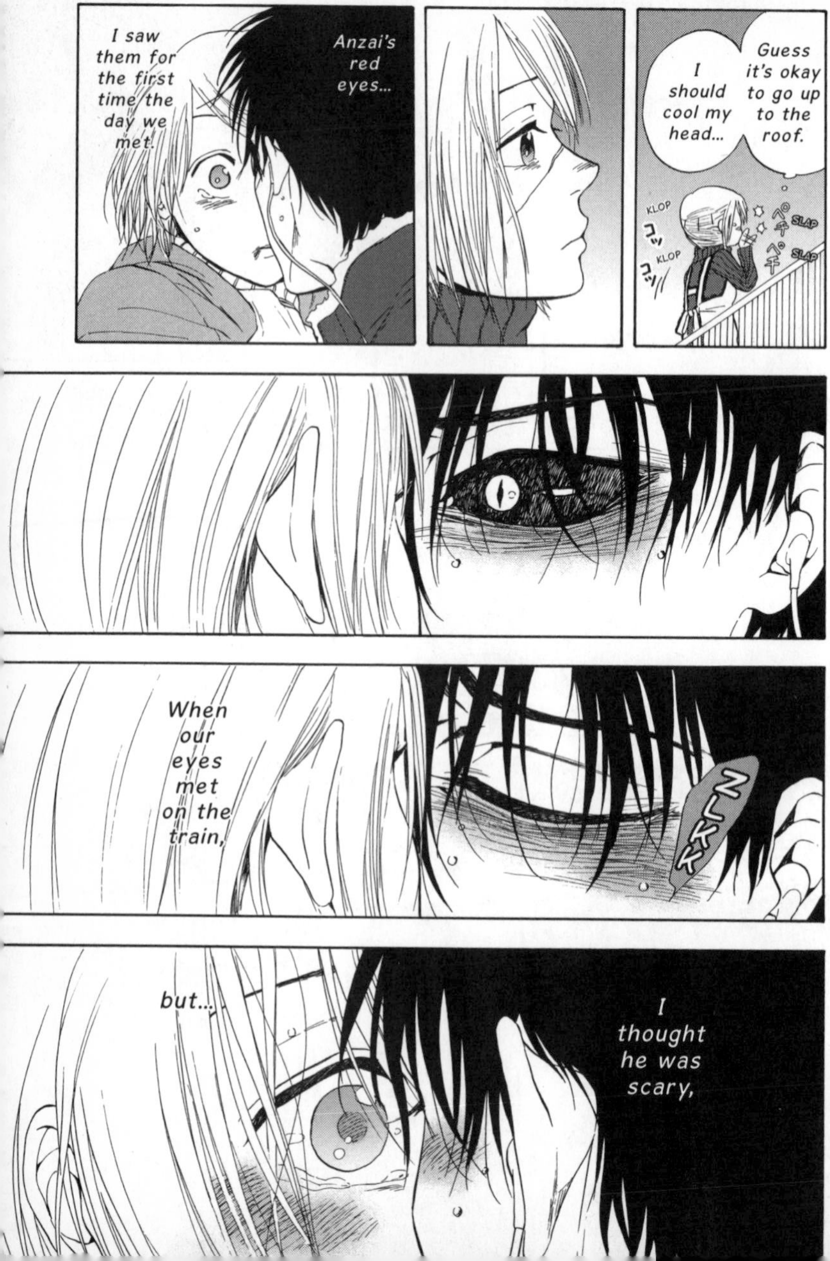
Guess it's okay to go up to the roof.
I should cool my head...
SLAP
ペチ
SLAP
ペチ
KLOP
コッ
KLOP
コッ
Anzai's red eyes...
I saw them for the first time the day we met.
ZLKK
When our eyes met on the train,
I thought he was scary,
but...

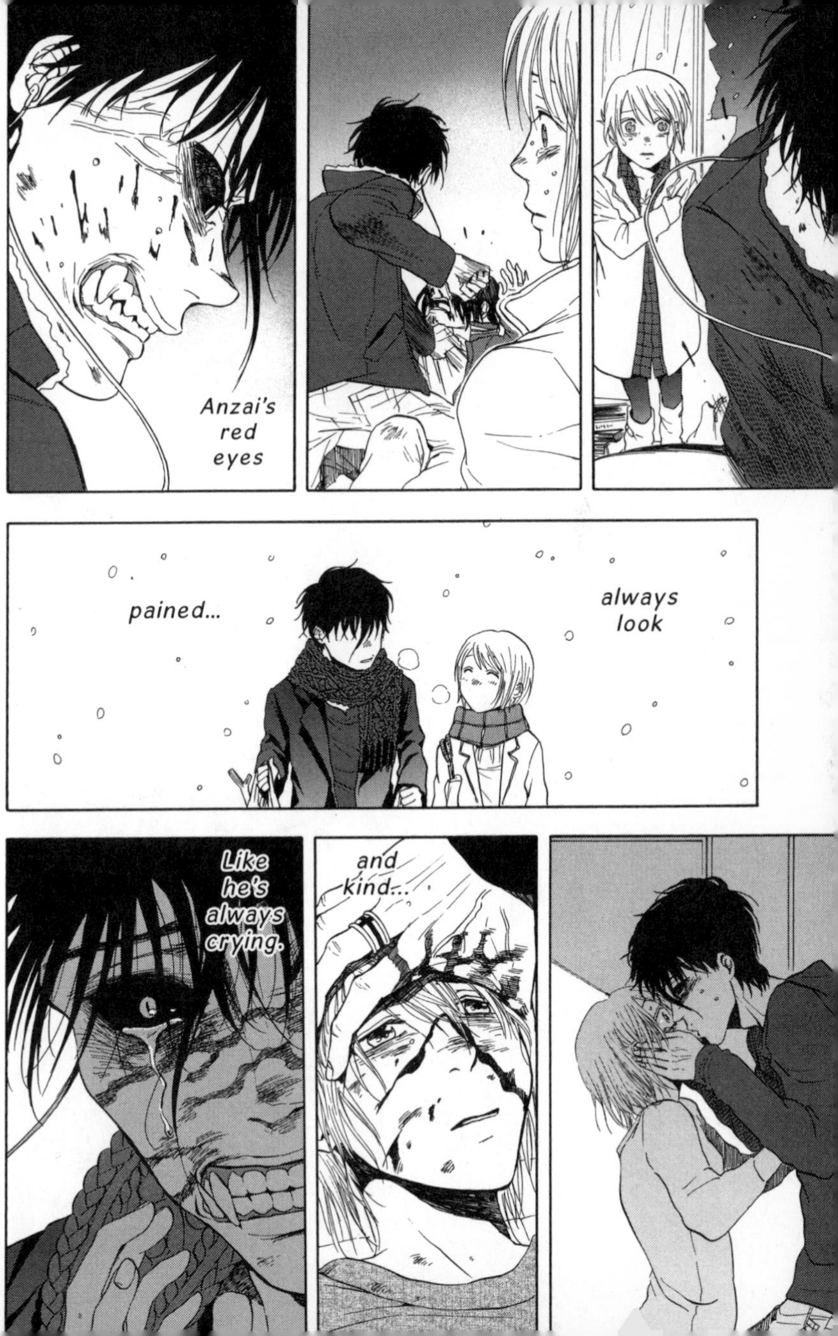
Anzai's red eyes
always look
pained...
and kind...
Like he's always crying.

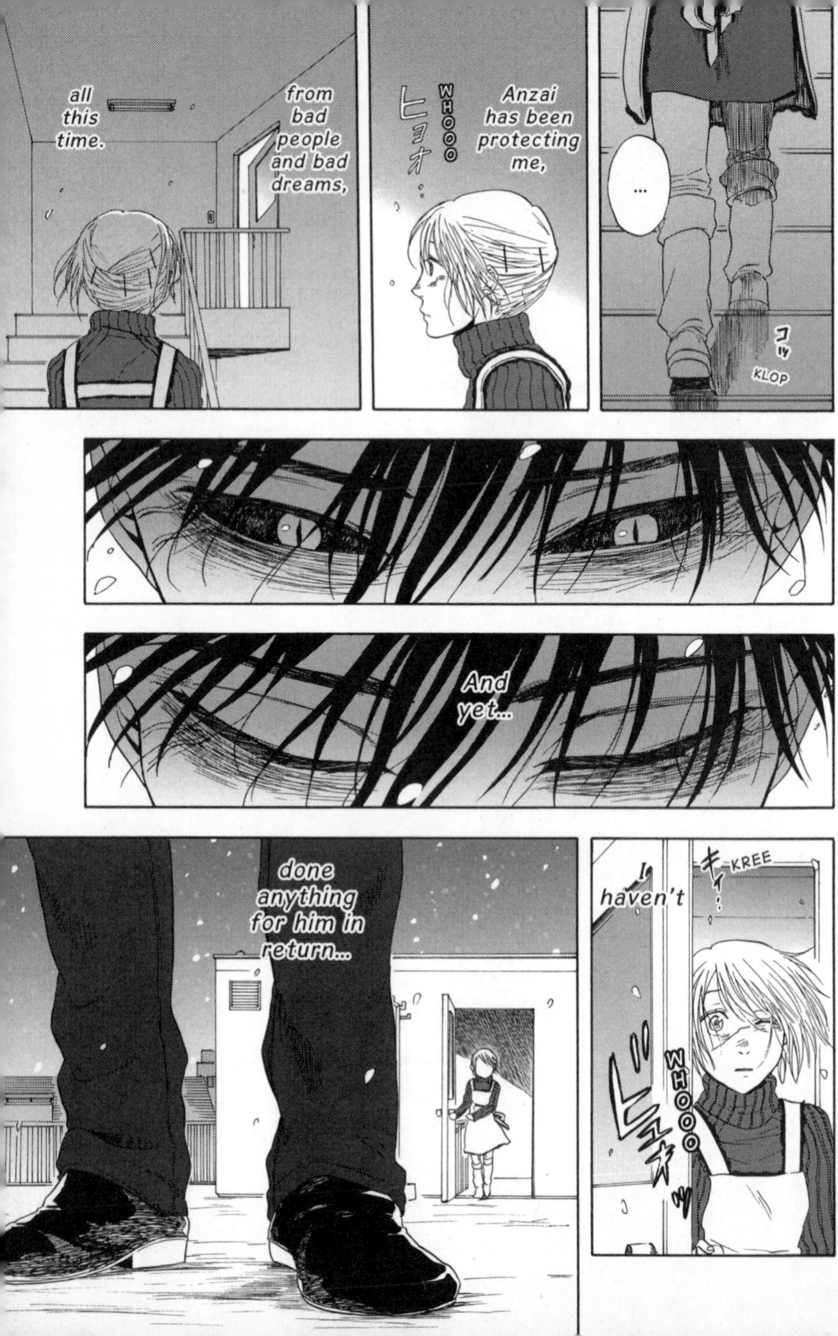
...
コッ
KLOP
Anzai has been protecting me,
ヒョオ
WHOOO
from bad people and bad dreams,
all this time.
And yet...
I haven't
キィ
KREE
ヒュオッ
WHOOO
done anything for him in return...

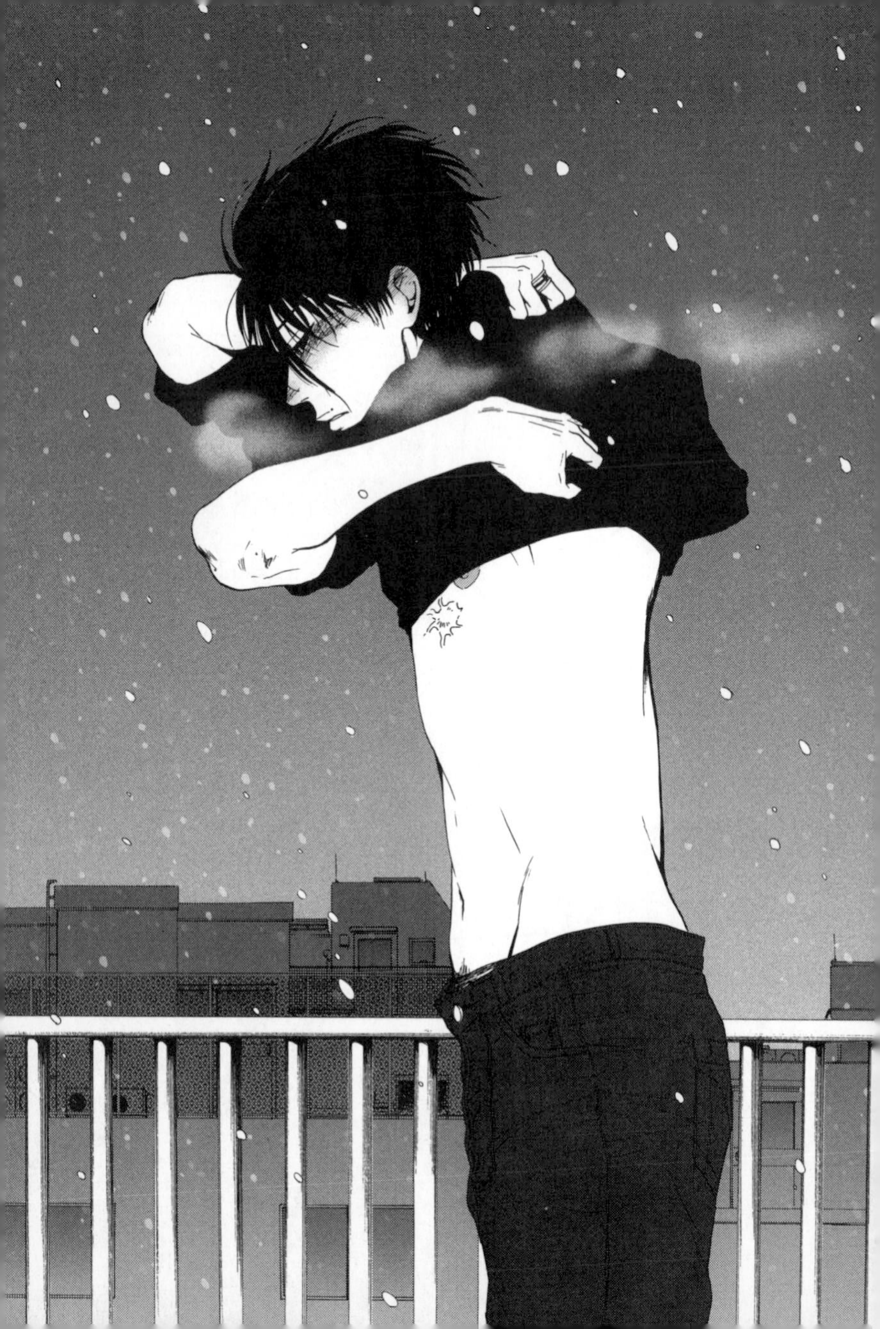

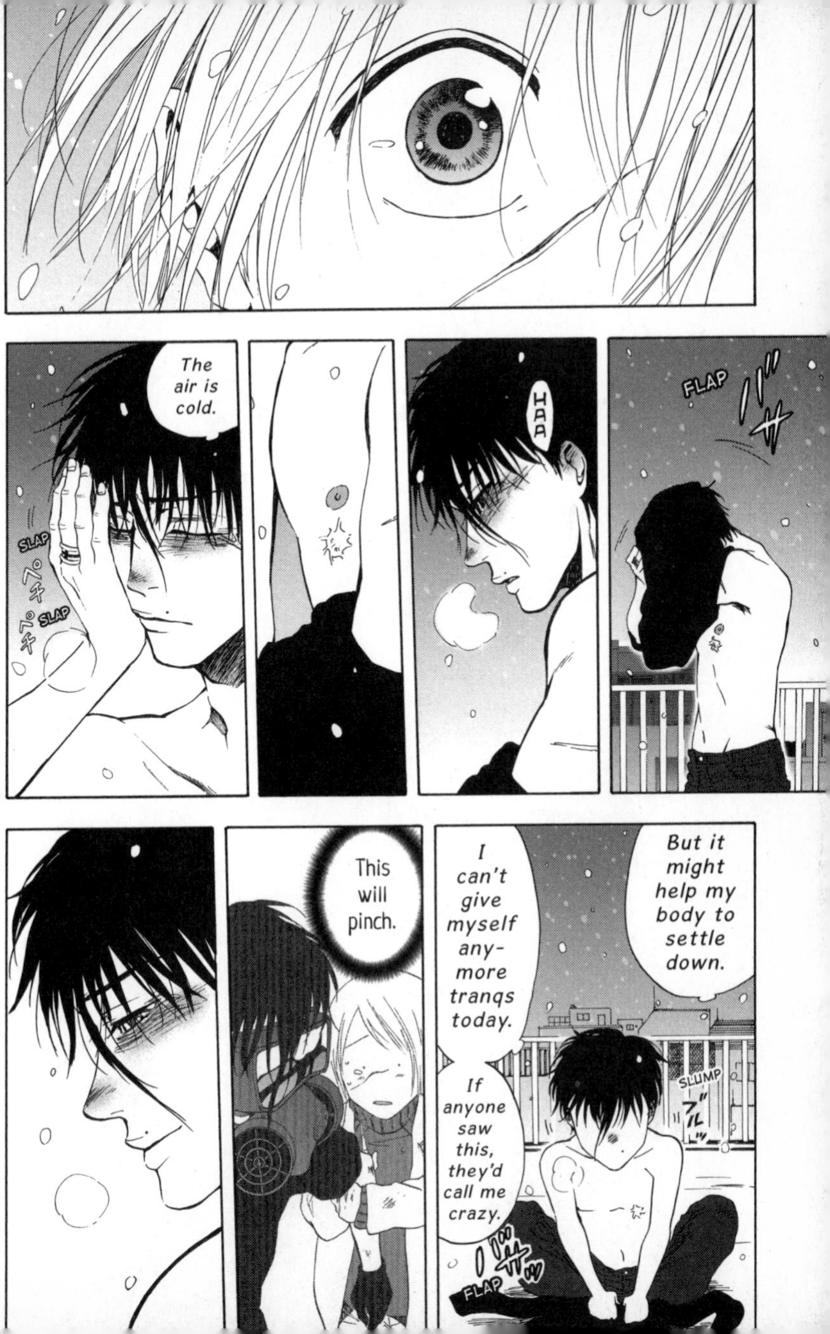
FLAP
HAA
The air is cold.
SLAP
SLAP
But it might help my body to settle down.
I can't give myself any-more tranqs today.
If anyone saw this, they'd call me crazy.
SLUMP
FLAP
This will pinch.

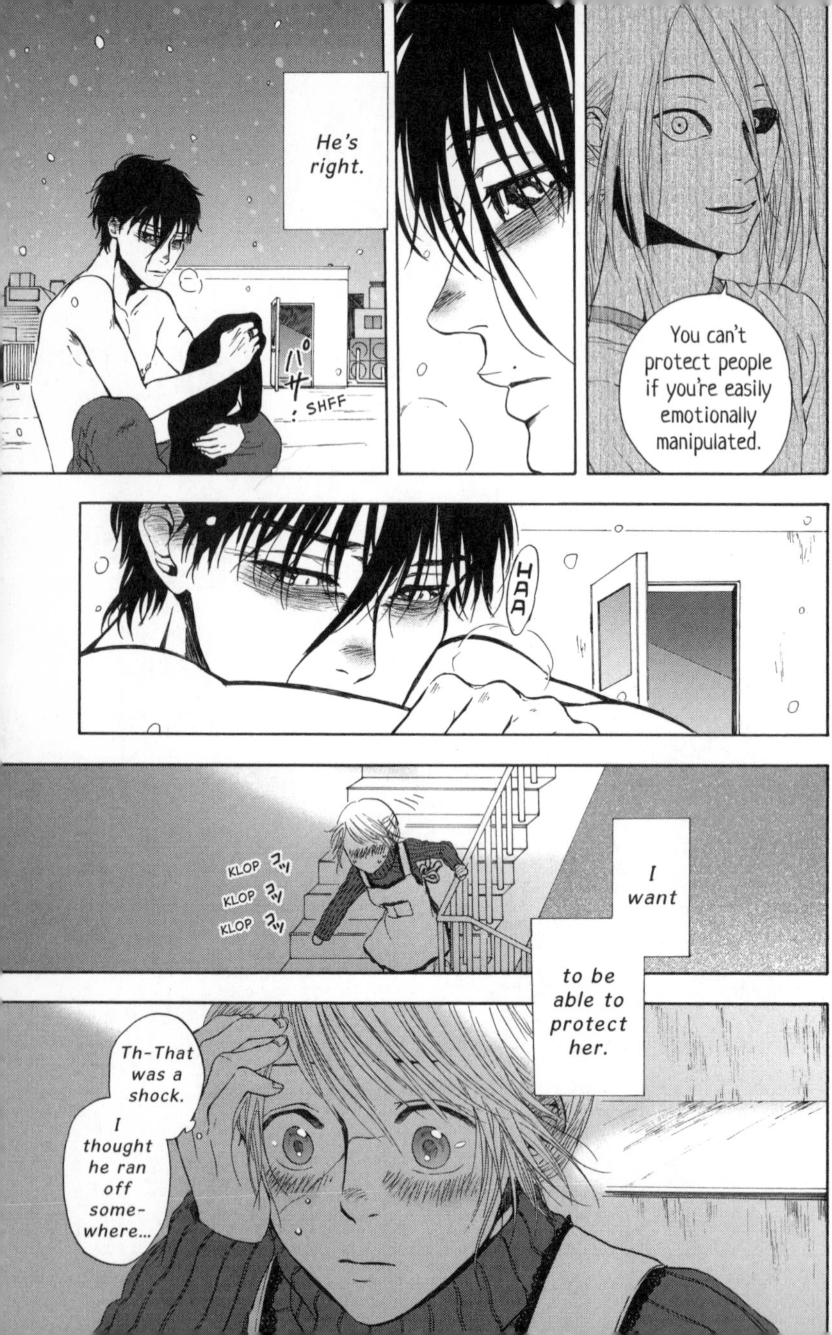
You can't protect people if you're easily emotionally manipulated.
He's right.
パサ
SHFF
HAA
I want
KLOP コッ
KLOP コッ
KLOP コッ
to be able to protect her.
Th-That was a shock.
I thought he ran off some-where...

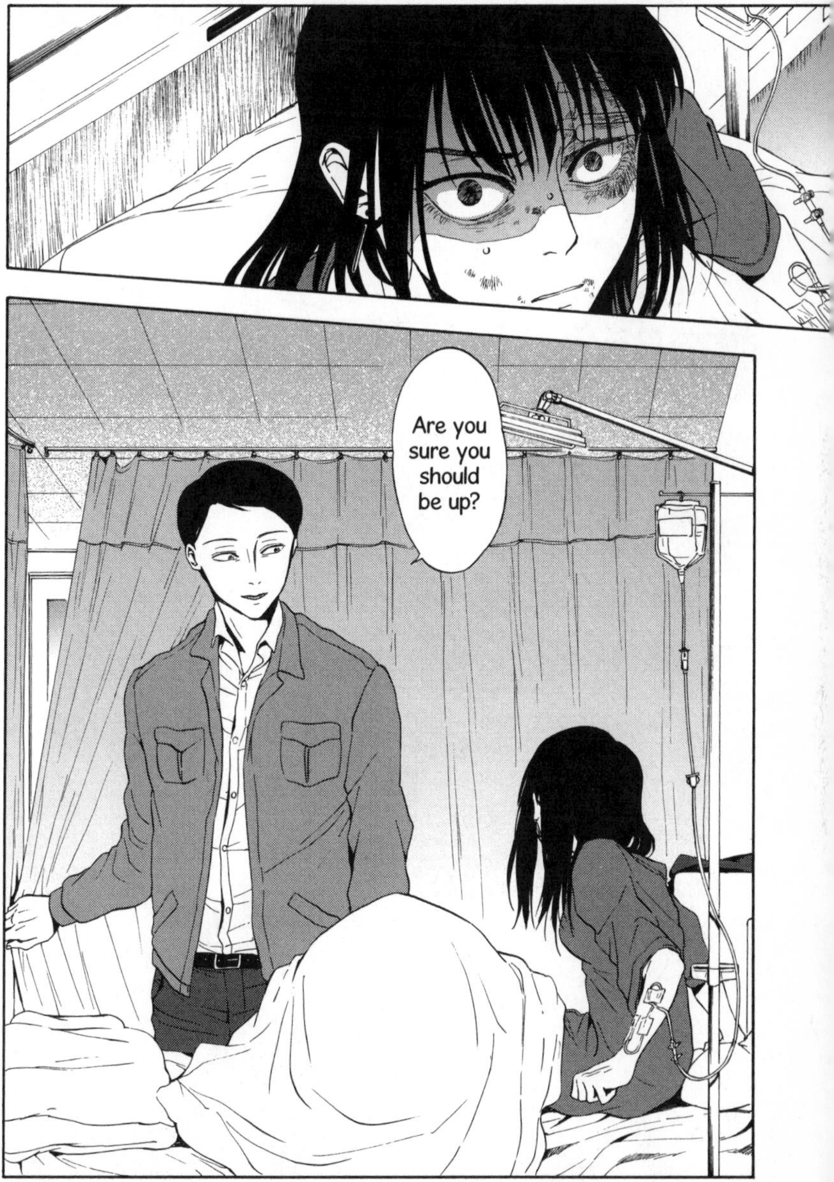
Are you sure you should be up?

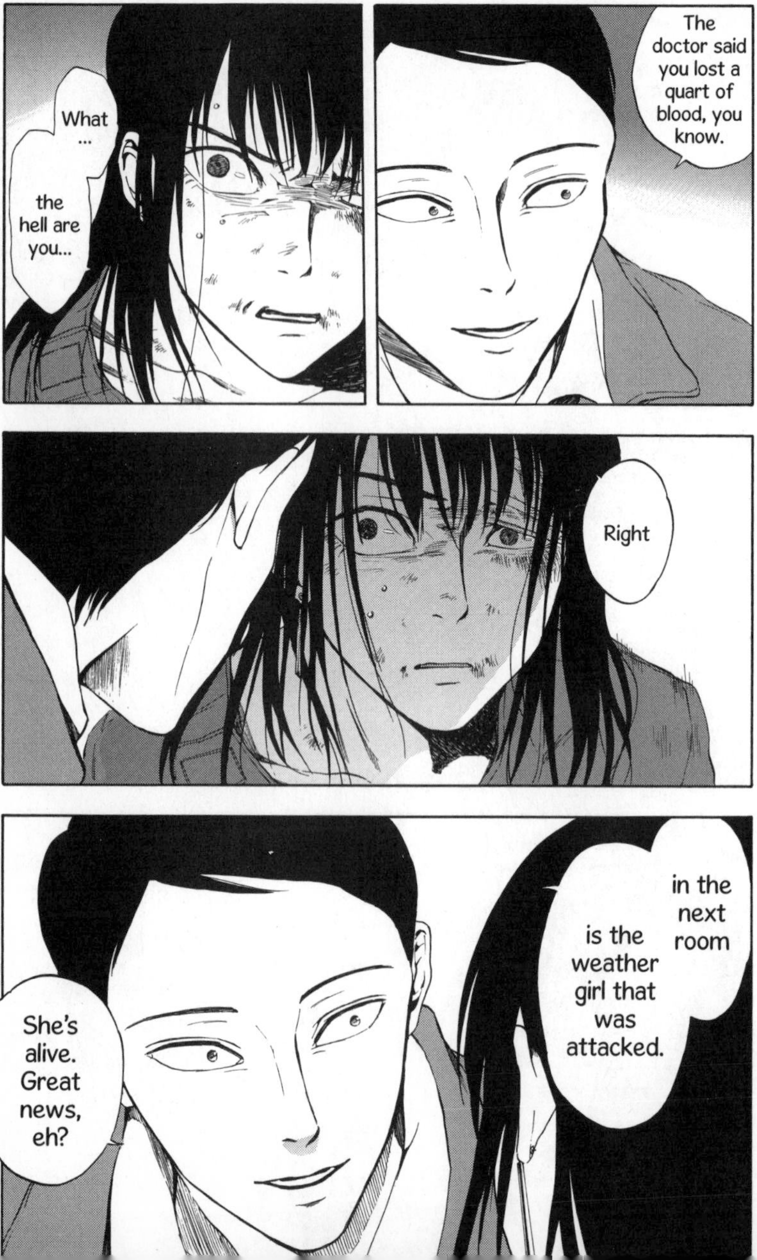
The doctor said you lost a quart of blood, you know.
What ... the hell are you...
Right
in the next room is the weather girl that was attacked.
She's alive. Great news, eh?

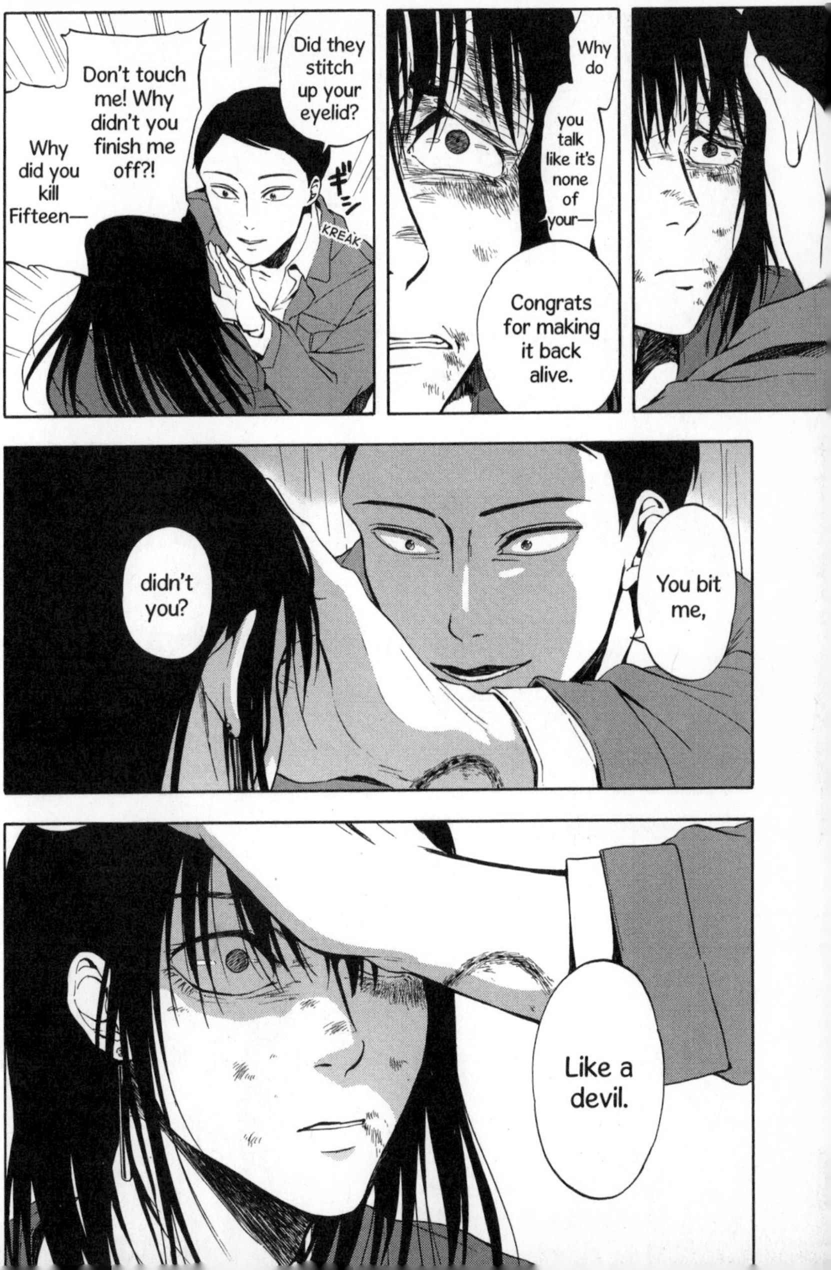
Why do you talk like it's none of your—
Congrats for making it back alive.
Did they stitch up your eyelid?
KREAK
Don't touch me! Why didn't you finish me off?!
Why did you kill Fifteen—
You bit me,
didn't you?
Like a devil.

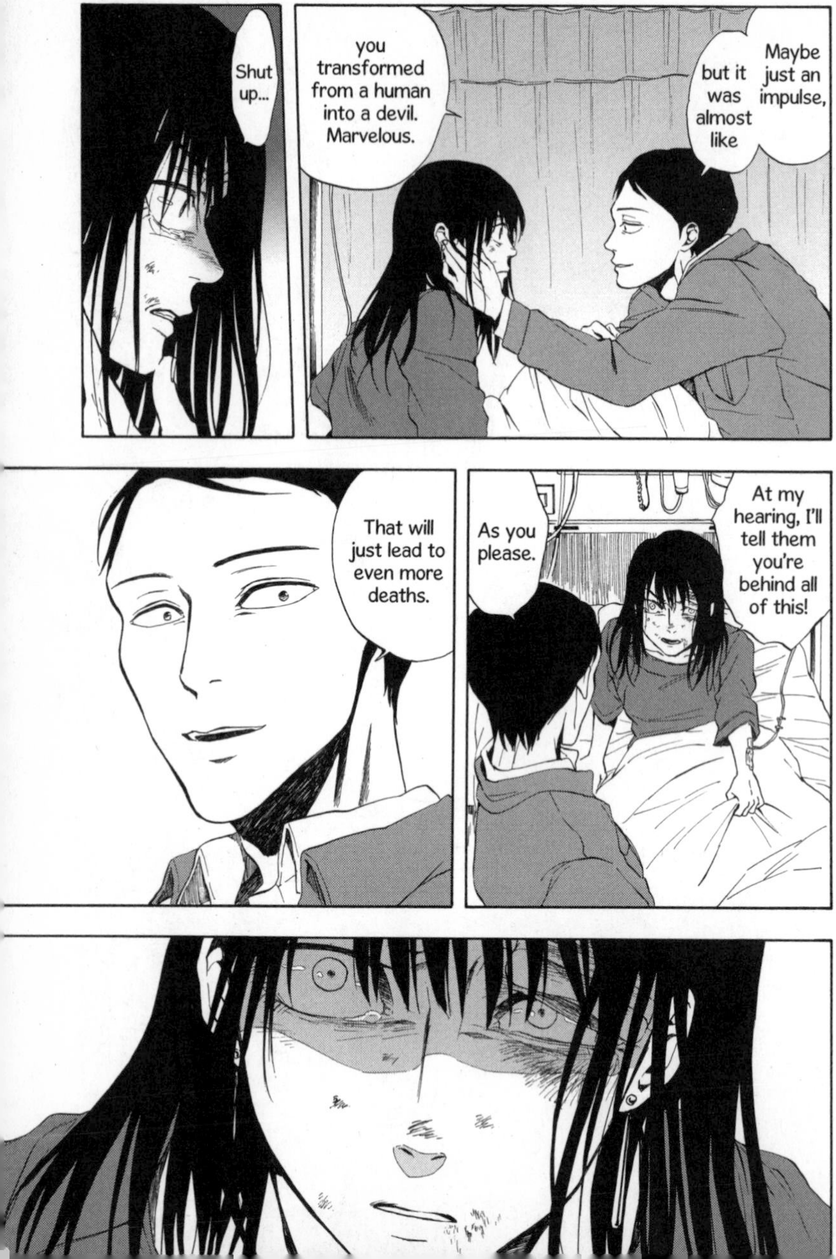
Maybe just an impulse,
but it was almost like
you transformed from a human into a devil. Marvelous.
Shut up...
At my hearing, I'll tell them you're behind all of this!
As you please.
That will just lead to even more deaths.

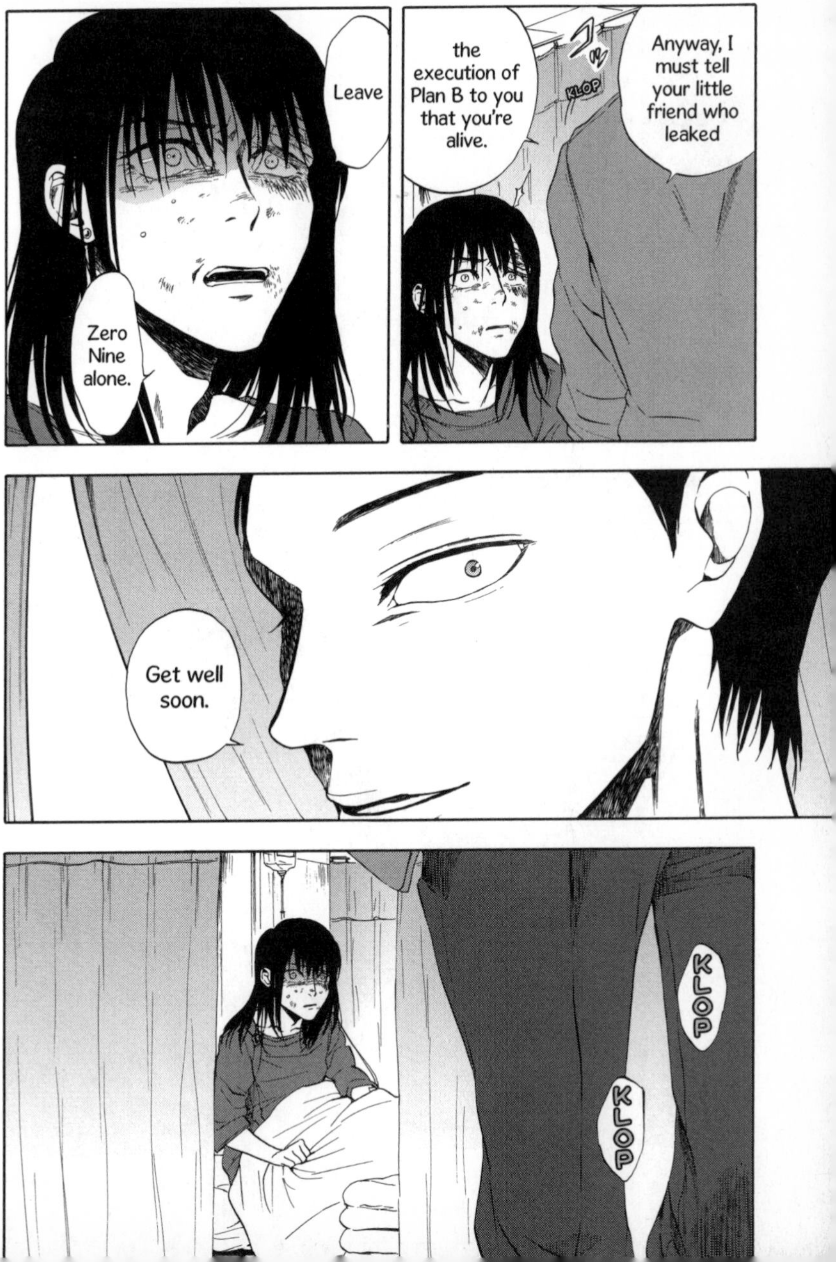
Anyway, I must tell your little friend who leaked
the execution of Plan B to you that you're alive.
KLOP
Leave
Zero Nine alone.
Get well soon.
KLOP
KLOP

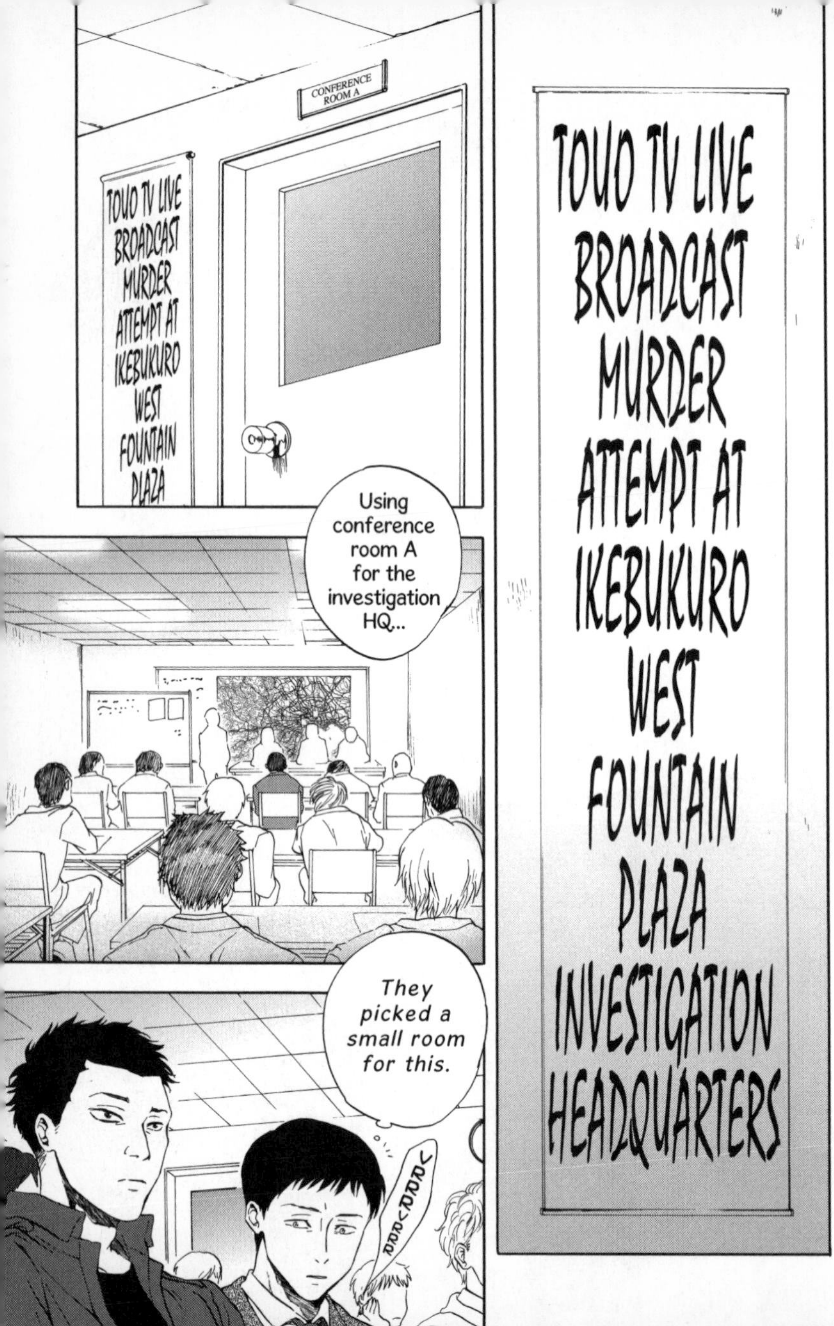
TOUO TV LIVE BROADCAST MURDER ATTEMPT AT IKEBUKURO WEST FOUNTAIN PLAZA INVESTIGATION HEADQUARTERS
CONFERENCE ROOM A
TOUO TV LIVE BROADCAST MURDER ATTEMPT AT IKEBUKURO WEST FOUNTAIN PLAZA
Using conference room A for the investigation HQ...
They picked a small room for this.

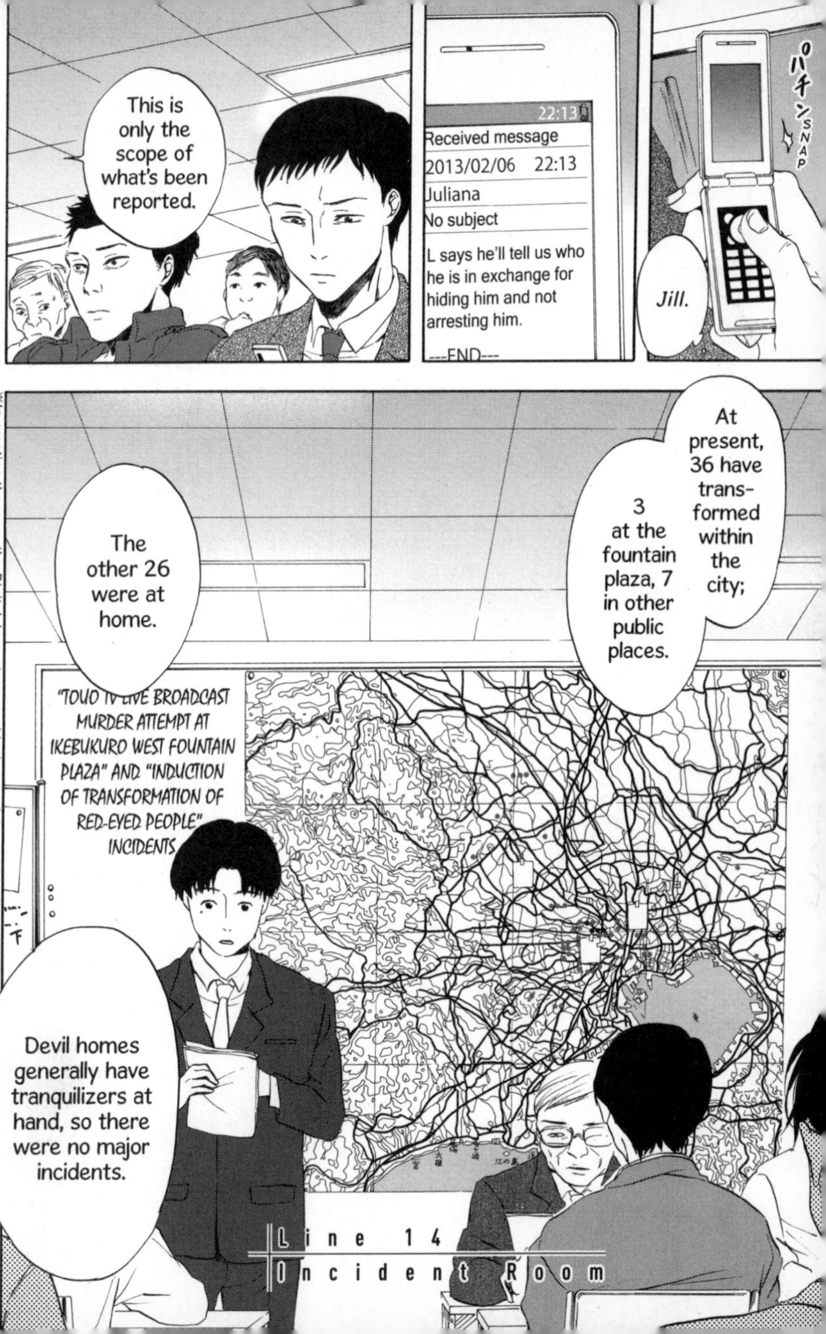
パチン
SNAP
Jill.
22:13
Received message
2013/02/06 22:13
Juliana
No subject
L says he'll tell us who he is in exchange for hiding him and not arresting him.
---END---
This is only the scope of what's been reported.
At present, 36 have transformed within the city;
3 at the fountain plaza, 7 in other public places.
The other 26 were at home.
"TOUO TV LIVE BROADCAST MURDER ATTEMPT AT IKEBUKURO WEST FOUNTAIN PLAZA" AND "INDUCTION OF TRANSFORMATION OF RED-EYED PEOPLE" INCIDENTS
Devil homes generally have tranquilizers at hand, so there were no major incidents.
Line 14
Incident Room

※In creating the map, the Digital Japan topographical map of the Geospatial Information Authority was used as reference.

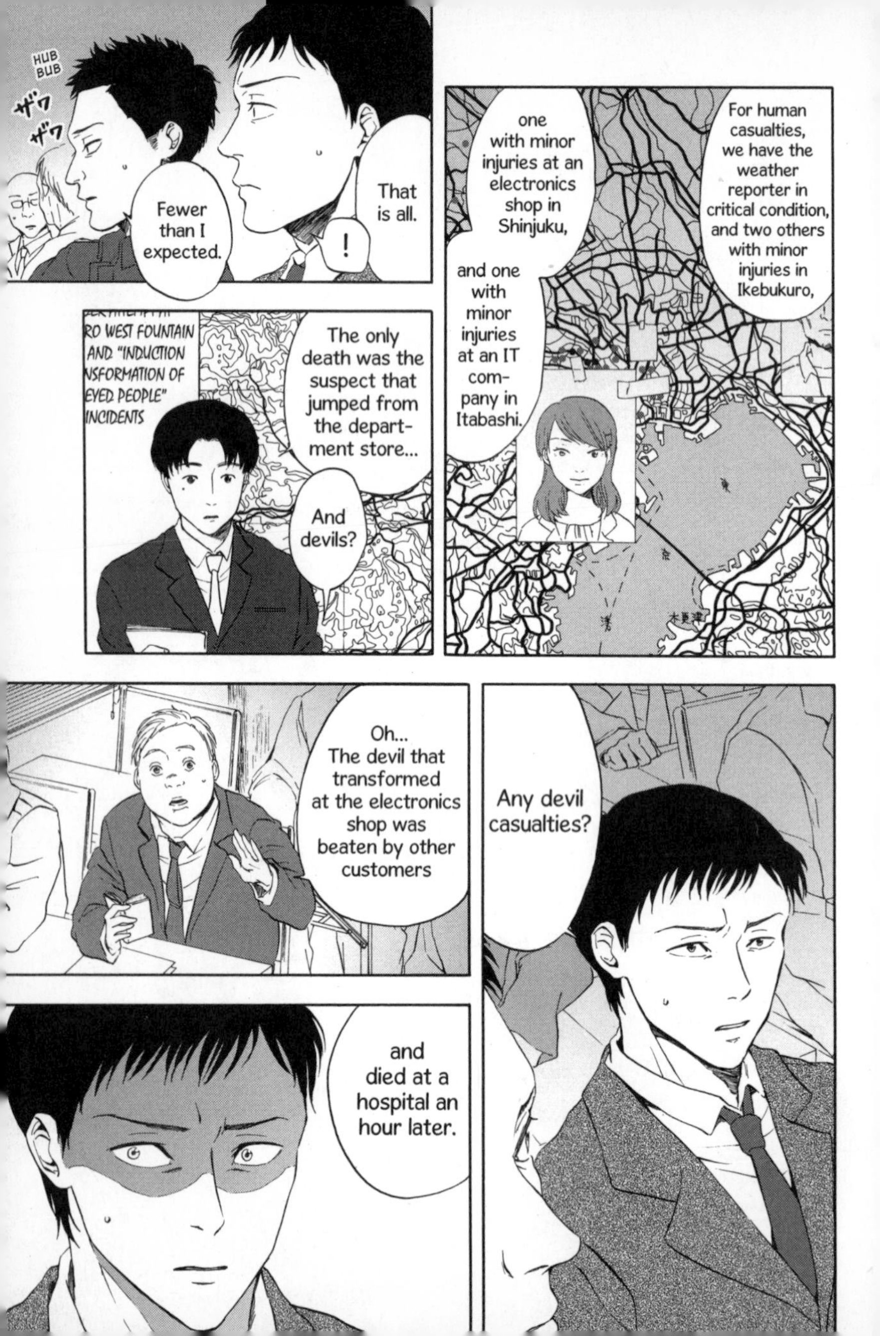
For human casualties, we have the weather reporter in critical condition, and two others with minor injuries in Ikebukuro,
one with minor injuries at an electronics shop in Shinjuku,
and one with minor injuries at an IT company in Itabashi.
That is all.
!
Fewer than I expected.
HUB BUB
ザワ ザワ
RO WEST FOUNTAIN AND "INDUCTION NSFORMATION OF EYED PEOPLE" INCIDENTS
The only death was the suspect that jumped from the department store...
And devils?
Any devil casualties?
Oh... The devil that transformed at the electronics shop was beaten by other customers
and died at a hospital an hour later.

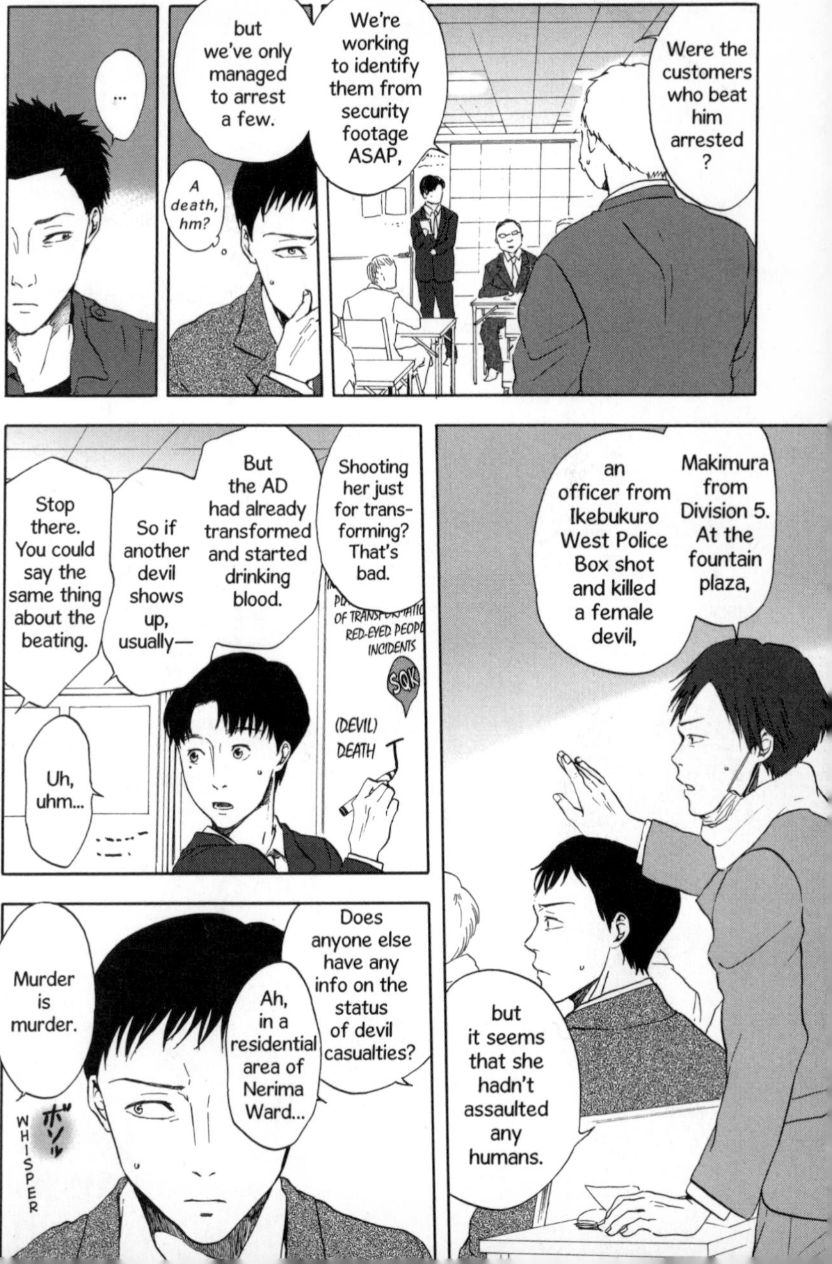

Were the customers who beat him arrested?
We're working to identify them from security footage ASAP,
but we've only managed to arrest a few.
A death, hm?
...
Makimura from Division 5. At the fountain plaza,
an officer from Ikebukuro West Police Box shot and killed a female devil,
but it seems that she hadn't assaulted any humans.
Shooting her just for transforming? That's bad.
But the AD had already transformed and started drinking blood.
So if another devil shows up, usually—
Stop there. You could say the same thing about the beating.
INCIDENTS
SQK
(DEVIL) DEATH
Uh, uhm...
Does anyone else have any info on the status of devil casualties?
Ah, in a residential area of Nerima Ward...
Murder is murder.
WHISPER

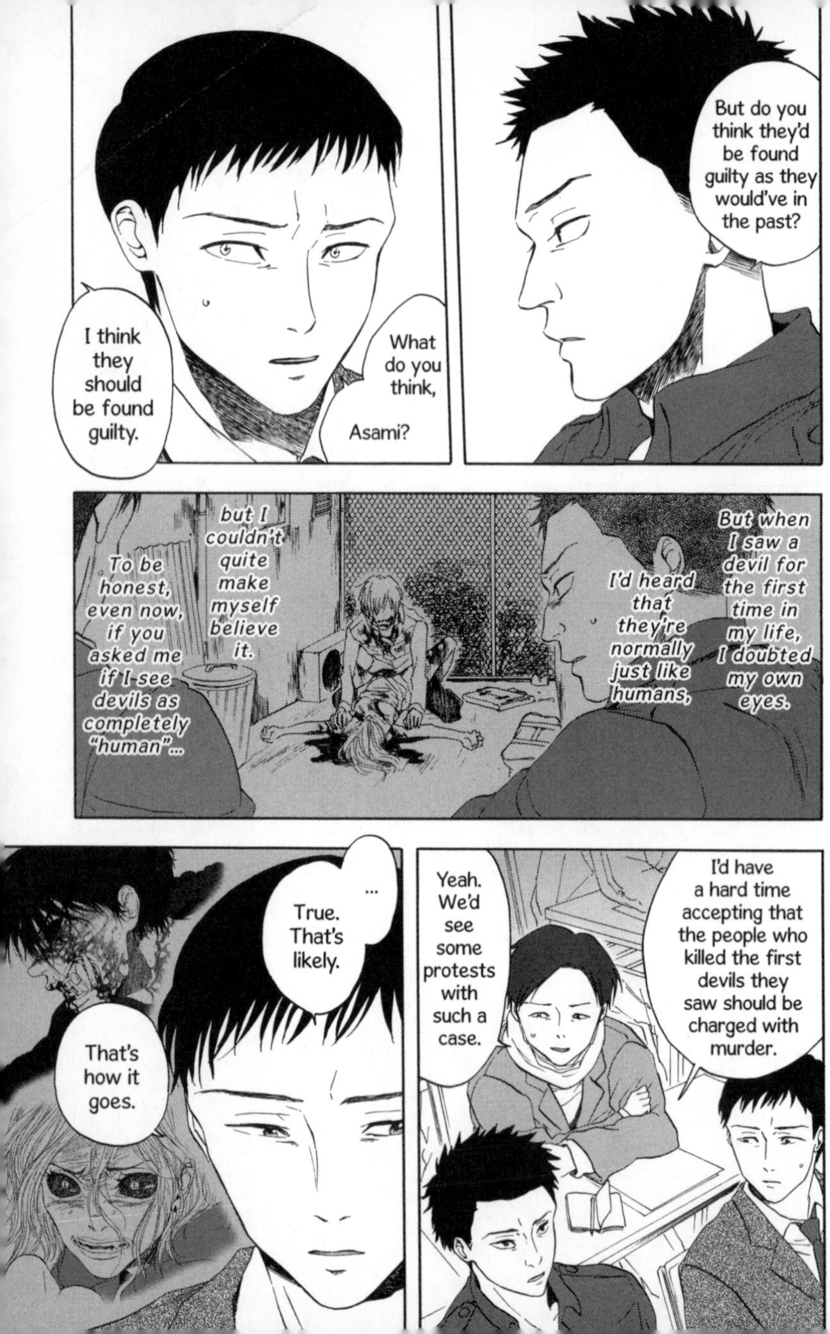

But do you think they'd be found guilty as they would've in the past?
What do you think, Asami?
I think they should be found guilty.
But when I saw a devil for the first time in my life, I doubted my own eyes.
I'd heard that they're normally just like humans,
but I couldn't quite make myself believe it.
To be honest, even now, if you asked me if I see devils as completely "human"...
I'd have a hard time accepting that the people who killed the first devils they saw should be charged with murder.
Yeah. We'd see some protests with such a case.
... True. That's likely.
That's how it goes.

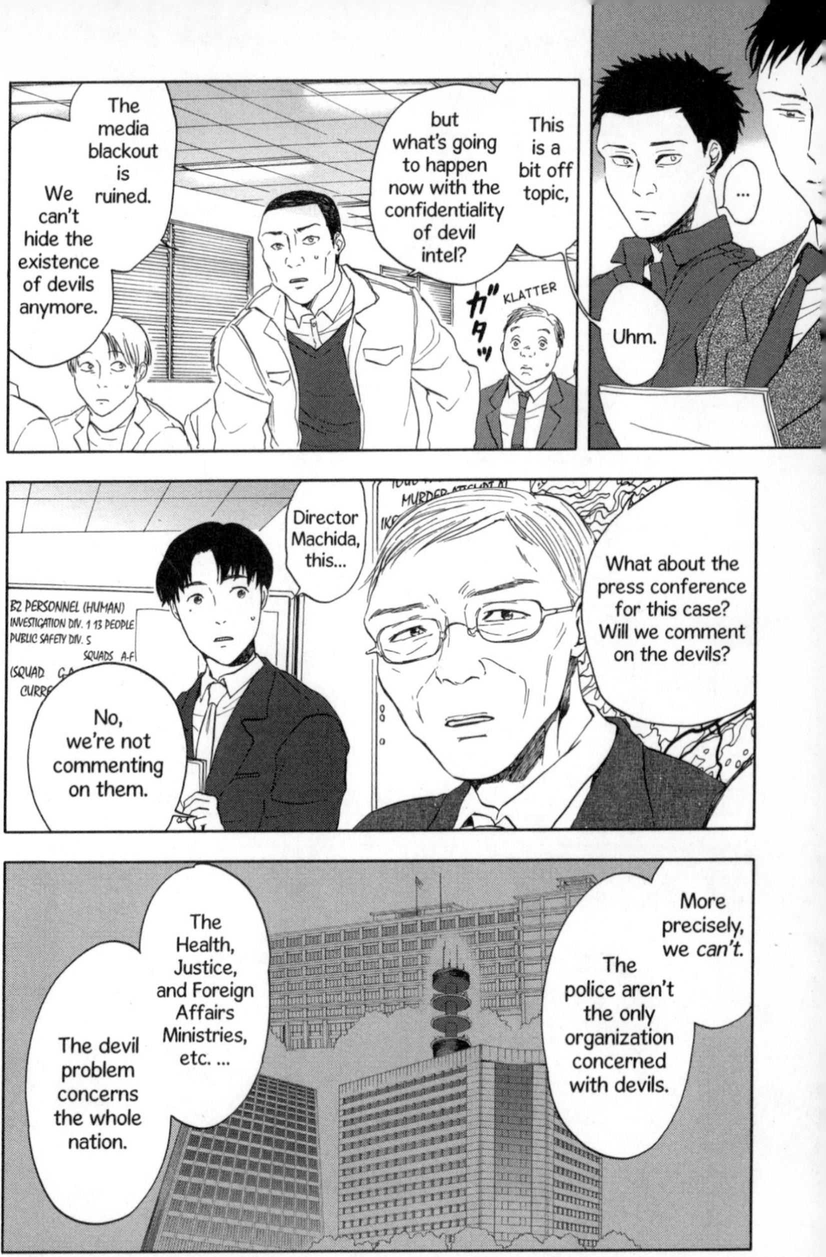
...
Uhm.
This is a bit off topic,
but what's going to happen now with the confidentiality of devil intel?
ガタッ
KLATTER
The media blackout is ruined.
We can't hide the existence of devils anymore.
What about the press conference for this case? Will we comment on the devils?
Director Machida, this...
B2 PERSONNEL (HUMAN)
INVESTIGATION DIV. 1 13 PEOPLE
PUBLIC SAFETY DIV. 5
SQUADS A-F
No, we're not commenting on them.
More precisely, we *can't*.
The police aren't the only organization concerned with devils.
The Health, Justice, and Foreign Affairs Ministries, etc. ...
The devil problem concerns the whole nation.

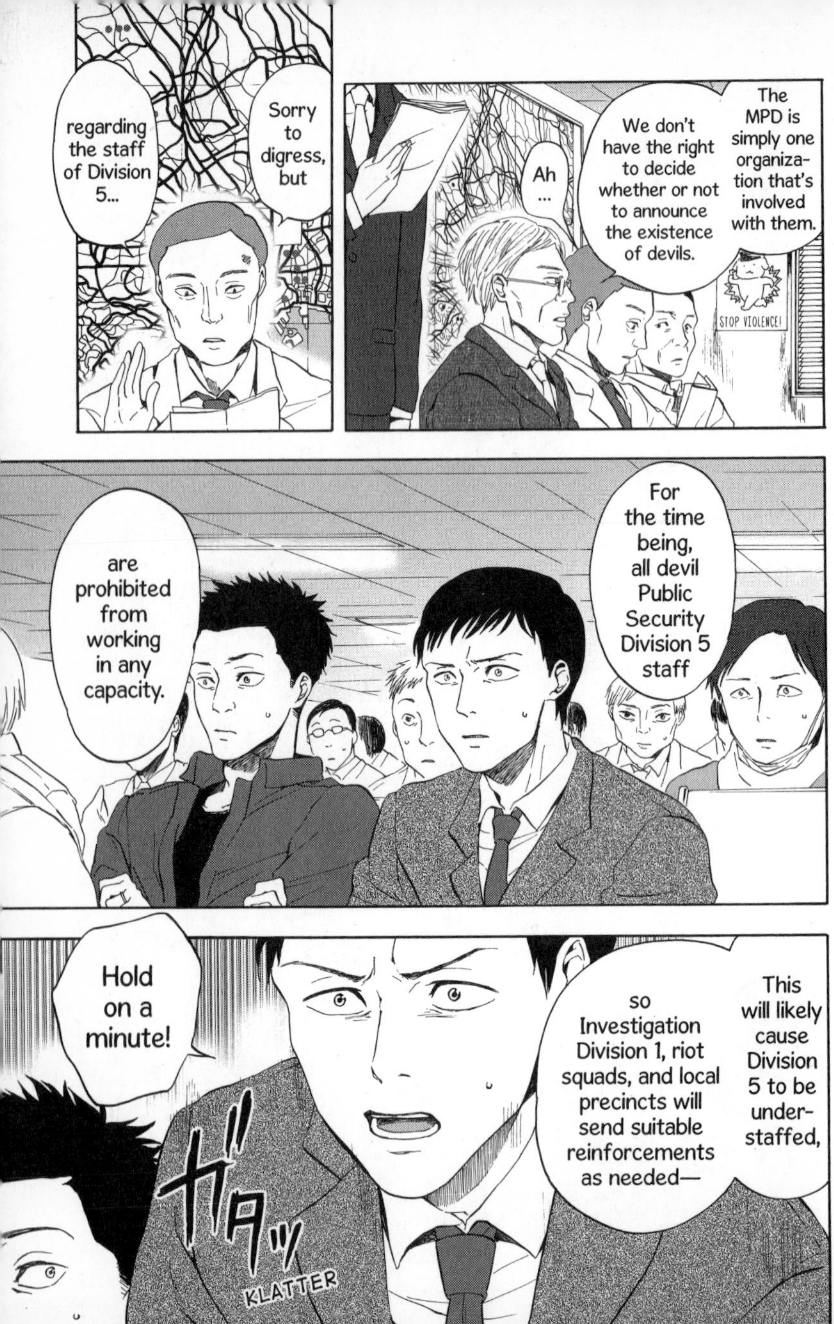
The MPD is simply one organiza-tion that's involved with them.
We don't have the right to decide whether or not to announce the existence of devils.
Ah ...
STOP VIOLENCE!
Sorry to digress, but
regarding the staff of Division 5...
For the time being, all devil Public Security Division 5 staff
are prohibited from working in any capacity.
This will likely cause Division 5 to be under-staffed,
so Investigation Division 1, riot squads, and local precincts will send suitable reinforcements as needed—
Hold on a minute!
KLATTER

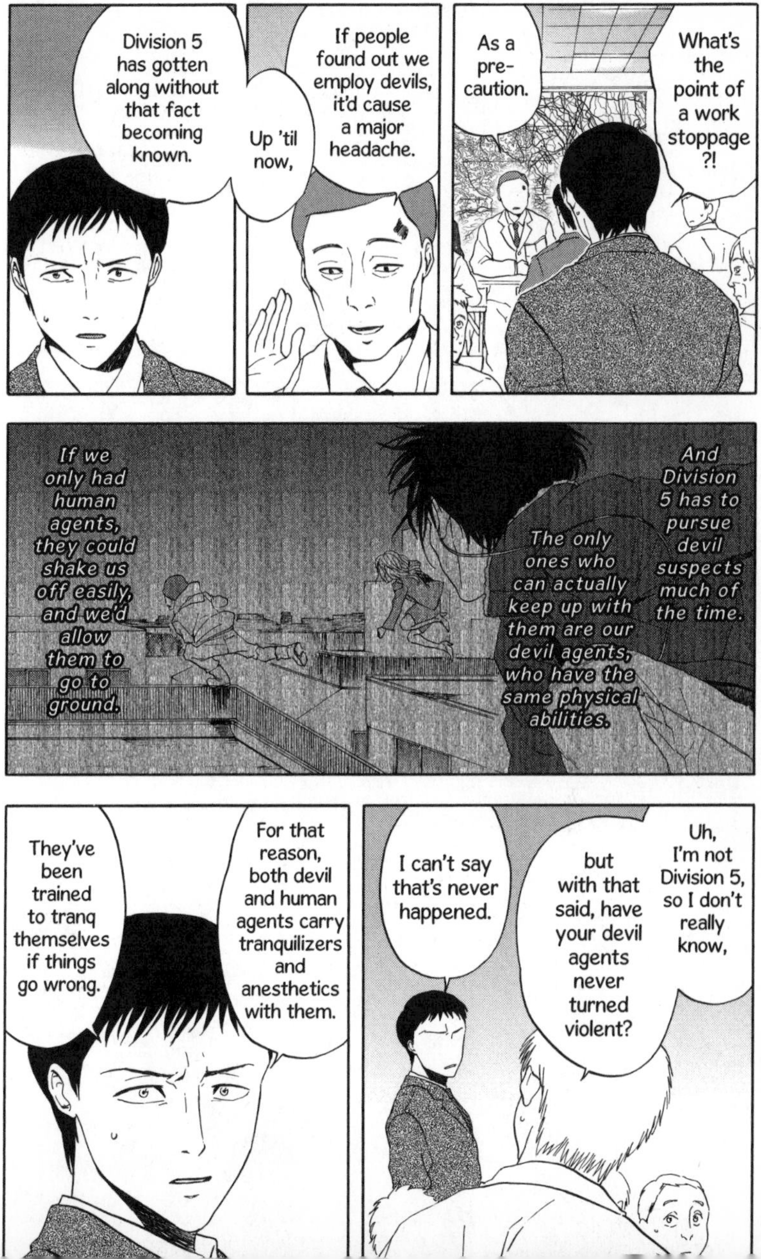
What's the point of a work stoppage?!
As a pre-caution.
If people found out we employ devils, it'd cause a major headache.
Up 'til now,
Division 5 has gotten along without that fact becoming known.
And Division 5 has to pursue devil suspects much of the time.
The only ones who can actually keep up with them are our devil agents, who have the same physical abilities.
If we only had human agents, they could shake us off easily, and we'd allow them to go to ground.
Uh, I'm not Division 5, so I don't really know,
but with that said, have your devil agents never turned violent?
I can't say that's never happened.
For that reason, both devil and human agents carry tranquilizers and anesthetics with them.
They've been trained to tranq themselves if things go wrong.

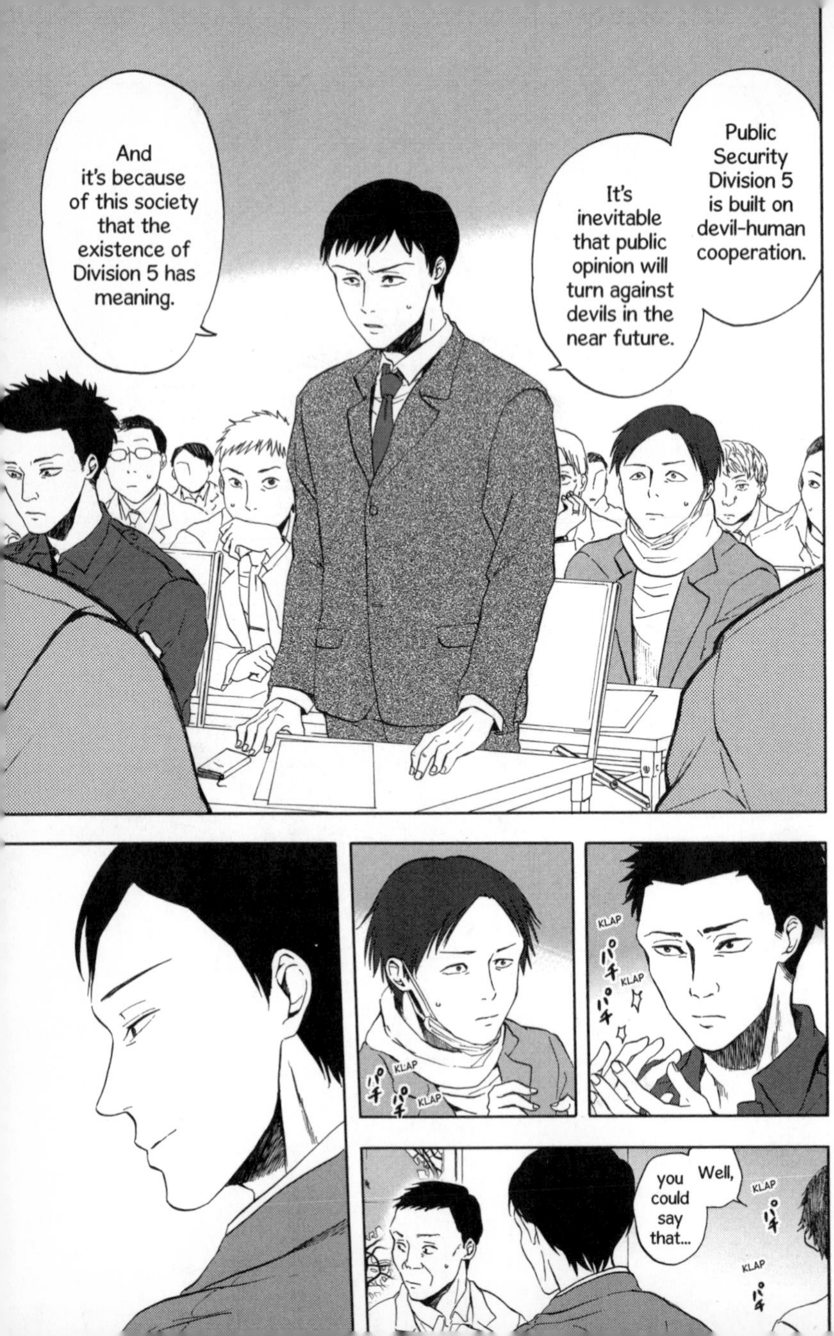
Public Security Division 5 is built on devil-human cooperation.
It's inevitable that public opinion will turn against devils in the near future.
And it's because of this society that the existence of Division 5 has meaning.
KLAP
パチ
KLAP
パチ
KLAP
パチ
パチ
KLAP
Well, you could say that...
KLAP
パチ
KLAP
パチ

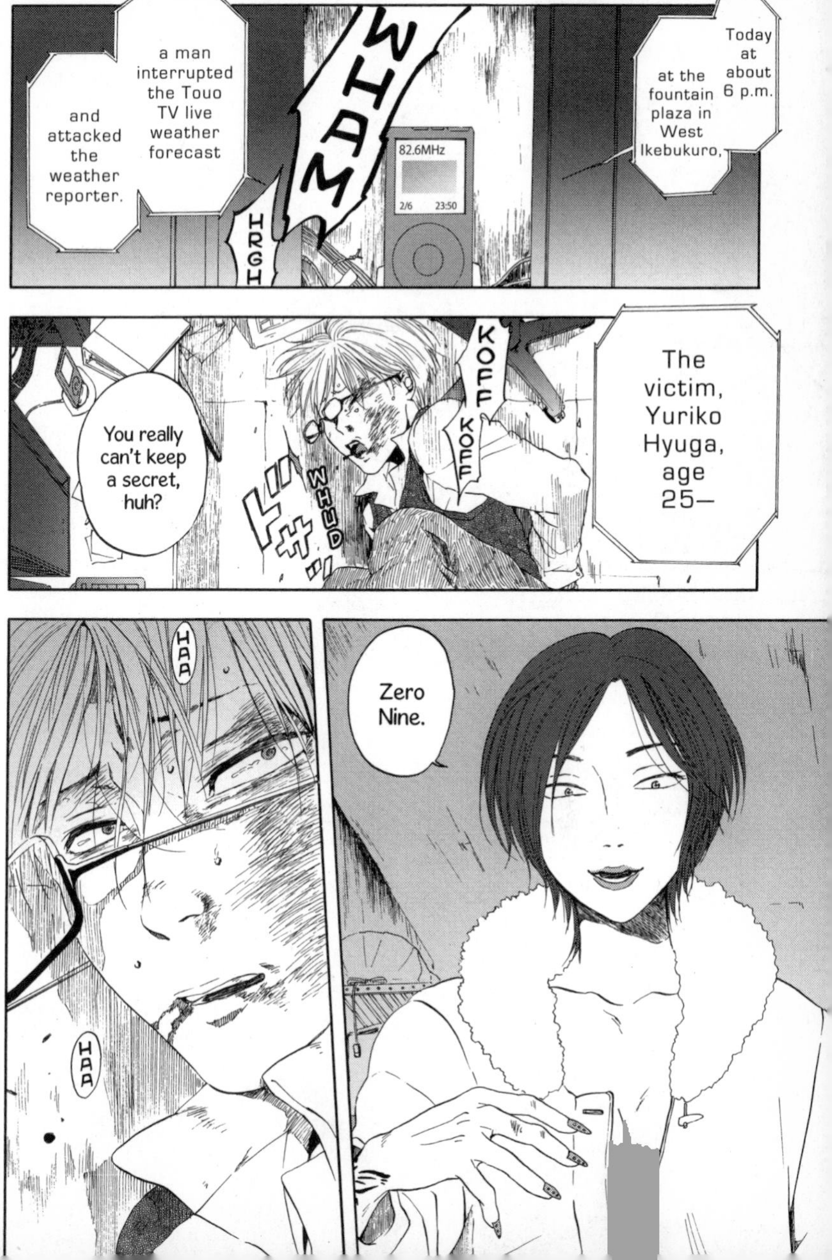
Today at about 6 p.m.
at the fountain plaza in West Ikebukuro,
a man interrupted the Touo TV live weather forecast
and attacked the weather reporter.
WHAM
82.6MHz
2/6 23:50
HRGH
The victim, Yuriko Hyuga, age 25—
KOFF
KOFF
WHUD
You really can't keep a secret, huh?
Zero Nine.
HAA
HAA

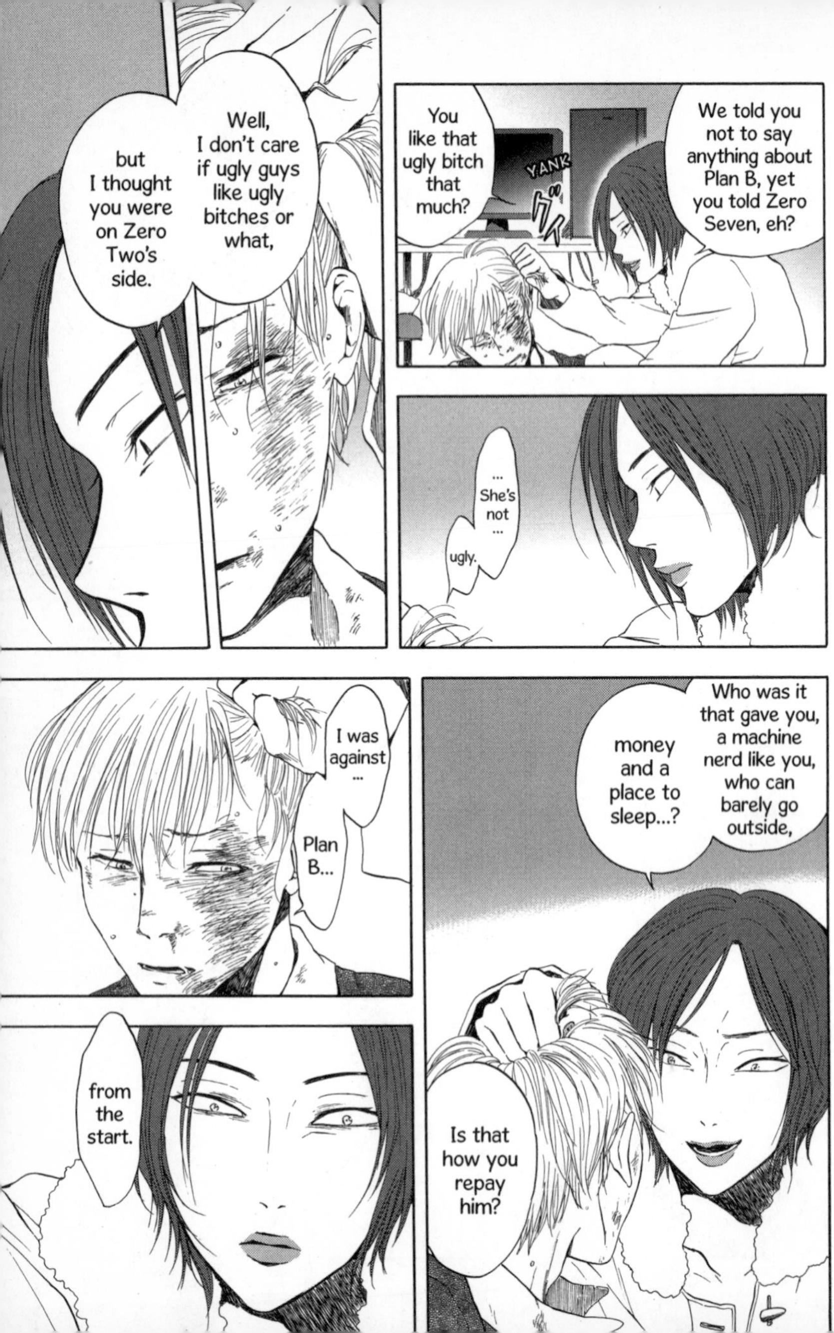

We told you not to say anything about Plan B, yet you told Zero Seven, eh?
YANK
グイ
You like that ugly bitch that much?
... She's not ...
ugly.
Well, I don't care if ugly guys like ugly bitches or what,
but I thought you were on Zero Two's side.
Who was it that gave you, a machine nerd like you, who can barely go outside,
money and a place to sleep...?
Is that how you repay him?
I was against ...
Plan B...
from the start.

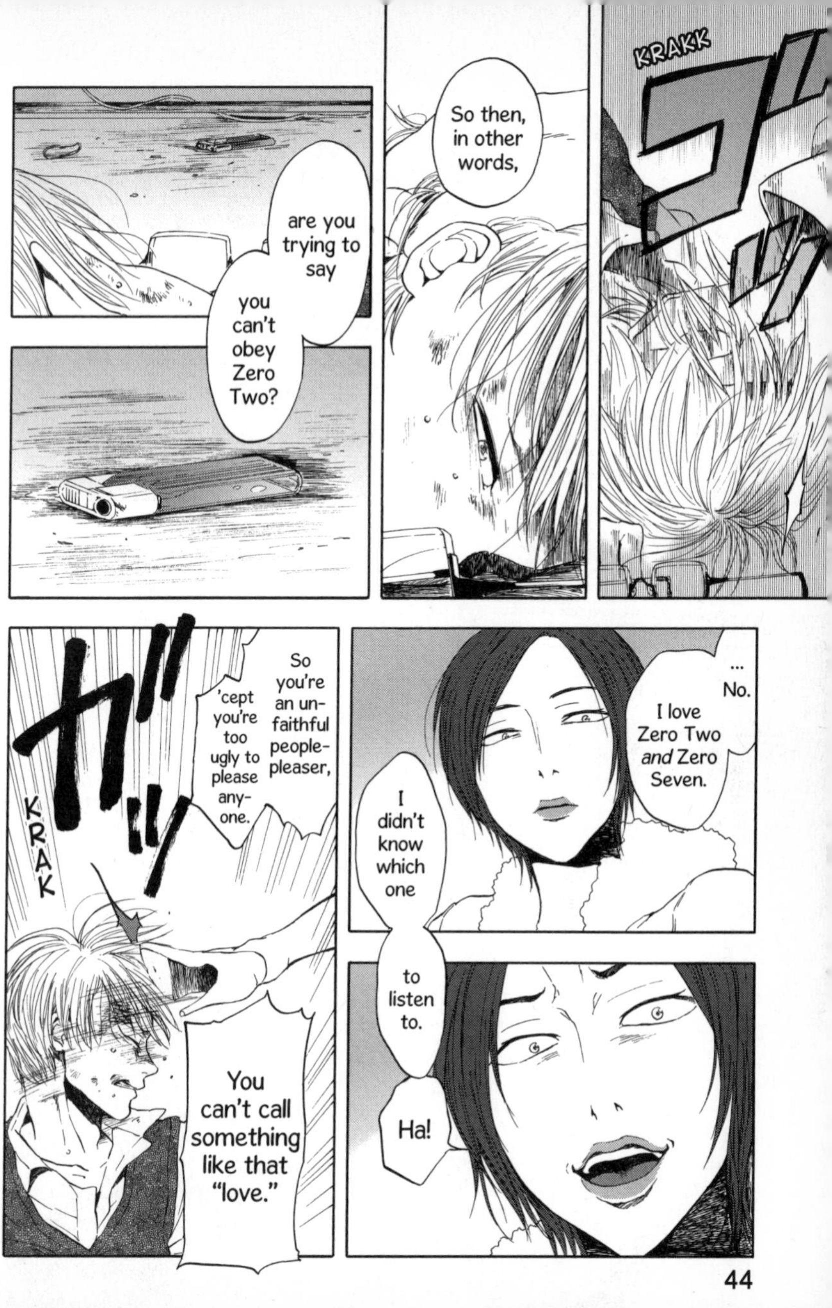
KRAKK
So then, in other words,
are you trying to say
you can't obey Zero Two?
... No.
I love Zero Two *and* Zero Seven.
I didn't know which one
to listen to.
Ha!
So you're an unfaithful people-pleaser,
'cept you're too ugly to please anyone.
KRAK
You can't call something like that "love."

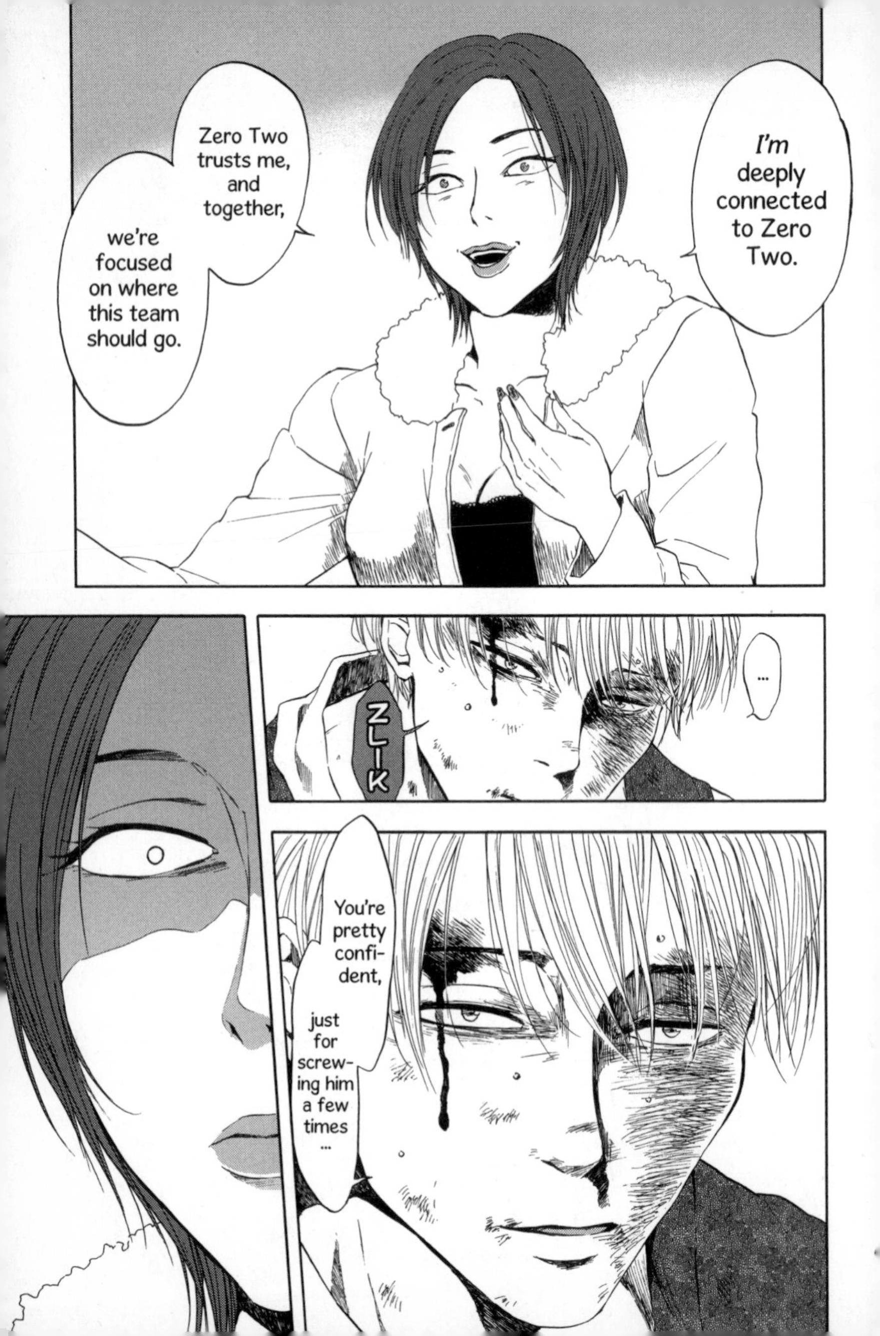
I'm deeply connected to Zero Two.
Zero Two trusts me, and together,
we're focused on where this team should go.
...
ZLIK
You're pretty confident,
just for screwing him a few times...

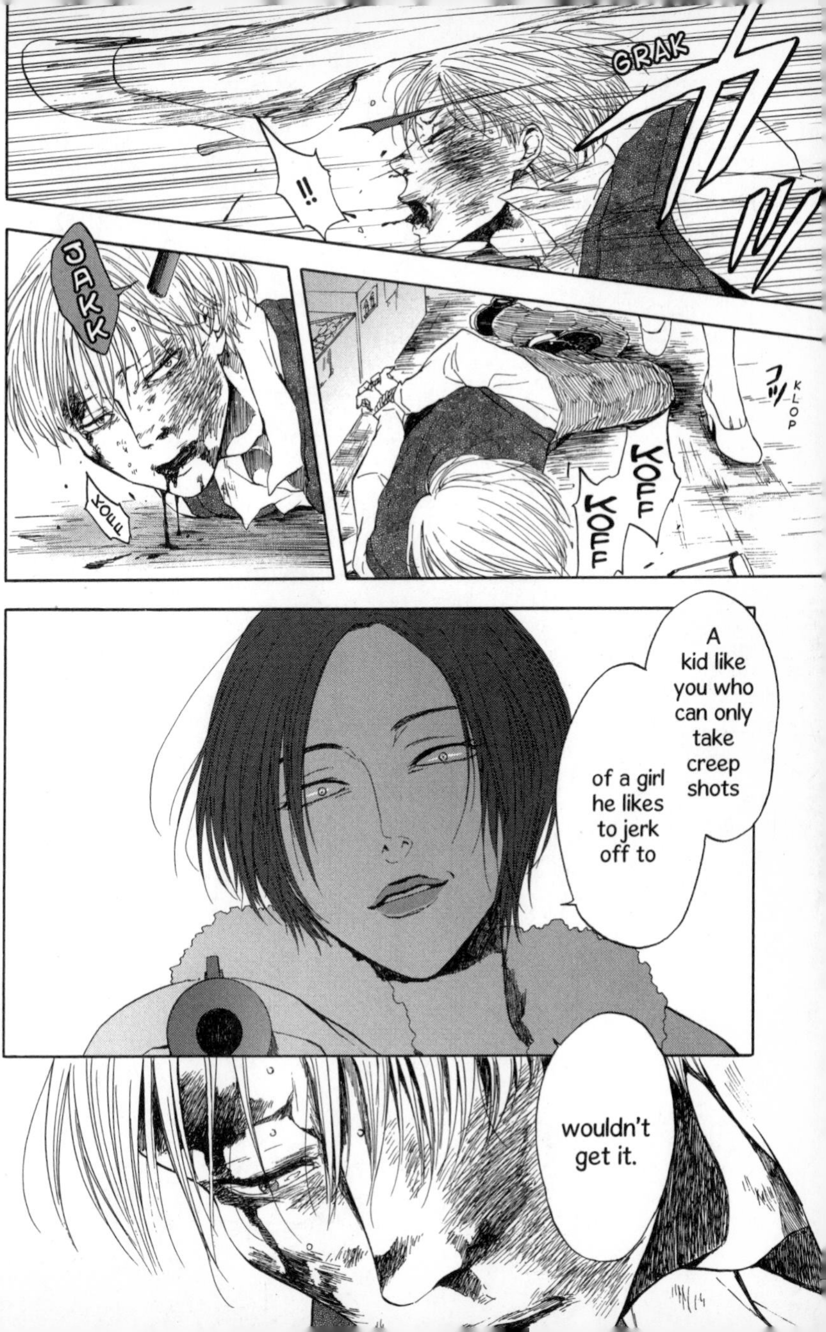
GRAK
!!
KLOP
KOFF KOFF
JAKK
A kid like you who can only take creep shots
of a girl he likes to jerk off to
wouldn't get it.

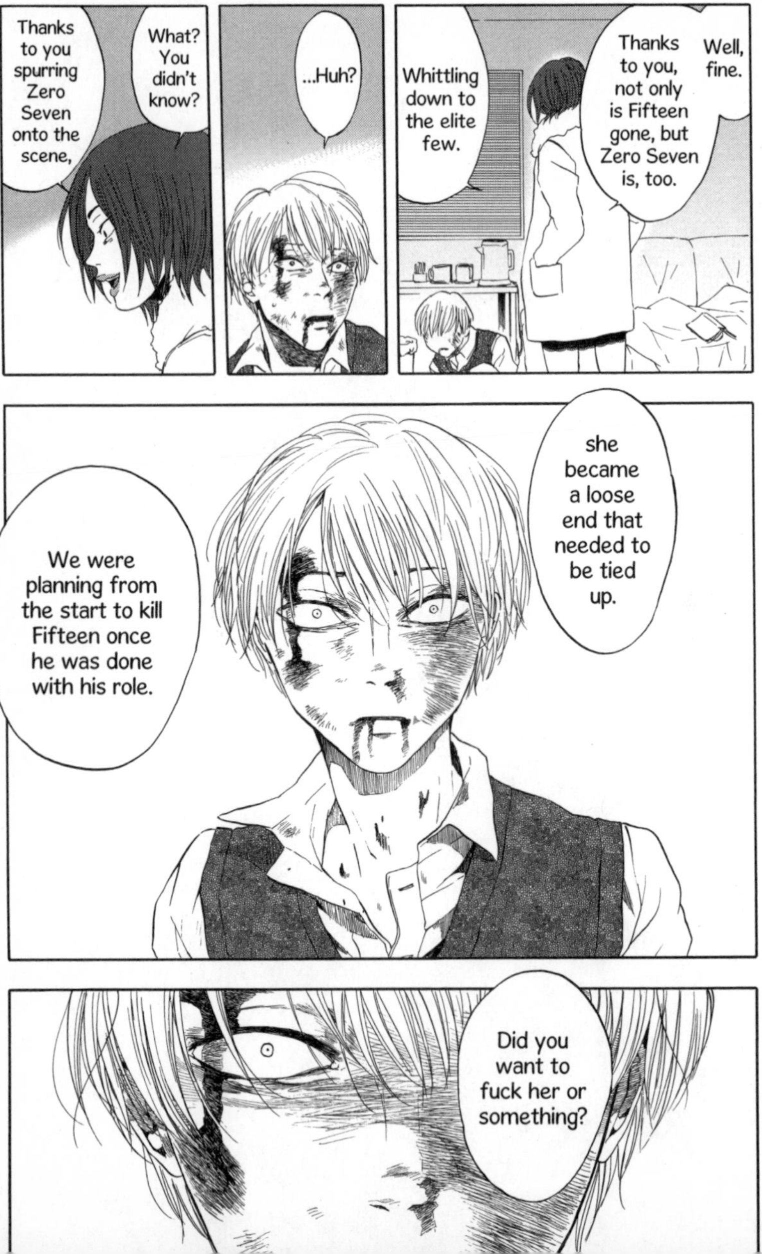
Well, fine.
Thanks to you, not only is Fifteen gone, but Zero Seven is, too.
Whittling down to the elite few.
...Huh?
What? You didn't know?
Thanks to you spurring Zero Seven onto the scene,
she became a loose end that needed to be tied up.
We were planning from the start to kill Fifteen once he was done with his role.
Did you want to fuck her or something?

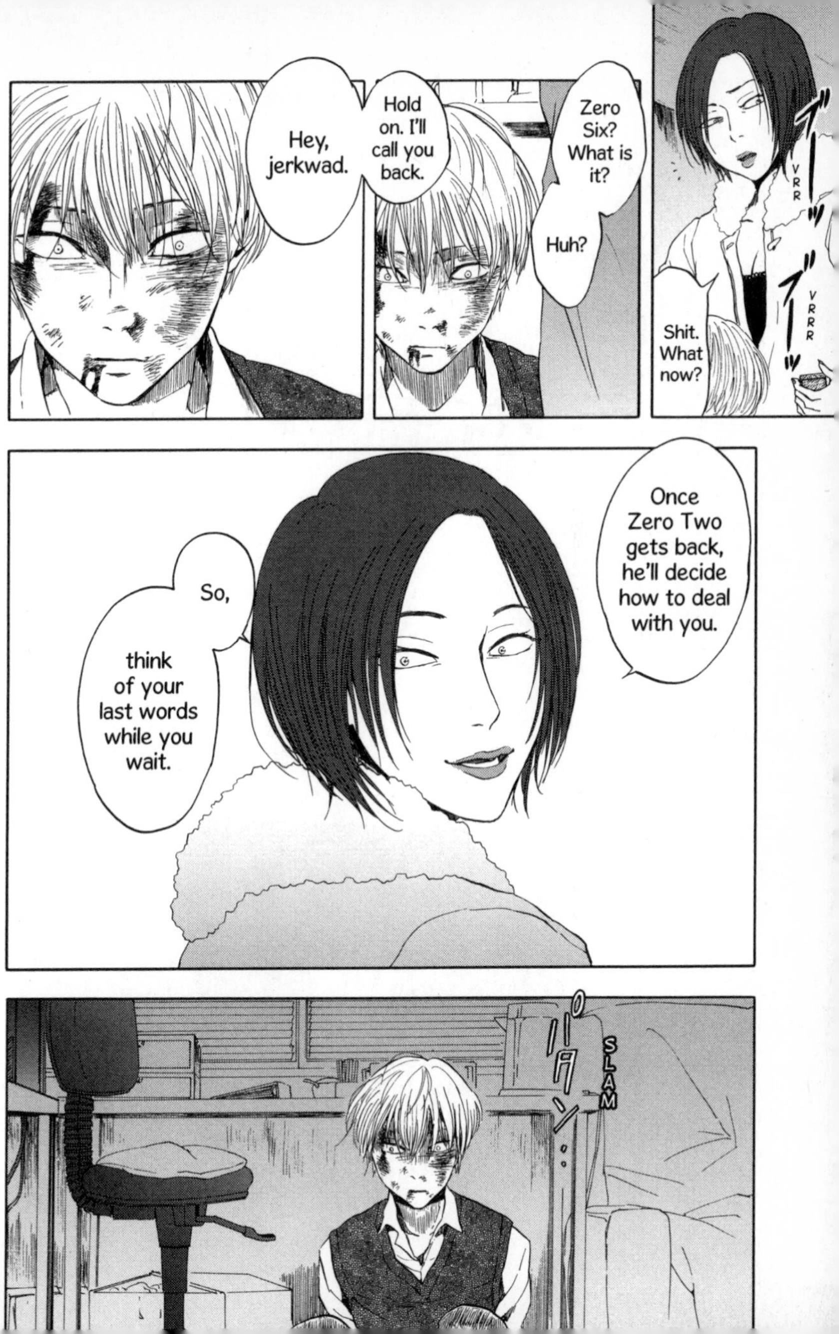
VRR
VRRR
Shit. What now?
Zero Six? What is it?
Huh?
Hold on. I'll call you back.
Hey, jerkwad.
Once Zero Two gets back, he'll decide how to deal with you.
So,
think of your last words while you wait.
SLAM

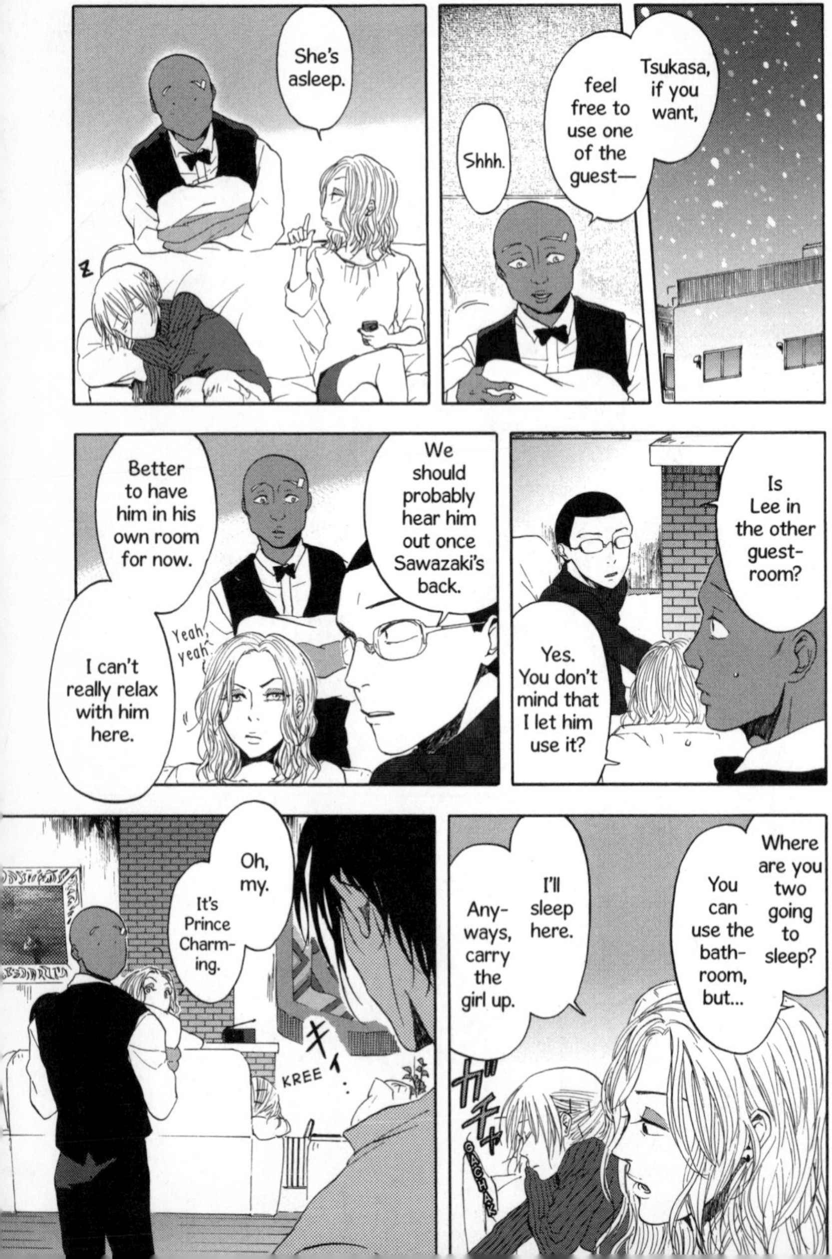
Tsukasa, if you want,
feel free to use one of the guest—
Shhh.
She's asleep.
Is Lee in the other guest-room?
Yes. You don't mind that I let him use it?
We should probably hear him out once Sawazaki's back.
Better to have him in his own room for now.
Yeah, yeah.
I can't really relax with him here.
Where are you two going to sleep?
You can use the bathroom, but...
I'll sleep here.
Anyways, carry the girl up.
GACHA
Oh, my.
It's Prince Charming.
KREE

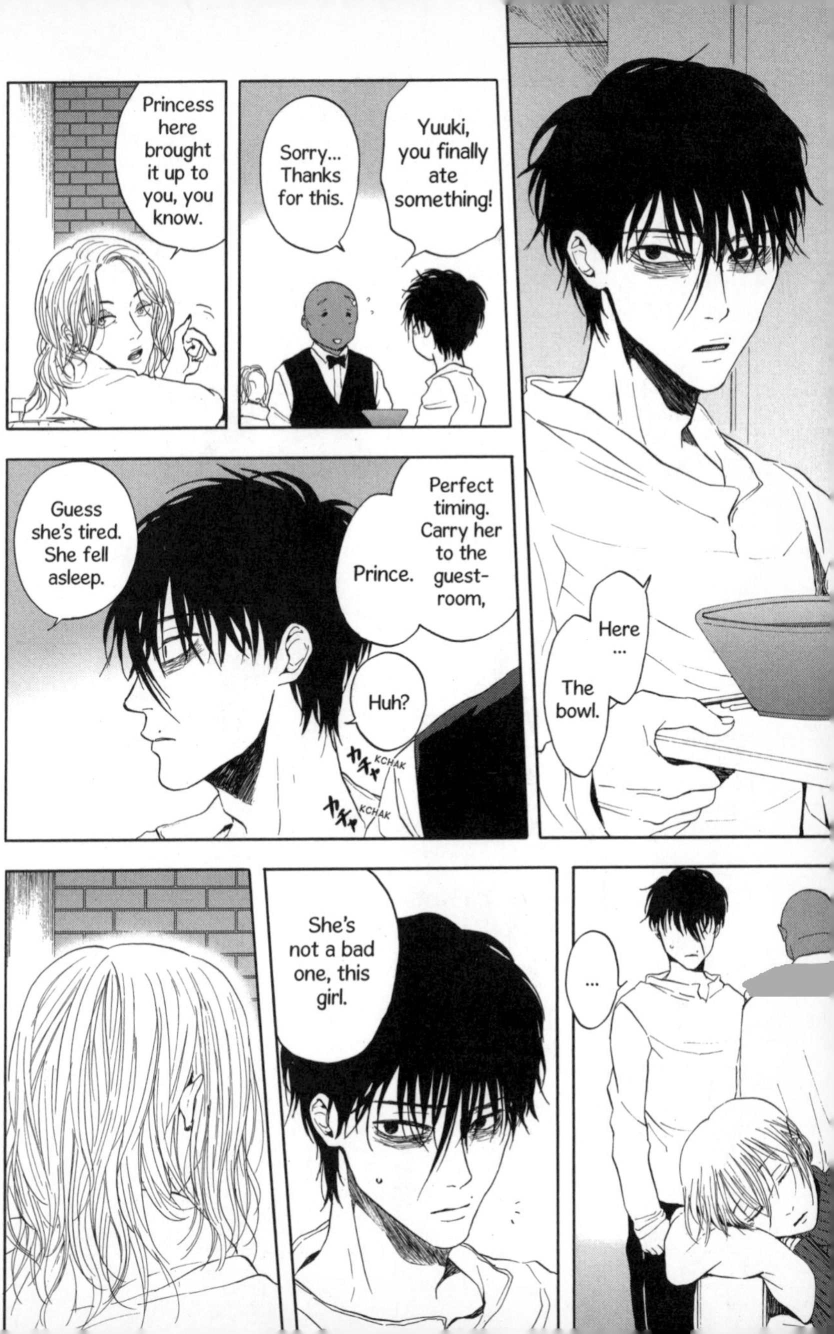
Here ... The bowl.
Yuuki, you finally ate something!
Sorry... Thanks for this.
Princess here brought it up to you, you know.
Perfect timing. Carry her to the guest-room, Prince.
Guess she's tired. She fell asleep.
Huh?
KCHAK
KCHAK
...
She's not a bad one, this girl.

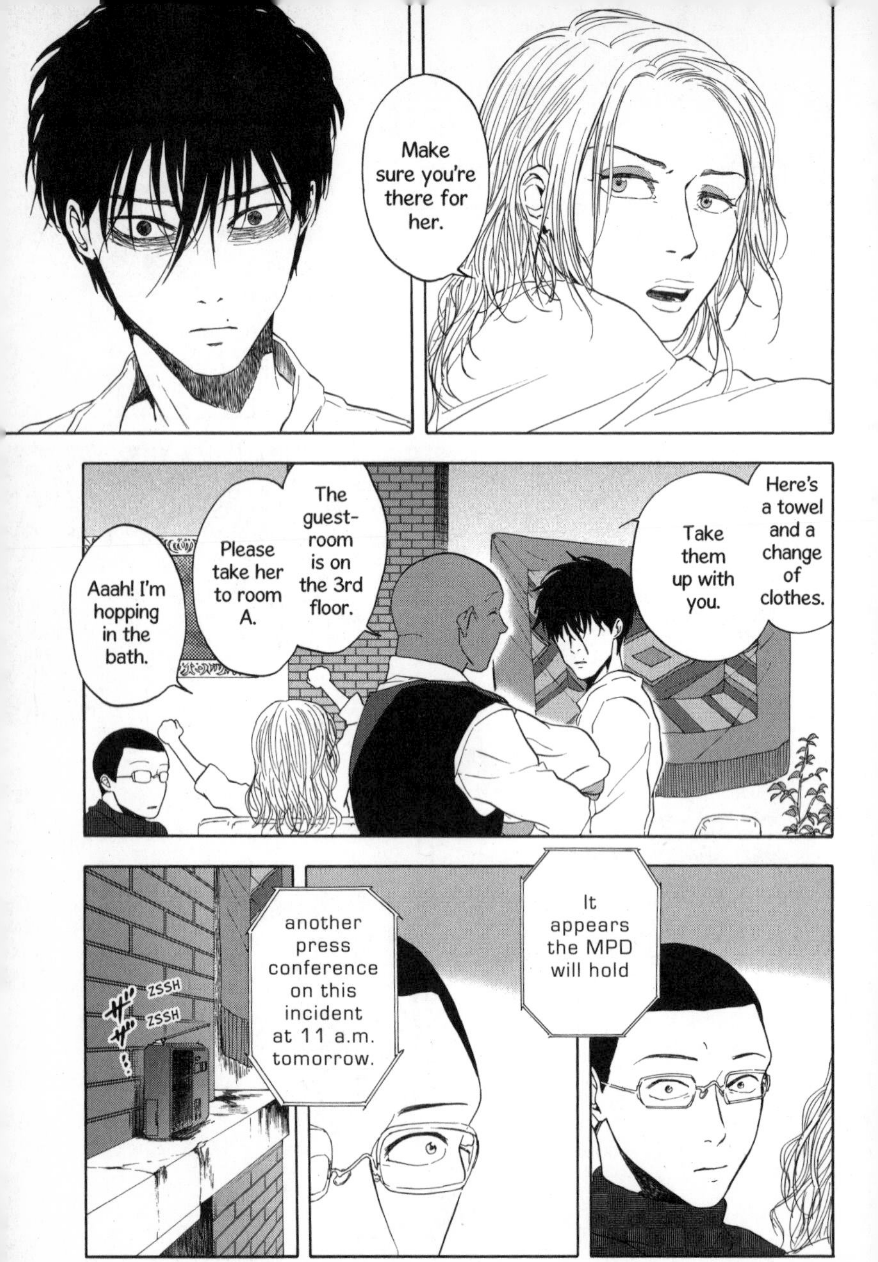
Make sure you're there for her.
Here's a towel and a change of clothes.
Take them up with you.
The guest-room is on the 3rd floor.
Please take her to room A.
Aaah! I'm hopping in the bath.
It appears the MPD will hold
another press conference on this incident at 11 a.m. tomorrow.
ZSSH
ZSSH

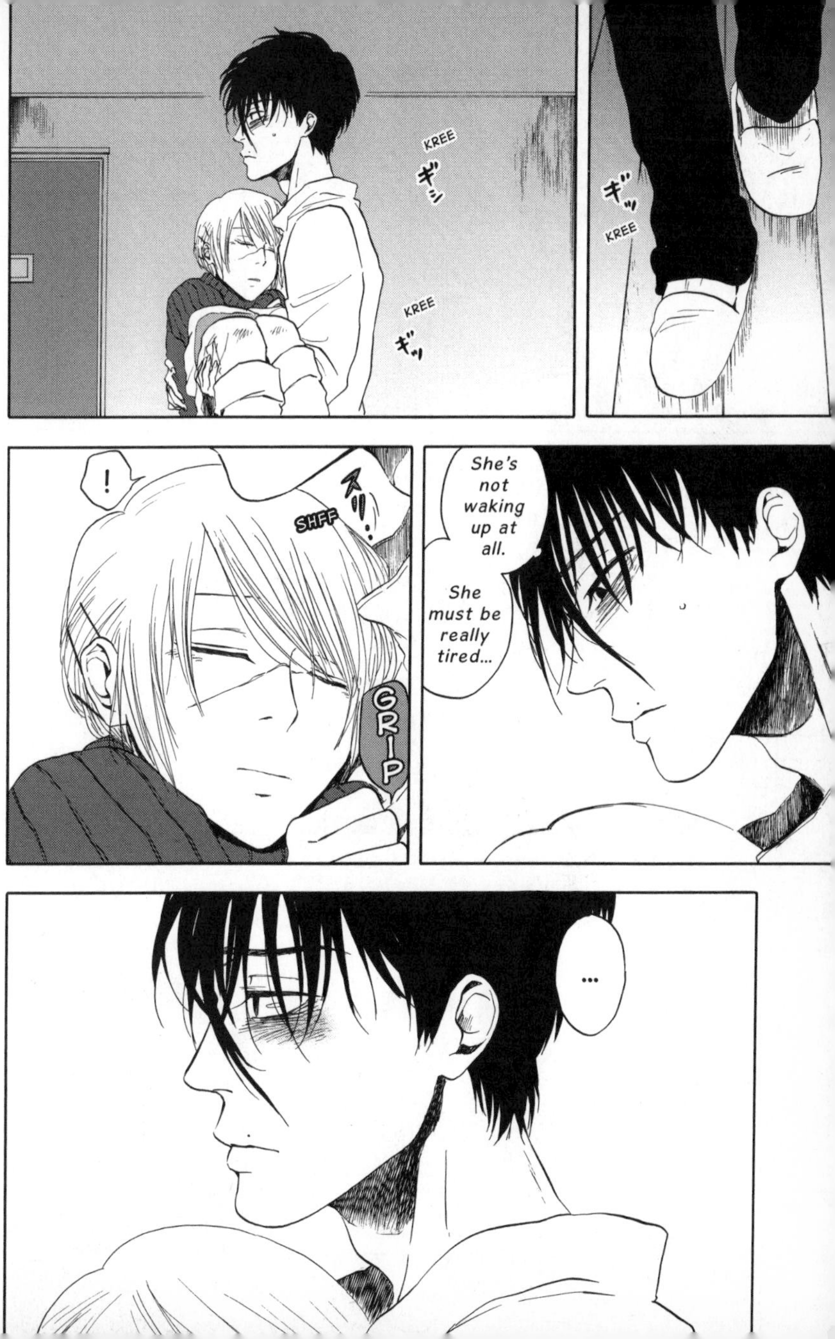
ギッ
KREE
KREE
ギシ
KREE
ギッ
She's not waking up at all.
She must be really tired...
!
スッ…
SHFF
GRIP
...

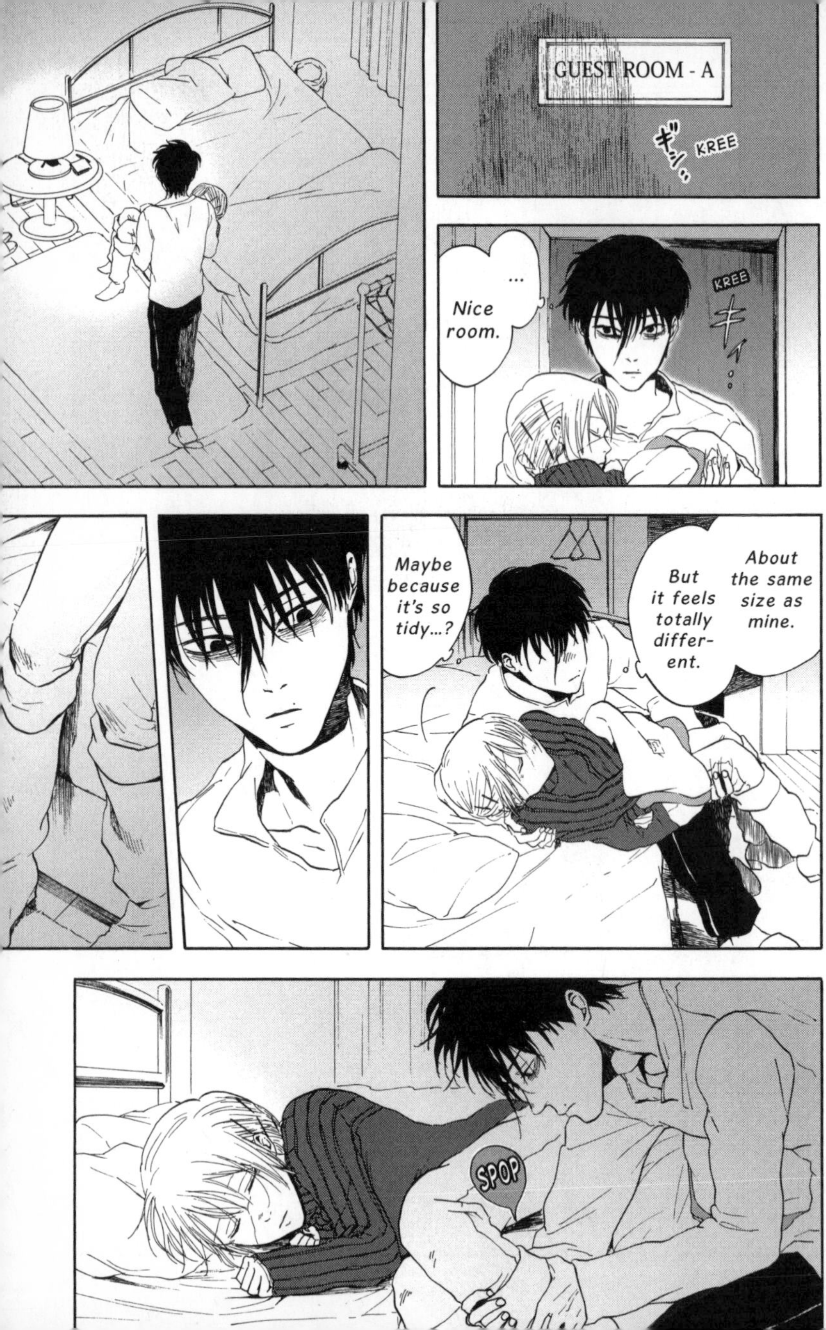
GUEST ROOM - A
ギシ
KREE
... Nice room.
KREE
キィ
About the same size as mine.
But it feels totally different.
Maybe because it's so tidy...?
SPOP

SPOP

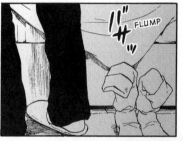

FLUMP

How

do I
take
them
out...

Oh.

Hair
pins
...

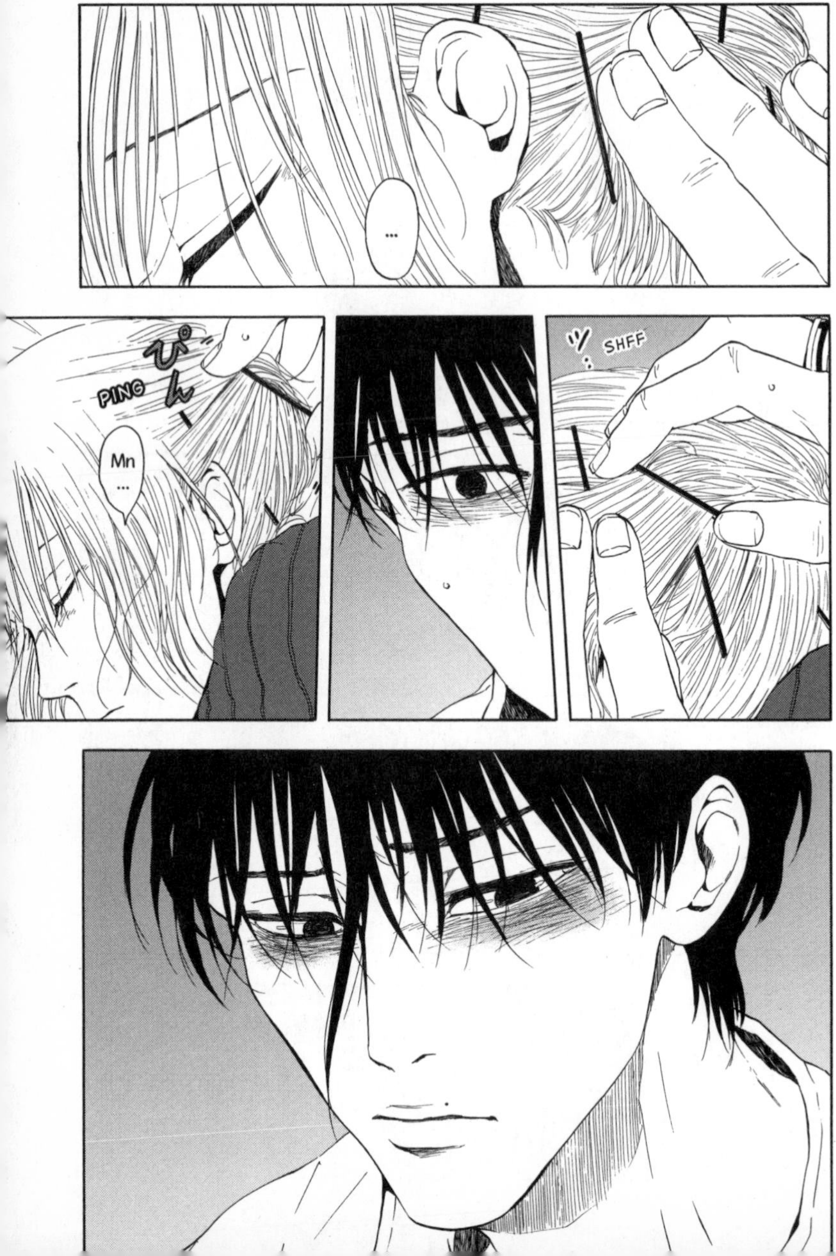
...
ツ
SHFF
ぴん
PING
Mn ...

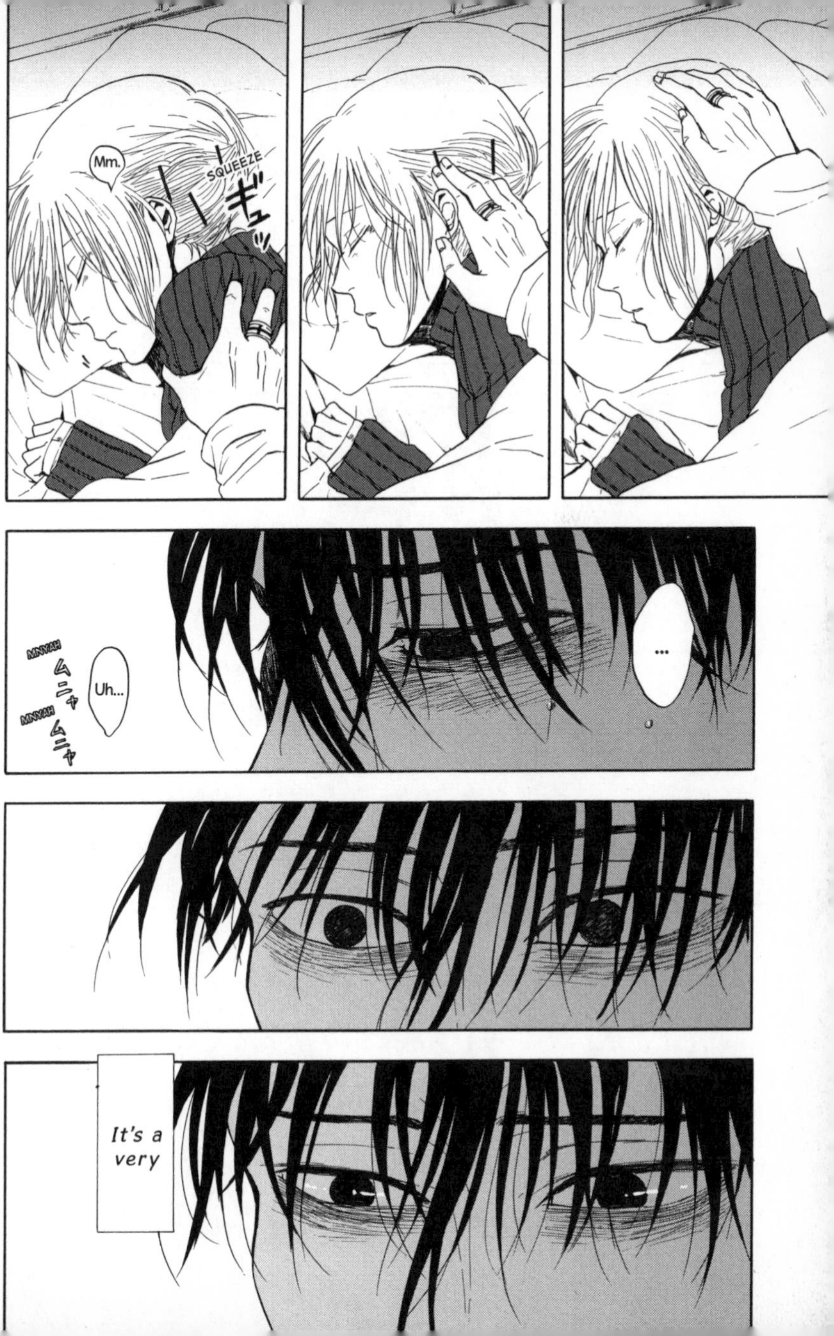
Mm.
SQUEEZE
ギュッ
...
Uh...
MNYAH
ムニャ
MNYAH
ムニャ
It's a very

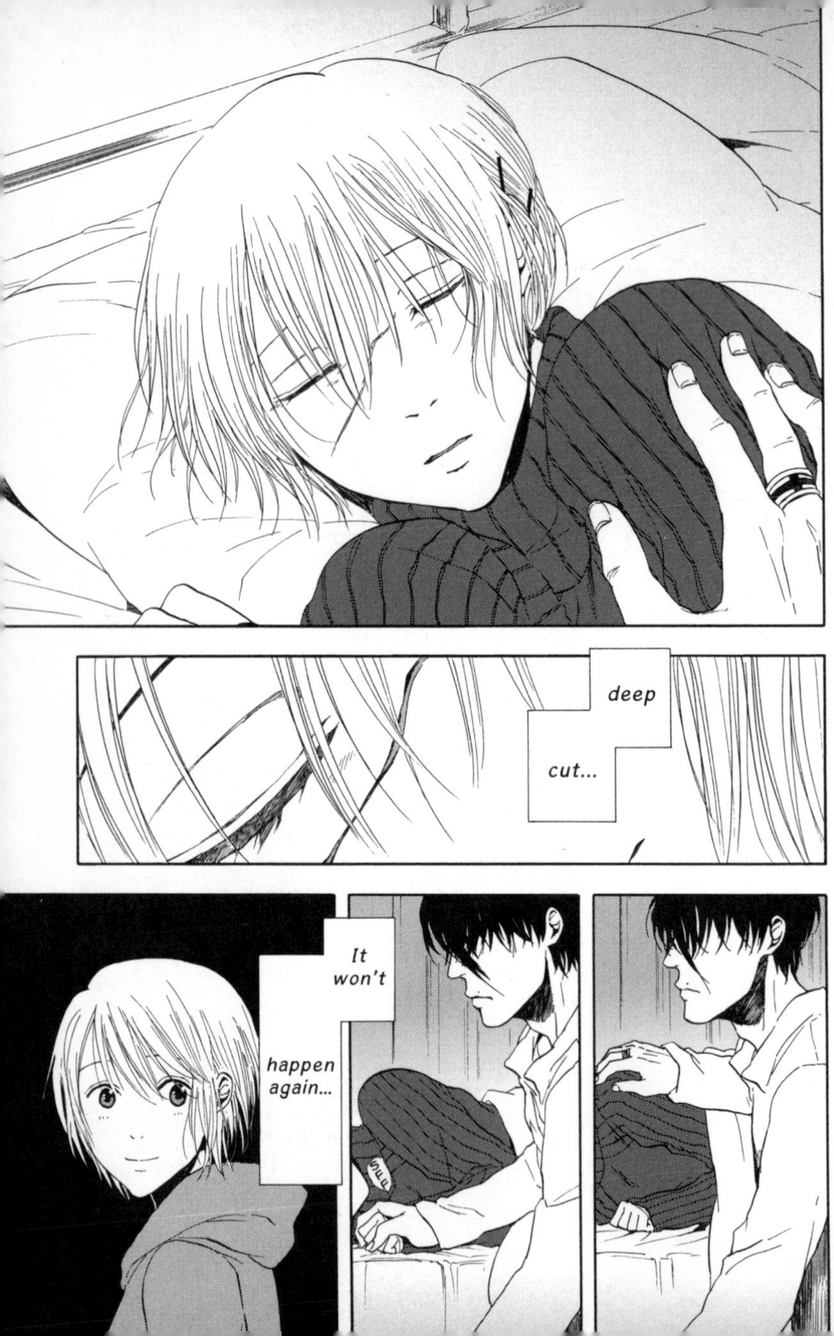
deep
cut...
It won't
happen again...

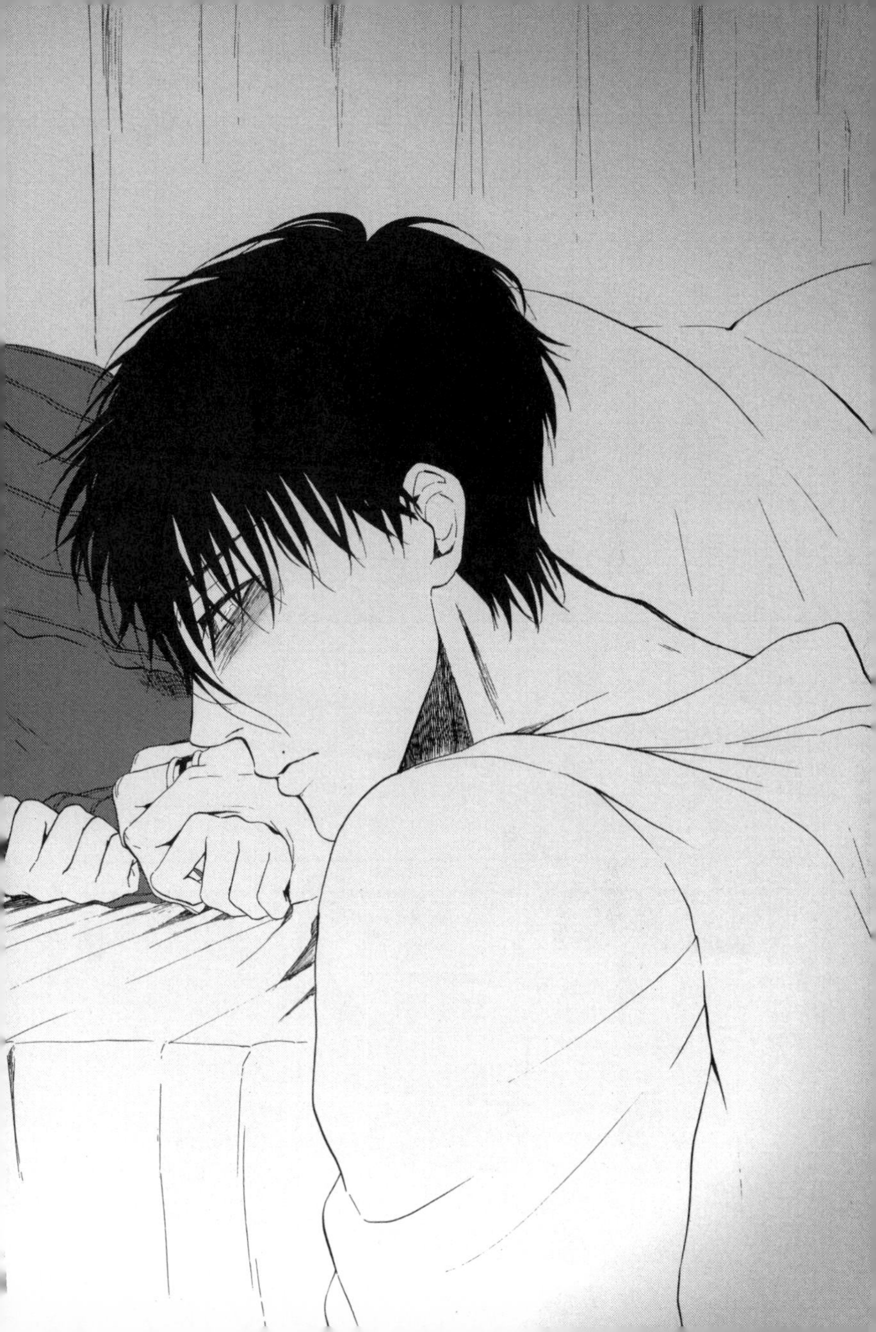

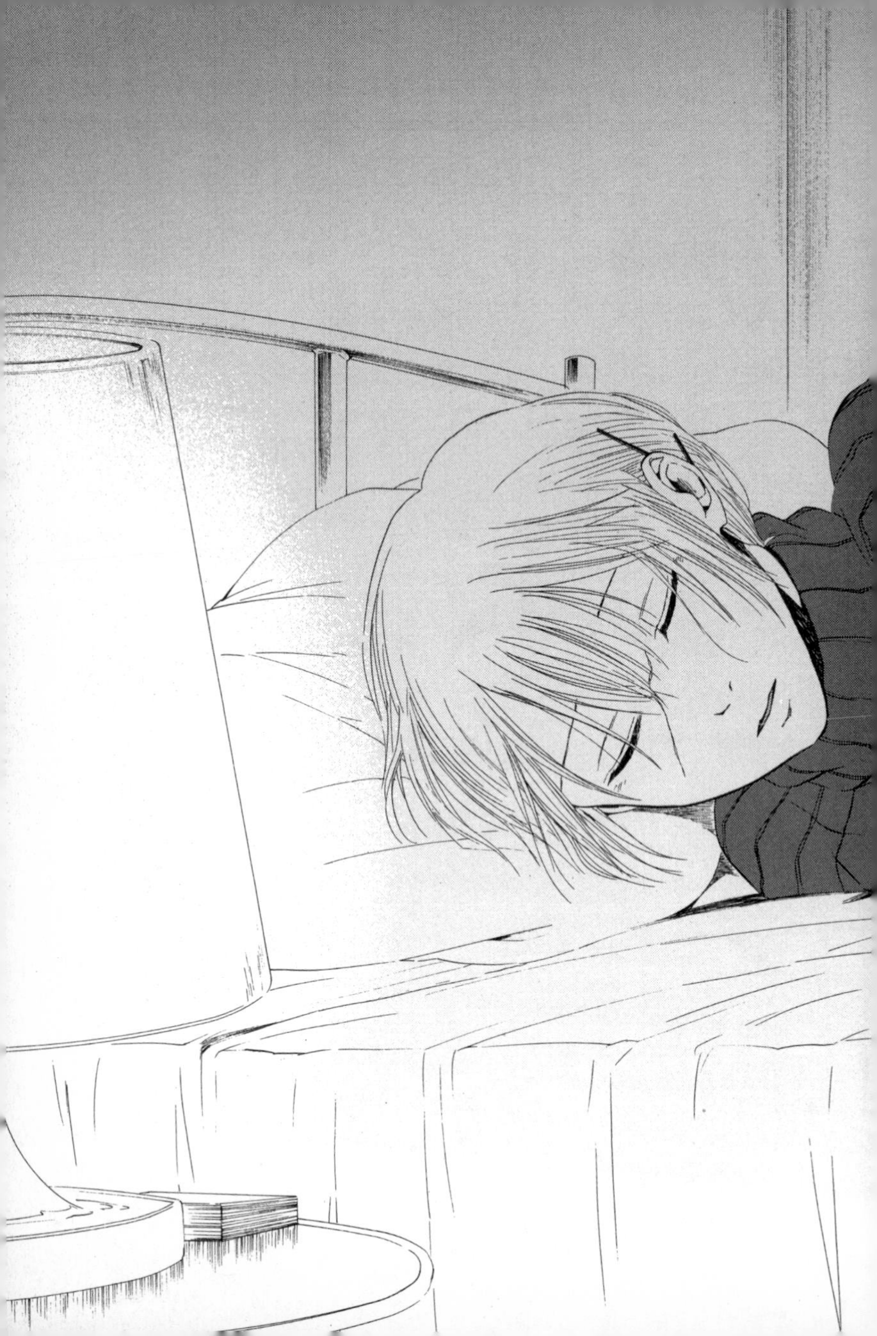

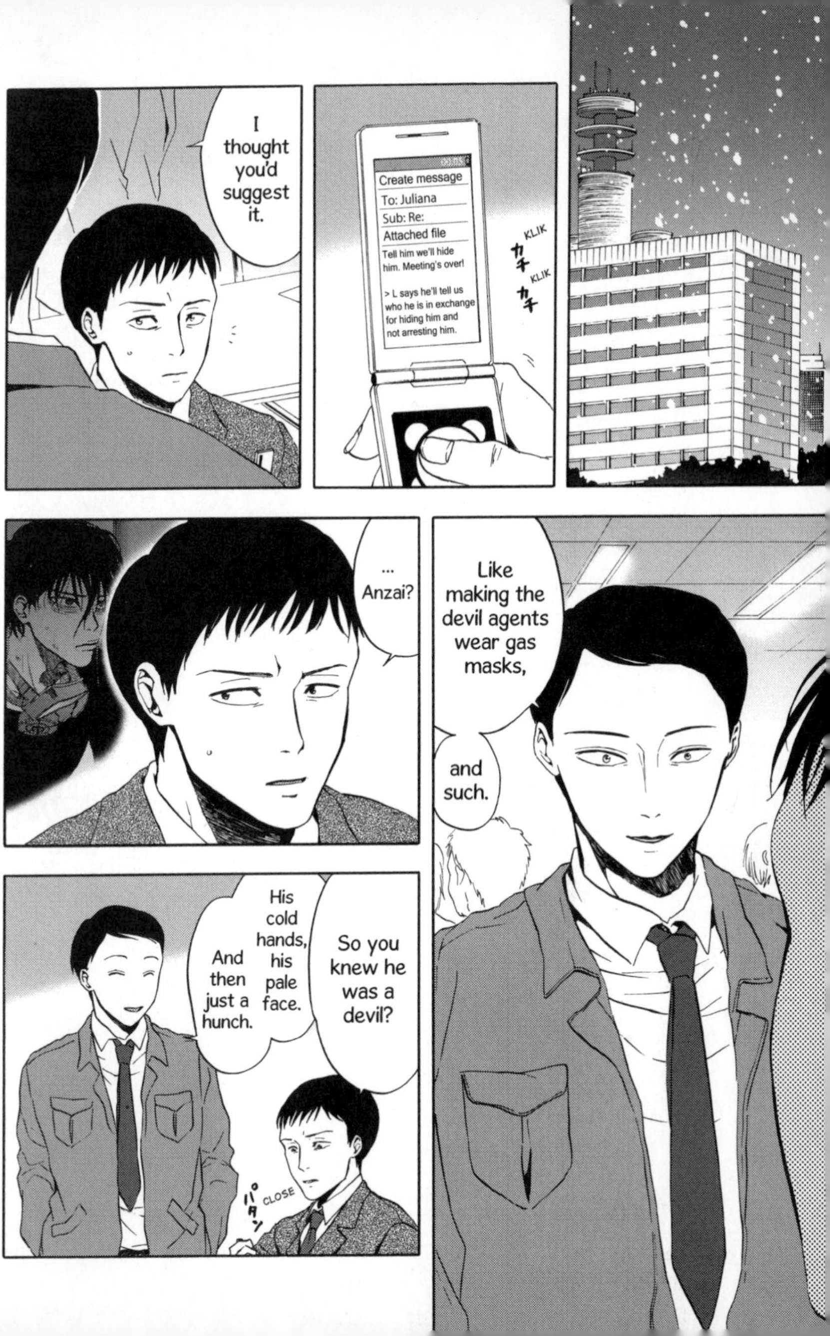
Create message
To: Juliana
Sub: Re:
Attached file
Tell him we'll hide him. Meeting's over!
> L says he'll tell us who he is in exchange for hiding him and not arresting him.
カチ KLIK
カチ KLIK
I thought you'd suggest it.
Like making the devil agents wear gas masks,
and such.
... Anzai?
So you knew he was a devil?
His cold hands, his pale face.
And then just a hunch.
パタン CLOSE

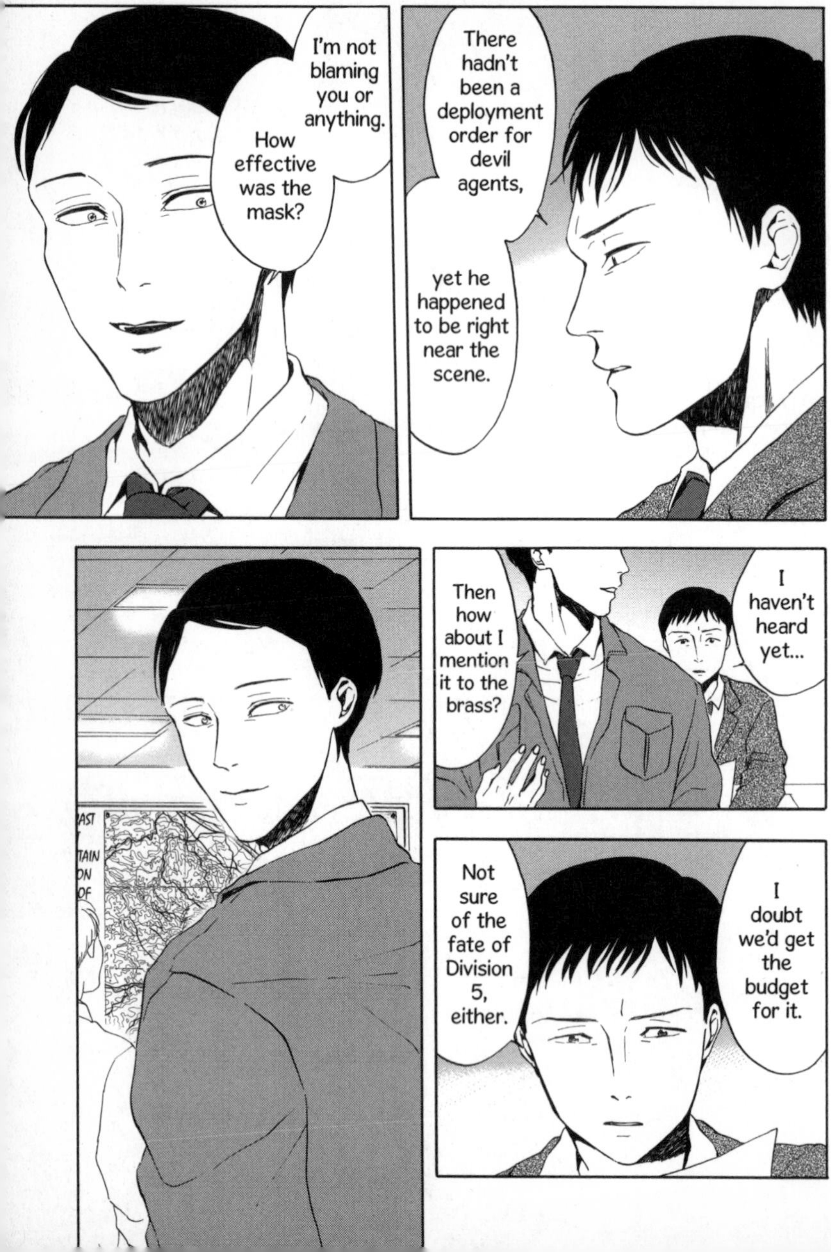
There hadn't been a deployment order for devil agents,
yet he happened to be right near the scene.
I'm not blaming you or anything.
How effective was the mask?
I haven't heard yet...
Then how about I mention it to the brass?
I doubt we'd get the budget for it.
Not sure of the fate of Division 5, either.

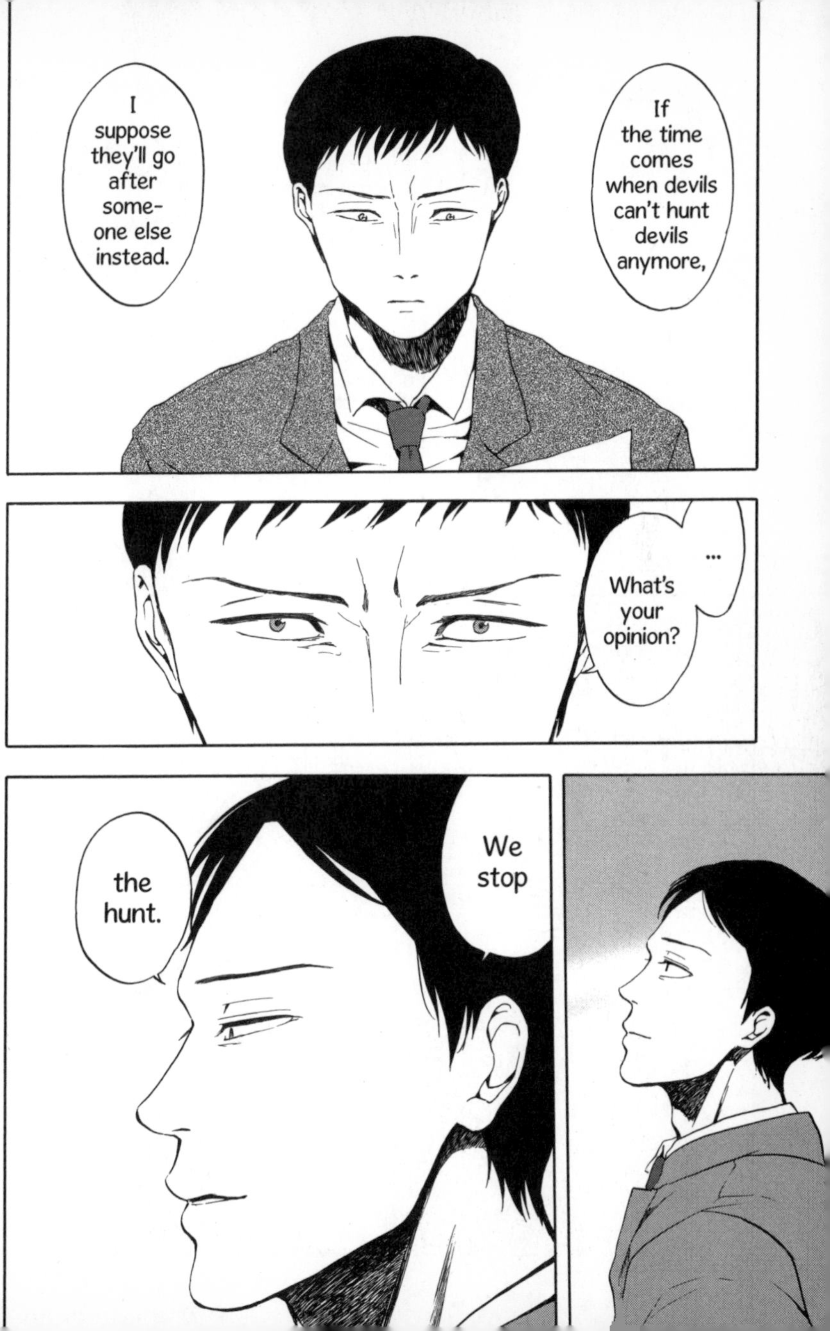
If the time comes when devils can't hunt devils anymore,
I suppose they'll go after some-one else instead.
... What's your opinion?
We stop
the hunt.

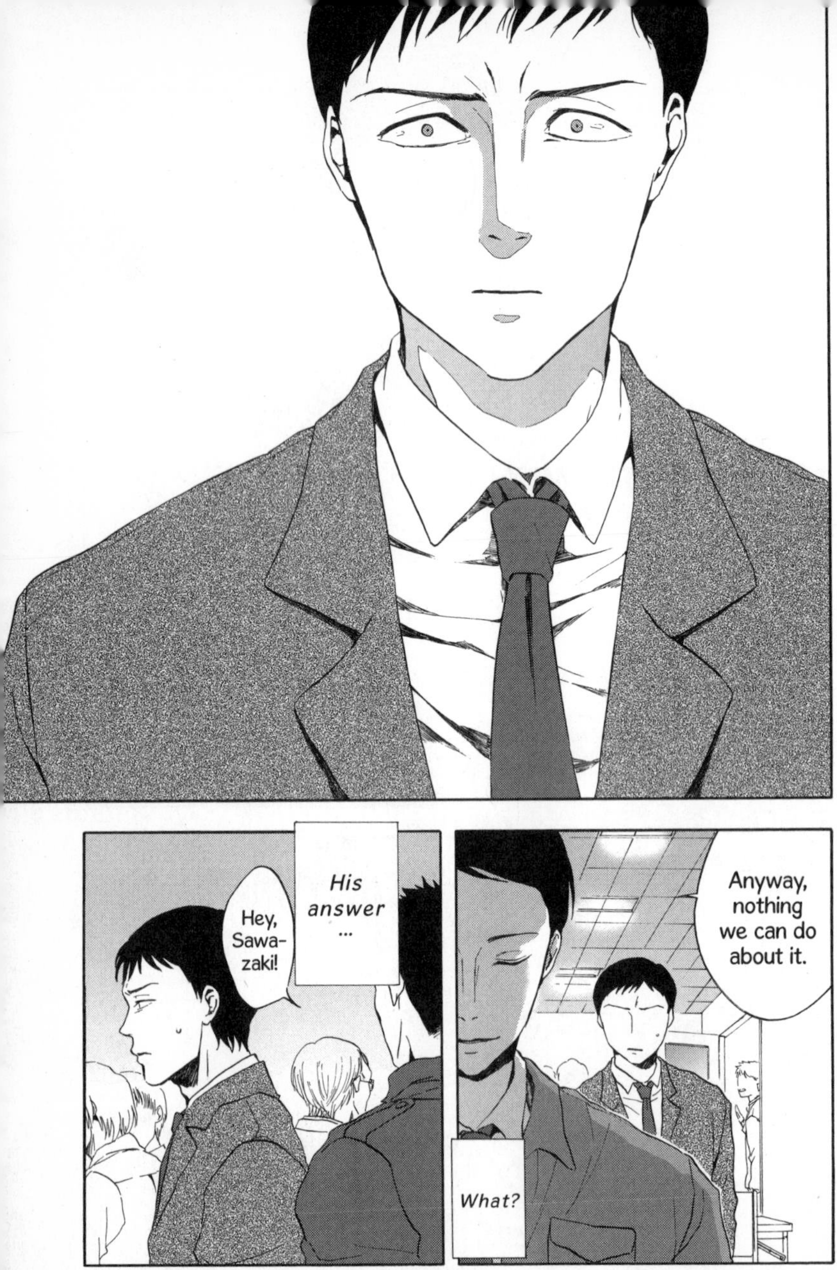
Anyway, nothing we can do about it.
What?
His answer ...
Hey, Sawa-zaki!

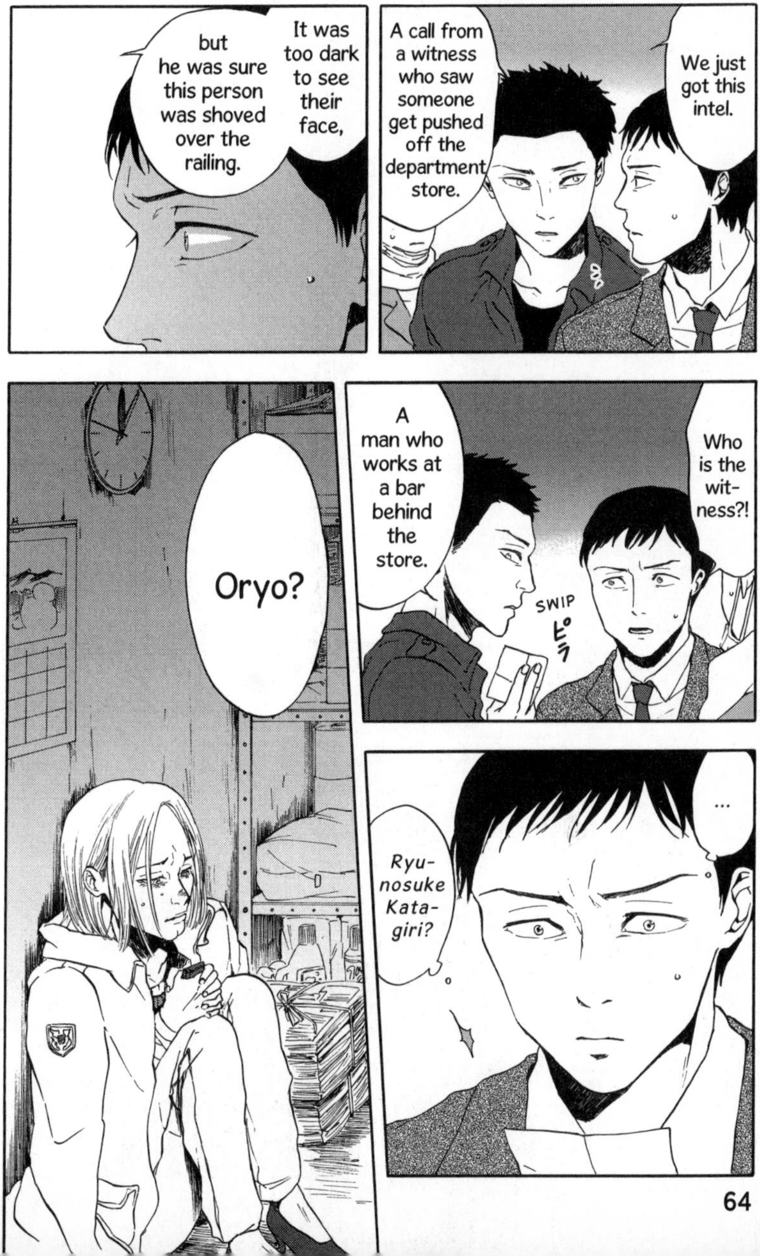
We just got this intel.
A call from a witness who saw someone get pushed off the department store.
It was too dark to see their face,
but he was sure this person was shoved over the railing.
Who is the witness?!
A man who works at a bar behind the store.
SWIP
ピラ
...
Ryunosuke Katagiri?
Oryo?

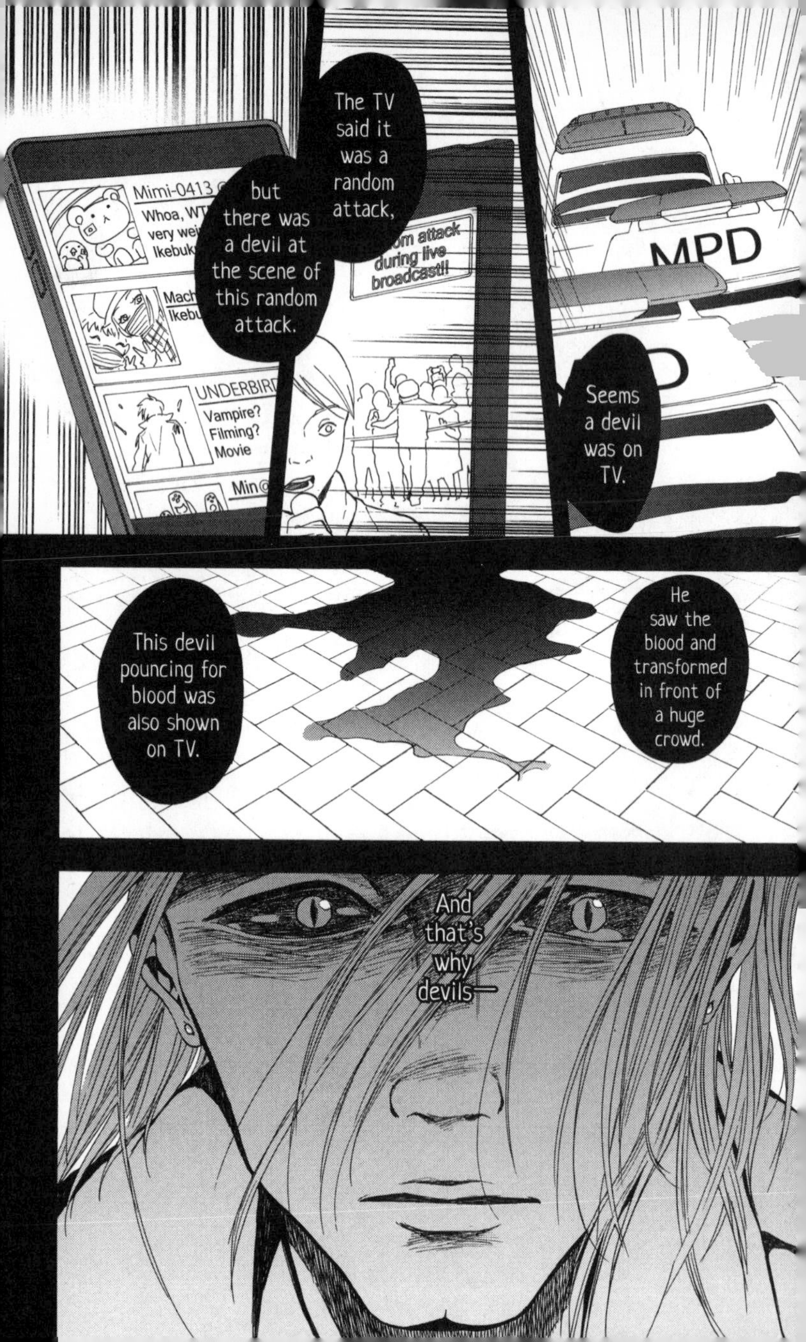
MPD
Seems a devil was on TV.
The TV said it was a random attack,
but there was a devil at the scene of this random attack.
Mimi-0413
Vampire? Filming? Movie
during live broadcast!!
He saw the blood and transformed in front of a huge crowd.
This devil pouncing for blood was also shown on TV.
And that's why devils—

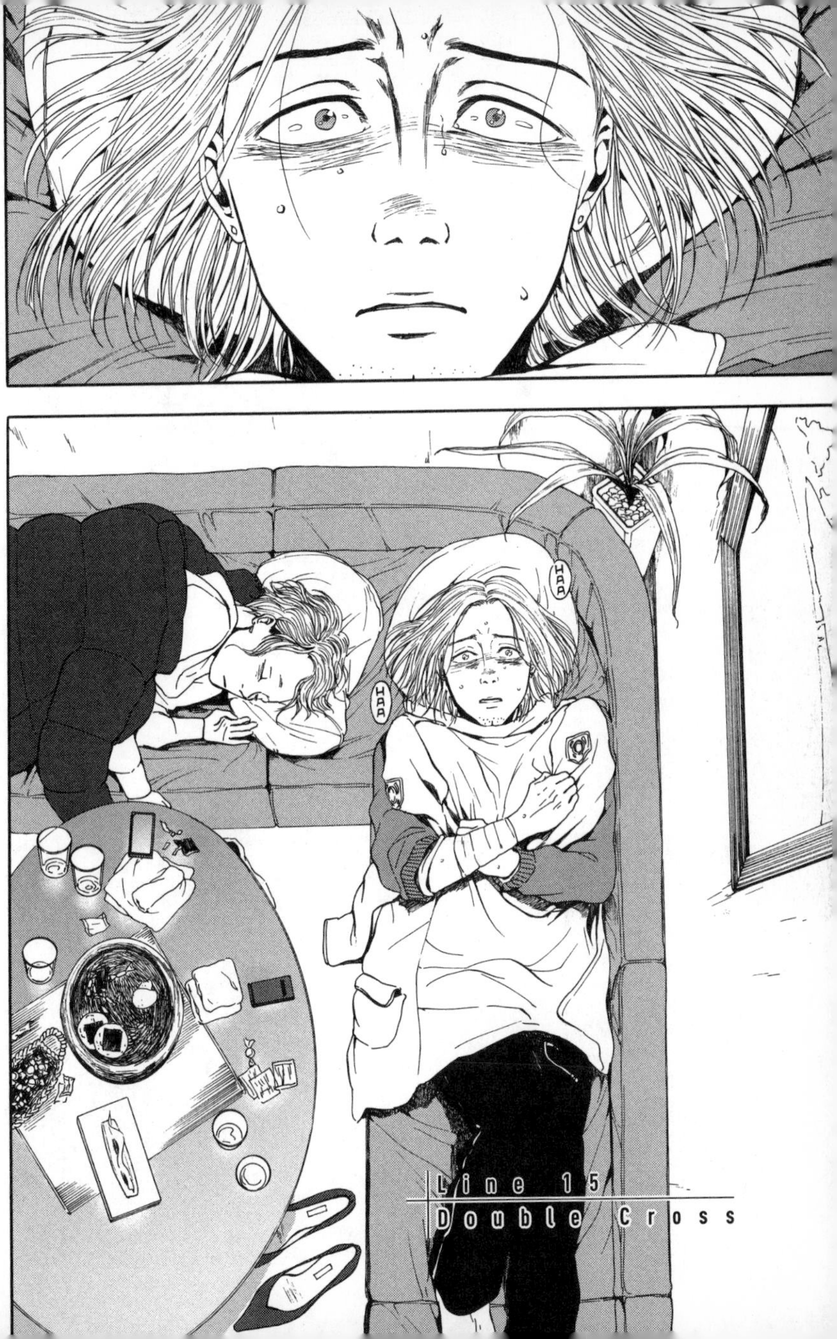
HAA
HAA
Line 15
Double Cross

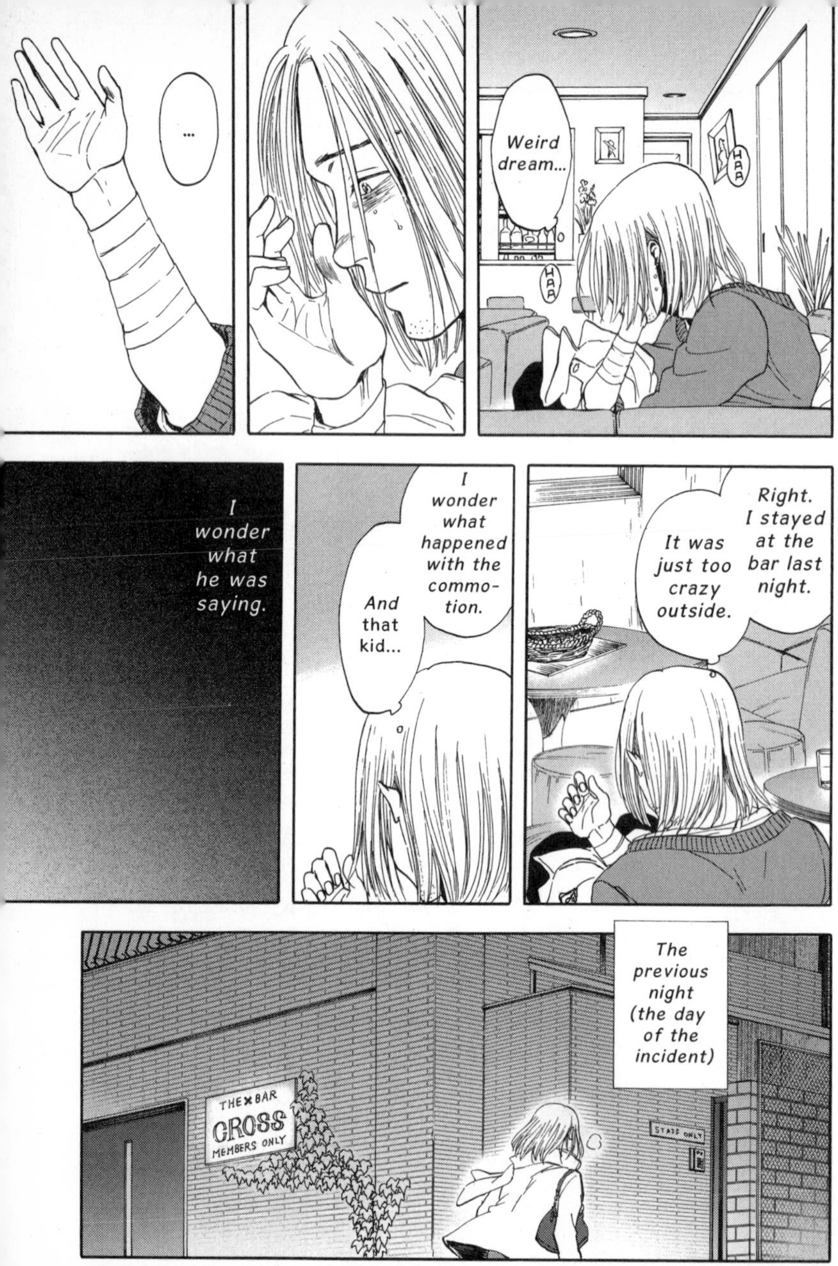
Weird dream...
HAA
HAA
...
Right. I stayed at the bar last night.
It was just too crazy outside.
I wonder what happened with the commotion.
And that kid...
I wonder what he was saying.
The previous night (the day of the incident)
THE BAR CROSS MEMBERS ONLY
STAFF ONLY

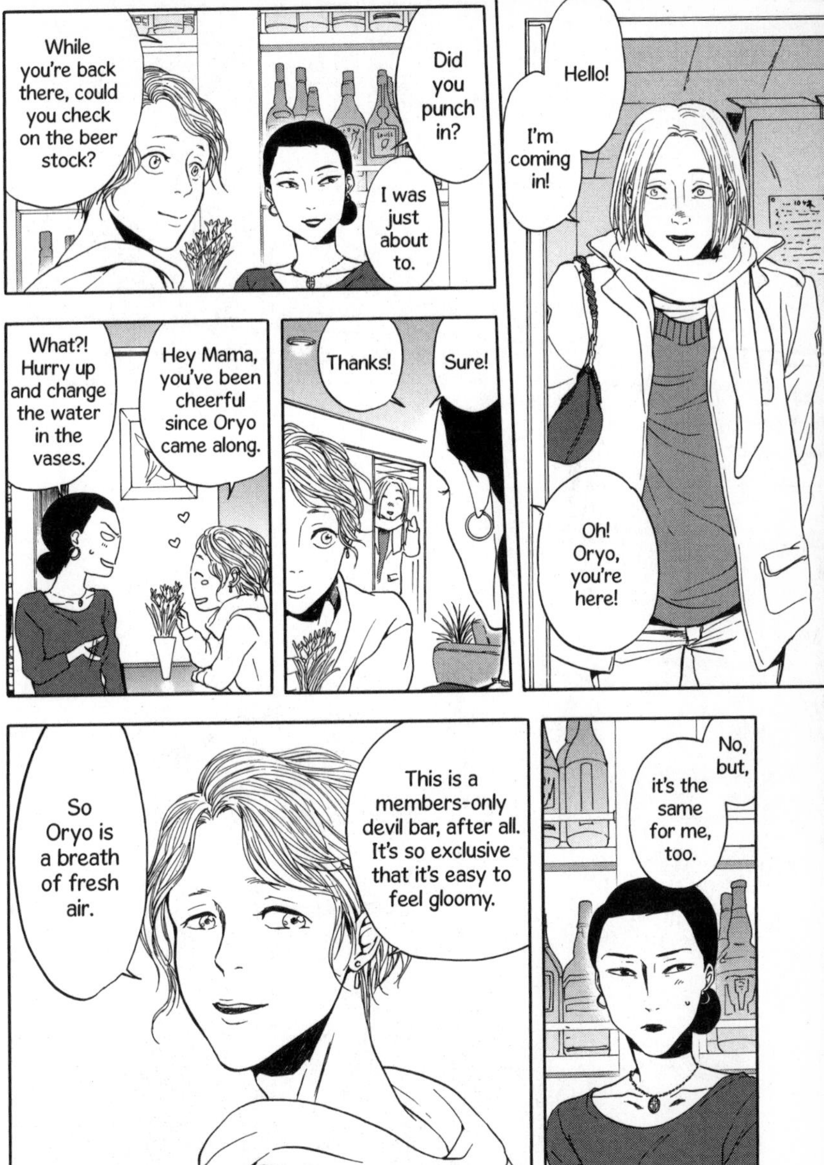
Hello!
I'm coming in!
Oh! Oryo, you're here!
Did you punch in?
I was just about to.
While you're back there, could you check on the beer stock?
Sure!
Thanks!
Hey Mama, you've been cheerful since Oryo came along.
What?! Hurry up and change the water in the vases.
No, but, it's the same for me, too.
This is a members-only devil bar, after all. It's so exclusive that it's easy to feel gloomy.
So Oryo is a breath of fresh air.

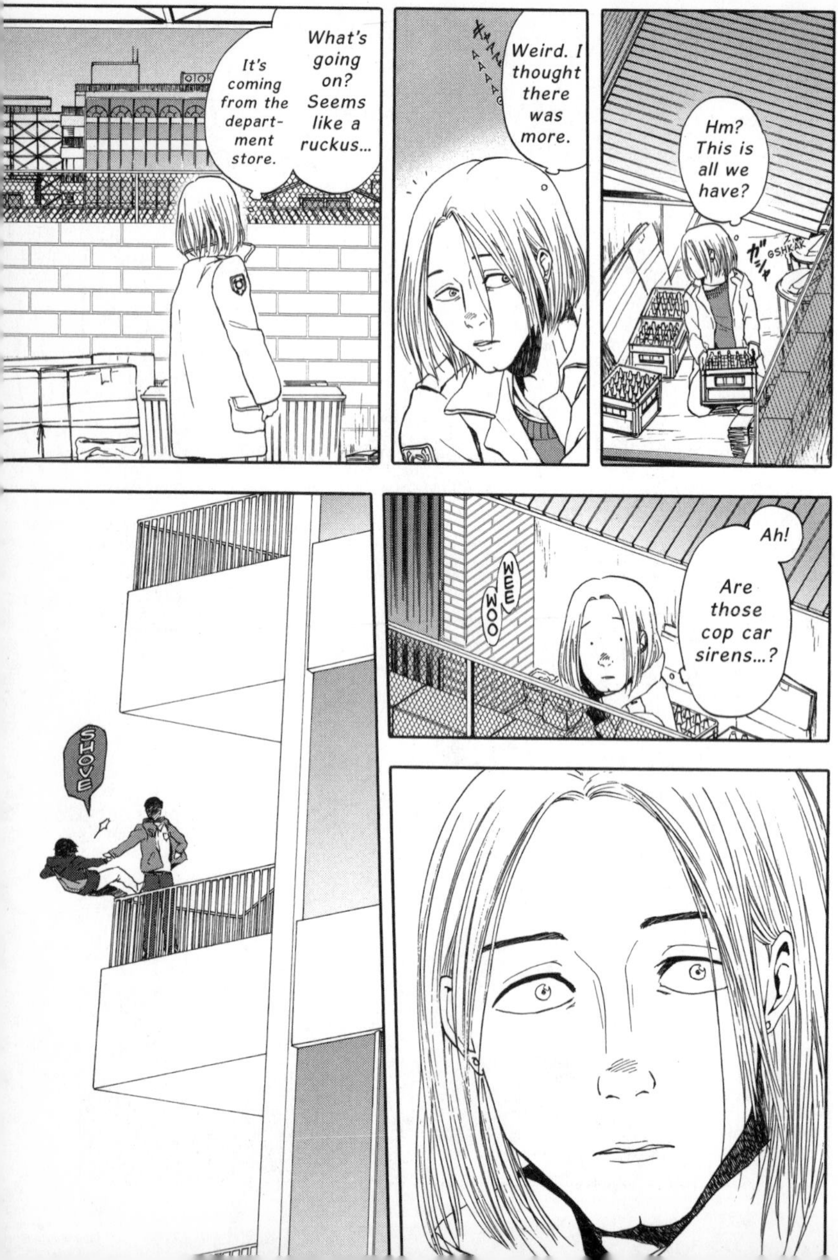
Hm? This is all we have?
ガシャ
GSHKAK
Weird. I thought there was more.
What's going on? Seems like a ruckus...
It's coming from the department store.
Ah!
Are those cop car sirens...?
WEE WOO
SHOVE

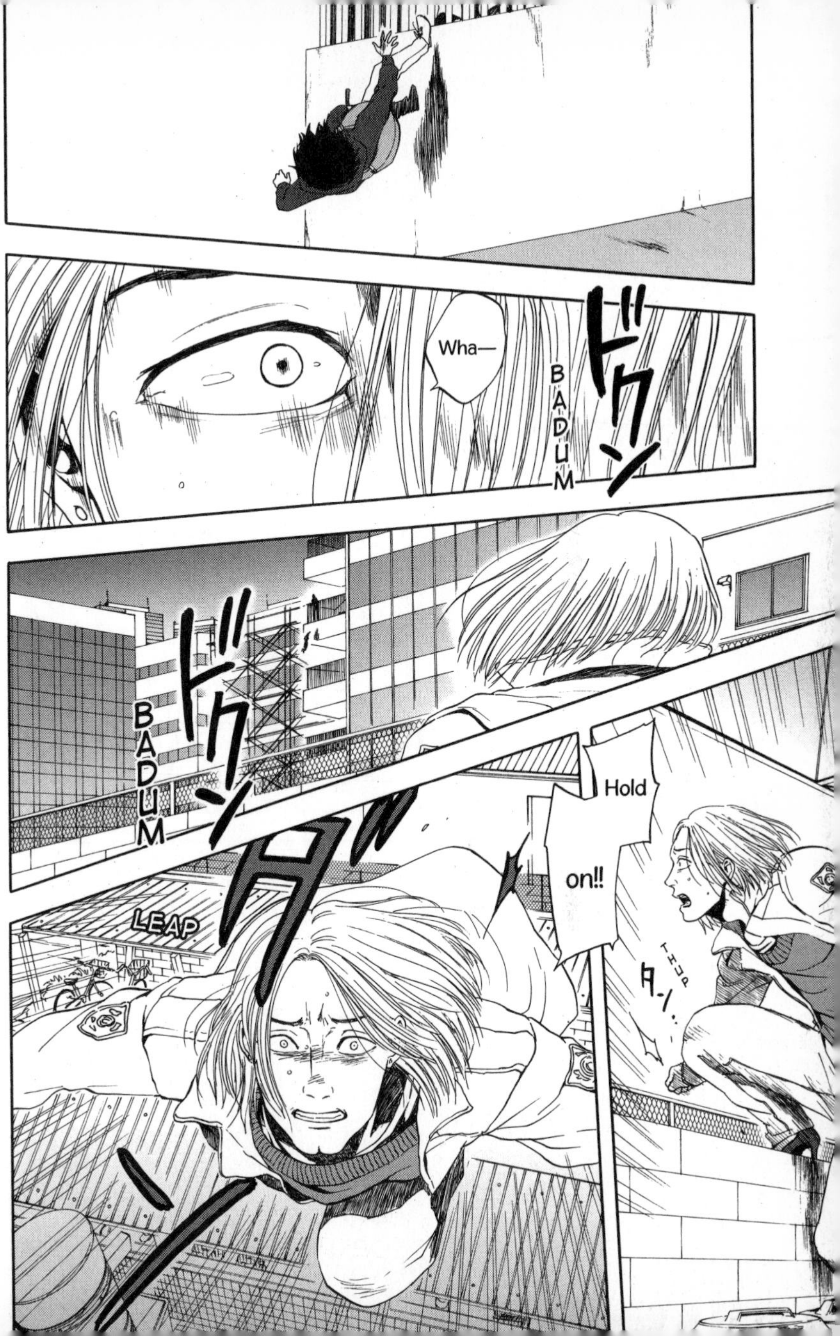
Wha—
ドクン
BADUM
ドクン
BADUM
Hold on!!
THUP
LEAP

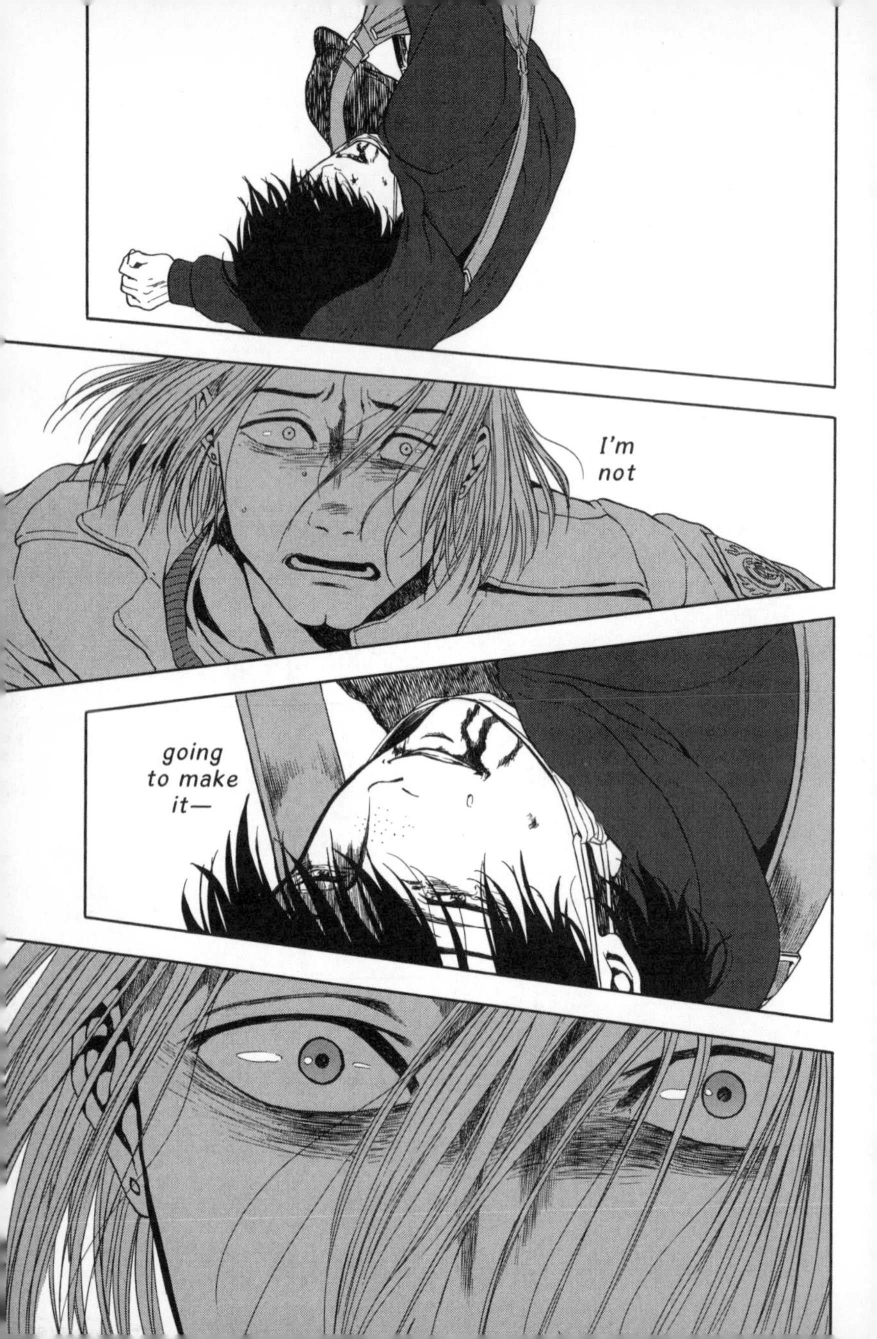
I'm not
going to make it—

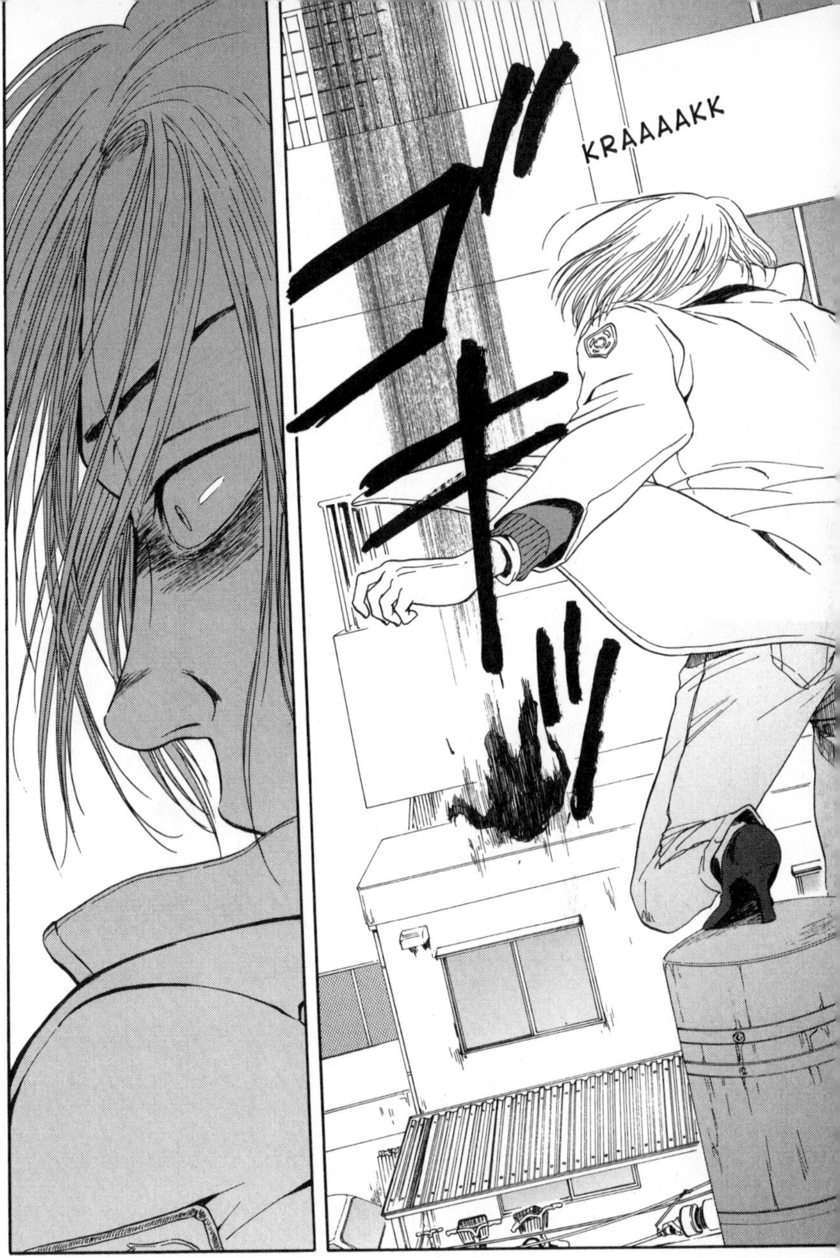
ゴキッ
KRAAAKK

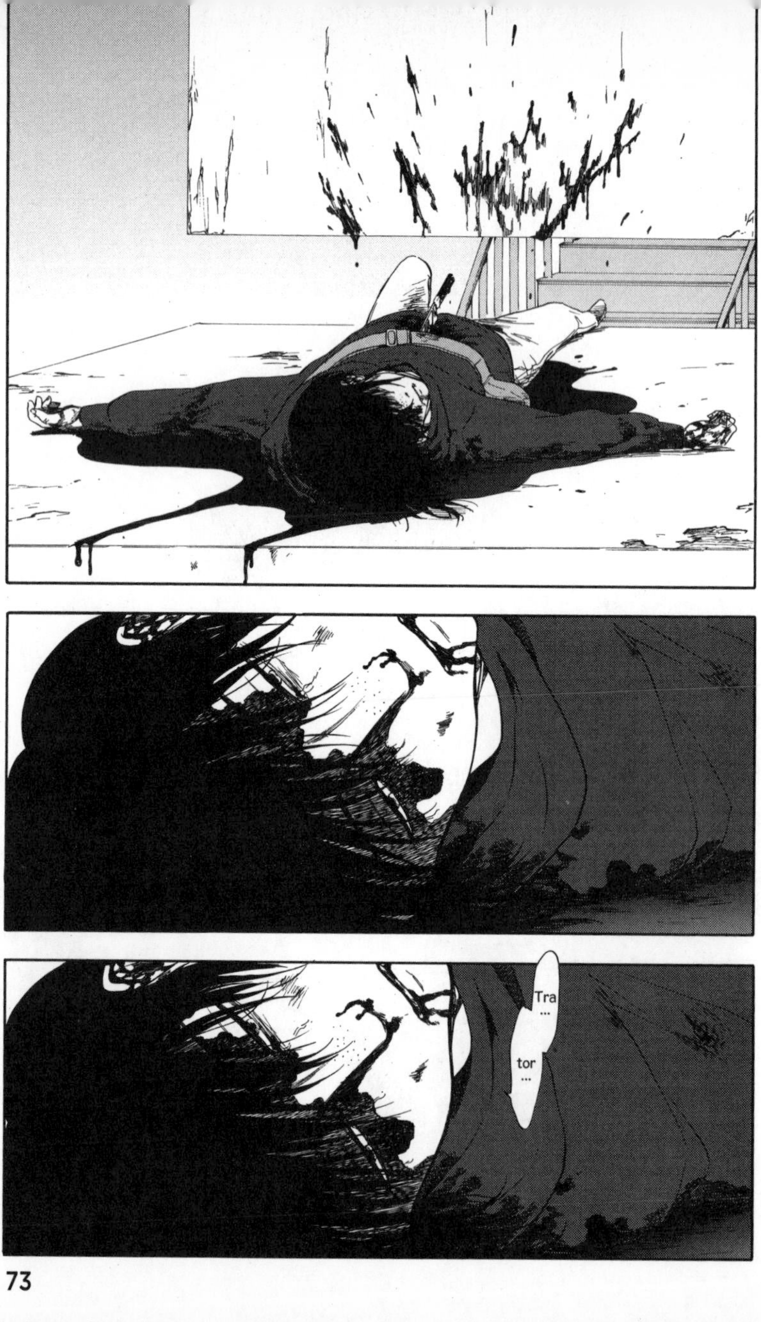
Tra… tor…

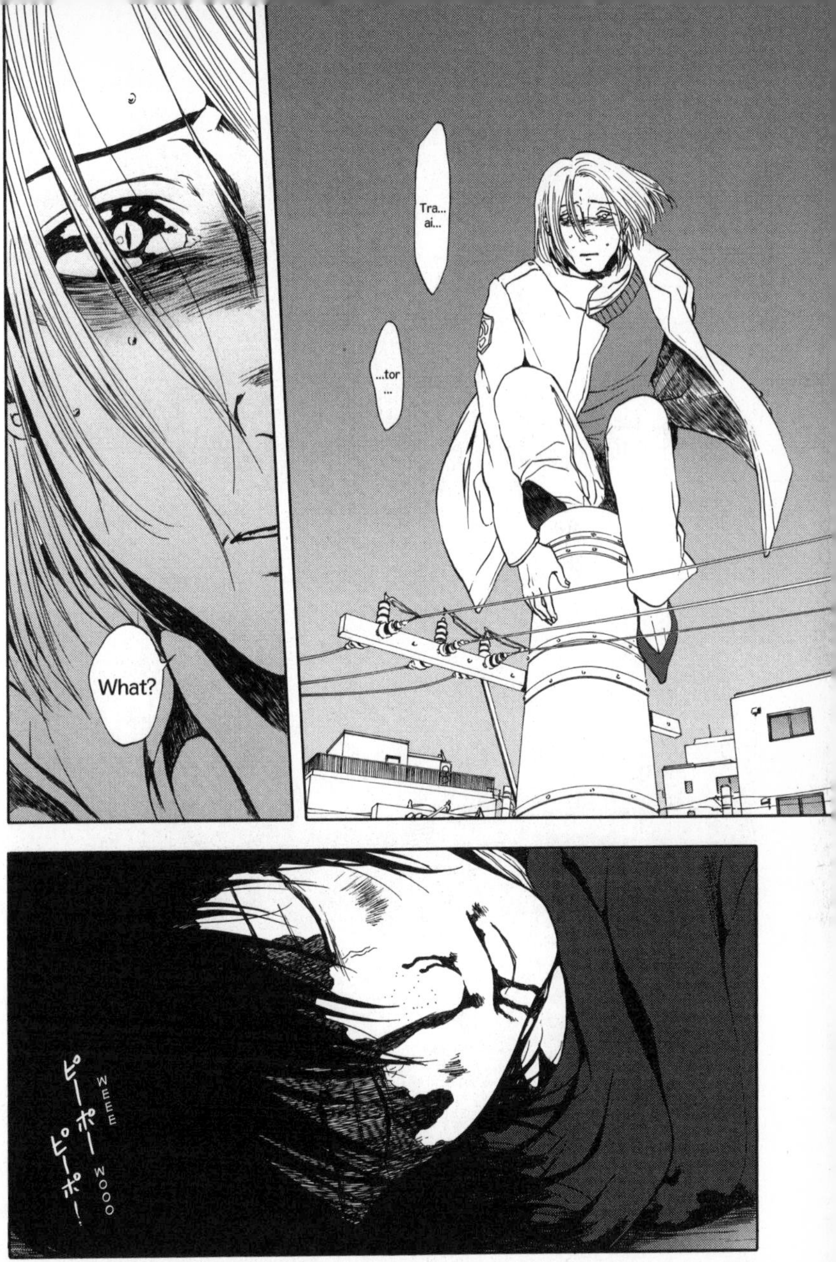
Tra... ai...
...tor ...
What?
ピーポーピーポー!
WEEE WOOO

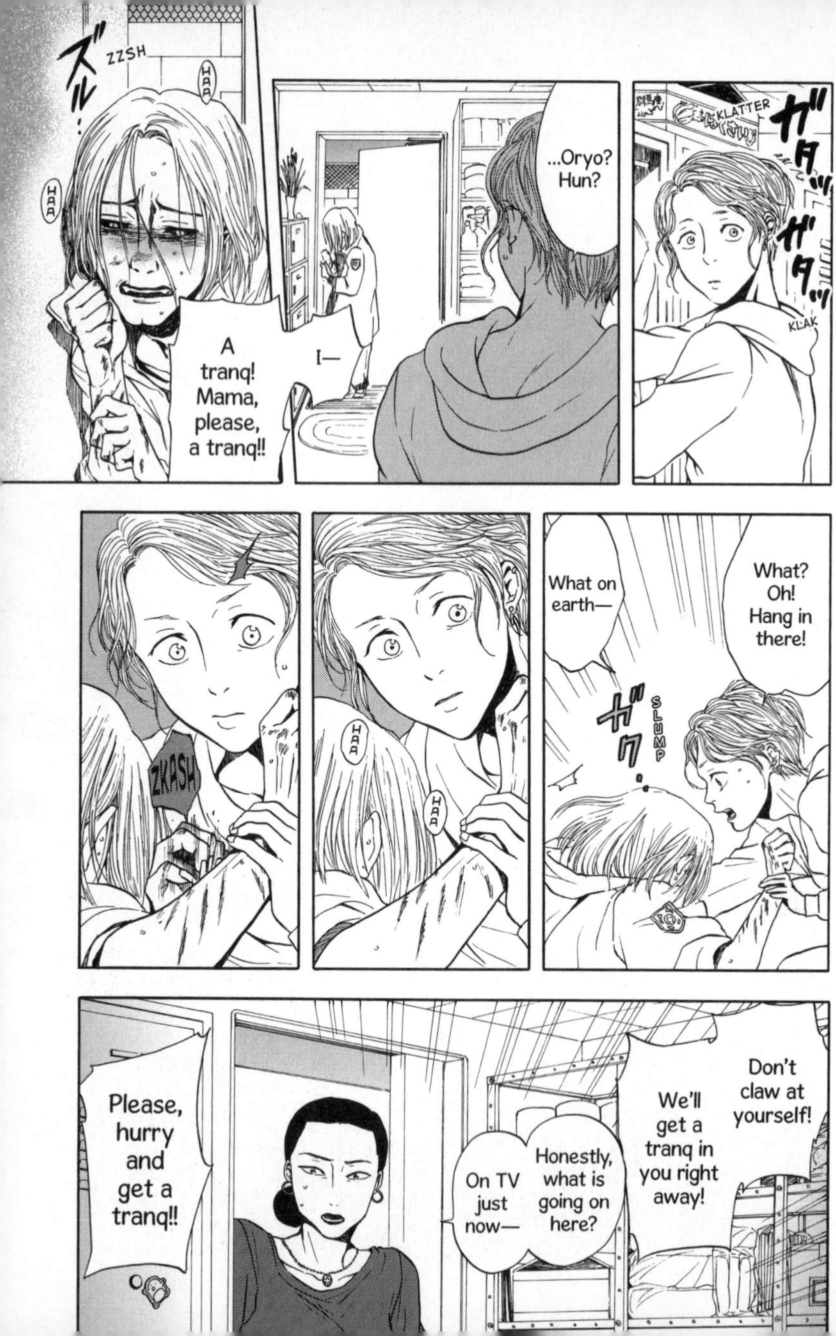
KLATTER
ガタッ
ガタッ
KLAK
...Oryo? Hun?
I—
ズル
ZZSH
HAA
HAA
A tranq! Mama, please, a tranq!!
What? Oh! Hang in there!
What on earth—
ガク
SLUMP
HAA
HAA
ZKASH
Don't claw at yourself!
We'll get a tranq in you right away!
Honestly, what is going on here?
On TV just now—
Please, hurry and get a tranq!!

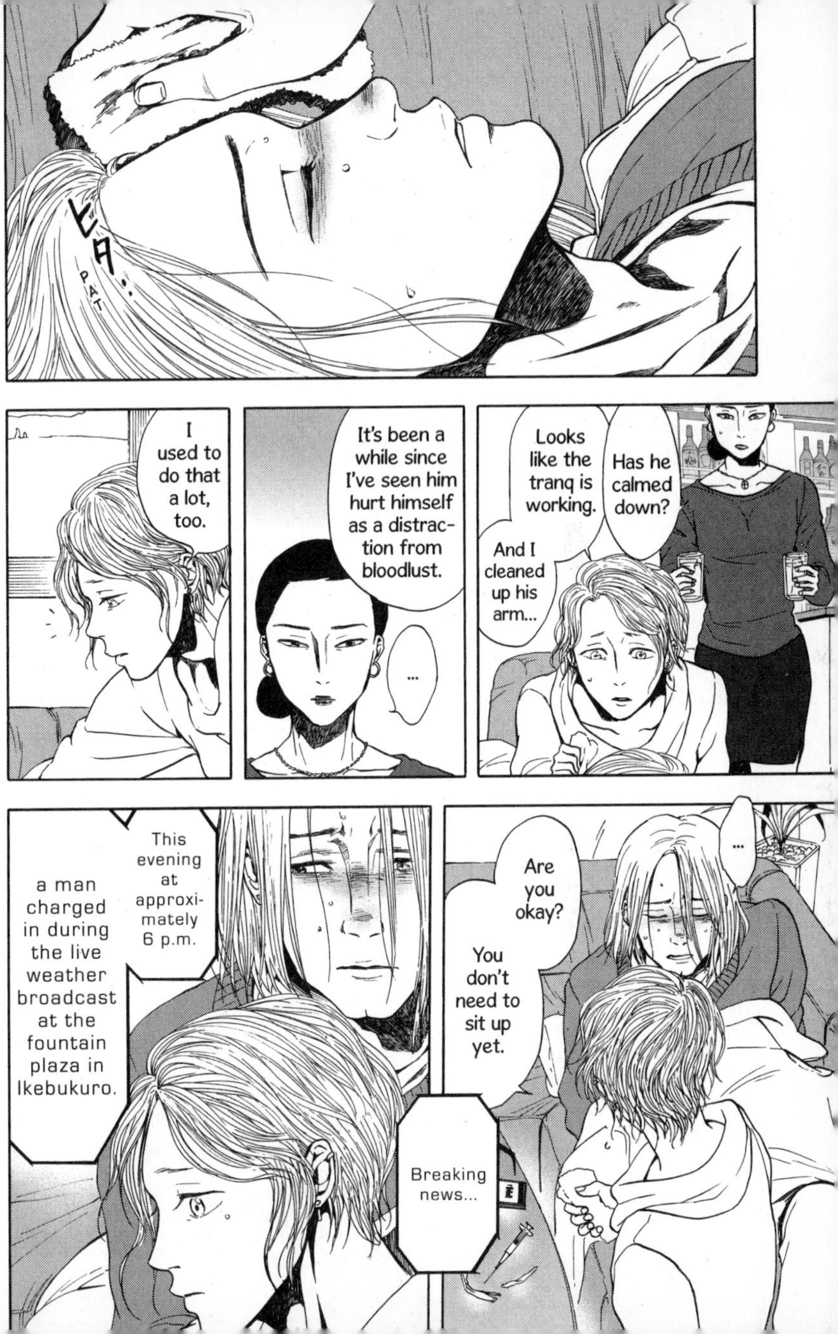
ピタ
PAT
Has he calmed down?
Looks like the tranq is working.
And I cleaned up his arm...
It's been a while since I've seen him hurt himself as a distraction from bloodlust.
...
I used to do that a lot, too.
...
Are you okay?
You don't need to sit up yet.
Breaking news...
This evening at approximately 6 p.m.
a man charged in during the live weather broadcast at the fountain plaza in Ikebukuro.

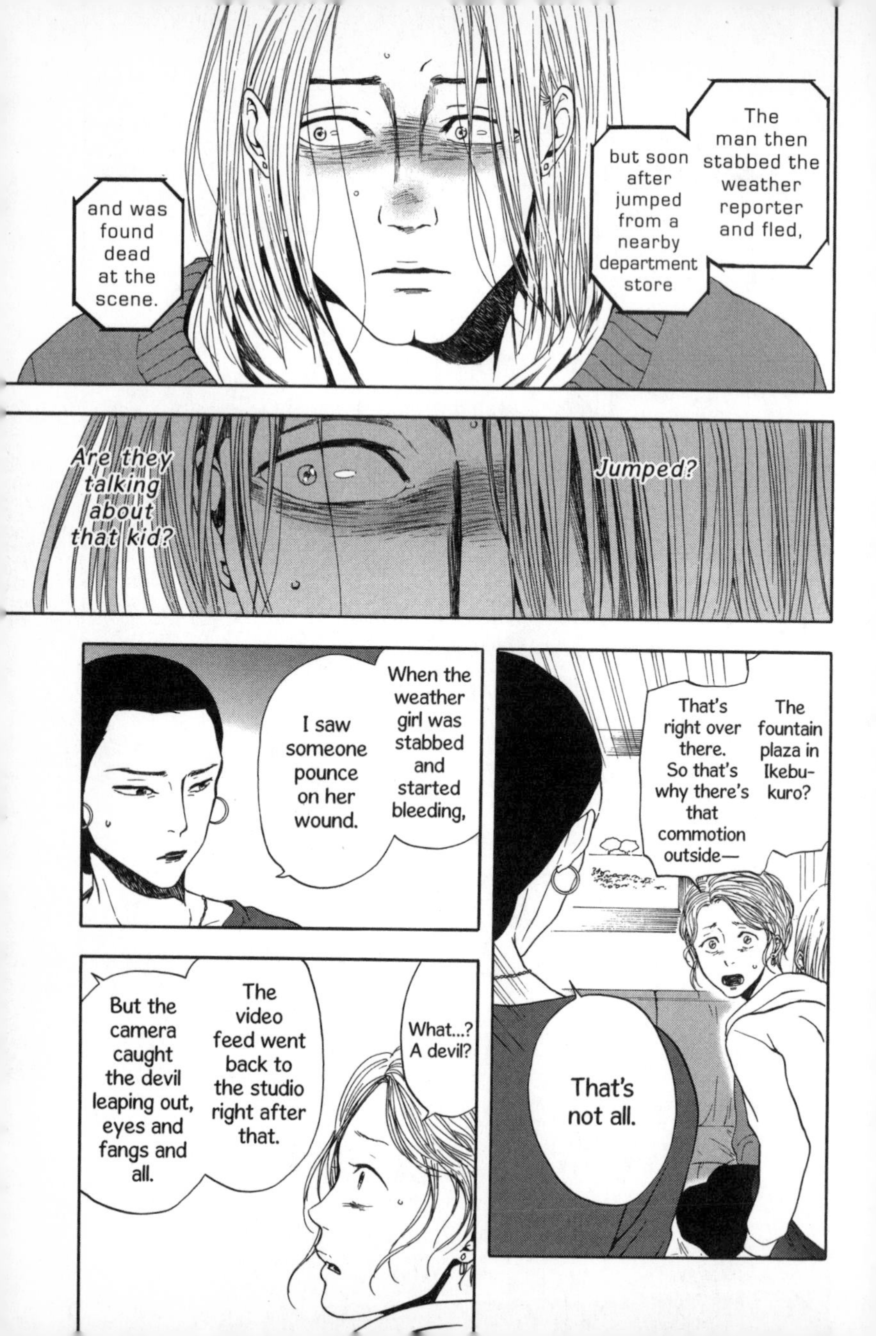
The man then stabbed the weather reporter and fled,
but soon after jumped from a nearby department store
and was found dead at the scene.
Jumped?
Are they talking about that kid?
The fountain plaza in Ikebu-kuro?
That's right over there. So that's why there's that commotion outside—
That's not all.
When the weather girl was stabbed and started bleeding,
I saw someone pounce on her wound.
What...? A devil?
The video feed went back to the studio right after that.
But the camera caught the devil leaping out, eyes and fangs and all.

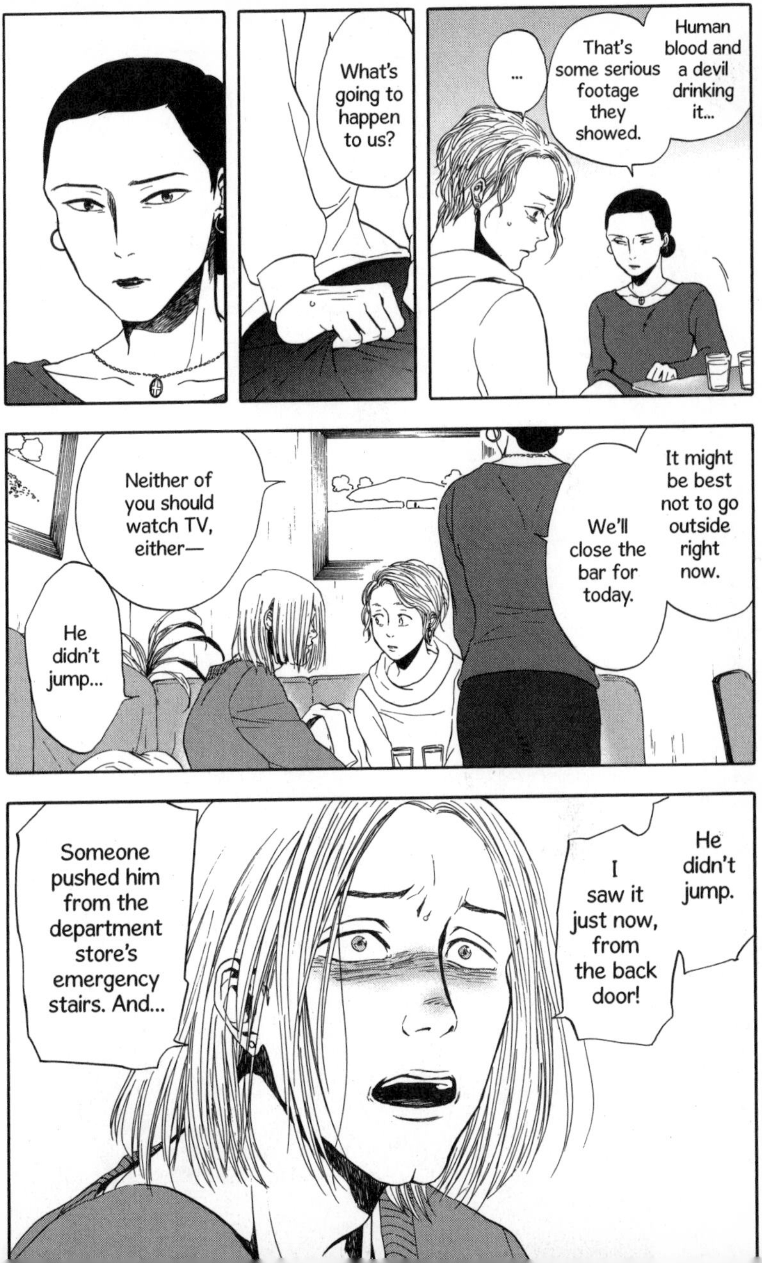
Human blood and a devil drinking it...
That's some serious footage they showed.
...
What's going to happen to us?
It might be best not to go outside right now.
We'll close the bar for today.
Neither of you should watch TV, either—
He didn't jump...
He didn't jump.
I saw it just now, from the back door!
Someone pushed him from the department store's emergency stairs. And...

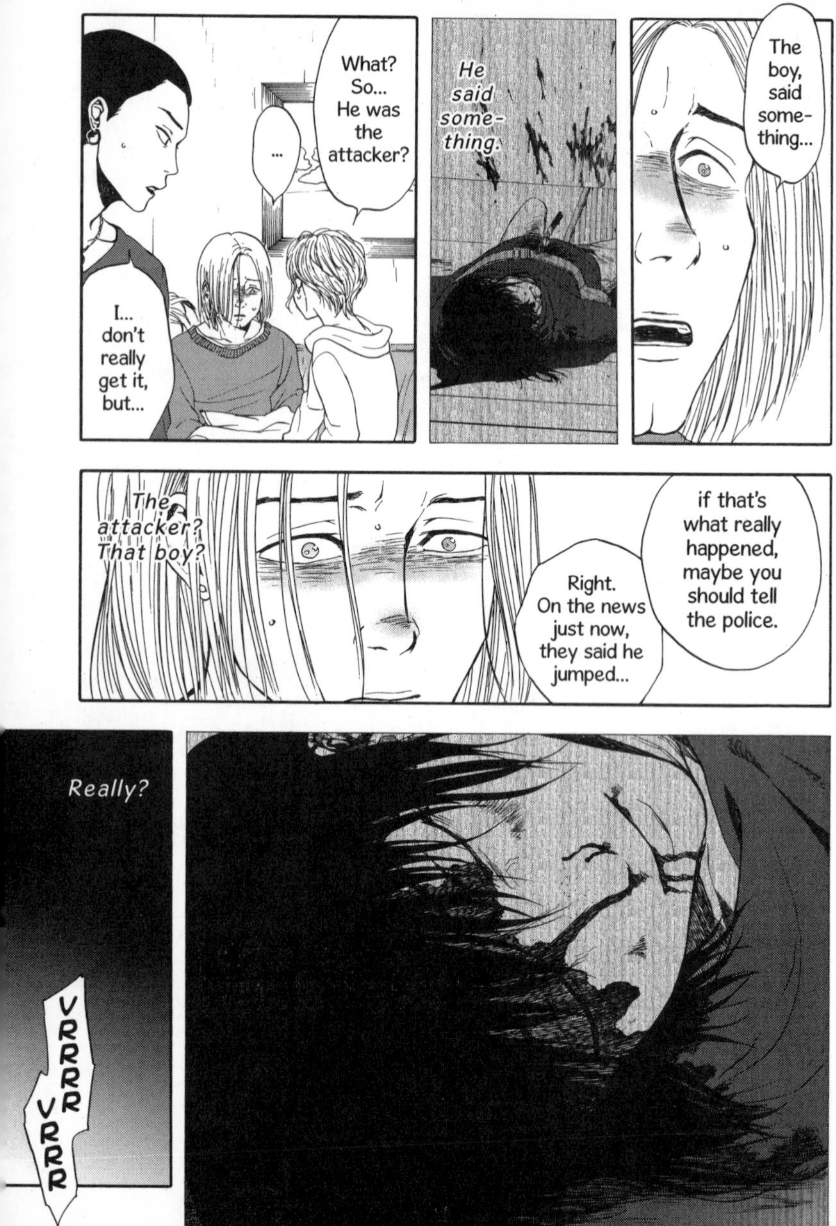
The boy, said some- thing...
He said some- thing.
What? So... He was the attacker?
...
I... don't really get it, but...
The attacker? That boy?
Right. On the news just now, they said he jumped...
if that's what really happened, maybe you should tell the police.
Really?
VRRRR VRRR

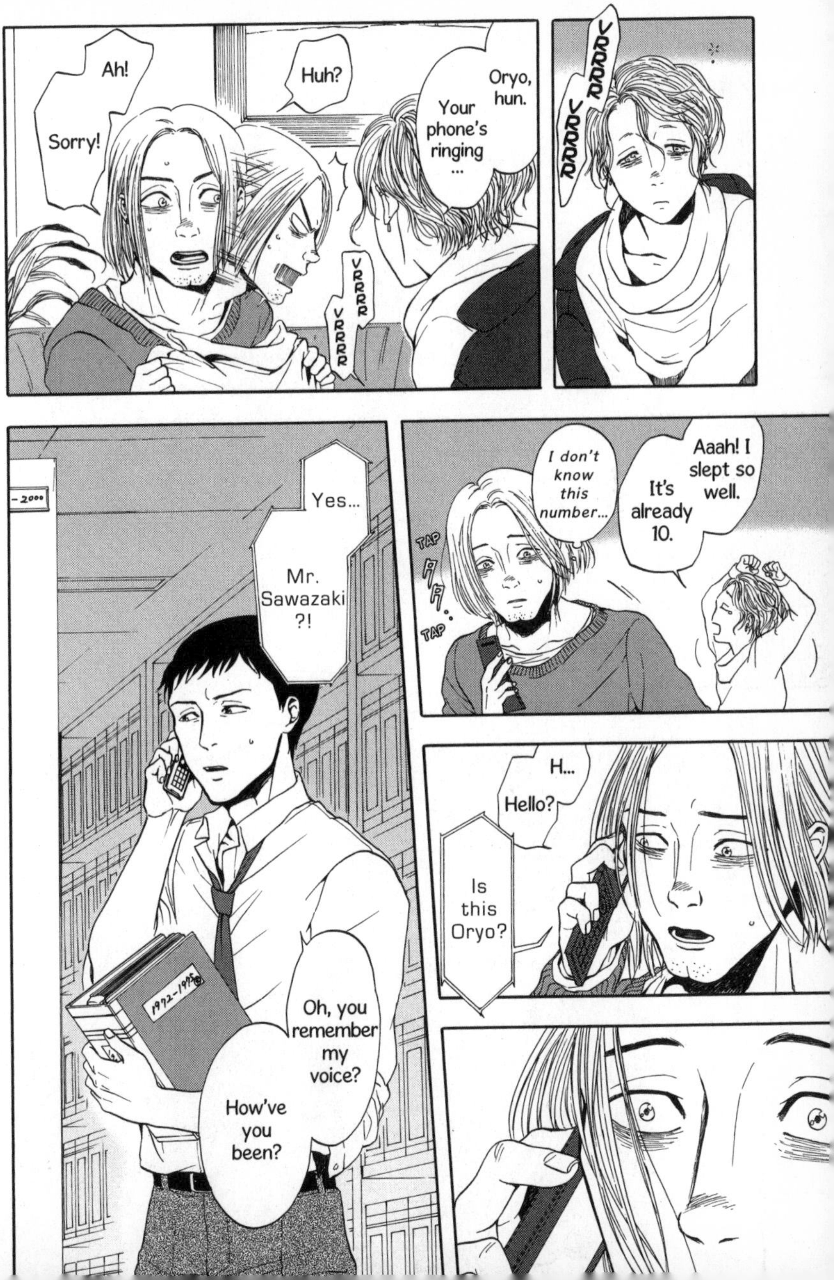
VRRRR
VRRRR
Oryo, hun.
Your phone's ringing ...
Huh?
Ah!
Sorry!
VRRRR
VRRRR
Aaah! I slept so well.
It's already 10.
I don't know this number...
TAP
TAP
H...
Hello?
Is this Oryo?
-2000
Yes...
Mr. Sawazaki?!
Oh, you remember my voice?
How've you been?
1972-1995

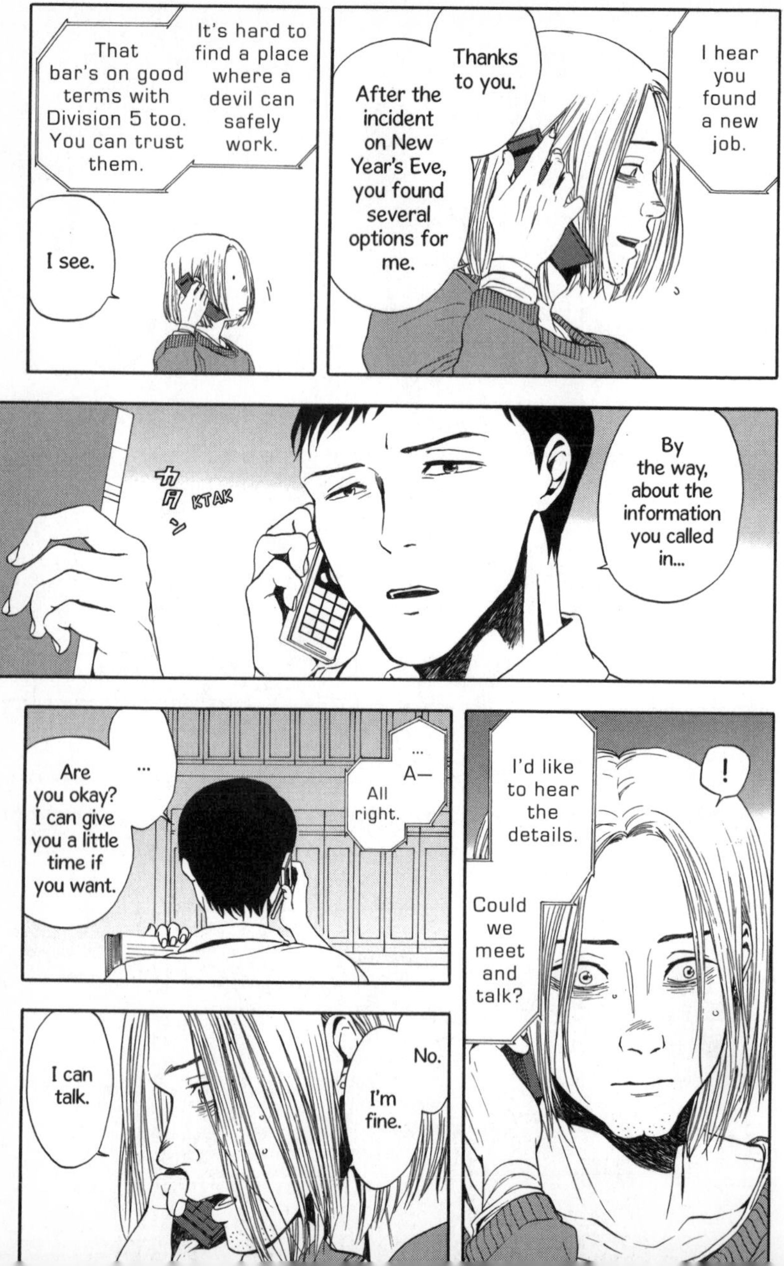
I hear you found a new job.
Thanks to you.
After the incident on New Year's Eve, you found several options for me.
It's hard to find a place where a devil can safely work.
That bar's on good terms with Division 5 too. You can trust them.
I see.
By the way, about the information you called in...
カタン KTAK
!
I'd like to hear the details.
Could we meet and talk?
... A— All right.
...
Are you okay? I can give you a little time if you want.
No.
I'm fine.
I can talk.

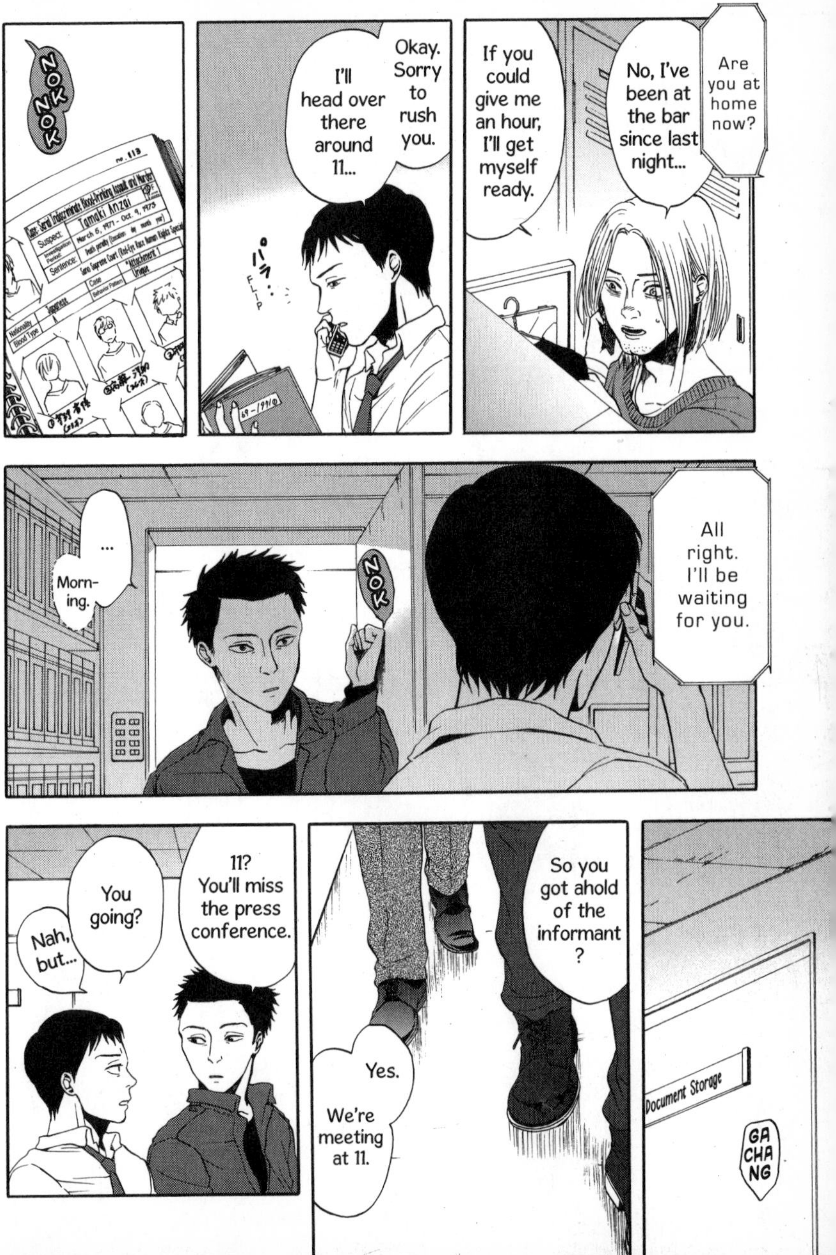
Are you at home now?
No, I've been at the bar since last night...
If you could give me an hour, I'll get myself ready.
Okay. Sorry to rush you.
I'll head over there around 11...
FLIP
NOK NOK
no. 113
Case: Serial Indiscriminate Blood-Drinking Assault and Murder
Suspect: Tamaki Anzai
Investigation Period: March 6, 1971 - Oct. 9, 1973
Sentence: Death penalty
Attachment 1
Case Behavior Pattern: Unique
Nationality: Japanese
Blood Type: A
All right. I'll be waiting for you.
NOK
...
Morning.
GA CHA NG
Document Storage
So you got ahold of the informant?
Yes.
We're meeting at 11.
11? You'll miss the press conference.
You going?
Nah, but...

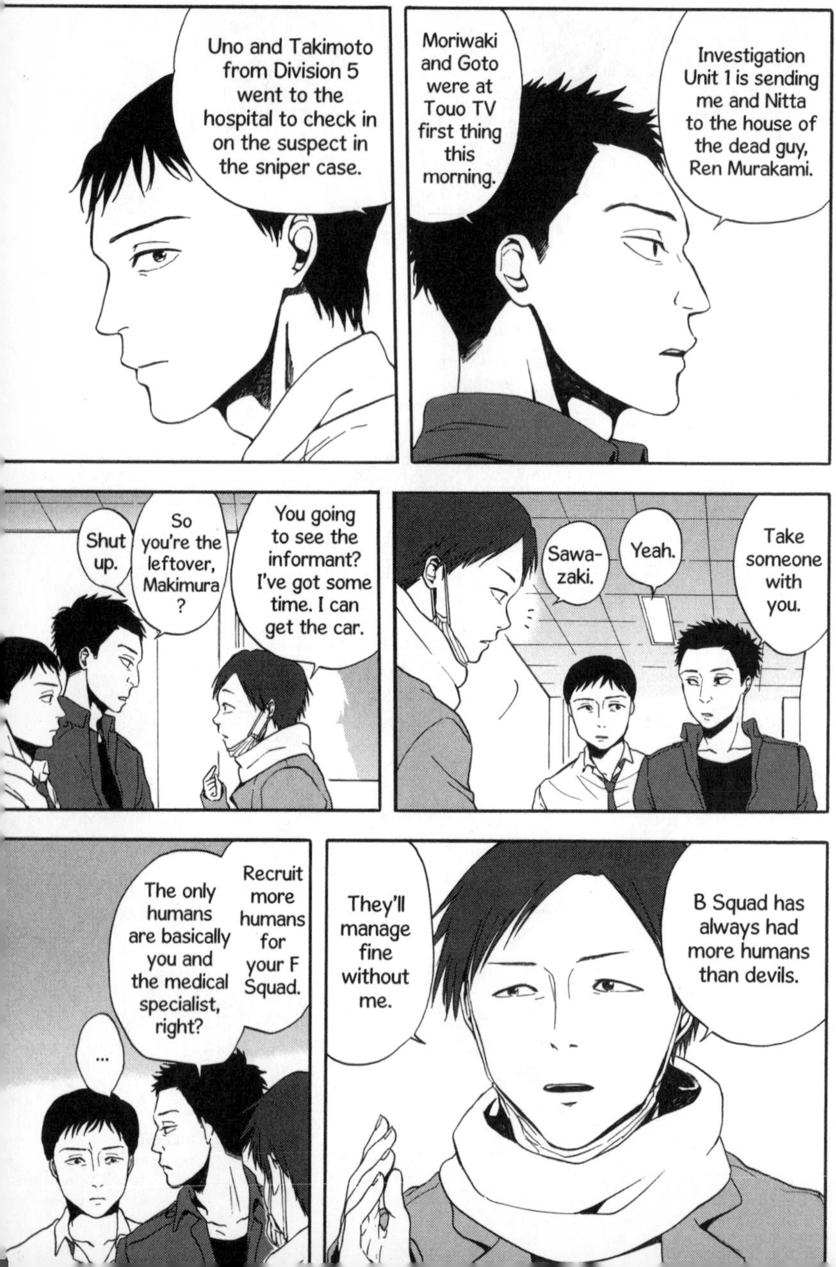
Investigation Unit 1 is sending me and Nitta to the house of the dead guy, Ren Murakami.
Moriwaki and Goto were at Touo TV first thing this morning.
Uno and Takimoto from Division 5 went to the hospital to check in on the suspect in the sniper case.
Take someone with you.
Yeah.
Sawa-zaki.
You going to see the informant? I've got some time. I can get the car.
So you're the leftover, Makimura?
Shut up.
B Squad has always had more humans than devils.
They'll manage fine without me.
Recruit more humans for your F Squad.
The only humans are basically you and the medical specialist, right?
...

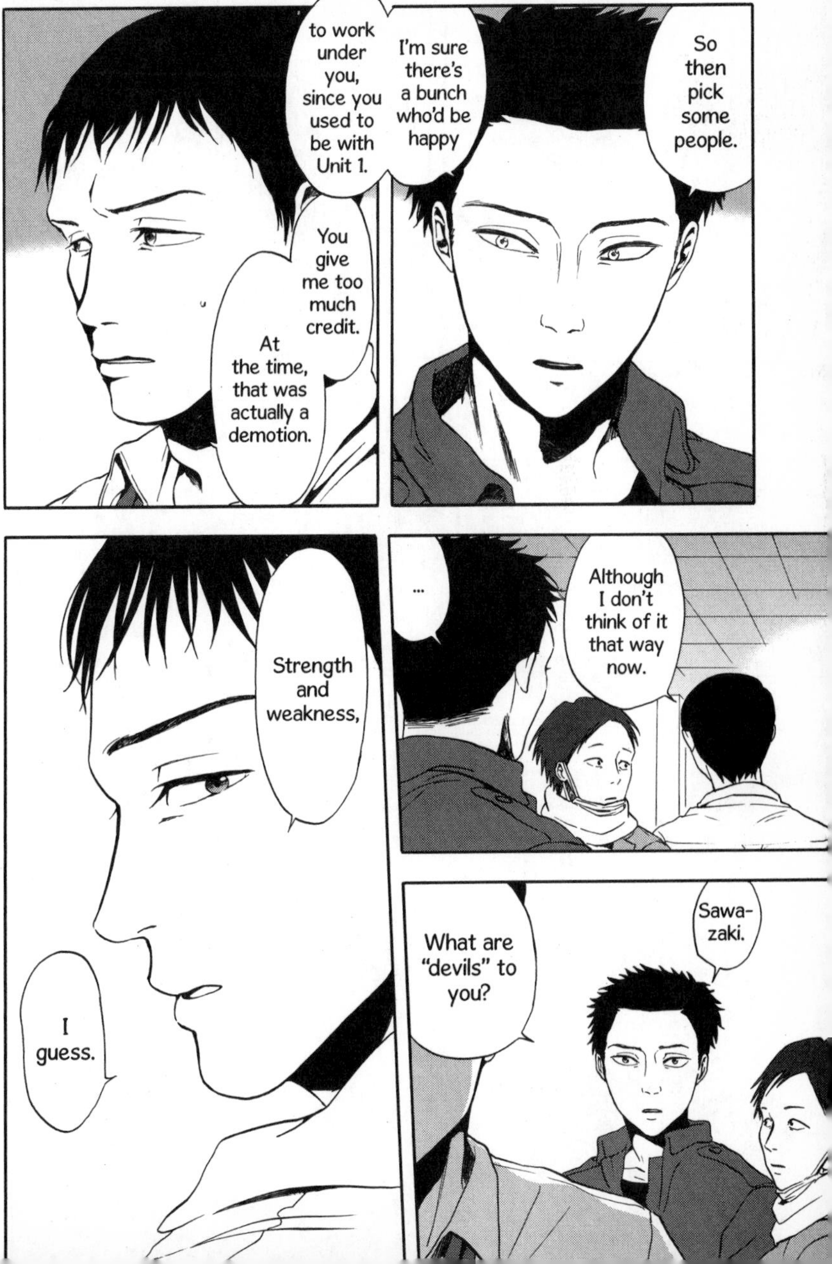
So then pick some people.
I'm sure there's a bunch who'd be happy
to work under you, since you used to be with Unit 1.
You give me too much credit.
At the time, that was actually a demotion.
Although I don't think of it that way now.
...
Sawa-zaki.
What are "devils" to you?
Strength and weakness,
I guess.

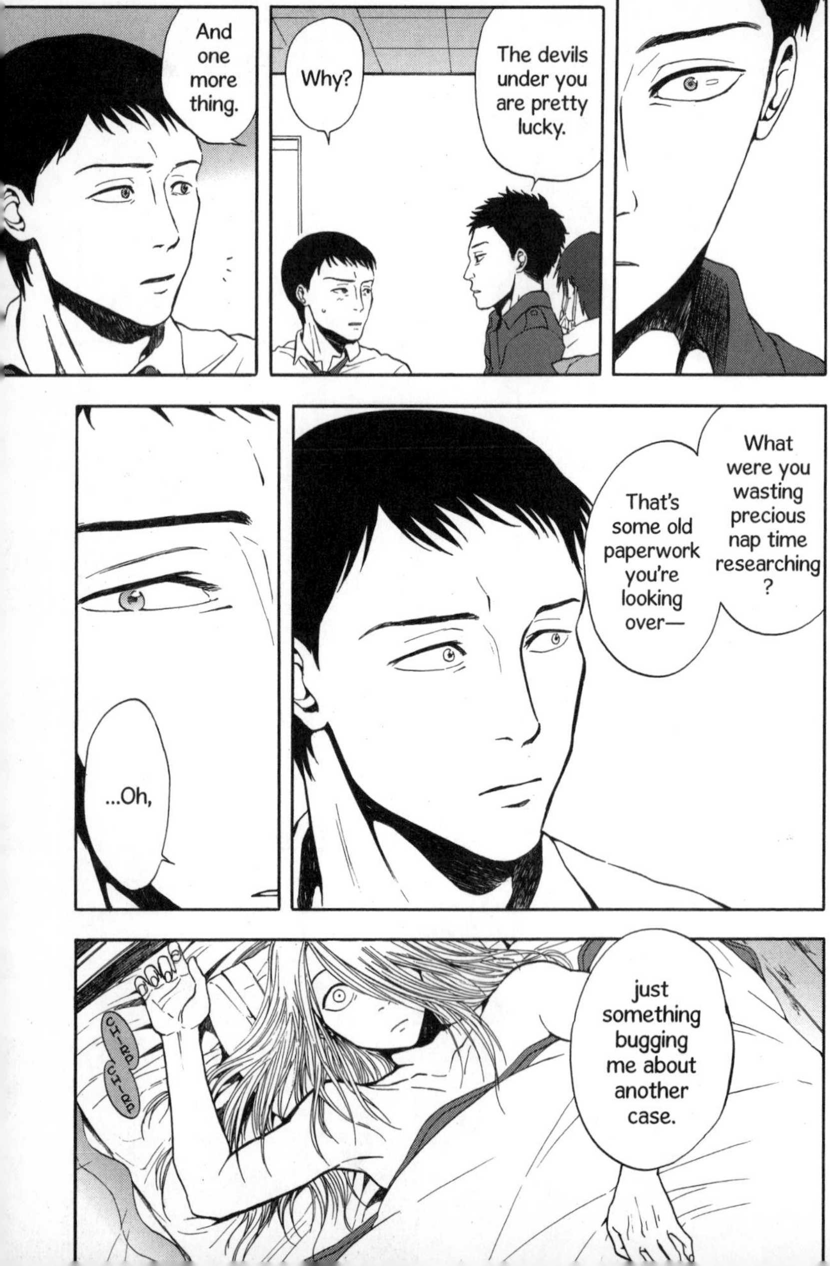
The devils under you are pretty lucky.
Why?
And one more thing.
What were you wasting precious nap time researching?
That's some old paperwork you're looking over—
...Oh,
just something bugging me about another case.
CHI-RR CHI-RR

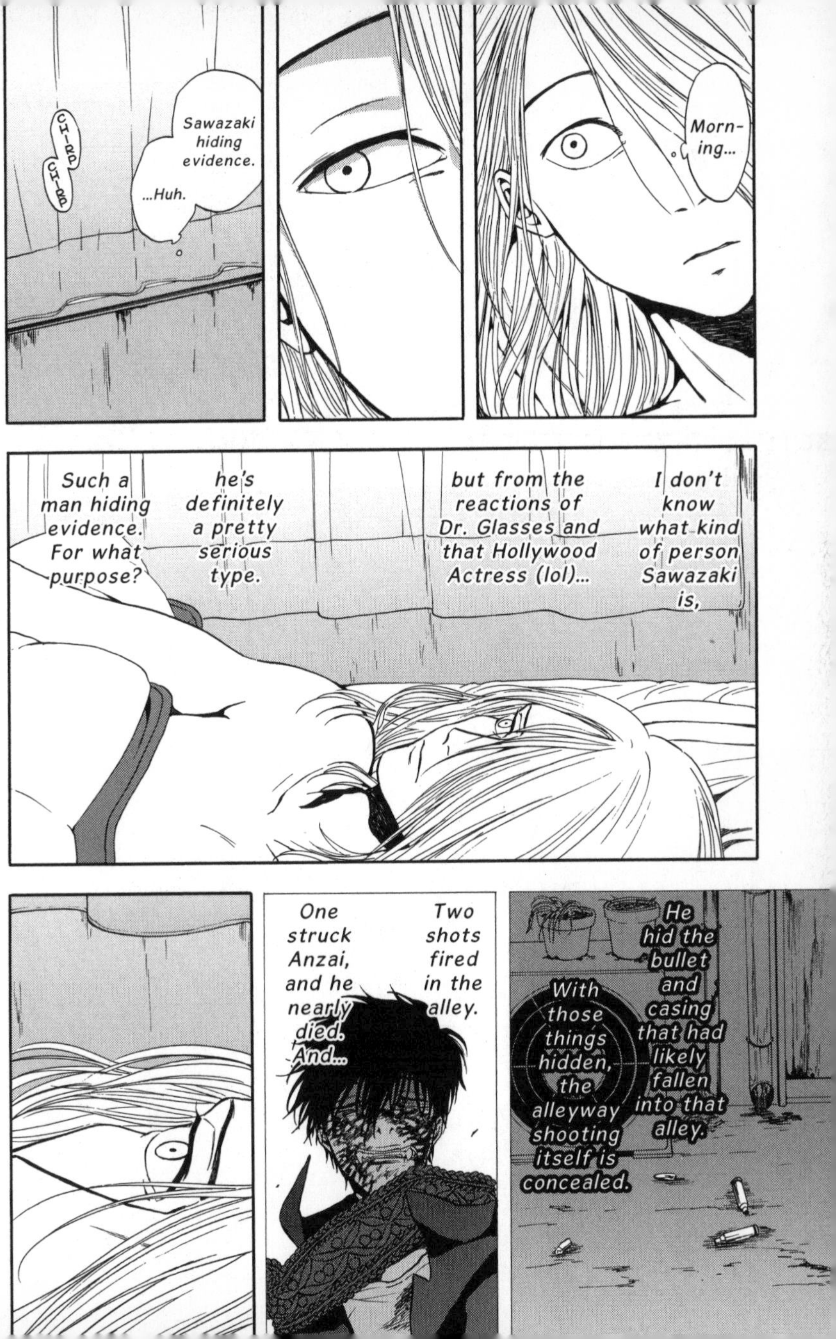
Morn-
ing...
Sawazaki hiding evidence.
...Huh.
CHIRP CHIRP
I don't know what kind of person Sawazaki is,
but from the reactions of Dr. Glasses and that Hollywood Actress (lol)...
he's definitely a pretty serious type.
Such a man hiding evidence. For what purpose?
He hid the bullet and casing that had likely fallen into that alley.
With those things hidden, the alleyway shooting itself is concealed.
Two shots fired in the alley.
One struck Anzai, and he nearly died. And...

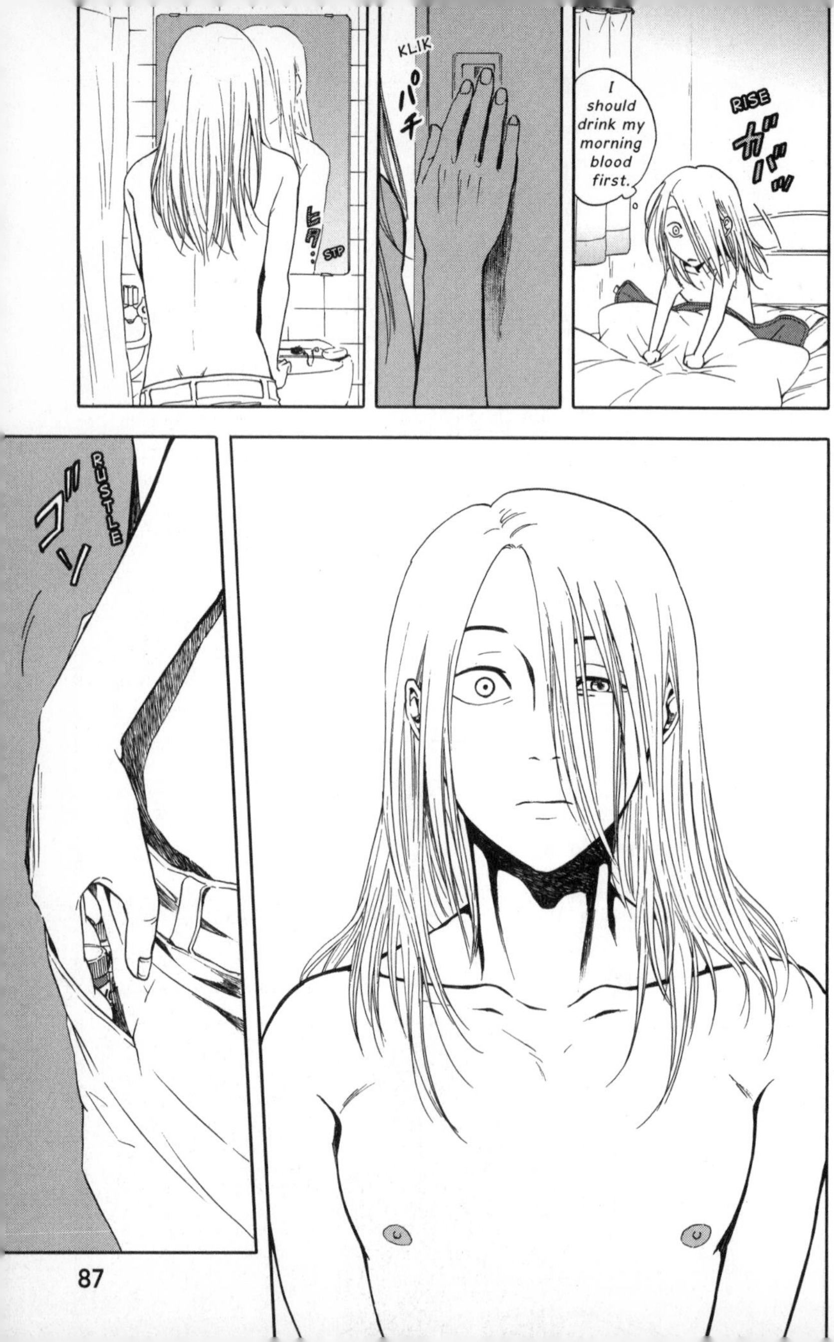

I should drink my morning blood first.
RISE
ガバッ
KLIK
パチ
ヒタ…
STP
RUSTLE
ゴソ

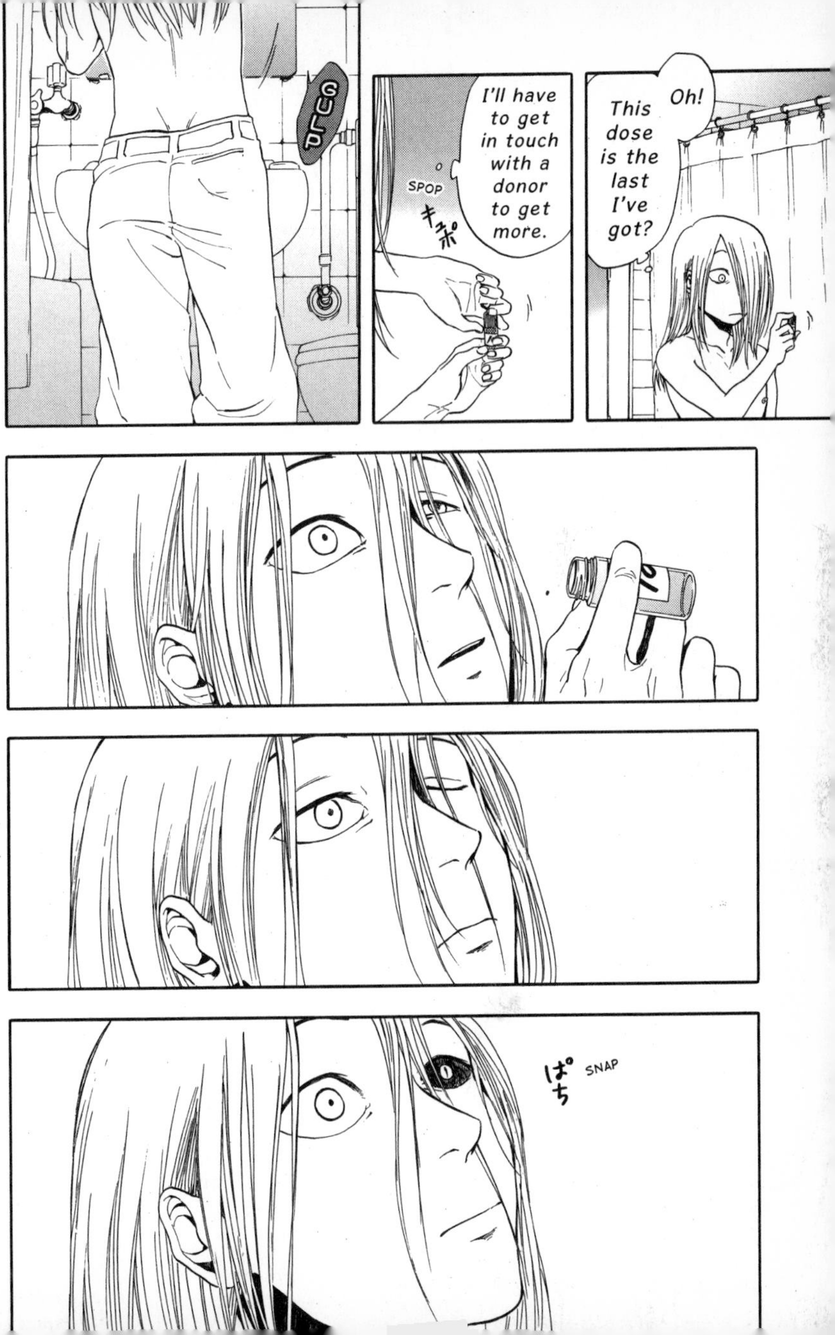

Oh!
This dose is the last I've got?
SPOP
キュポ
I'll have to get in touch with a donor to get more.
GULP
ぱち
SNAP

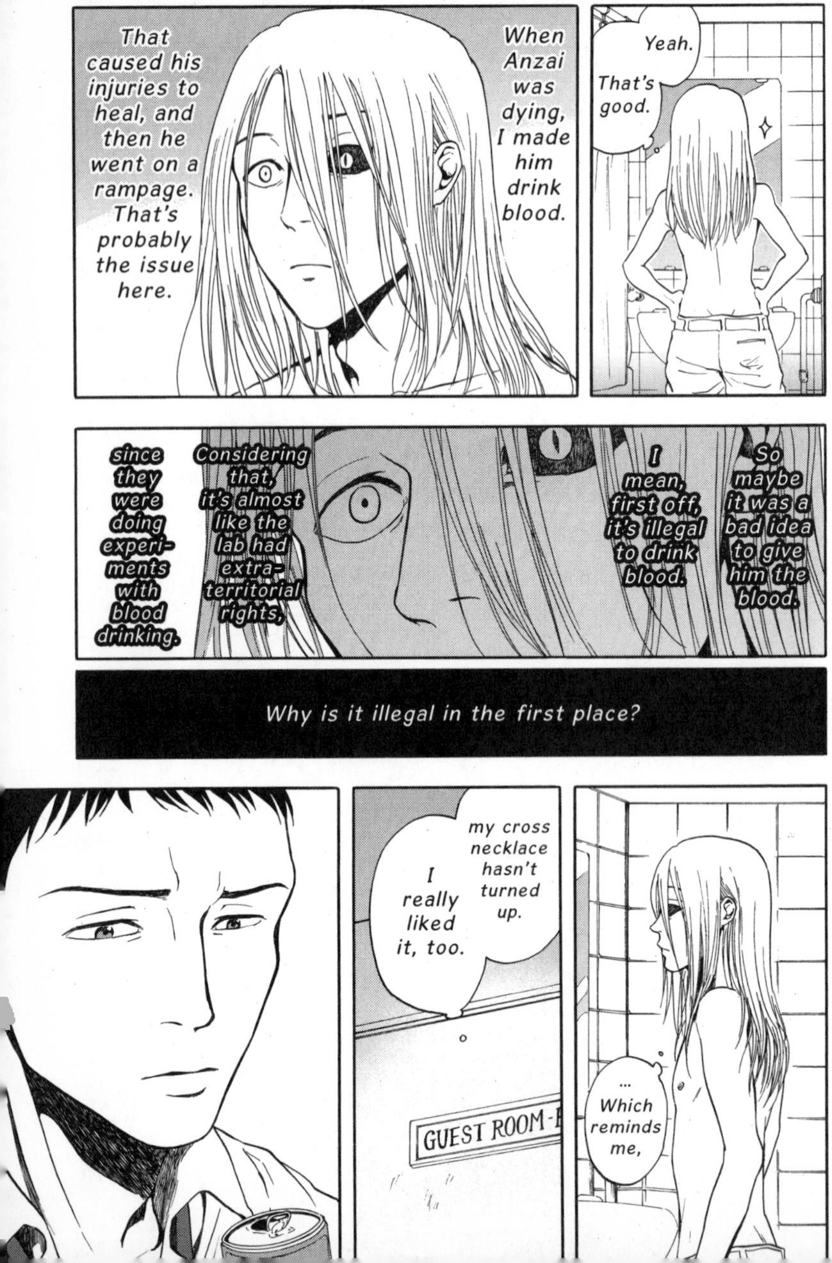
Yeah.
That's good.
When Anzai was dying, I made him drink blood.
That caused his injuries to heal, and then he went on a rampage. That's probably the issue here.
So maybe it was a bad idea to give him the blood.
I mean, first off, it's illegal to drink blood.
Considering that, it's almost like the lab had extra-territorial rights,
since they were doing experi-ments with blood drinking.
Why is it illegal in the first place?
... Which reminds me,
my cross necklace hasn't turned up.
I really liked it, too.
GUEST ROOM-

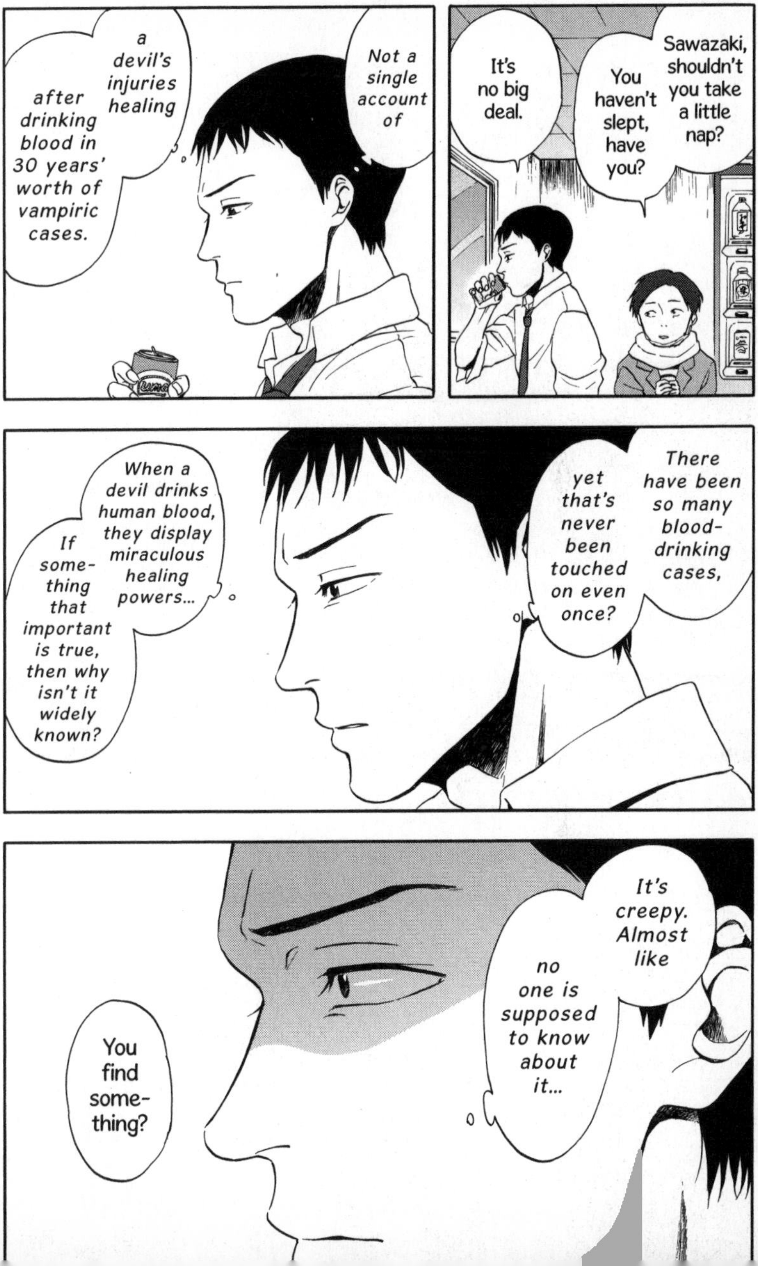
Sawazaki, shouldn't you take a little nap?
You haven't slept, have you?
It's no big deal.
Not a single account of
a devil's injuries healing
after drinking blood in 30 years' worth of vampiric cases.
There have been so many blood-drinking cases,
yet that's never been touched on even once?
When a devil drinks human blood, they display miraculous healing powers...
If something that important is true, then why isn't it widely known?
It's creepy. Almost like
no one is supposed to know about it...
You find something?

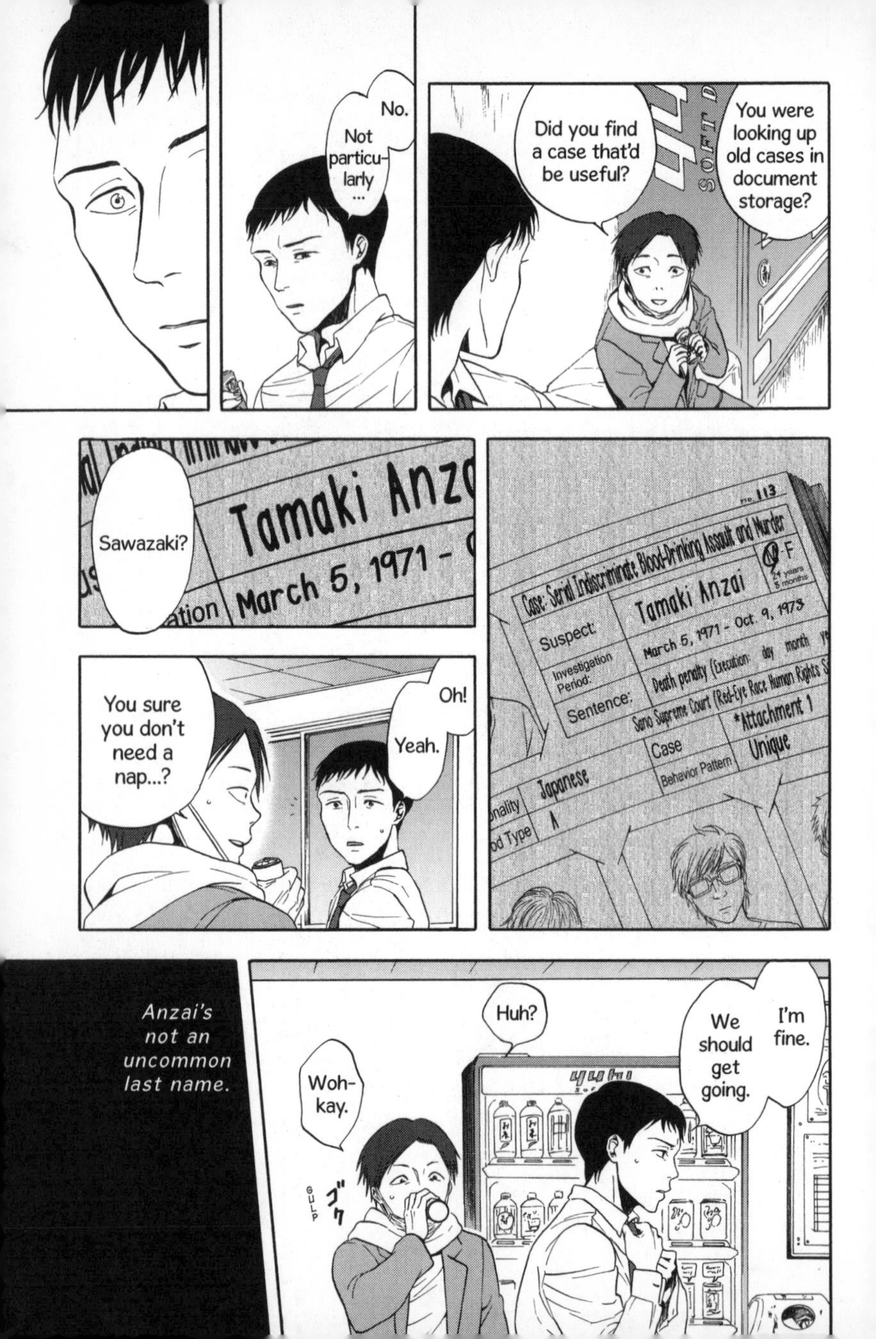
You were looking up old cases in document storage?
Did you find a case that'd be useful?
No.
Not particu-larly ...
No. 113
Case: Serial Indiscriminate Blood-Drinking Assault and Murder
M·F
21 years 5 months
Suspect:
Tamaki Anzai
Investigation Period:
March 5, 1971 - Oct. 9, 1973
Sentence:
Case
*Attachment 1
Behavior Pattern
Unique
Japanese
Tamaki Anz
March 5, 1971 -
Sawazaki?
Oh!
Yeah.
You sure you don't need a nap...?
I'm fine.
We should get going.
Huh?
Woh-kay.
GULP
Anzai's not an uncommon last name.

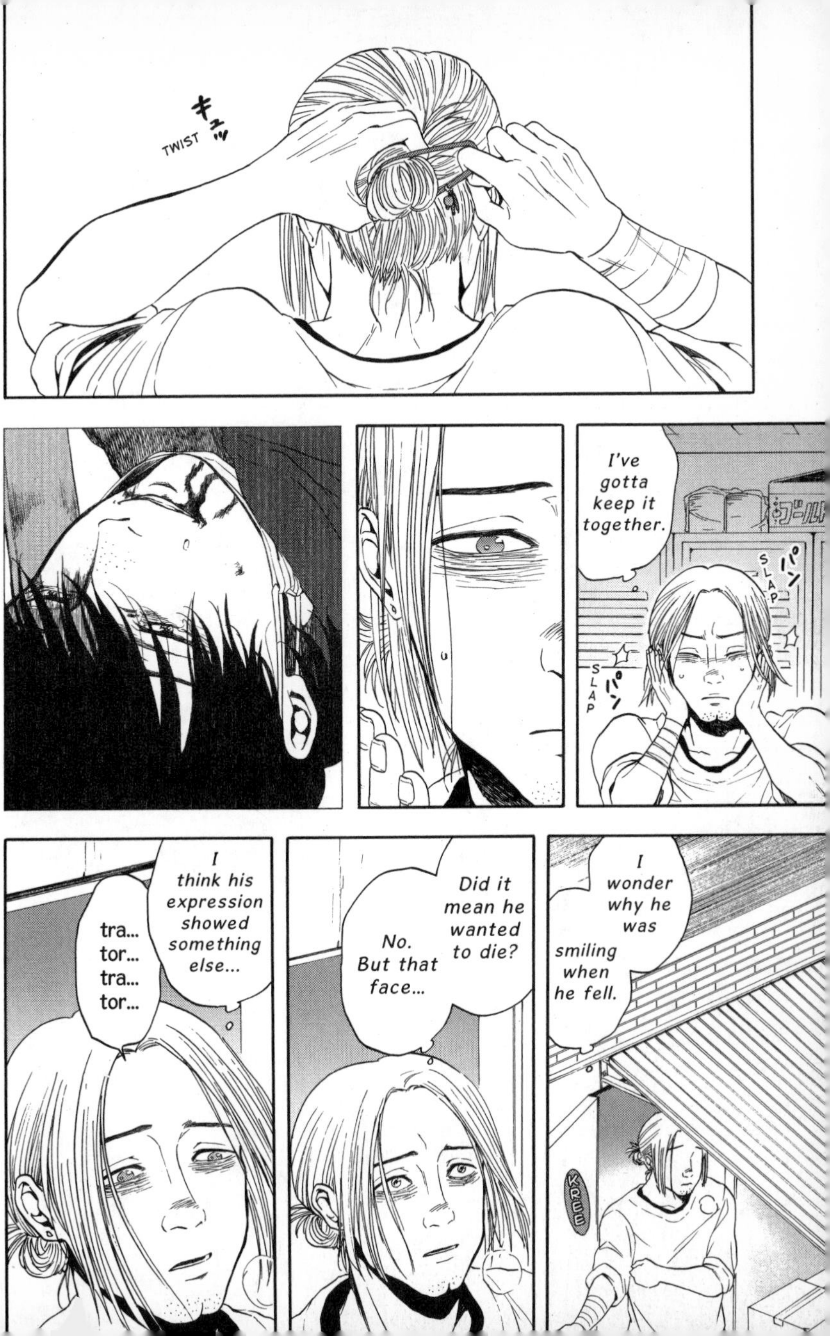
キュッ
TWIST
I've gotta keep it together.
パン
SLAP
パン
SLAP
I wonder why he was smiling when he fell.
KREE
Did it mean he wanted to die?
No. But that face...
I think his expression showed something else...
tra... tor... tra... tor...

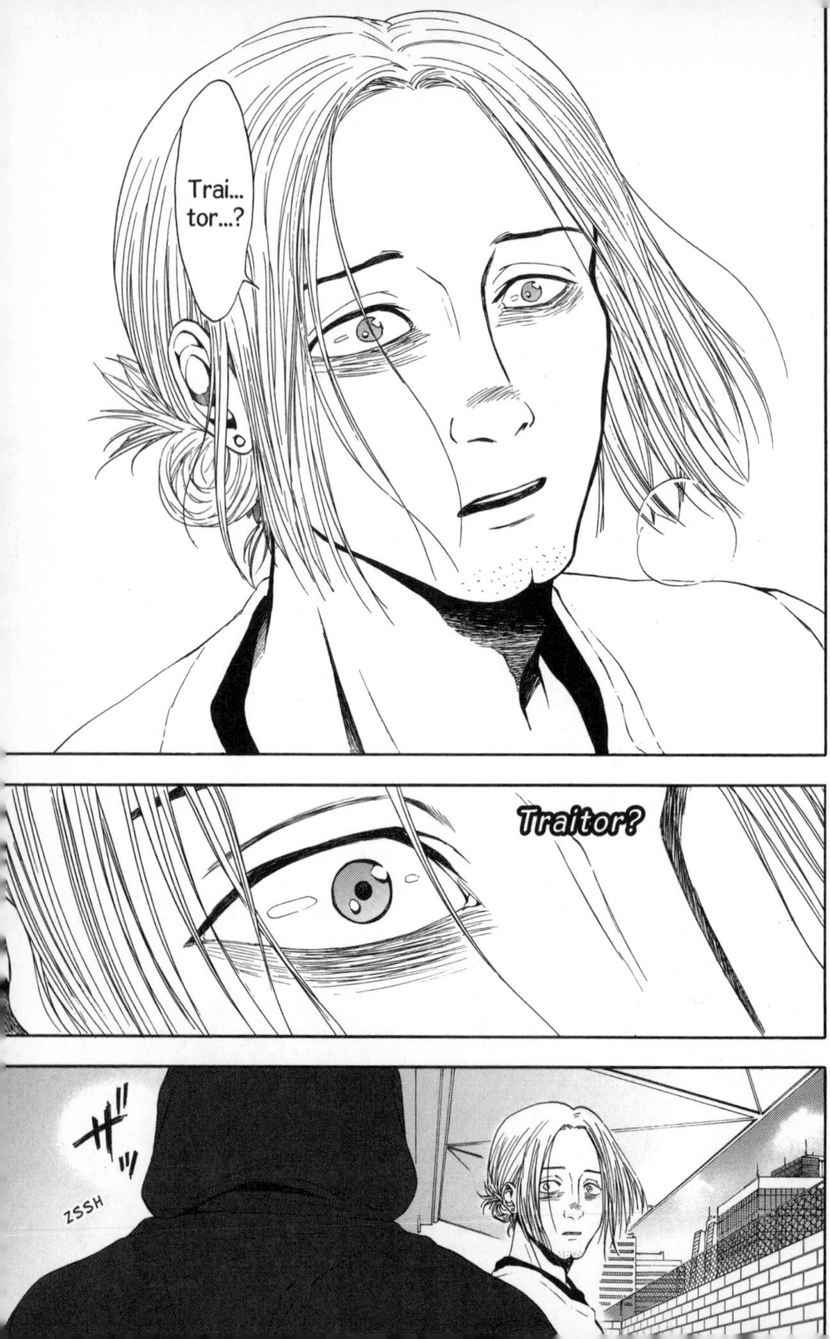

Trai...
tor...?
Traitor?
ZSSH

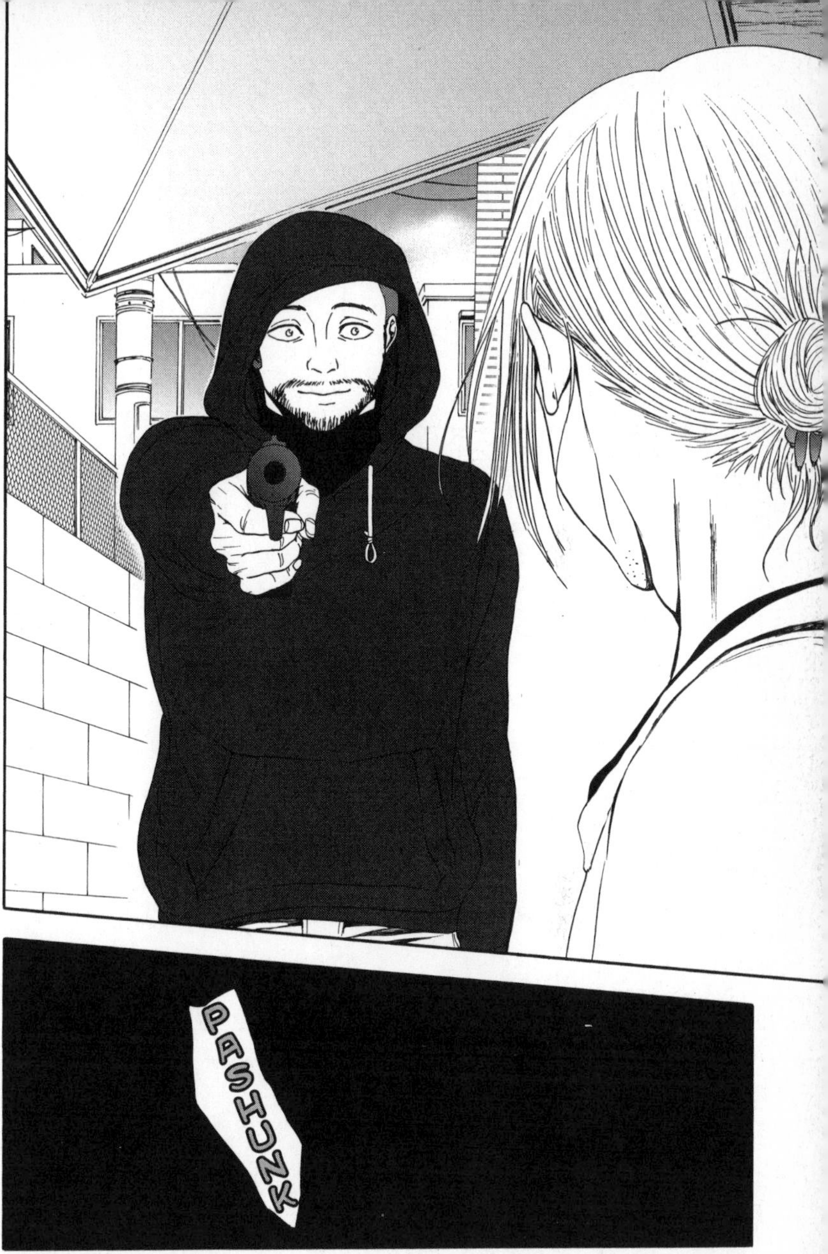
PASHUNK

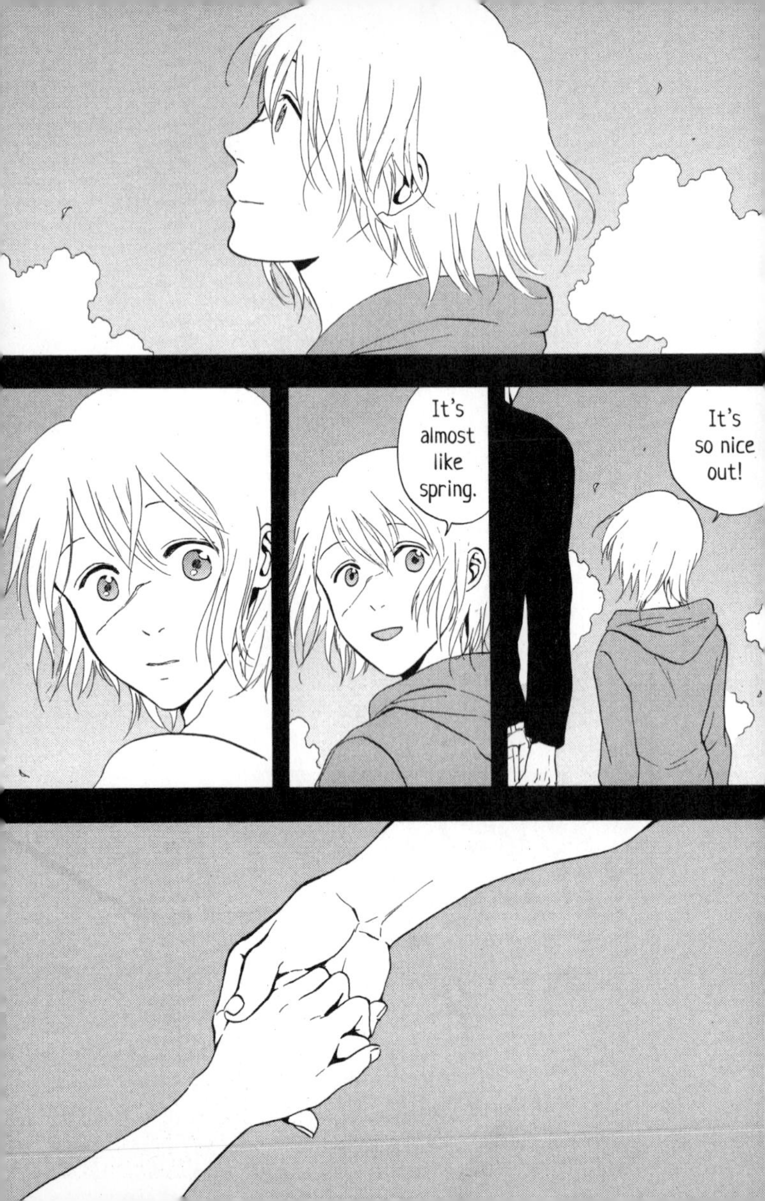
It's so nice out!
It's almost like spring.

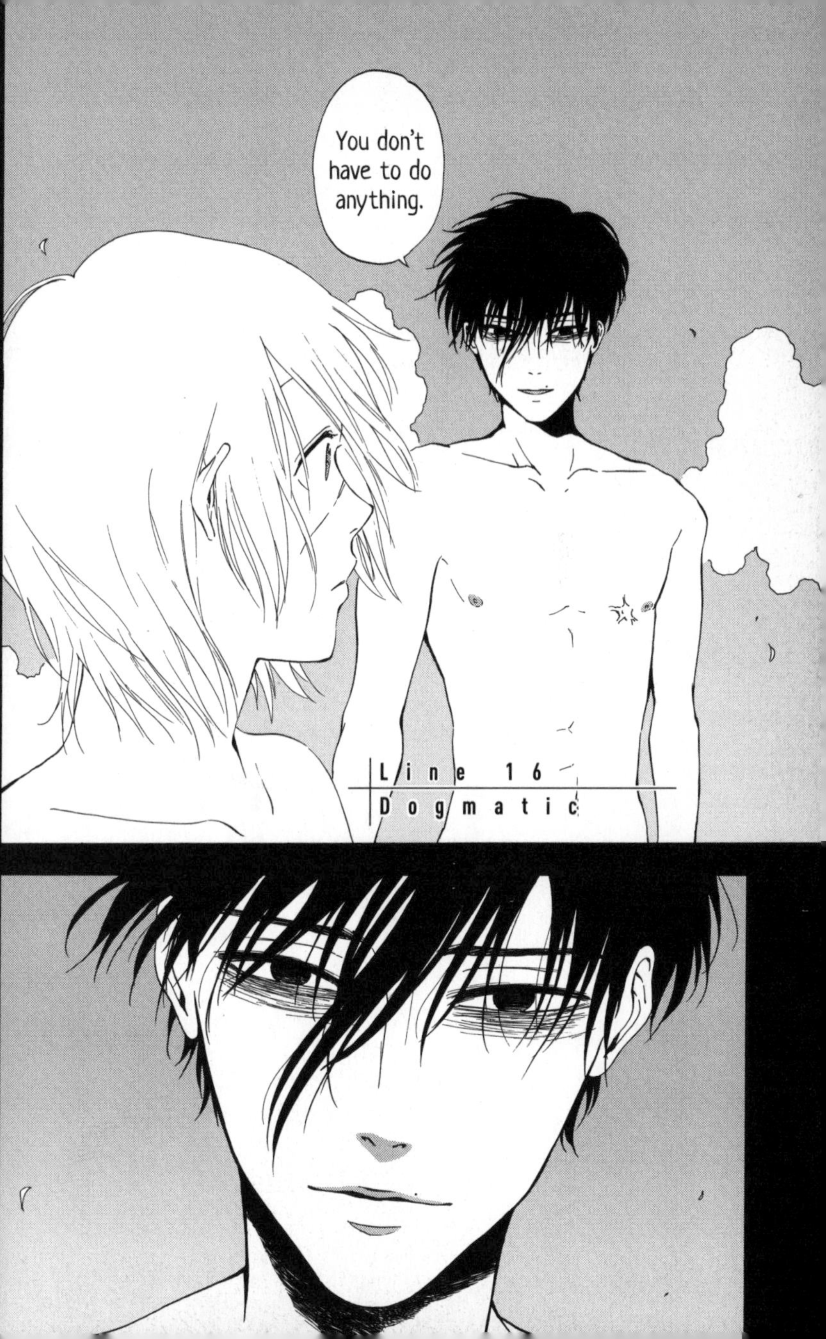
You don't have to do anything.
Line 16
Dogmatic

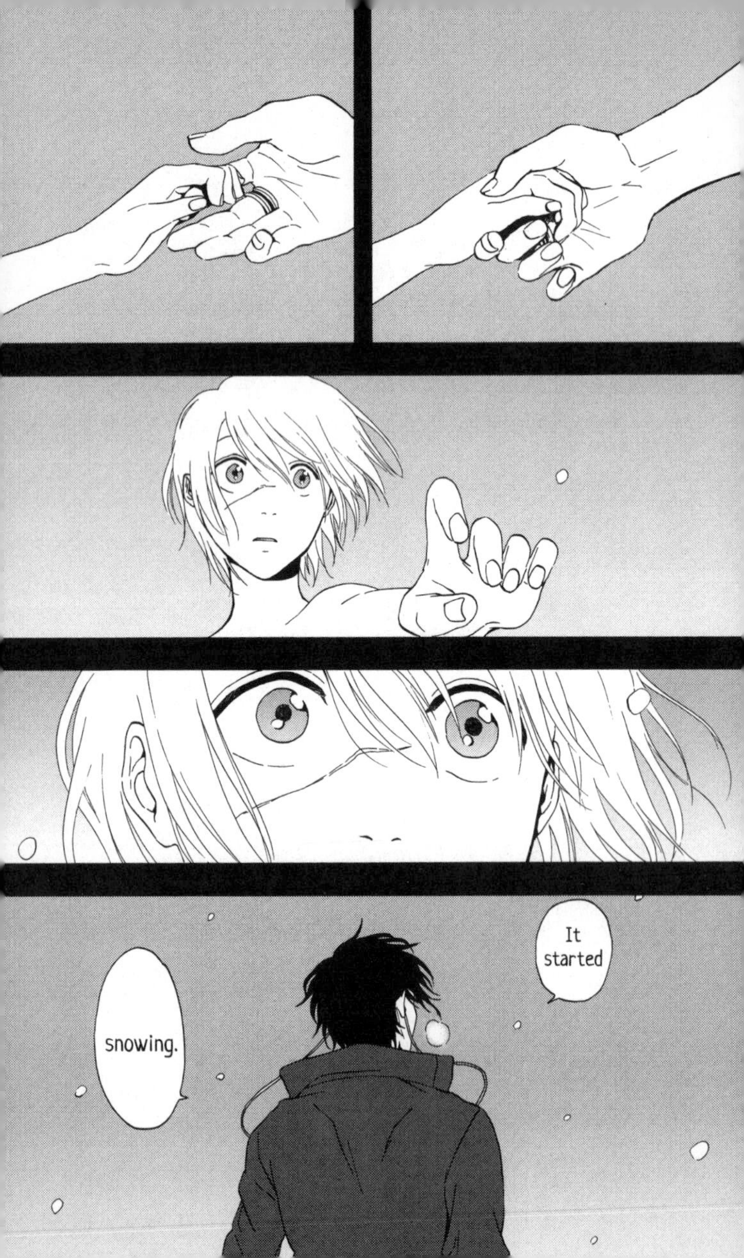

It started
snowing.

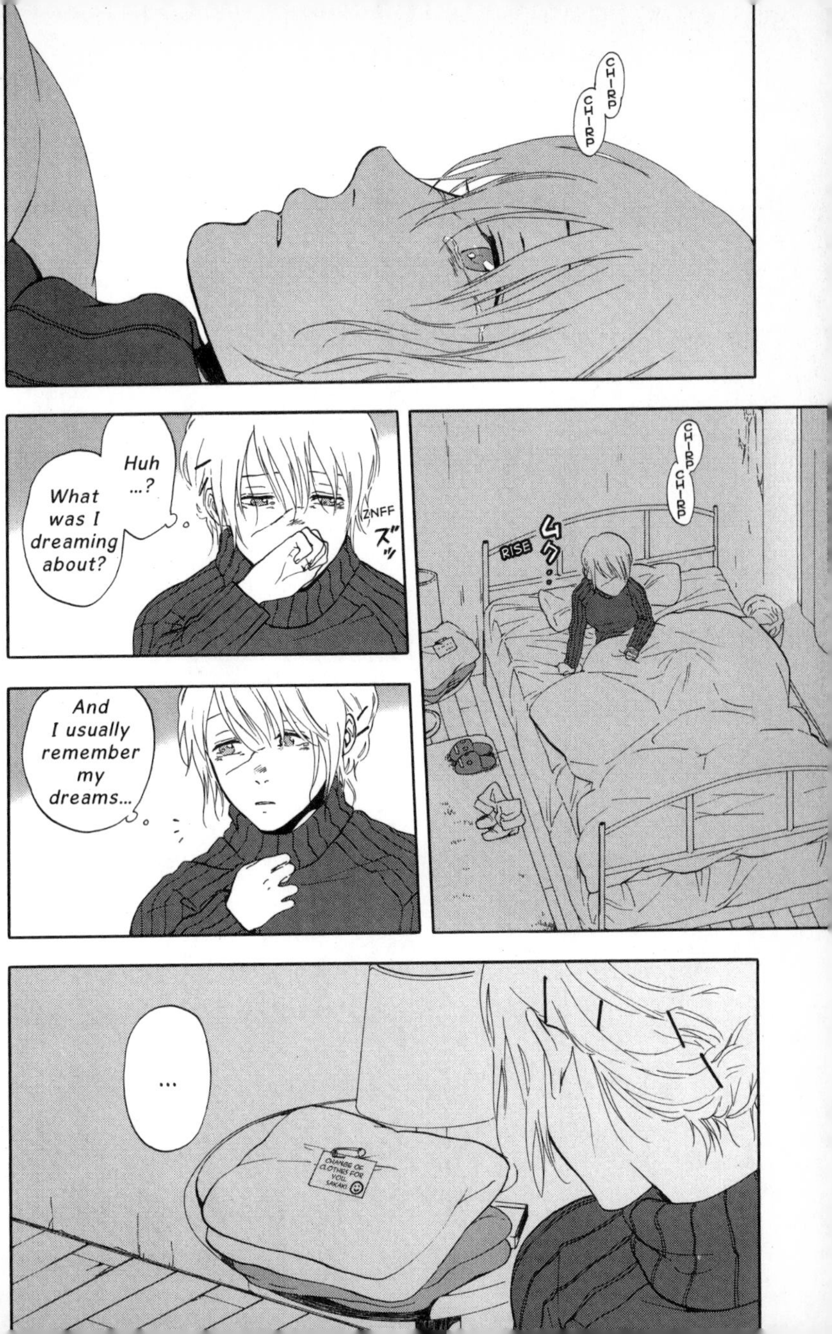
CHIRP
CHIRP
CHIRP
CHIRP
RISE
Huh ...?
What was I dreaming about?
ZNFF
And I usually remember my dreams...
...
CHANGE OF CLOTHES FOR YOU, SAKAKI

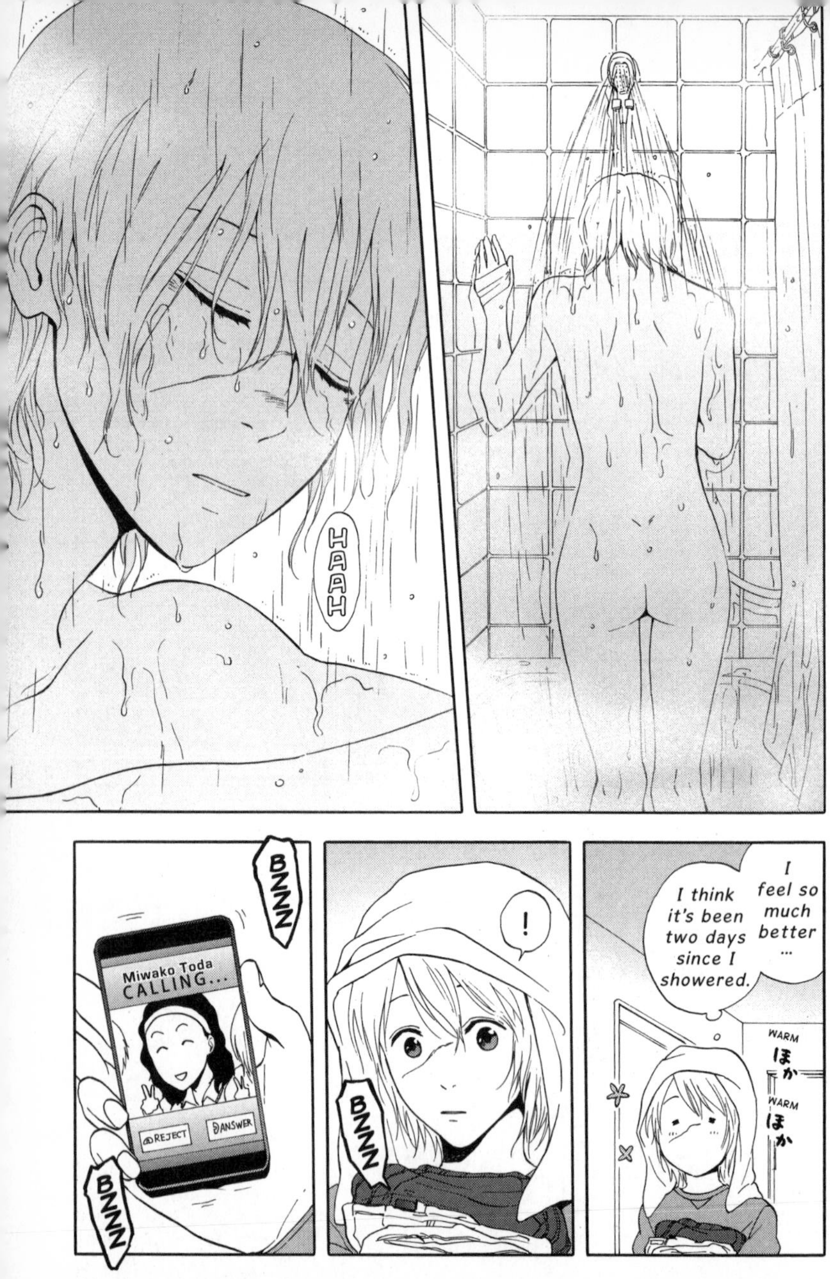
HAAAH
I feel so much better ...
I think it's been two days since I showered.
WARM ほか WARM ほか
!
BZZZ
BZZZ
Miwako Toda CALLING...
REJECT
ANSWER
BZZZ

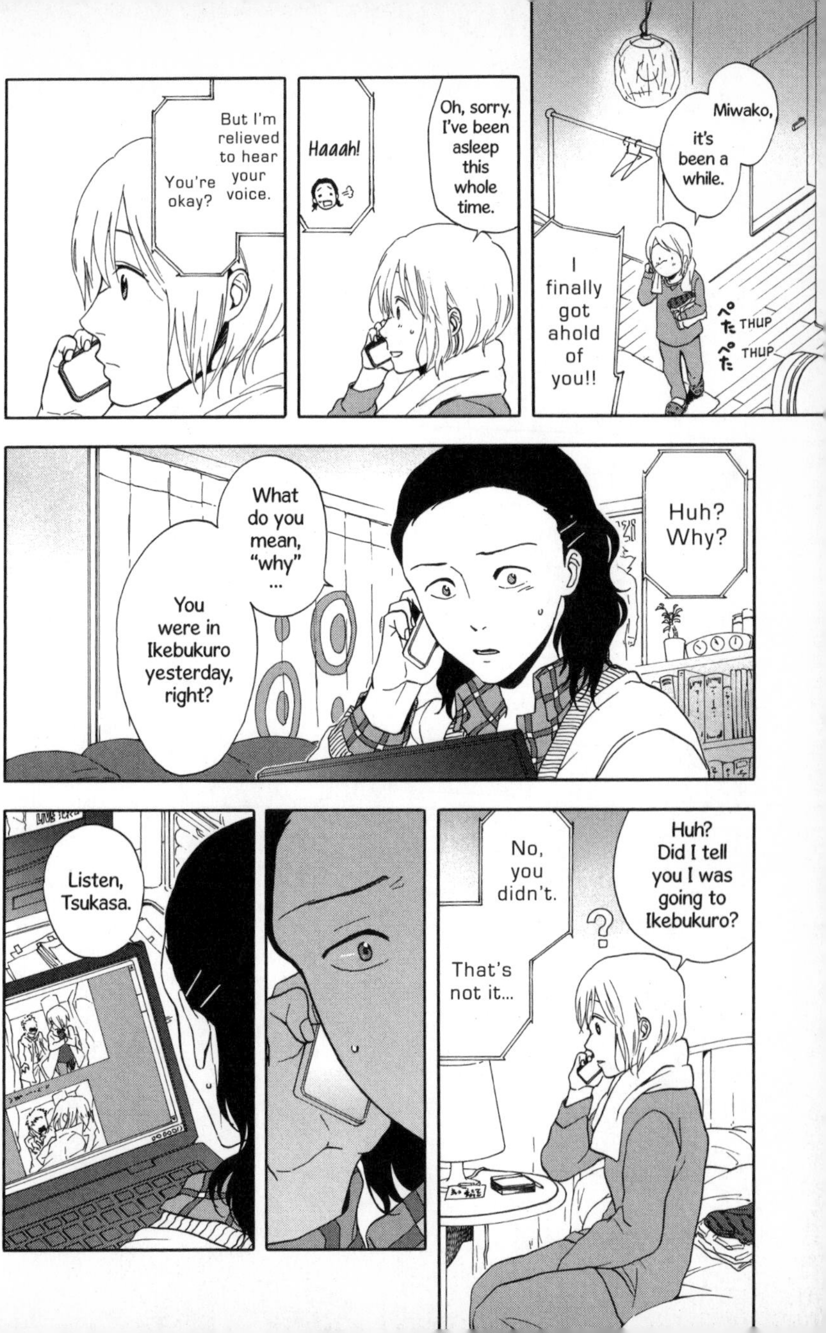
Miwako,
it's been a while.
I finally got ahold of you!!
ぺた THUP
ぺた THUP
Oh, sorry. I've been asleep this whole time.
Haaah!
But I'm relieved to hear your voice.
You're okay?
Huh? Why?
What do you mean, "why" ...
You were in Ikebukuro yesterday, right?
Huh? Did I tell you I was going to Ikebukuro?
?
No, you didn't.
That's not it...
Listen, Tsukasa.

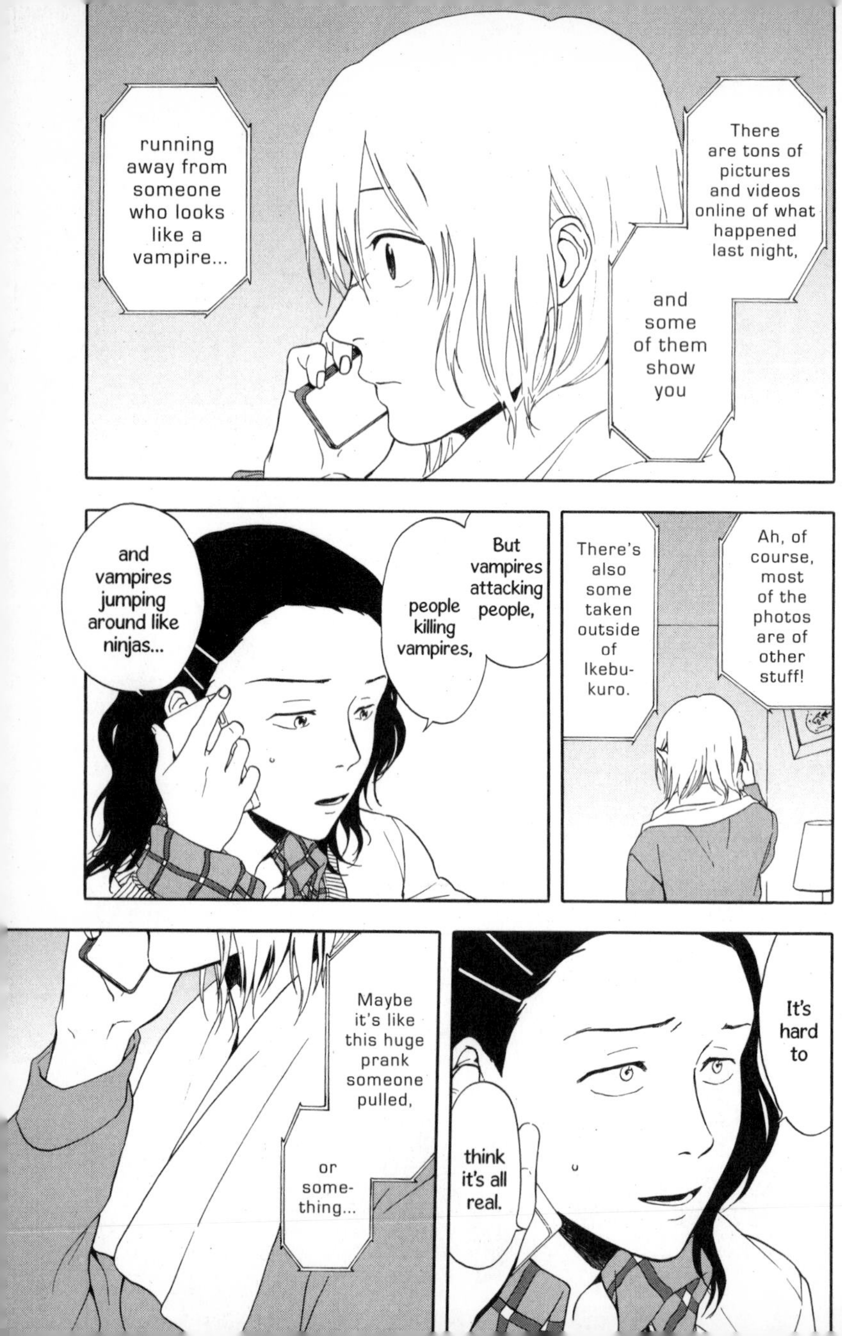
There are tons of pictures and videos online of what happened last night,
and some of them show you
running away from someone who looks like a vampire...
Ah, of course, most of the photos are of other stuff!
There's also some taken outside of Ikebu-kuro.
But vampires attacking people,
people killing vampires,
and vampires jumping around like ninjas...
It's hard to
think it's all real.
Maybe it's like this huge prank someone pulled,
or some-thing...

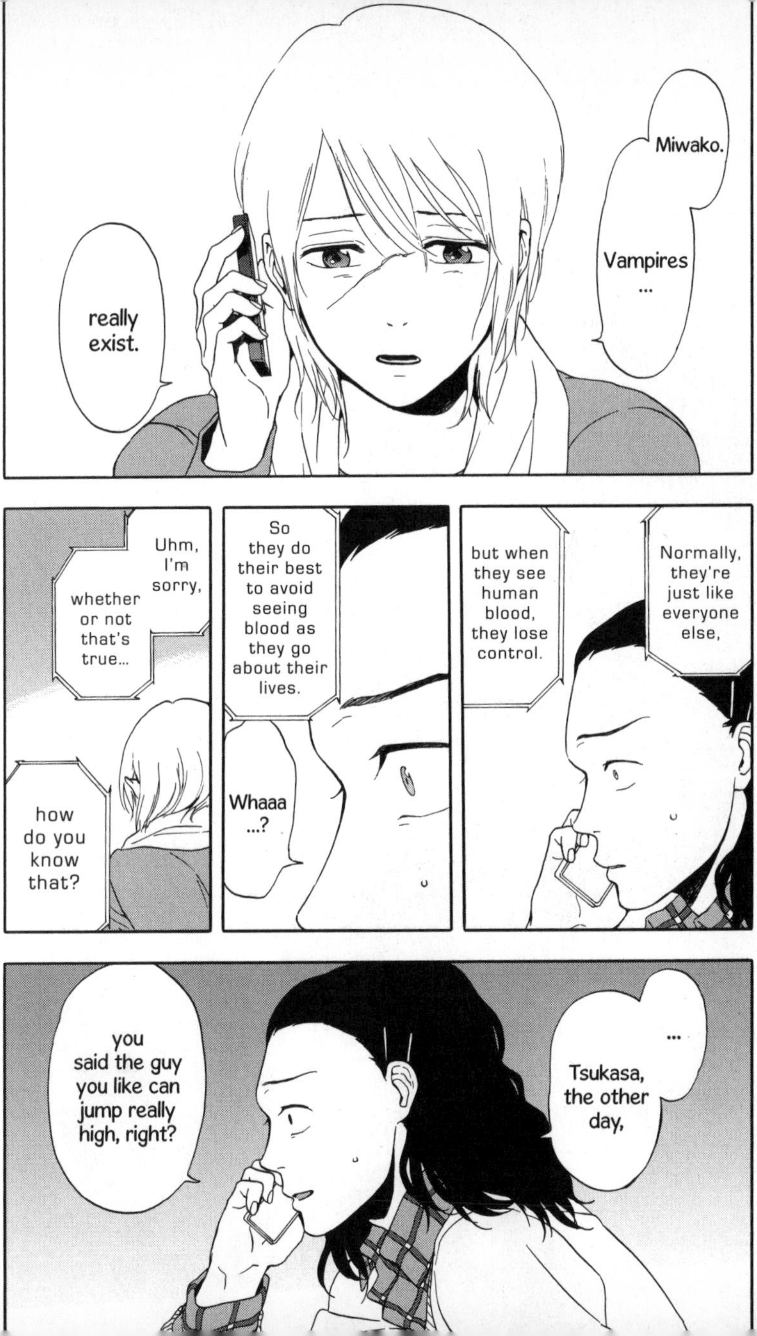
Miwako.
Vampires ...
really exist.
Normally, they're just like everyone else,
but when they see human blood, they lose control.
So they do their best to avoid seeing blood as they go about their lives.
Whaaa ...?
Uhm, I'm sorry,
whether or not that's true...
how do you know that?
...
Tsukasa, the other day,
you said the guy you like can jump really high, right?

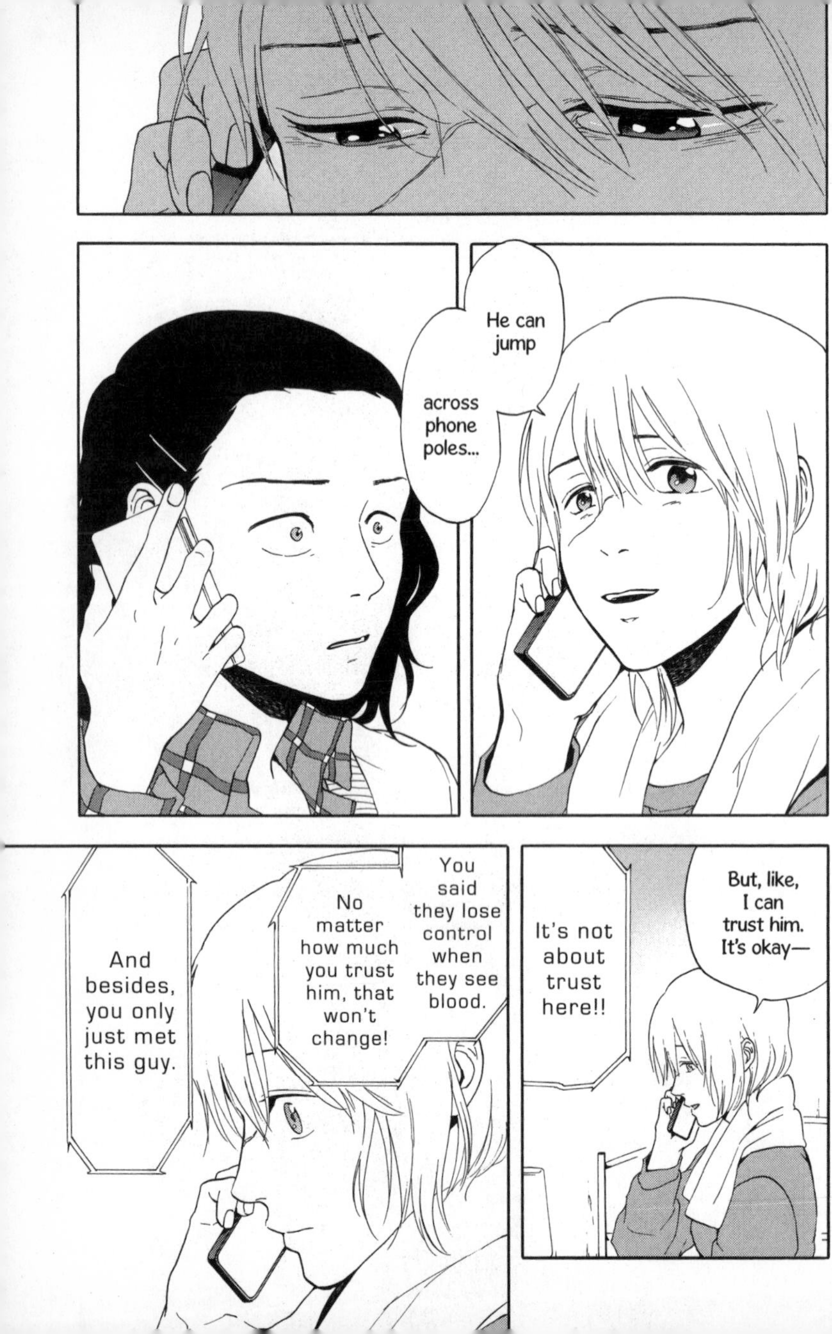
He can jump
across phone poles...
But, like, I can trust him. It's okay—
It's not about trust here!!
You said they lose control when they see blood.
No matter how much you trust him, that won't change!
And besides, you only just met this guy.

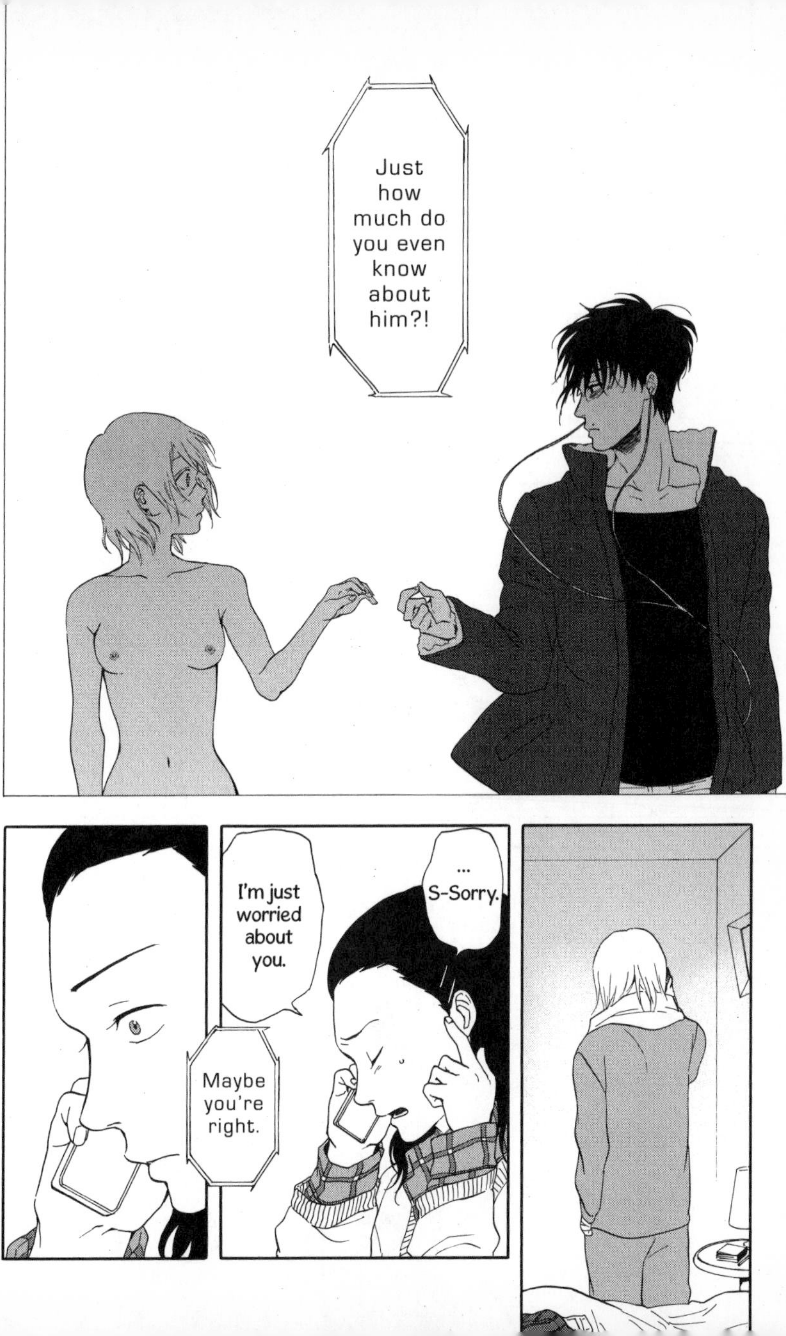
Just how much do you even know about him?!
... S-Sorry.
I'm just worried about you.
Maybe you're right.

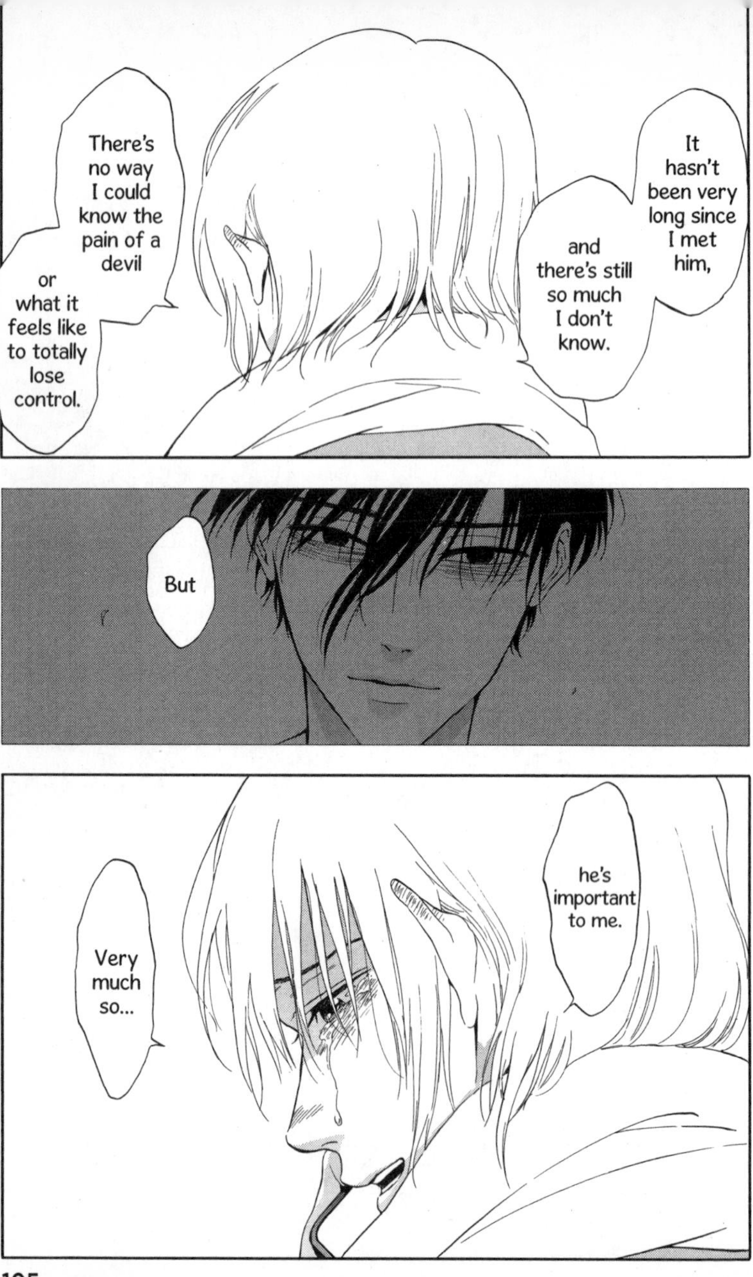
It hasn't been very long since I met him,
and there's still so much I don't know.
There's no way I could know the pain of a devil
or what it feels like to totally lose control.
But
he's important to me.
Very much so...

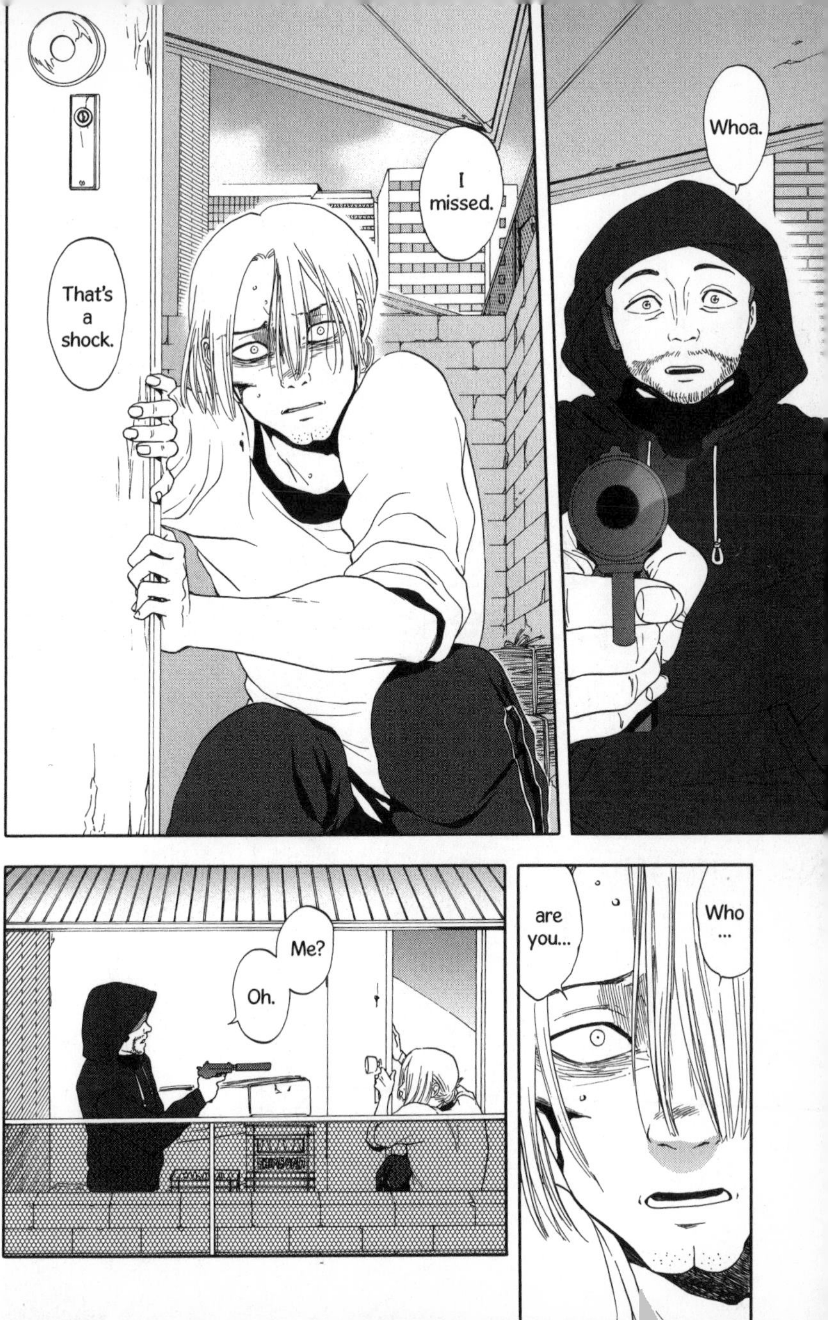
Whoa.
I missed.
That's a shock.
Who...
are you...
Me?
Oh.

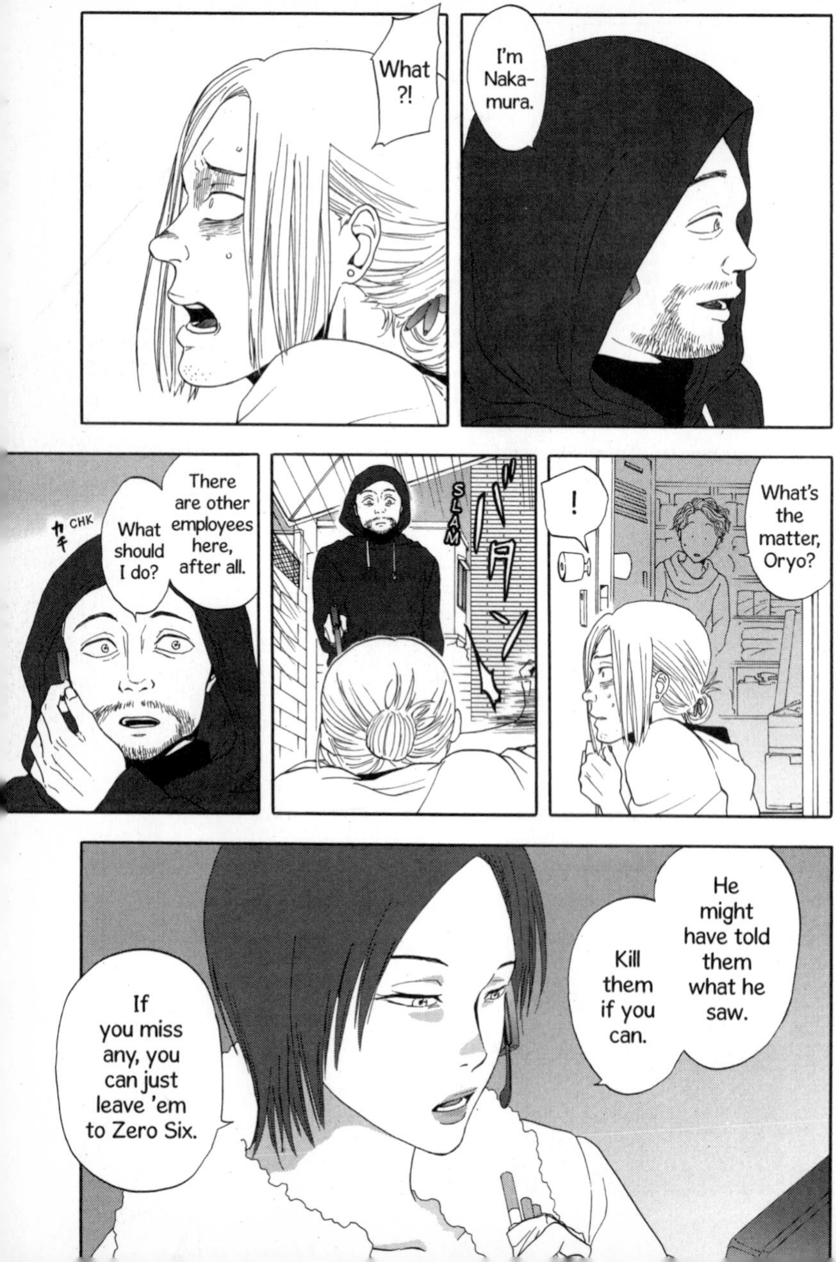
I'm Naka-mura.
What ?!
What's the matter, Oryo?
!
SLAM
There are other employees here, after all.
What should I do?
CHK
He might have told them what he saw.
Kill them if you can.
If you miss any, you can just leave 'em to Zero Six.

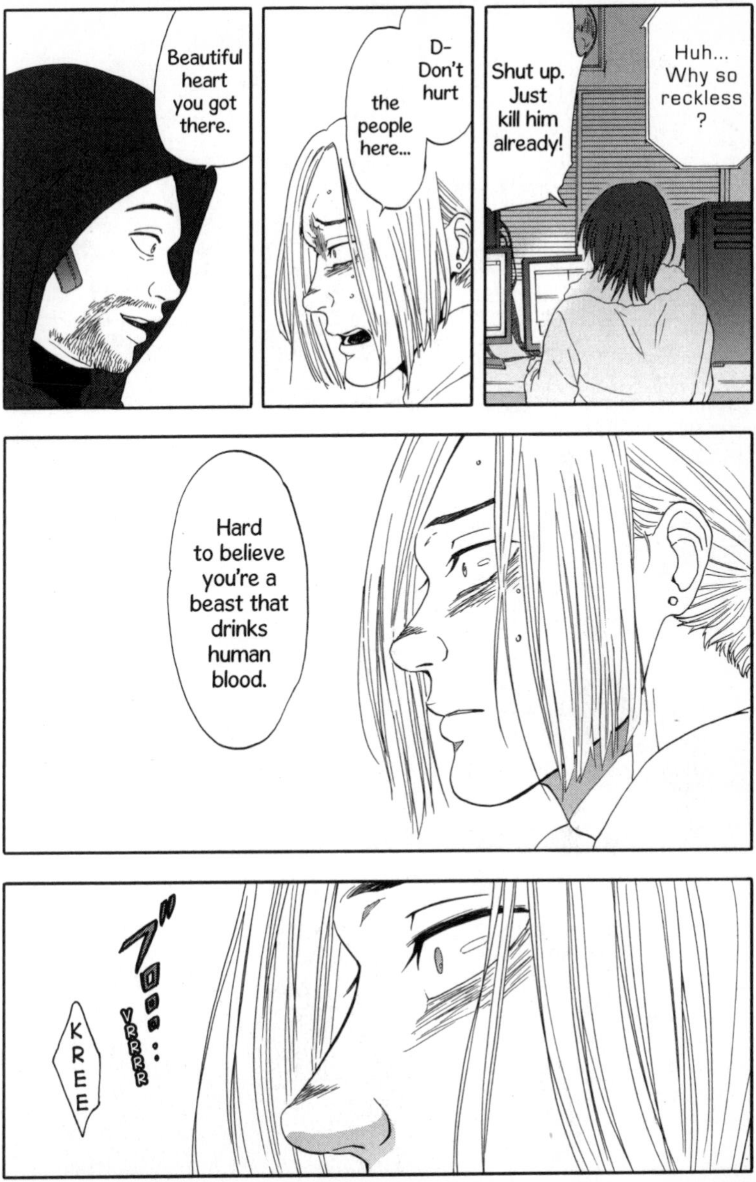
Huh... Why so reckless ?
Shut up. Just kill him already!
D- Don't hurt the people here...
Beautiful heart you got there.
Hard to believe you're a beast that drinks human blood.
ブロロ..
VRRRR
KREE

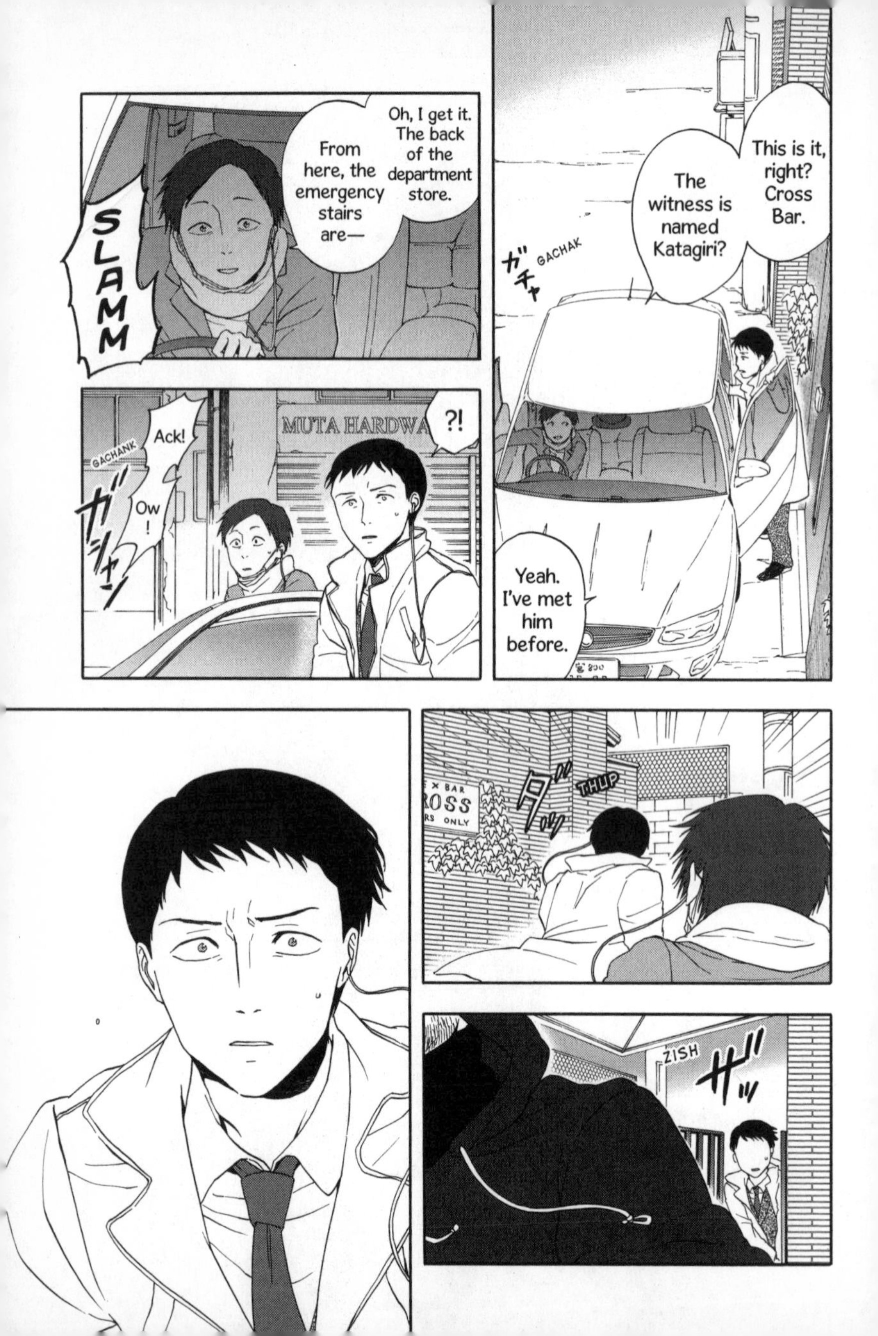
This is it, right? Cross Bar.
The witness is named Katagiri?
ガチャ GACHAK
Yeah. I've met him before.
Oh, I get it. The back of the department store.
From here, the emergency stairs are—
SLAMM
?!
MUTA HARDWA
Ack!
Ow!
ガシャン GACHANK
× BAR
ROSS
RS ONLY
THUP
ZISH

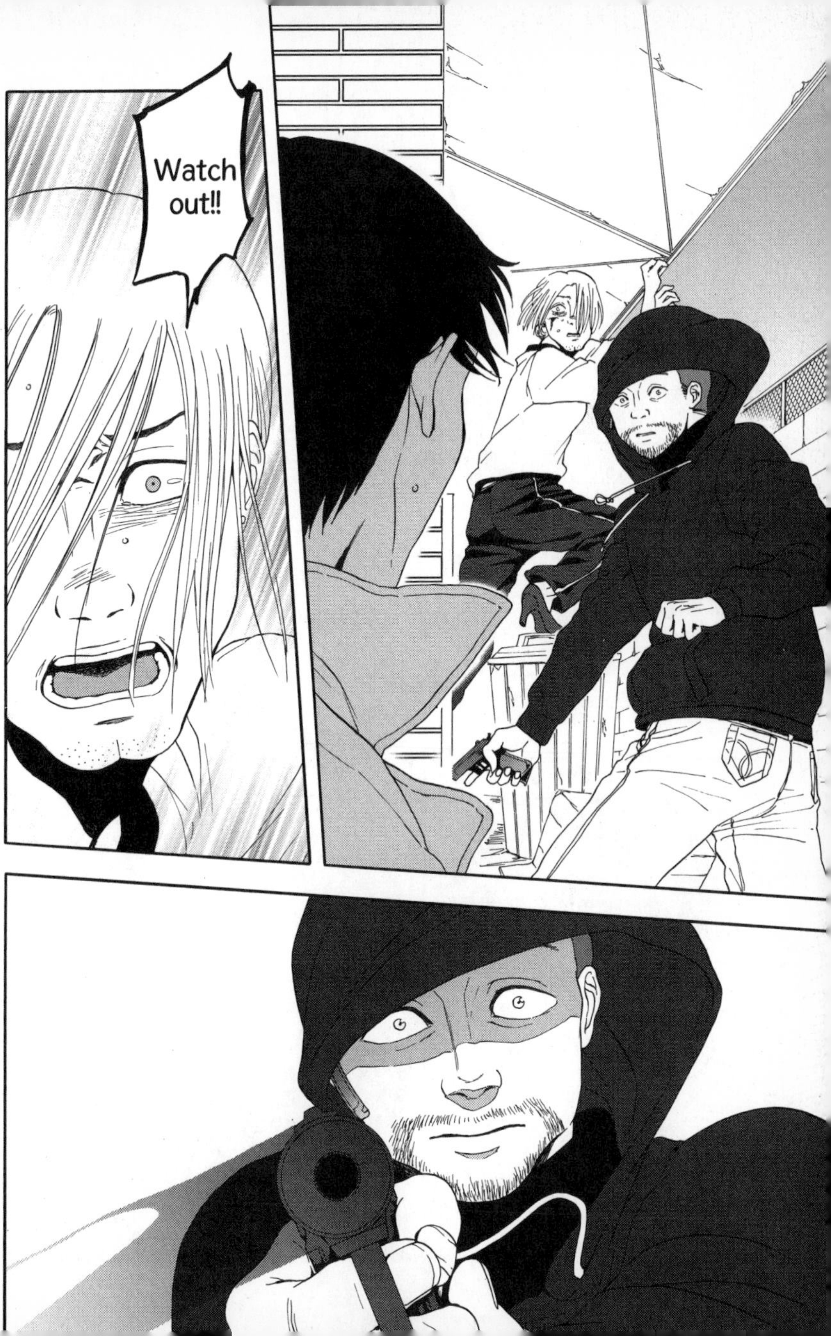
Watch out!!

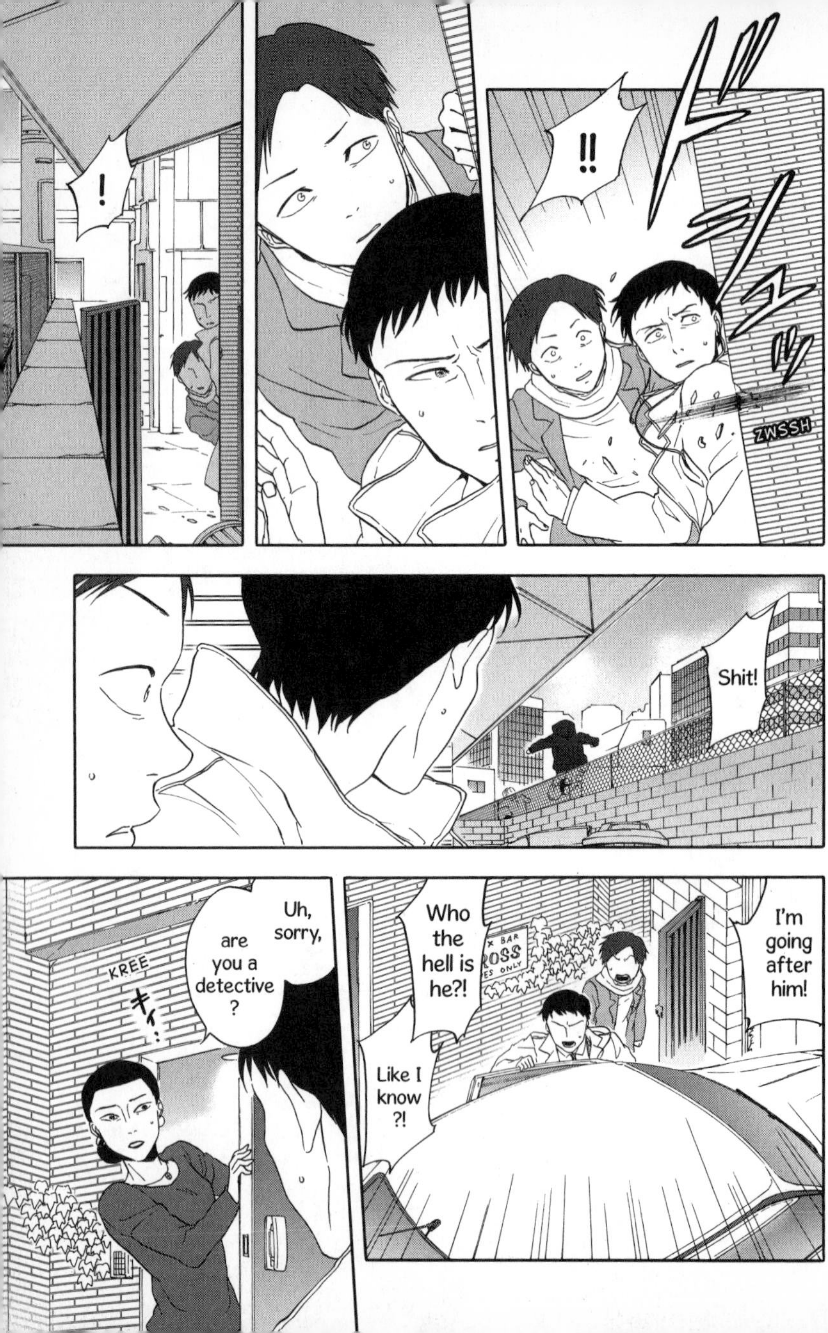
!!
ZWSSH
!
Shit!
I'm going after him!
Who the hell is he?!
Like I know?!
Uh, sorry,
are you a detective?
KREE
キィ…

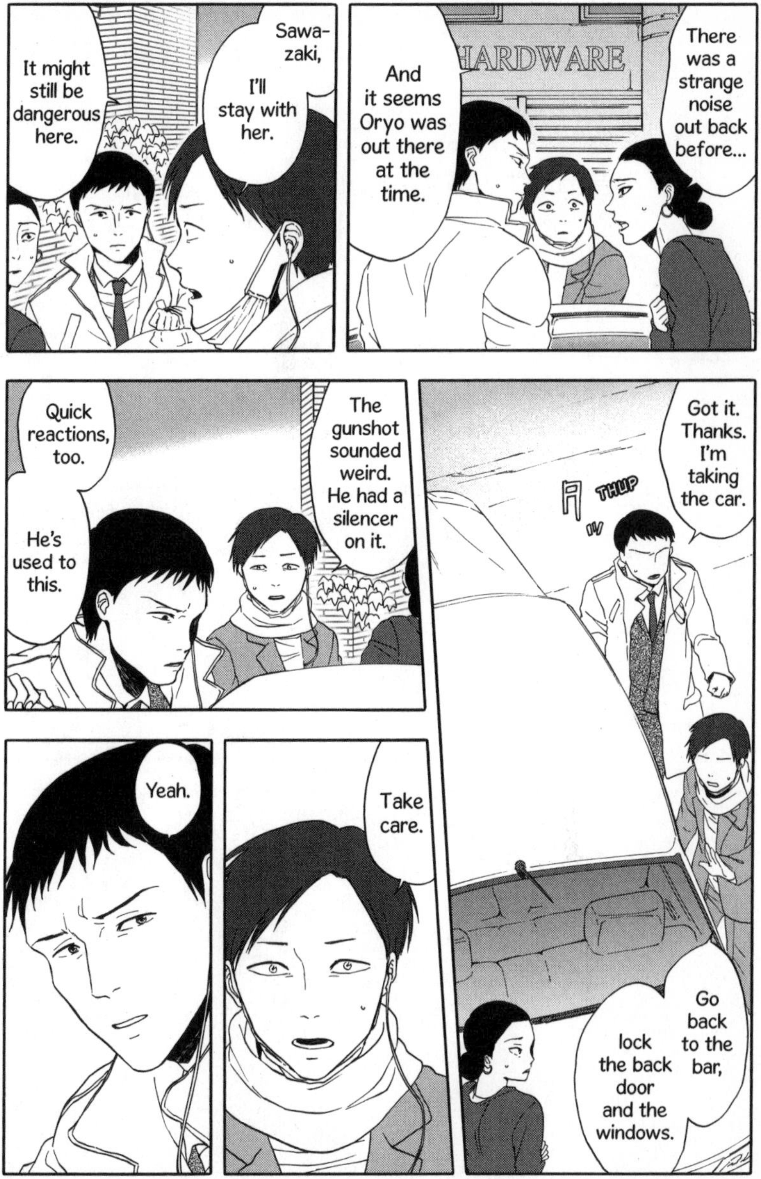
There was a strange noise out back before...
And it seems Oryo was out there at the time.
Sawa-zaki, I'll stay with her.
It might still be dangerous here.
HARDWARE
Got it. Thanks. I'm taking the car.
THUP
Go back to the bar, lock the back door and the windows.
The gunshot sounded weird. He had a silencer on it.
Quick reactions, too.
He's used to this.
Take care.
Yeah.

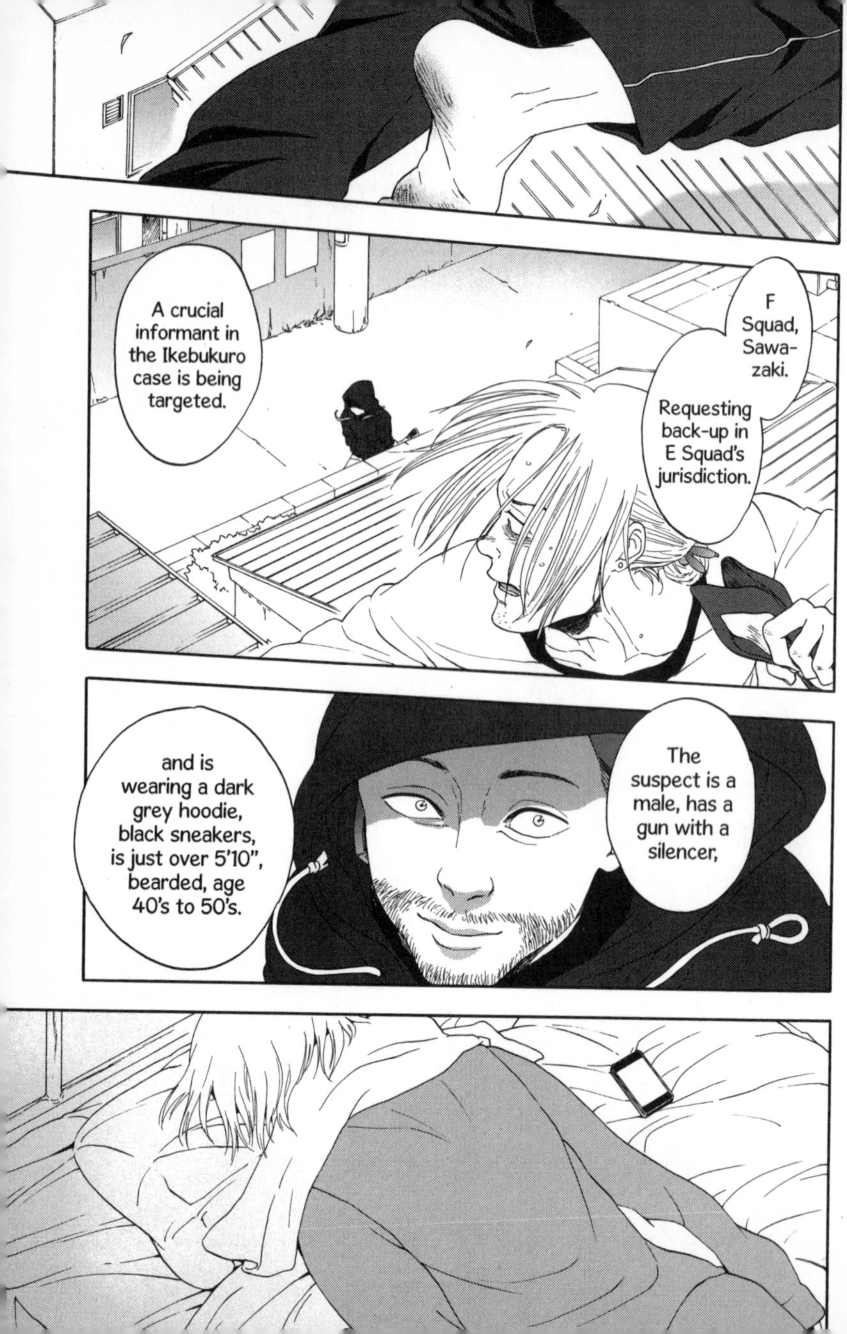
F Squad, Sawazaki.
Requesting back-up in E Squad's jurisdiction.
A crucial informant in the Ikebukuro case is being targeted.
The suspect is a male, has a gun with a silencer,
and is wearing a dark grey hoodie, black sneakers, is just over 5'10", bearded, age 40's to 50's.

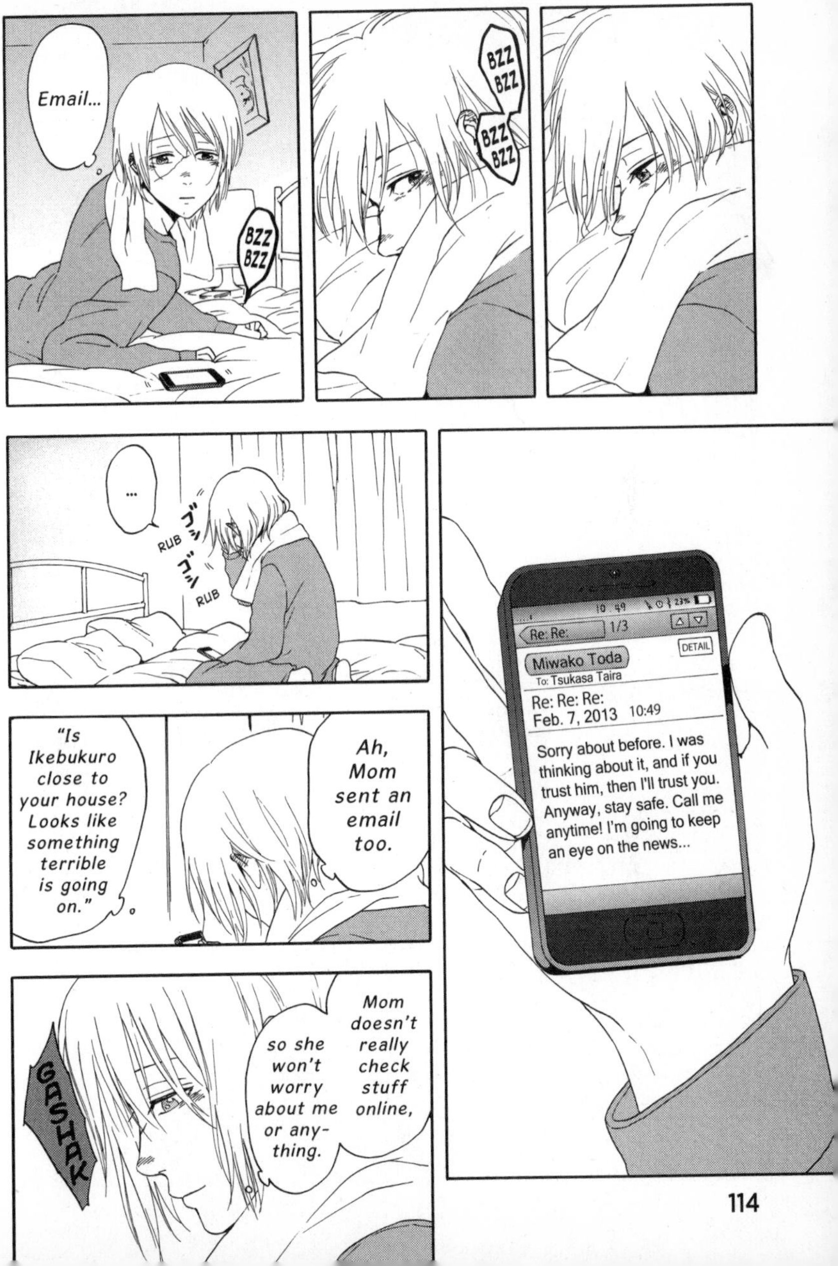
BZZ BZZ
BZZ BZZ
Email...
BZZ BZZ
10:49
23%
Re: Re:
1/3
DETAIL
Miwako Toda
To: Tsukasa Taira
Re: Re: Re:
Feb. 7, 2013 10:49
Sorry about before. I was thinking about it, and if you trust him, then I'll trust you. Anyway, stay safe. Call me anytime! I'm going to keep an eye on the news...
...
ゴッ RUB
ゴッ RUB
Ah, Mom sent an email too.
"Is Ikebukuro close to your house? Looks like something terrible is going on."
Mom doesn't really check stuff online,
so she won't worry about me or anything.
GASHAK

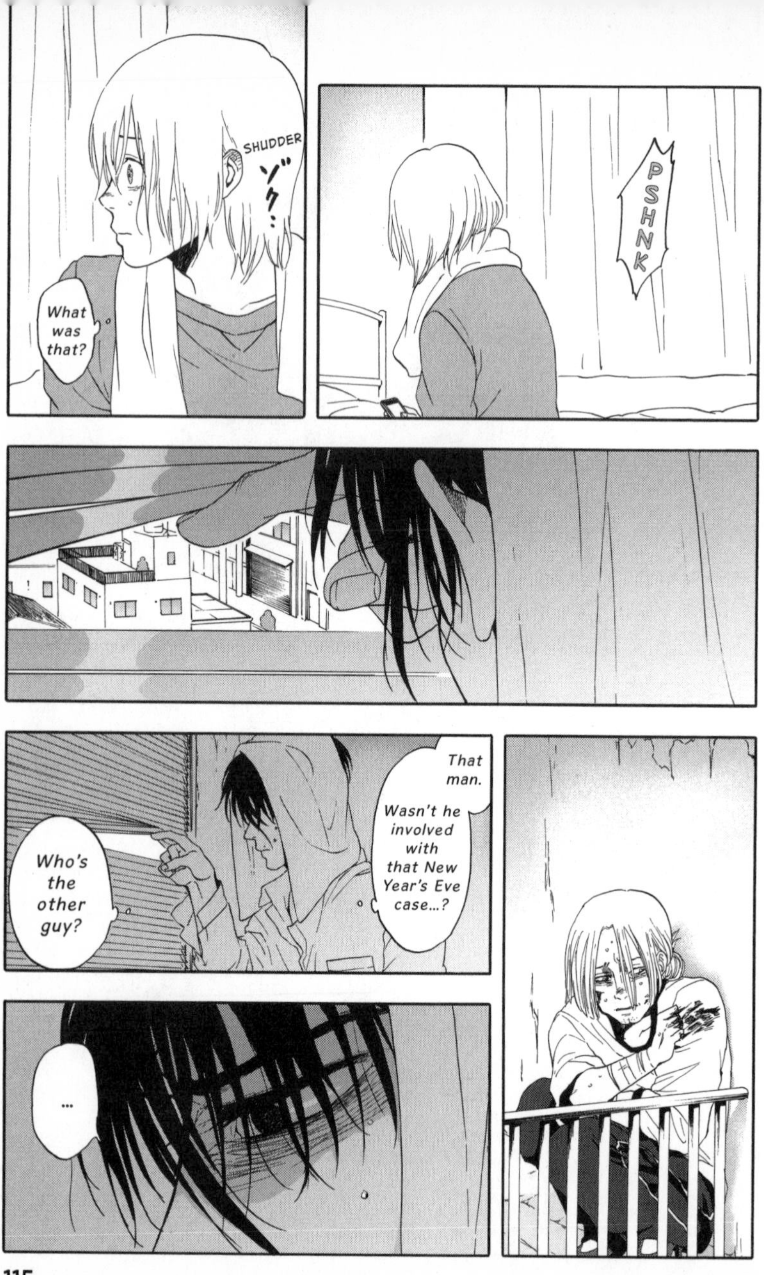
PSHNK
SHUDDER
ゾク…
What was that?
That man.
Wasn't he involved with that New Year's Eve case...?
Who's the other guy?
...

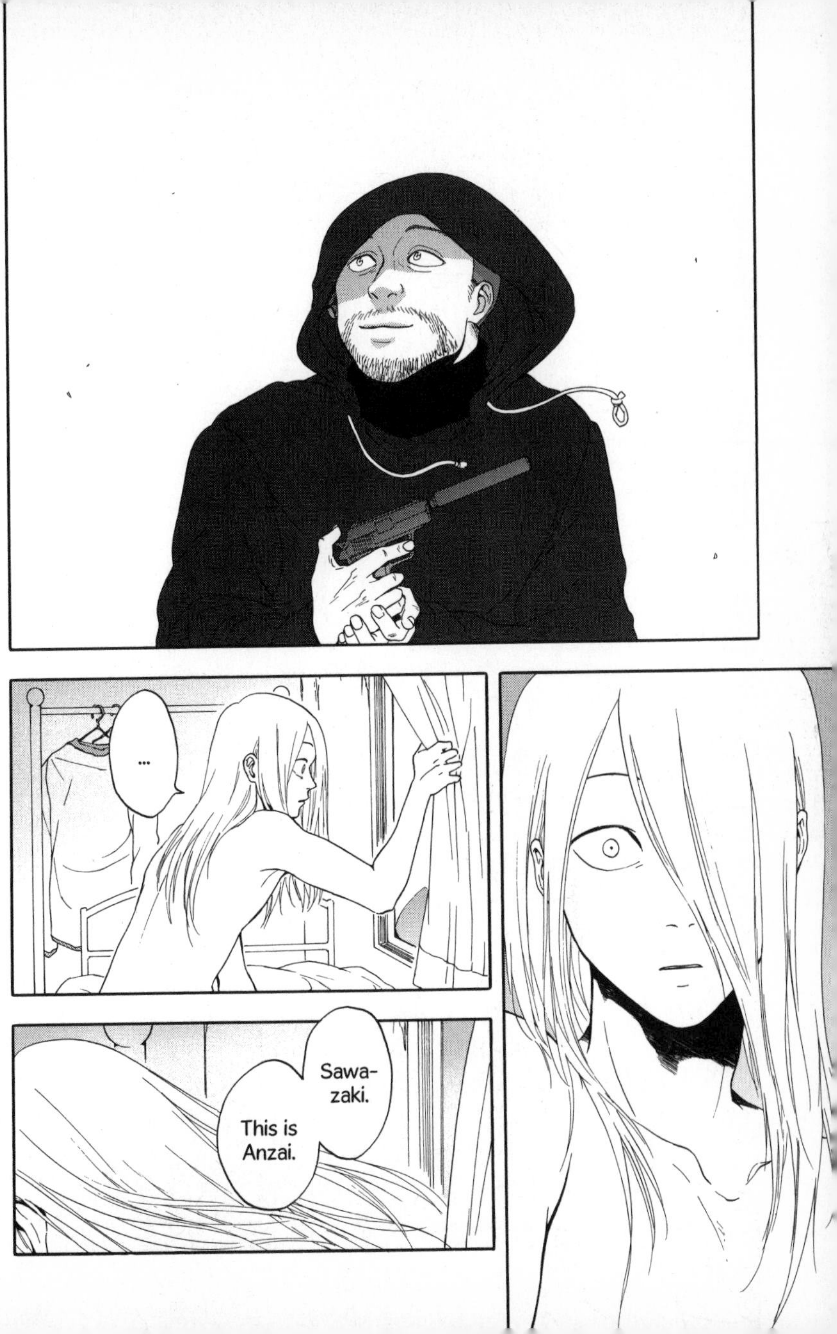
...
Sawa-
zaki.
This is
Anzai.

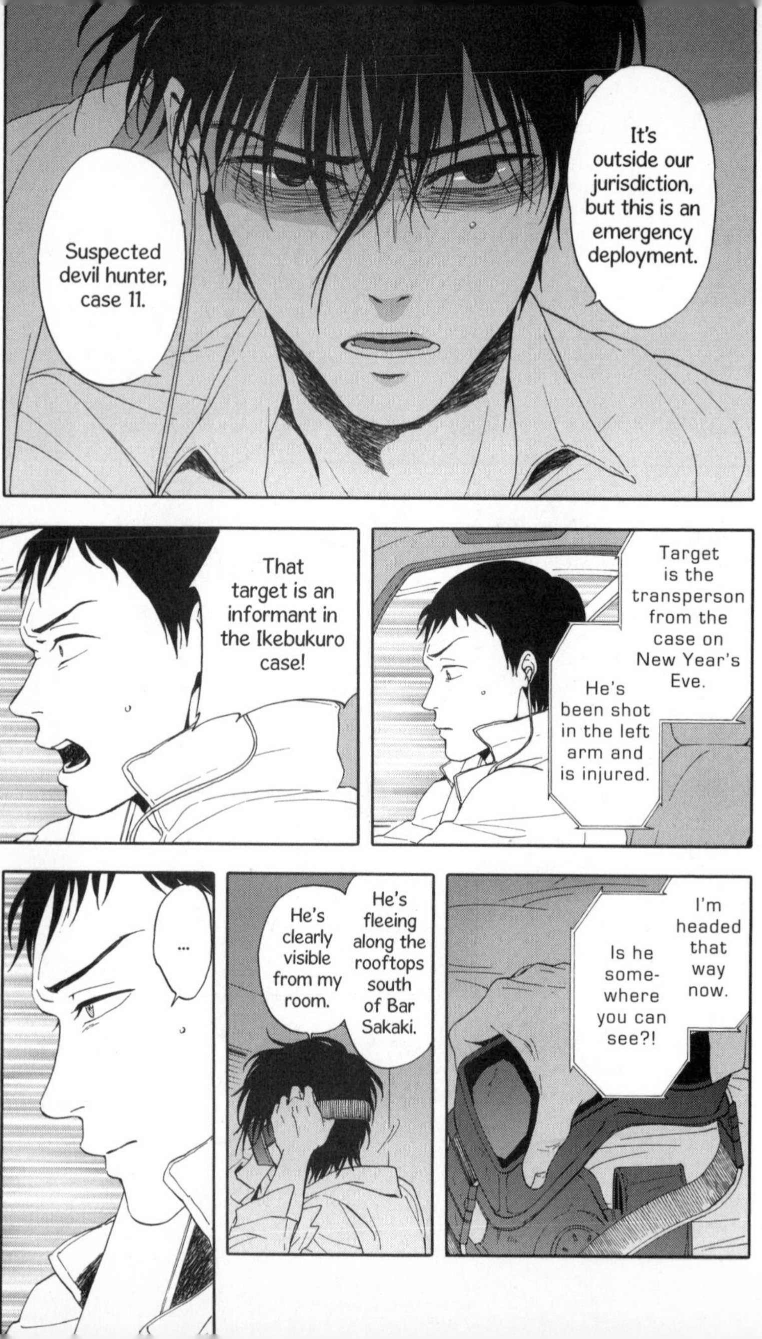
It's outside our jurisdiction, but this is an emergency deployment.
Suspected devil hunter, case 11.
Target is the transperson from the case on New Year's Eve.
He's been shot in the left arm and is injured.
That target is an informant in the Ikebukuro case!
I'm headed that way now.
Is he some-where you can see?!
He's fleeing along the rooftops south of Bar Sakaki.
He's clearly visible from my room.
...

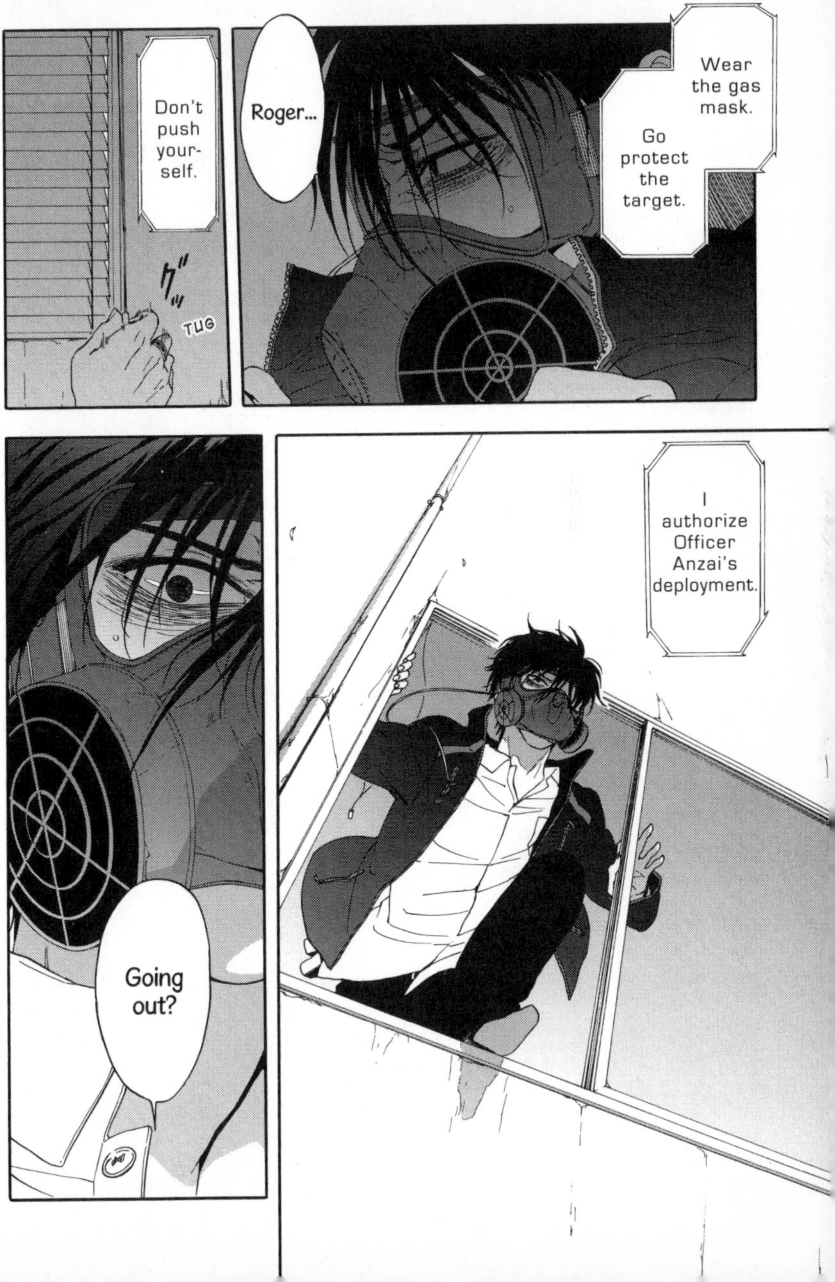

Wear the gas mask.
Go protect the target.
Roger...
Don't push your-self.
TUG
I authorize Officer Anzai's deployment.
Going out?

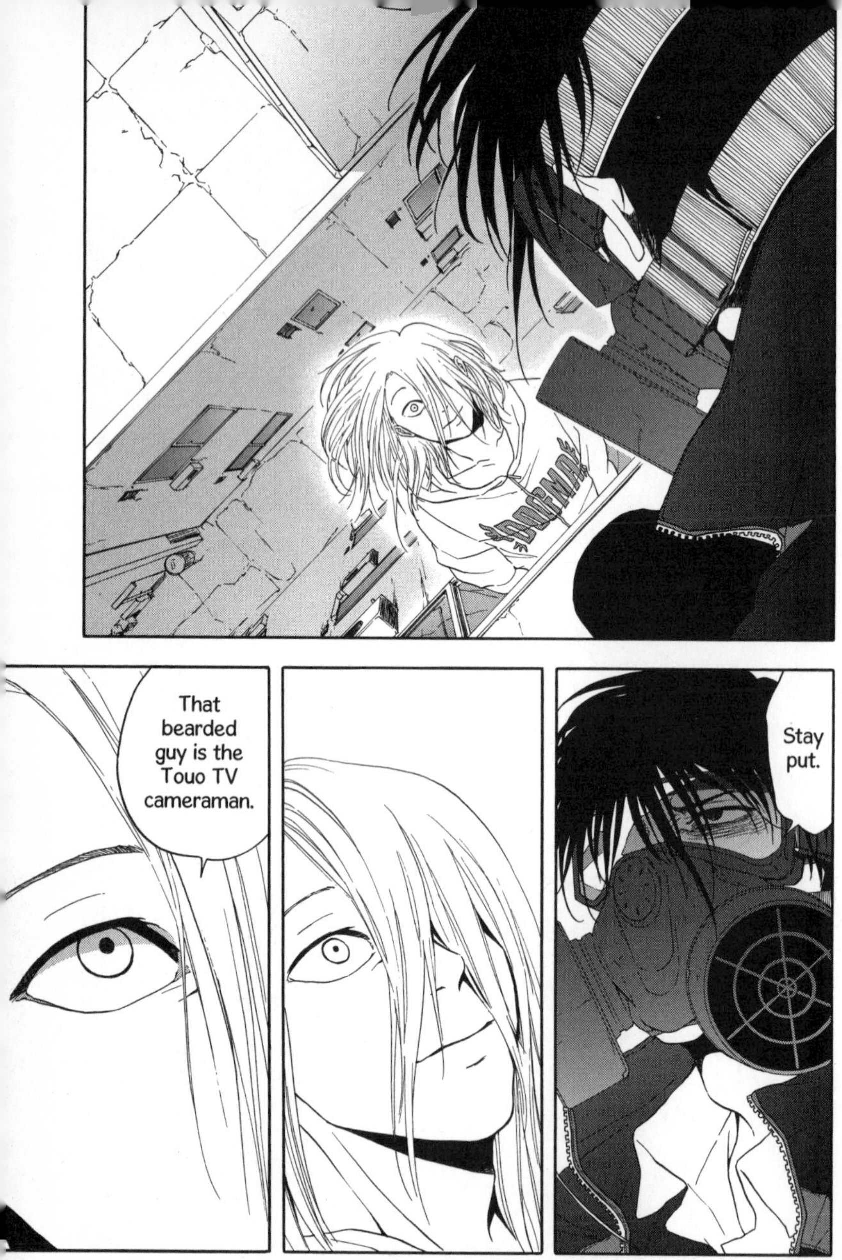
Stay put.
That bearded guy is the Touo TV cameraman.

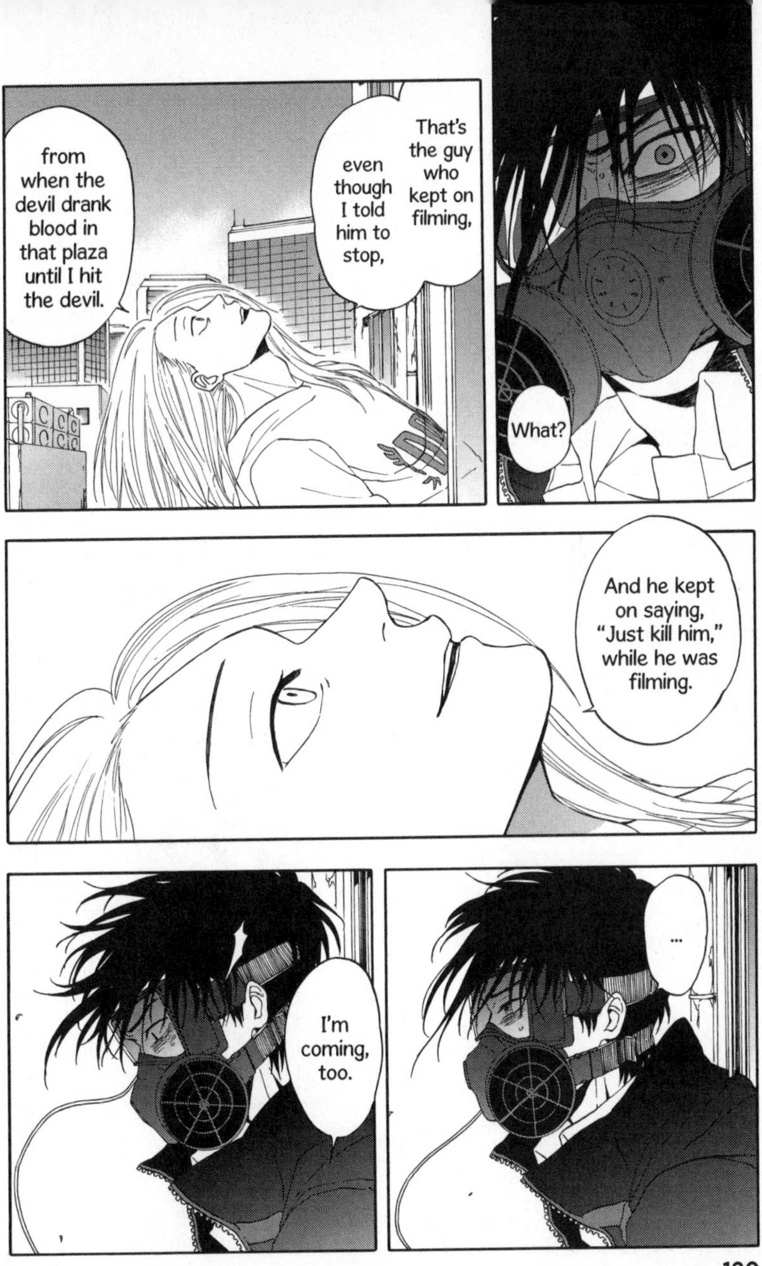
What?
That's the guy who kept on filming,
even though I told him to stop,
from when the devil drank blood in that plaza until I hit the devil.
And he kept on saying, "Just kill him," while he was filming.
...
I'm coming, too.

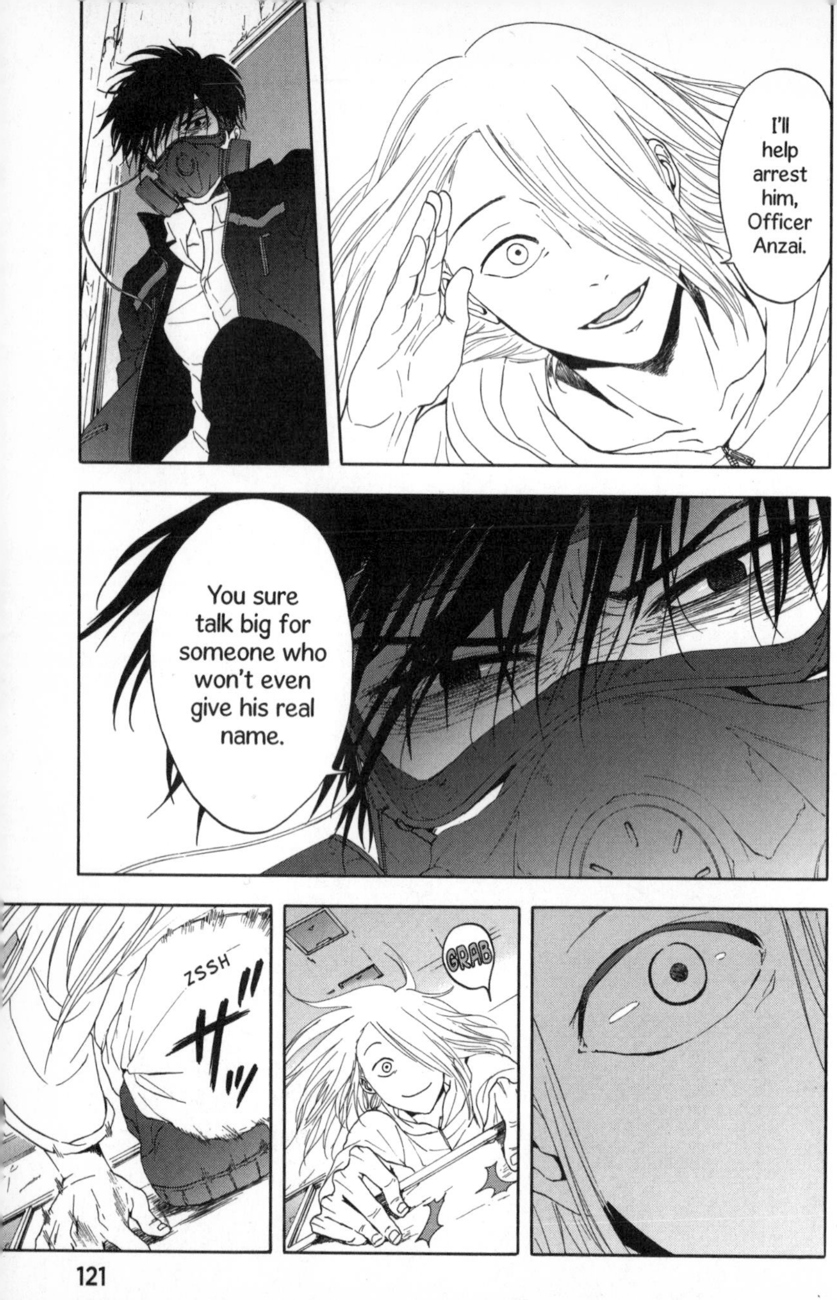
I'll help arrest him, Officer Anzai.
You sure talk big for someone who won't even give his real name.
GRAB
ZSSH

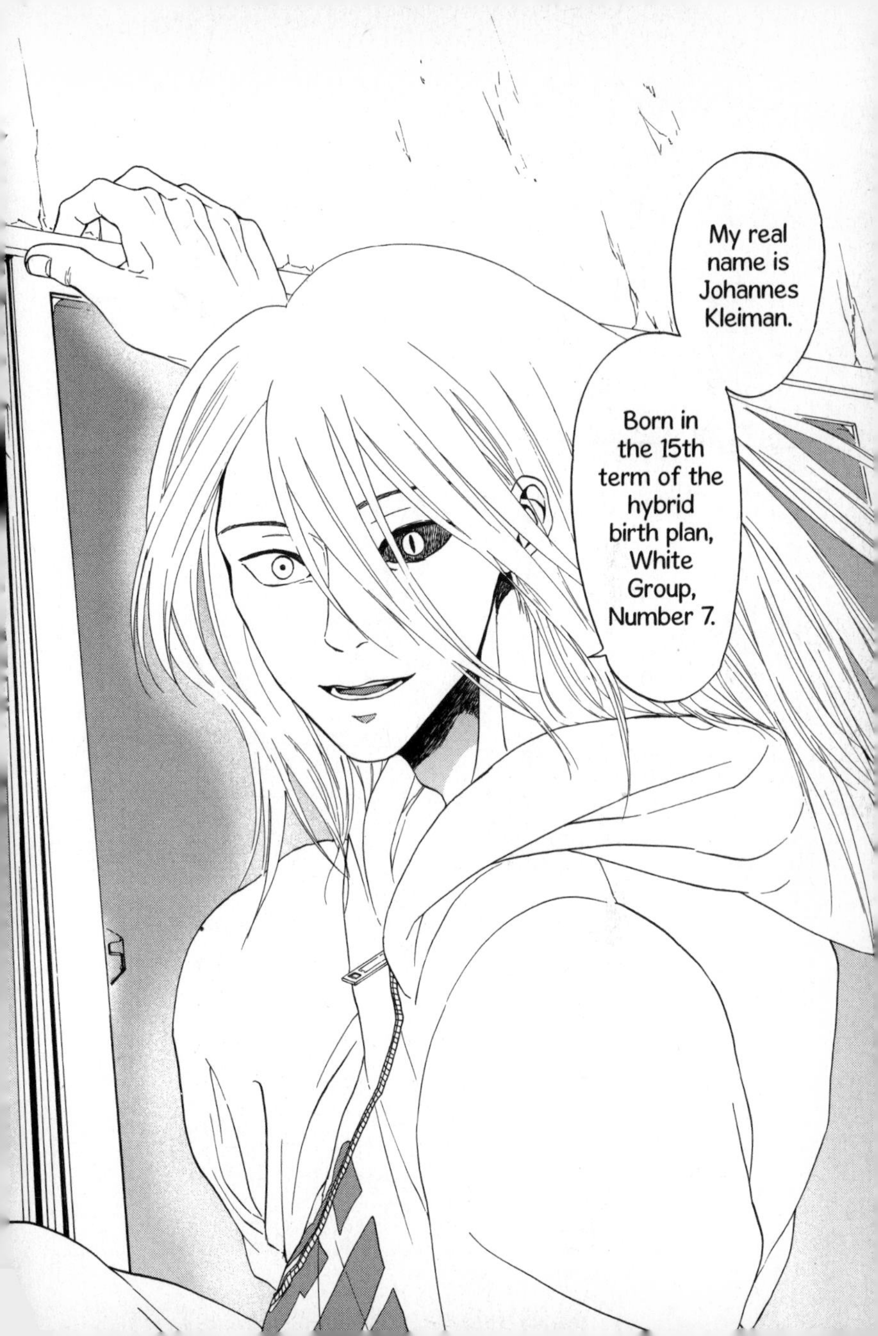
My real name is Johannes Kleiman.
Born in the 15th term of the hybrid birth plan, White Group, Number 7.

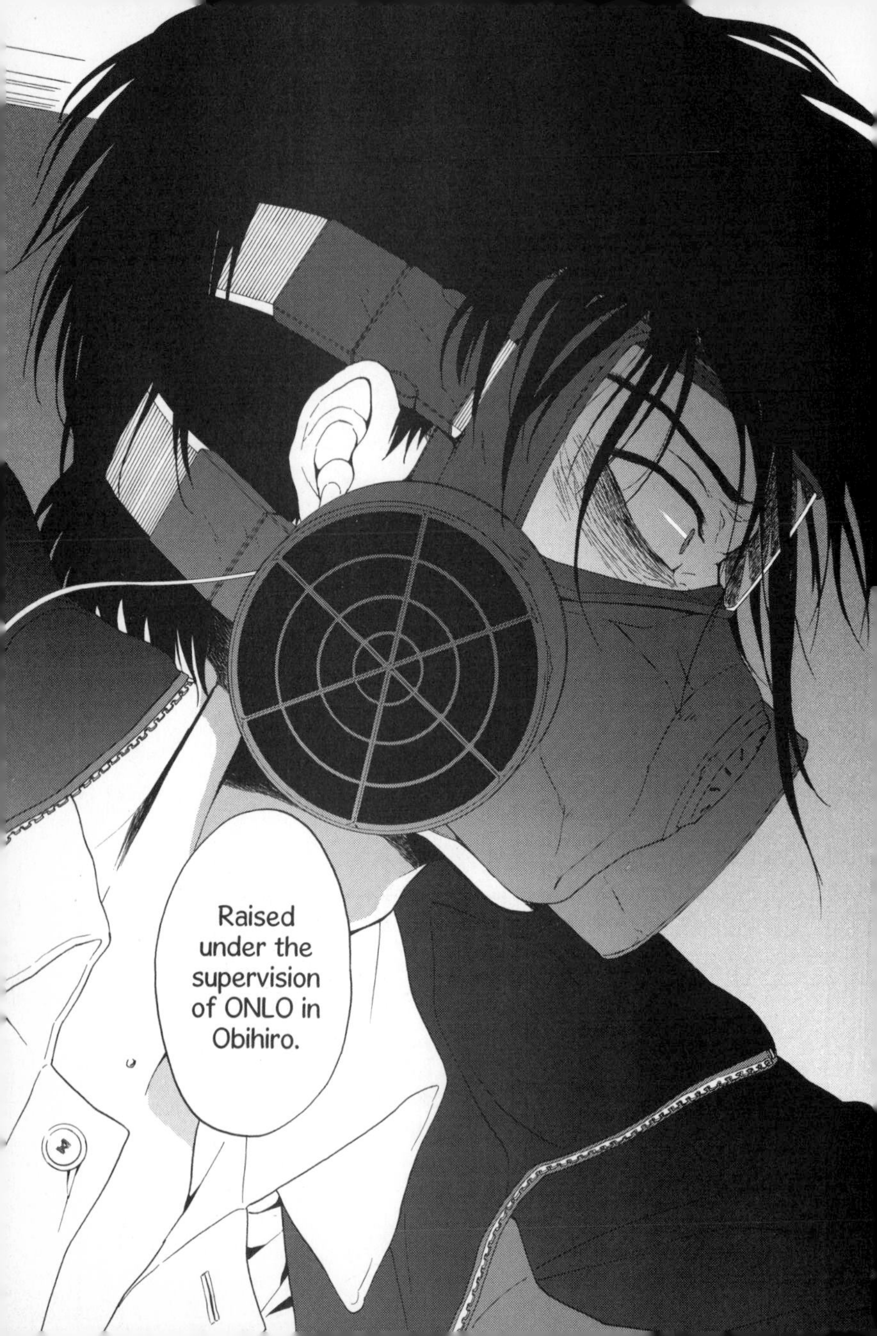
Raised under the supervision of ONLO in Obihiro.

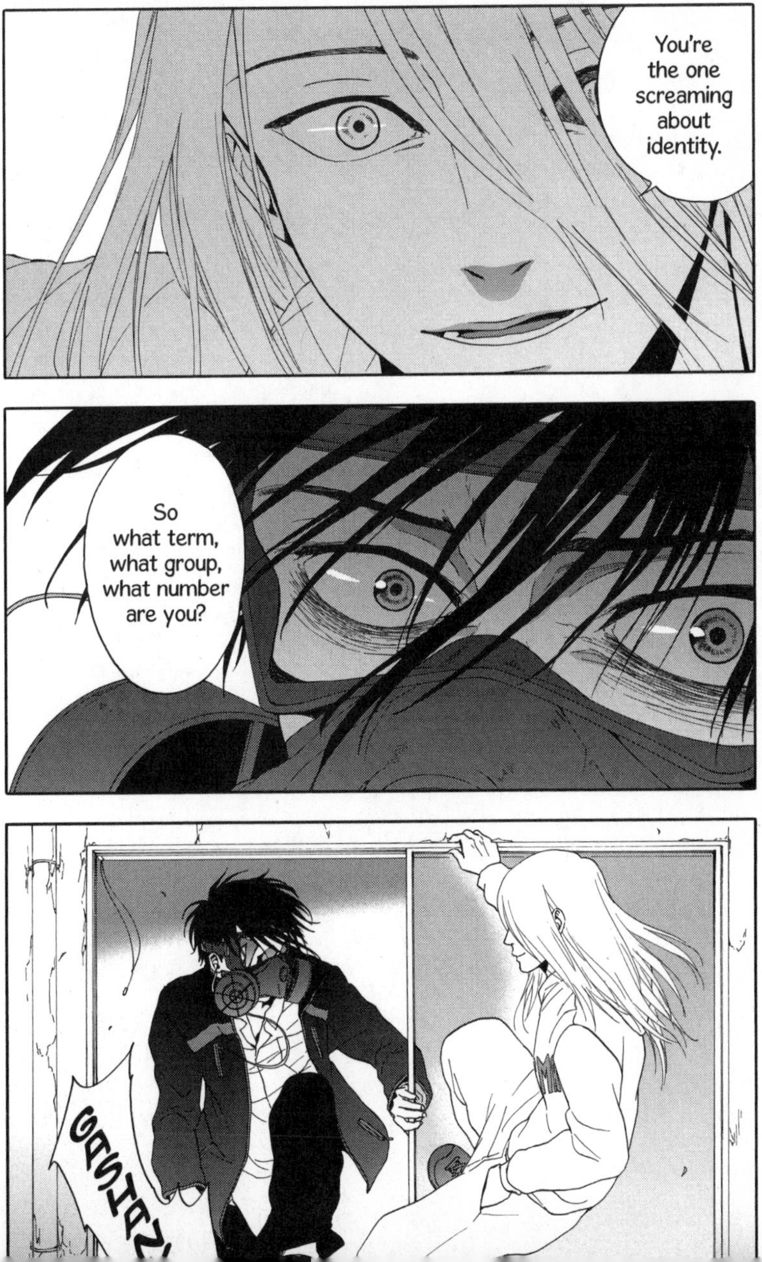
You're the one screaming about identity.
So what term, what group, what number are you?
GASHAN

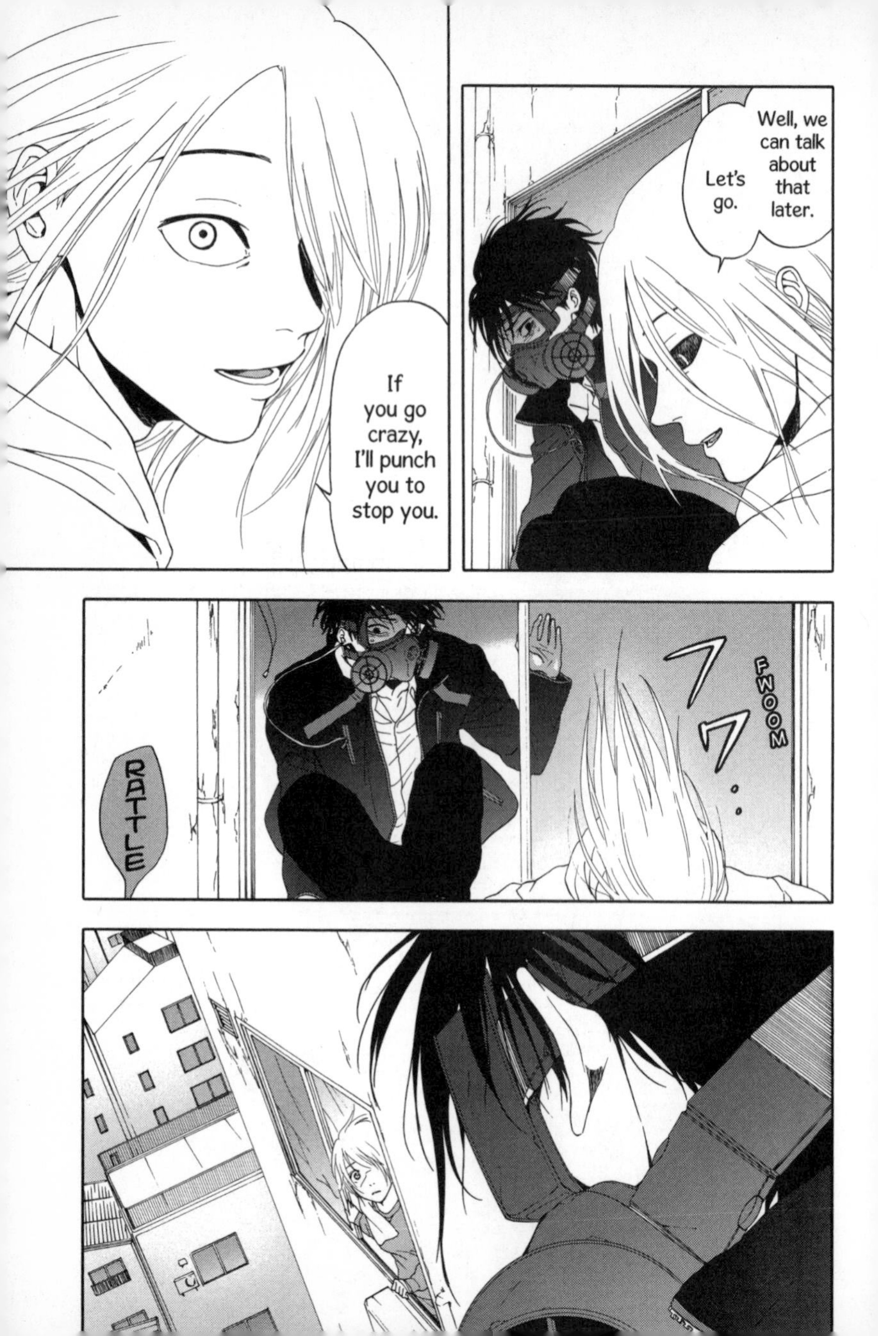
Well, we can talk about that later.
Let's go.
If you go crazy, I'll punch you to stop you.
FWOOM
RATTLE

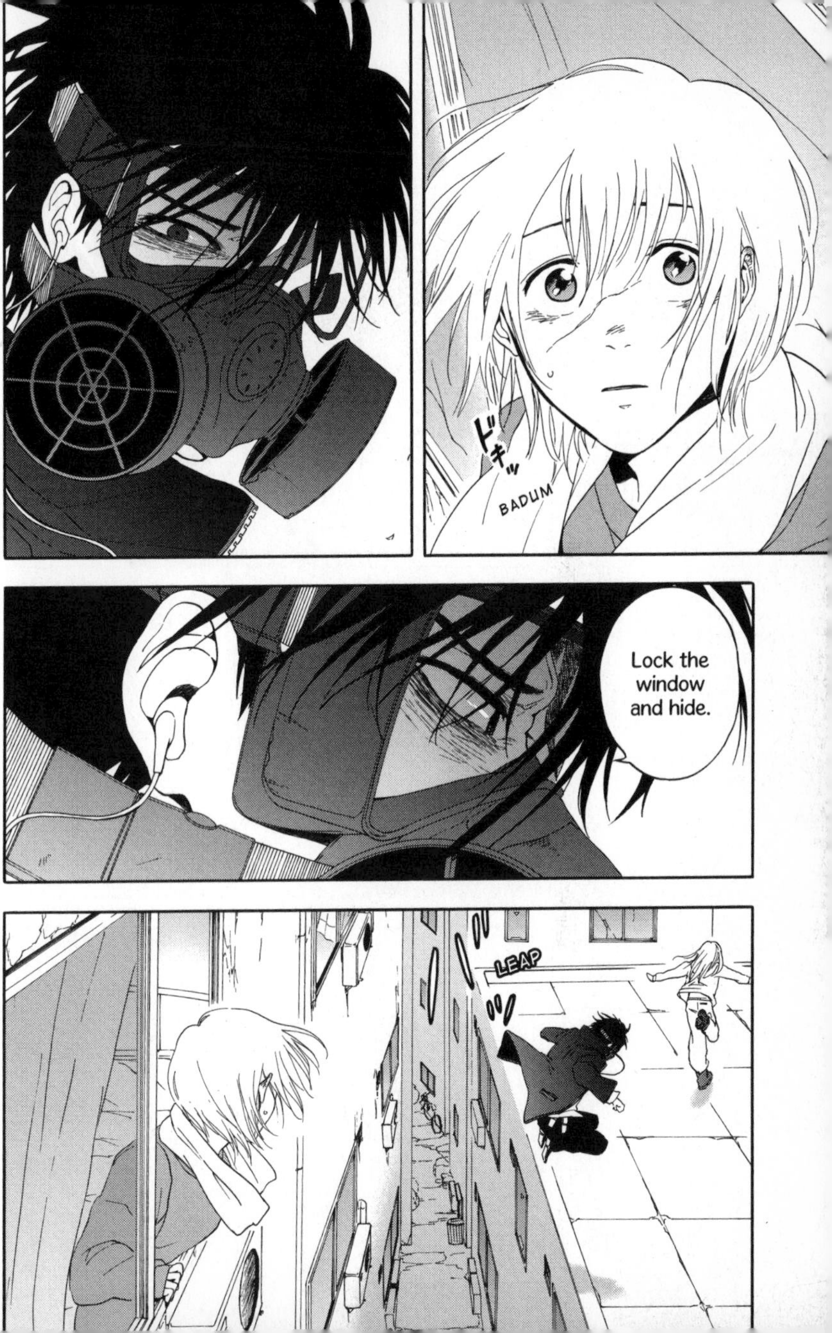
ドキッ
BADUM
Lock the window and hide.
LEAP

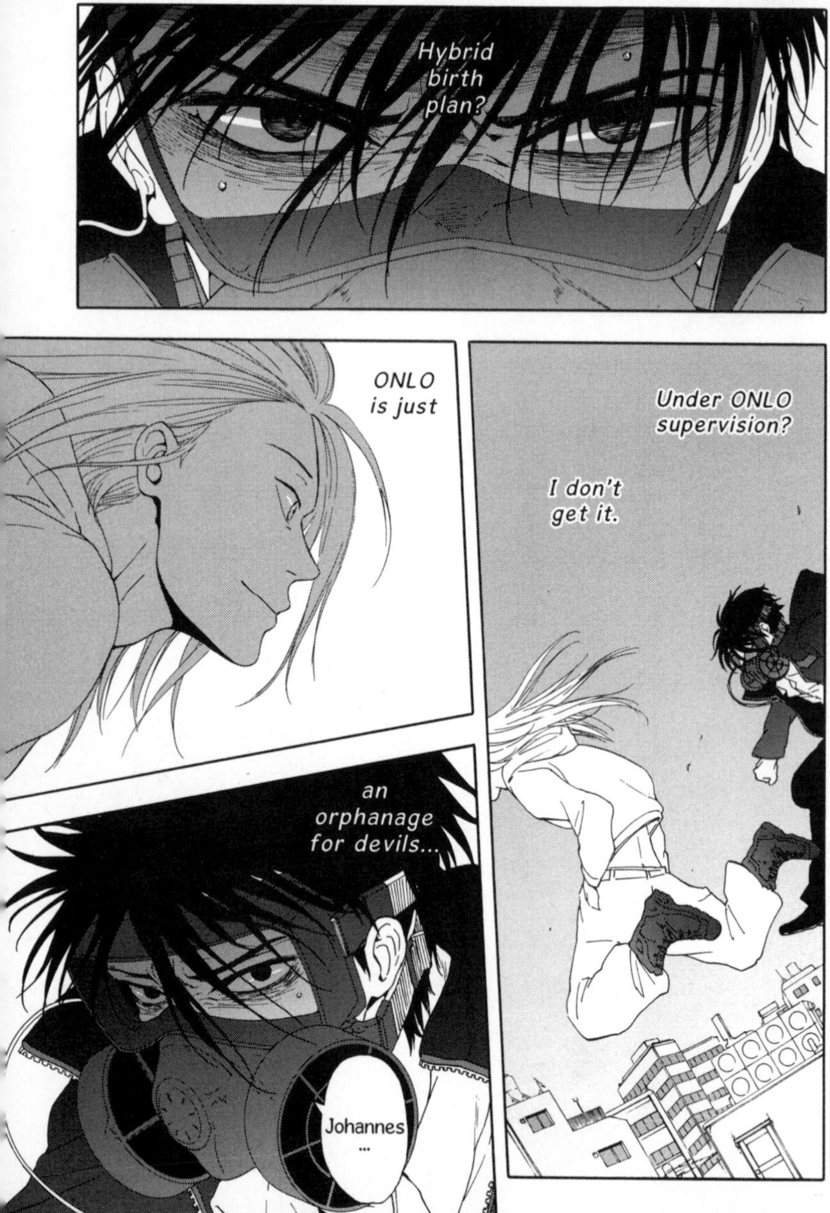
Hybrid birth plan?
Under ONLO supervision?
I don't get it.
ONLO is just
an orphanage for devils...
Johannes...

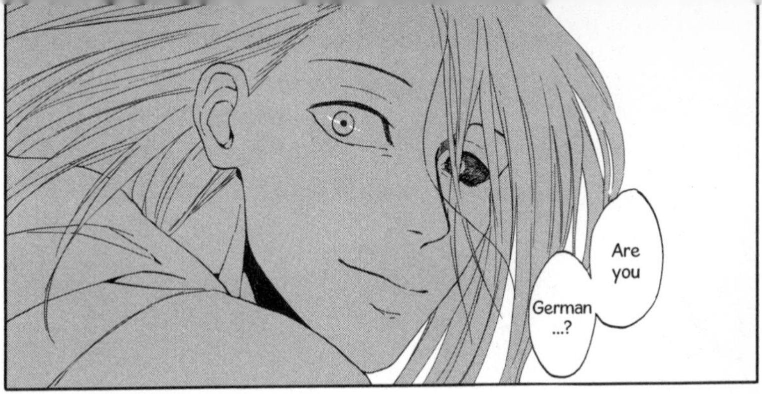

Are you
German ...?

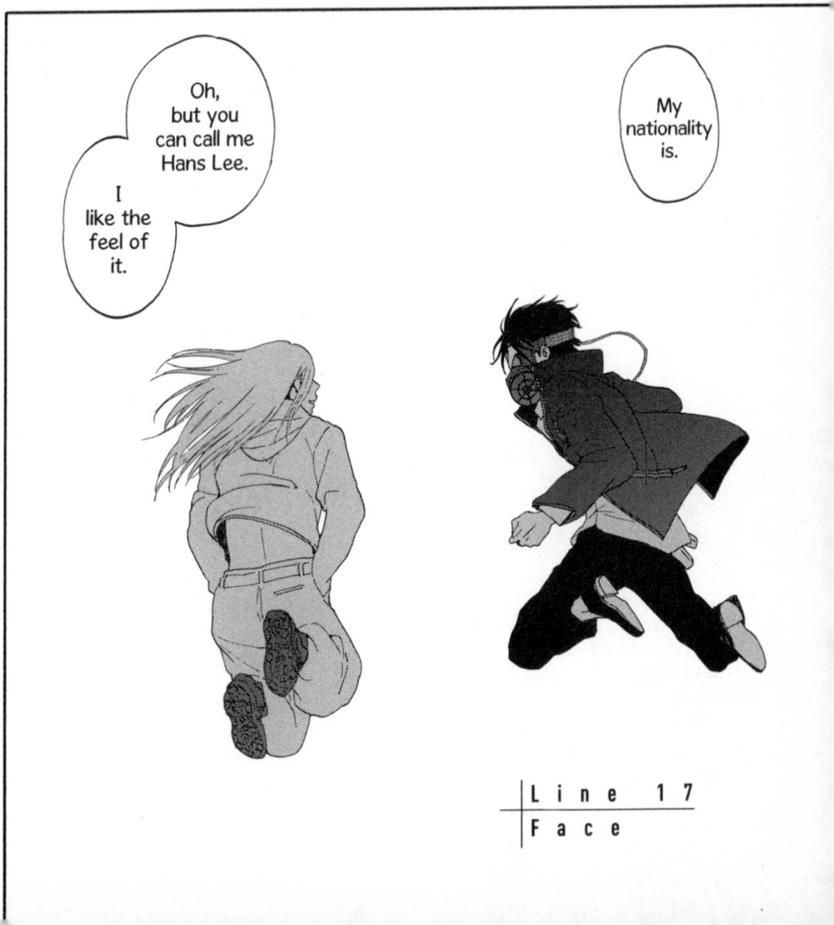

My nationality is.
Oh, but you can call me Hans Lee.
I like the feel of it.
Line 17
Face

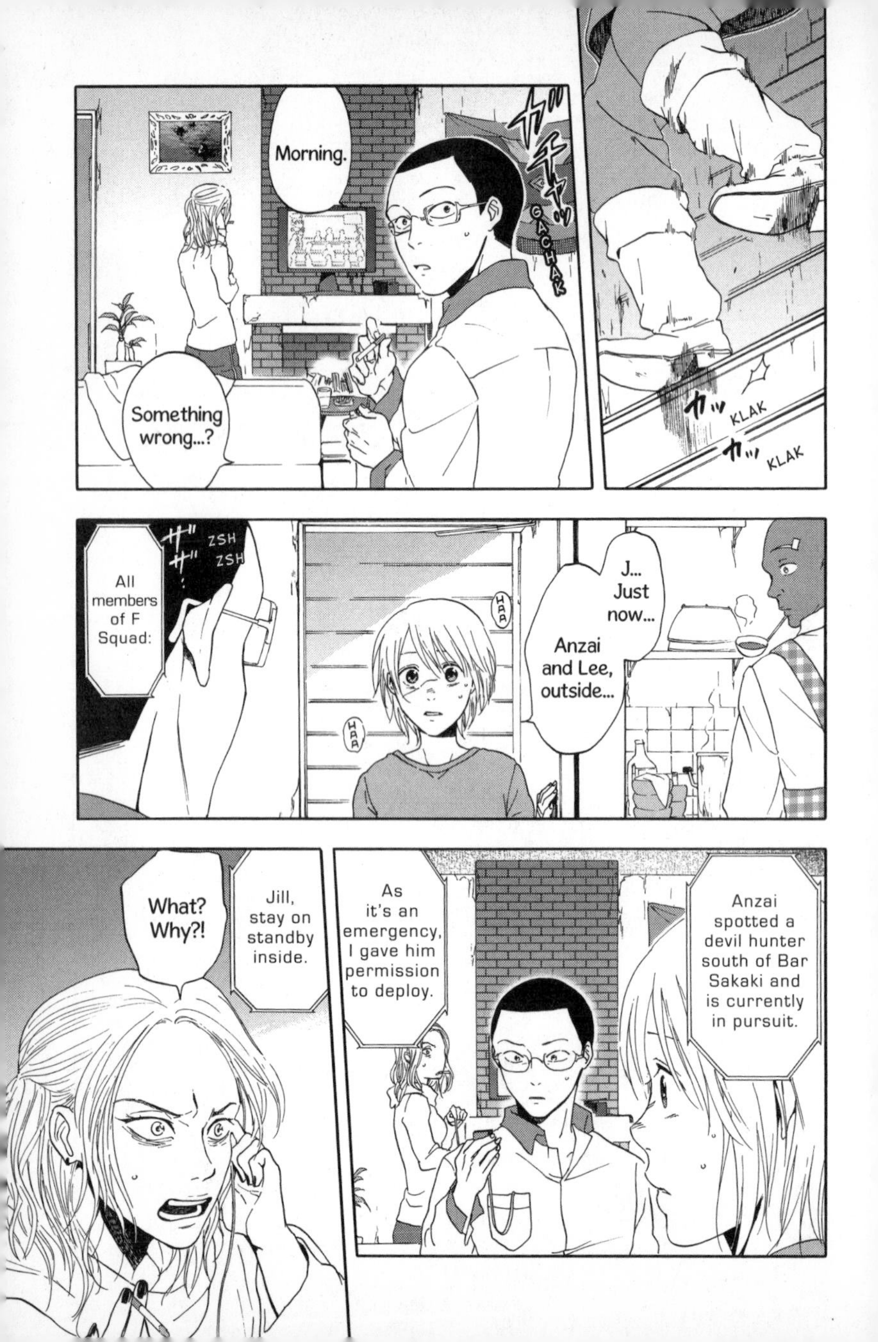
KLAK
KLAK
GACHAK
Morning.
Something wrong...?
J... Just now...
Anzai and Lee, outside...
HAA
HAA
ZSH
ZSH
All members of F Squad:
Anzai spotted a devil hunter south of Bar Sakaki and is currently in pursuit.
As it's an emergency, I gave him permission to deploy.
Jill, stay on standby inside.
What? Why?!

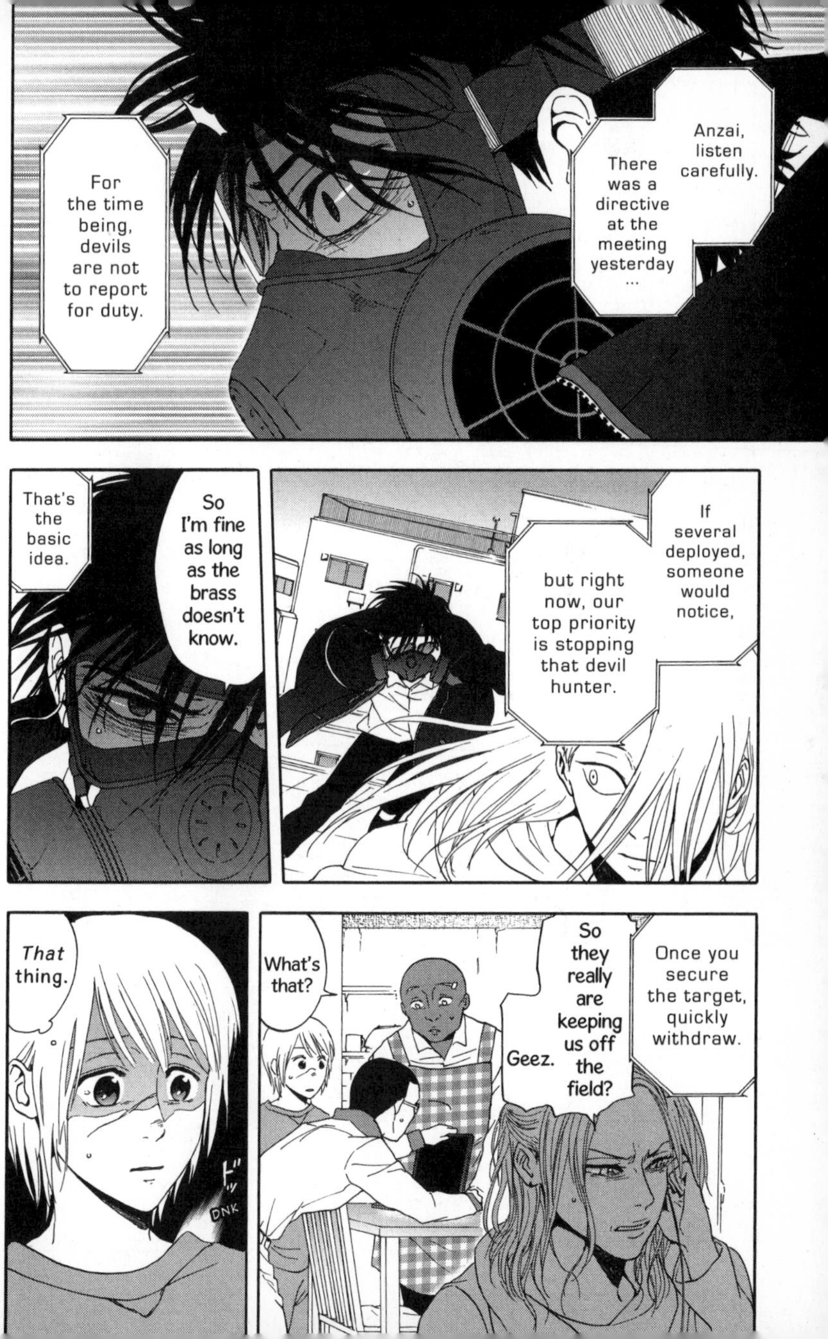
Anzai, listen carefully.
There was a directive at the meeting yesterday ...
For the time being, devils are not to report for duty.
If several deployed, someone would notice,
but right now, our top priority is stopping that devil hunter.
So I'm fine as long as the brass doesn't know.
That's the basic idea.
Once you secure the target, quickly withdraw.
So they really are keeping us off the field?
Geez.
What's that?
That thing.
ドッ
DNK

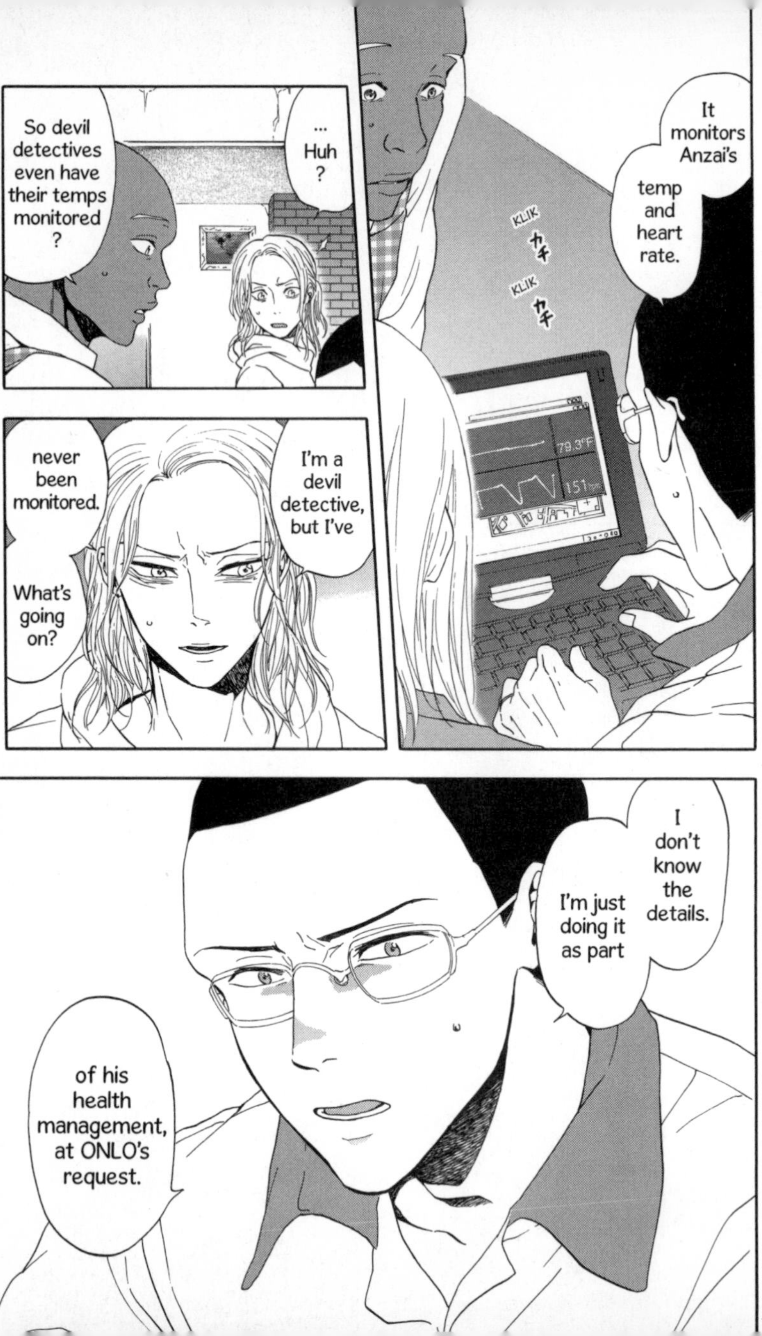
It monitors Anzai's temp and heart rate.
KLIK
カチ
KLIK
カチ
79.3°F
151
... Huh ?
So devil detectives even have their temps monitored ?
I'm a devil detective, but I've
never been monitored.
What's going on?
I don't know the details.
I'm just doing it as part
of his health management, at ONLO's request.

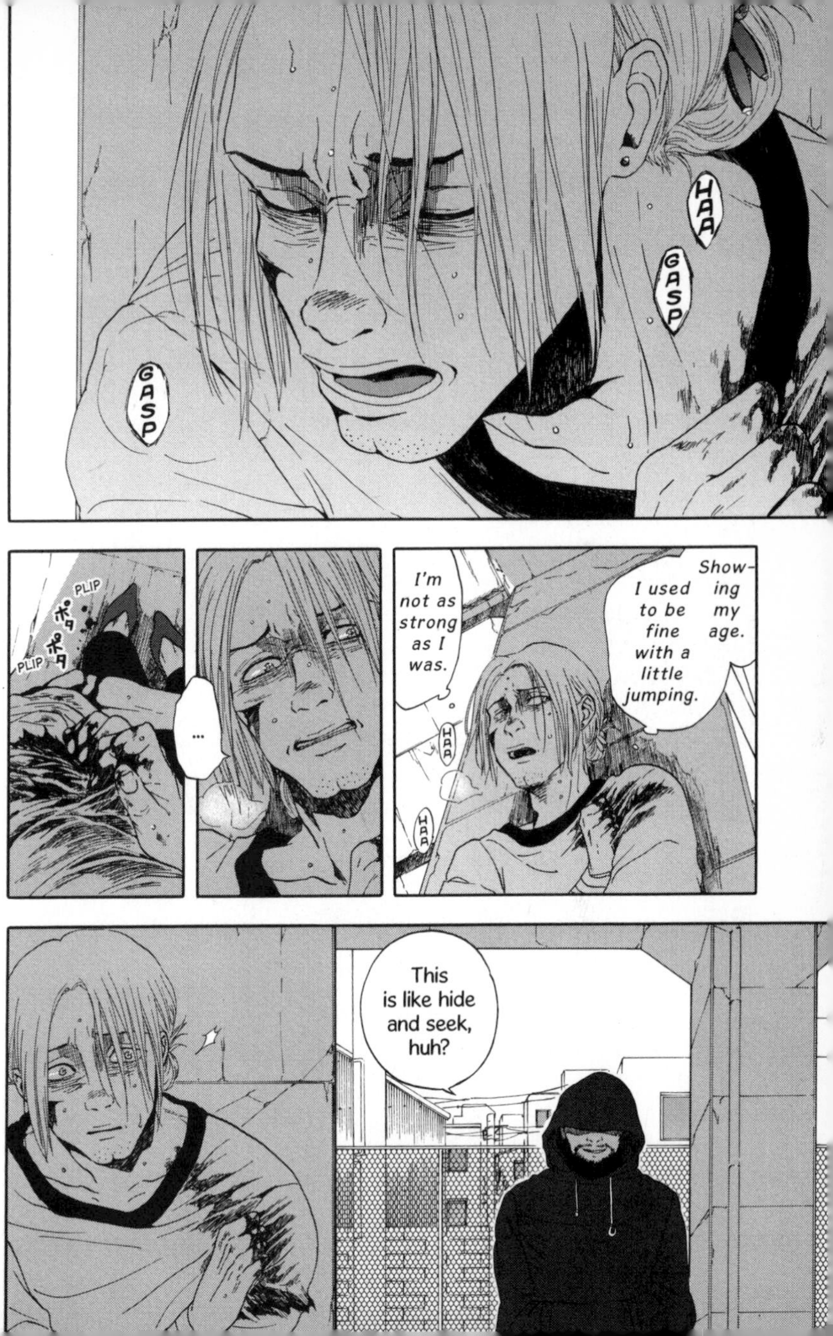
HAA
GASP
GASP
Show-ing my age.
I used to be fine with a little jumping.
I'm not as strong as I was.
HAA
HAA
...
PLIP
ポタ
PLIP
ポタ
This is like hide and seek, huh?

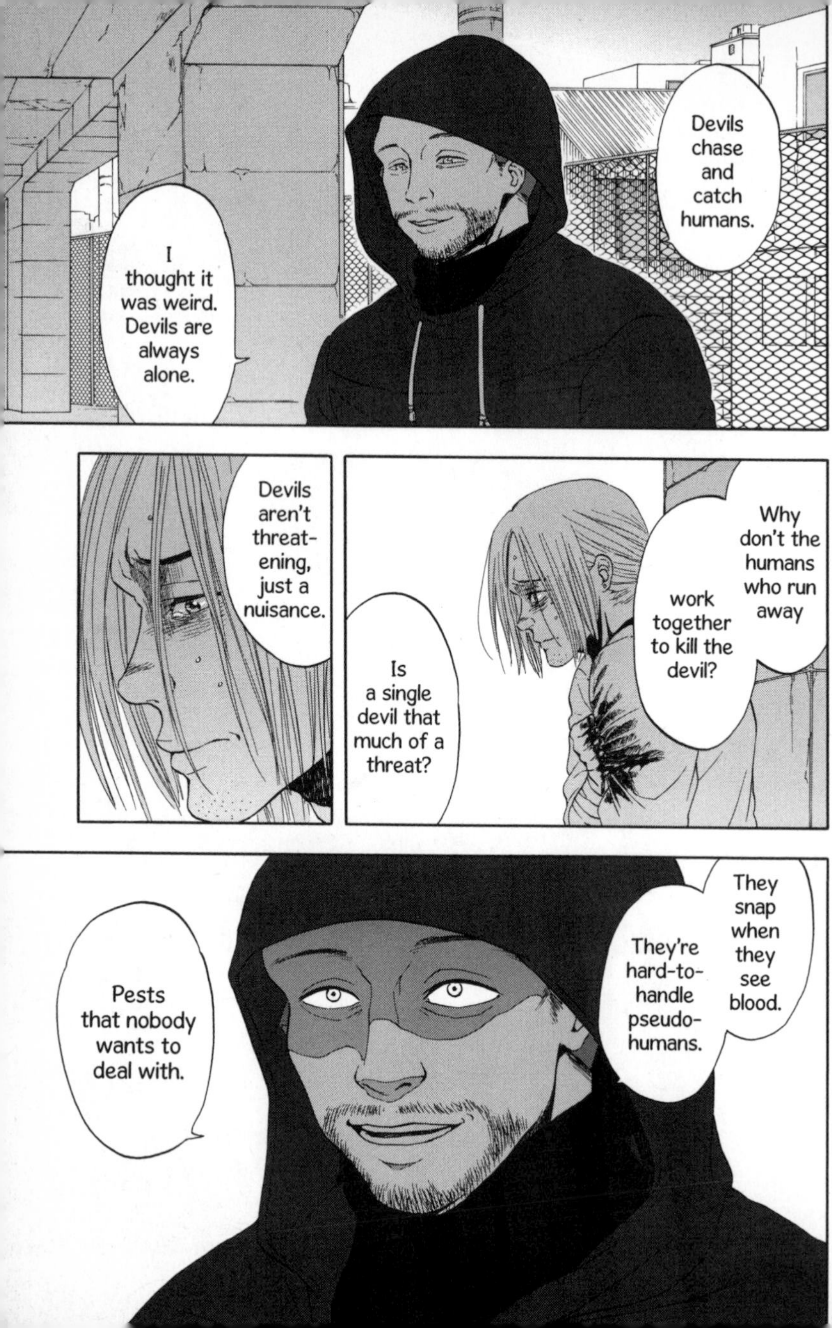
Devils chase and catch humans.
I thought it was weird. Devils are always alone.
Why don't the humans who run away
work together to kill the devil?
Is a single devil that much of a threat?
Devils aren't threat-ening, just a nuisance.
They snap when they see blood.
They're hard-to-handle pseudo-humans.
Pests that nobody wants to deal with.

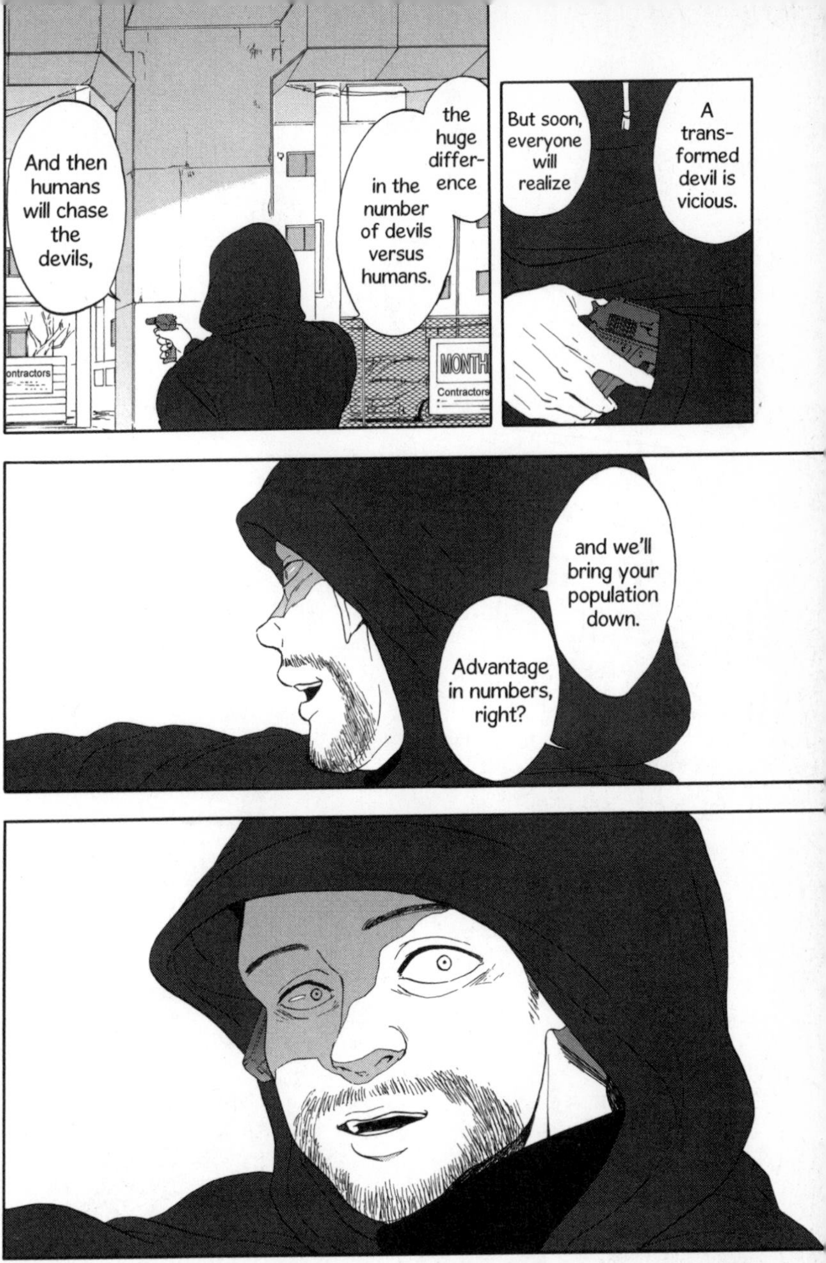
A transformed devil is vicious.
But soon, everyone will realize
the huge difference
in the number of devils versus humans.
And then humans will chase the devils,
Contractors
and we'll bring your population down.
Advantage in numbers, right?

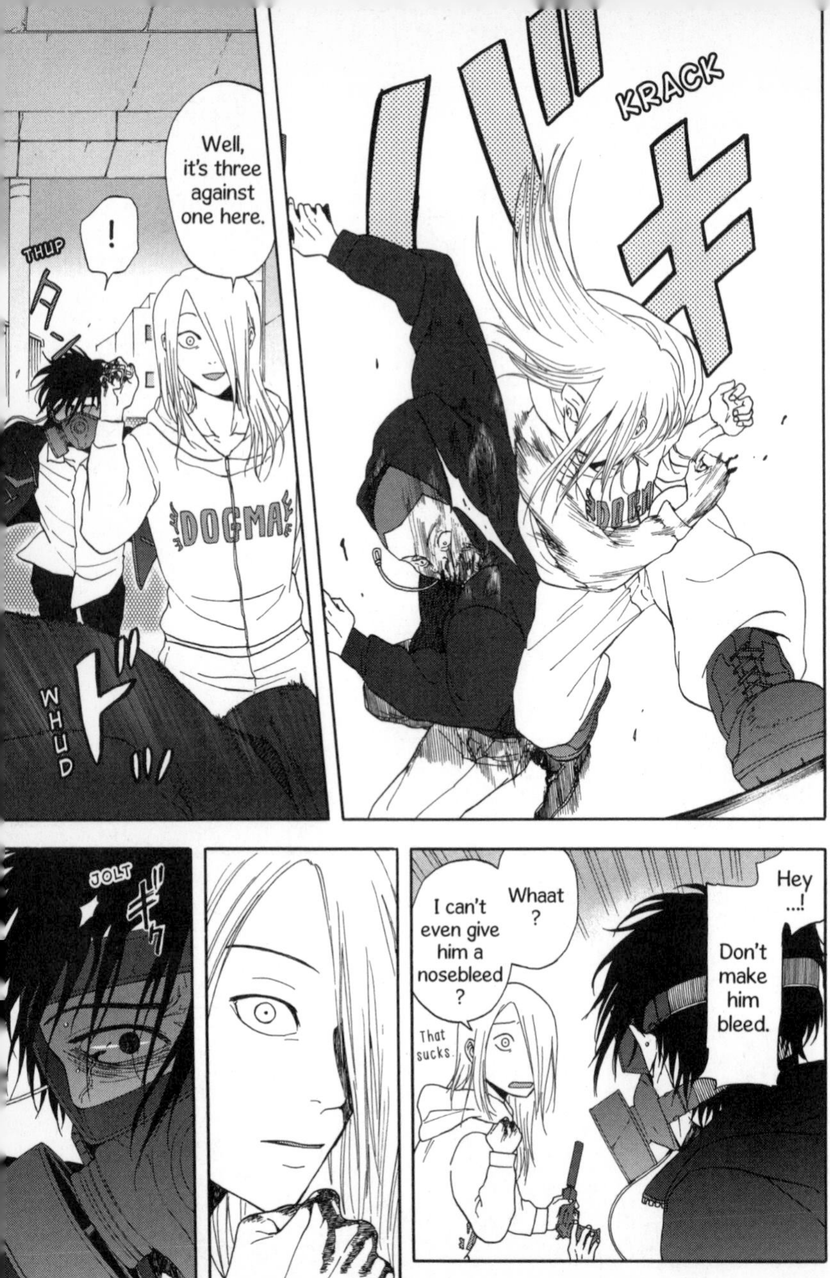
KRACK
Well, it's three against one here.
!
THUP
WHUD
Hey ...!
Don't make him bleed.
Whaat?
I can't even give him a nosebleed?
That sucks.
JOLT

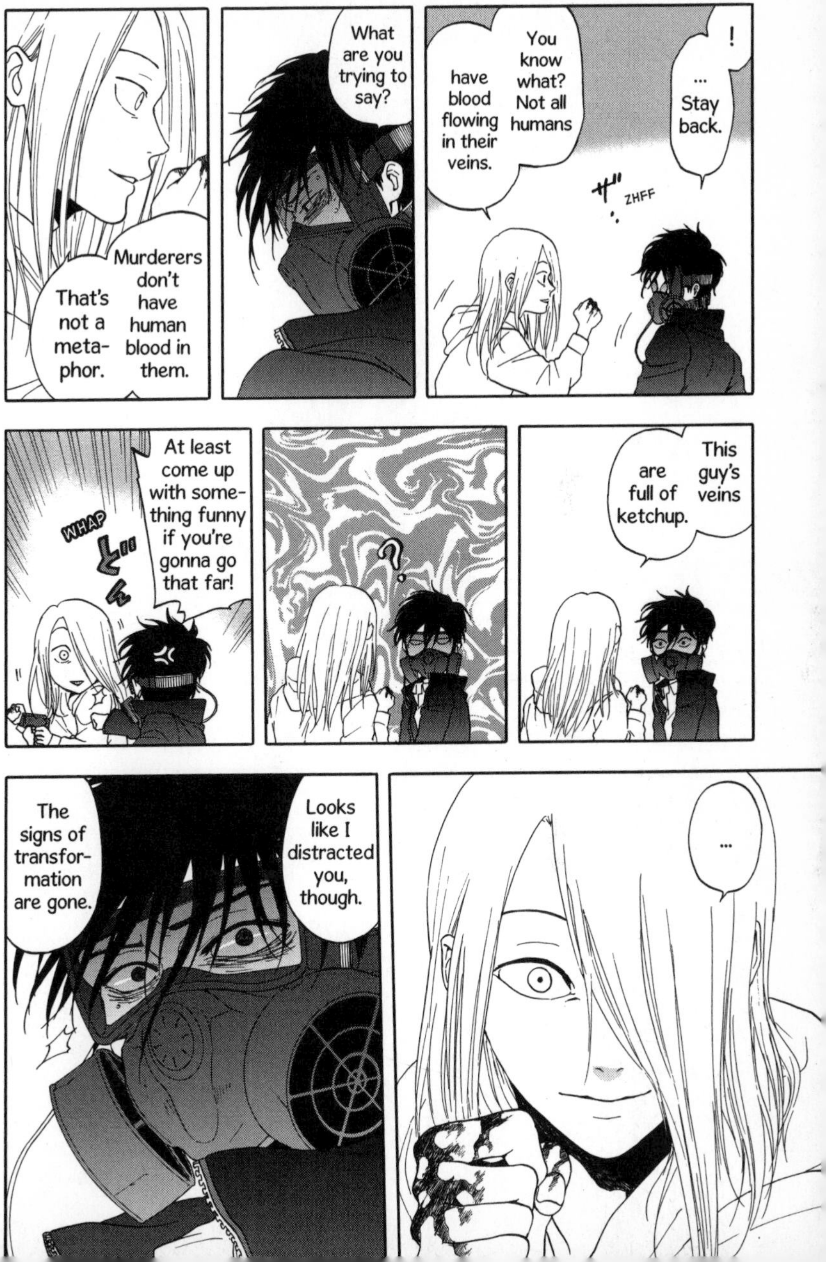
!
... Stay back.
ZHFF
You know what? Not all humans
have blood flowing in their veins.
What are you trying to say?
Murderers don't have human blood in them.
That's not a metaphor.
This guy's veins
are full of ketchup.
?
At least come up with some-thing funny if you're gonna go that far!
WHAP
...
Looks like I distracted you, though.
The signs of transfor-mation are gone.

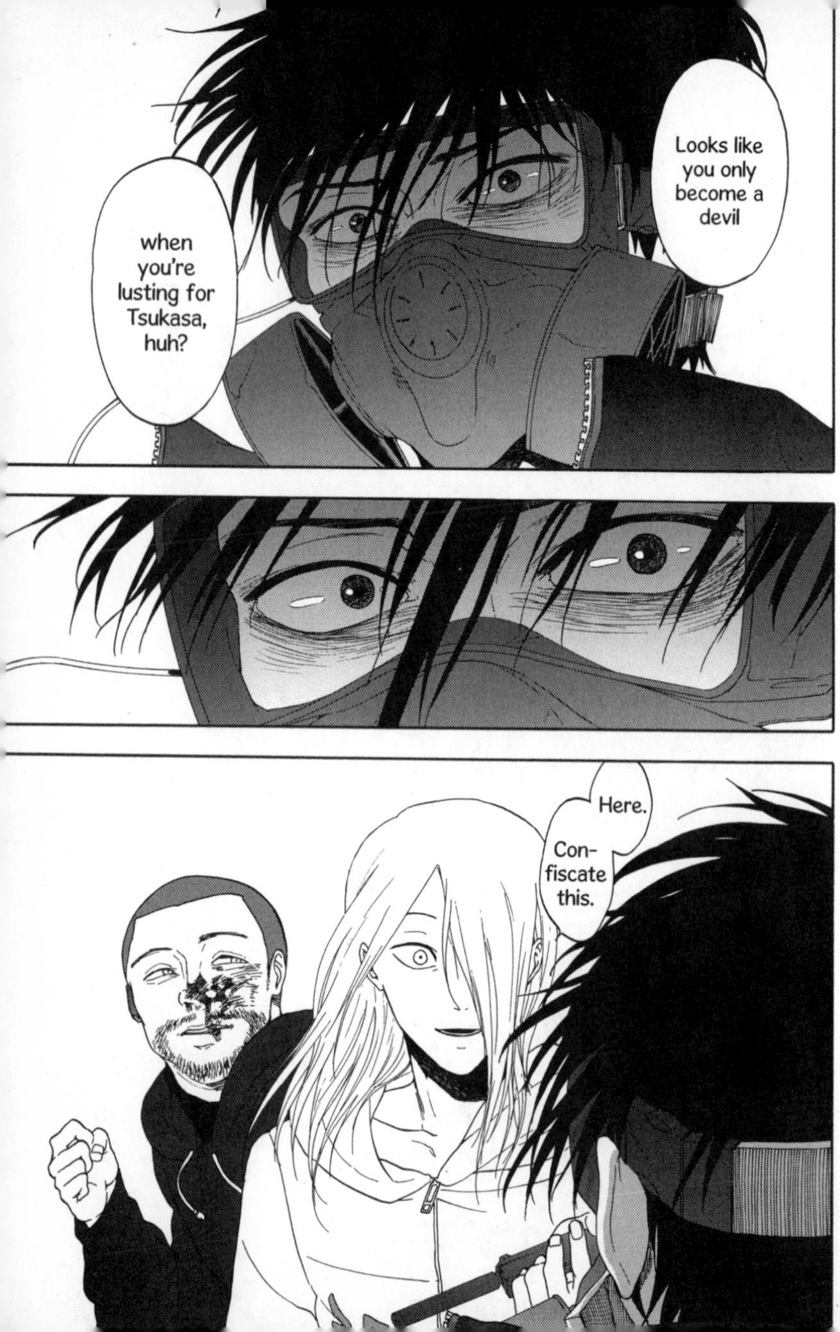
Looks like you only become a devil
when you're lusting for Tsukasa, huh?
Here. Con-fiscate this.

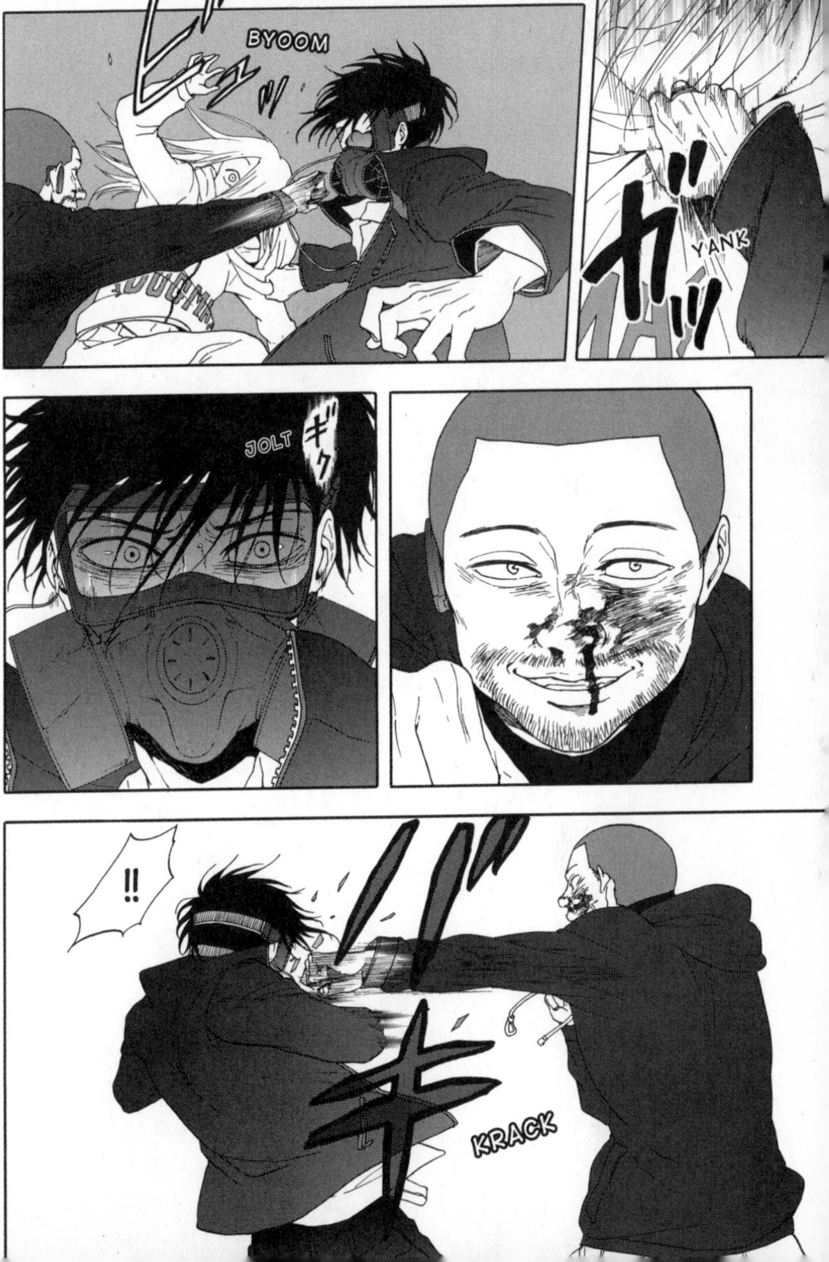
ガッ
YANK
ビュッ
BYOOM
ギク
JOLT
!!
バキ
KRACK

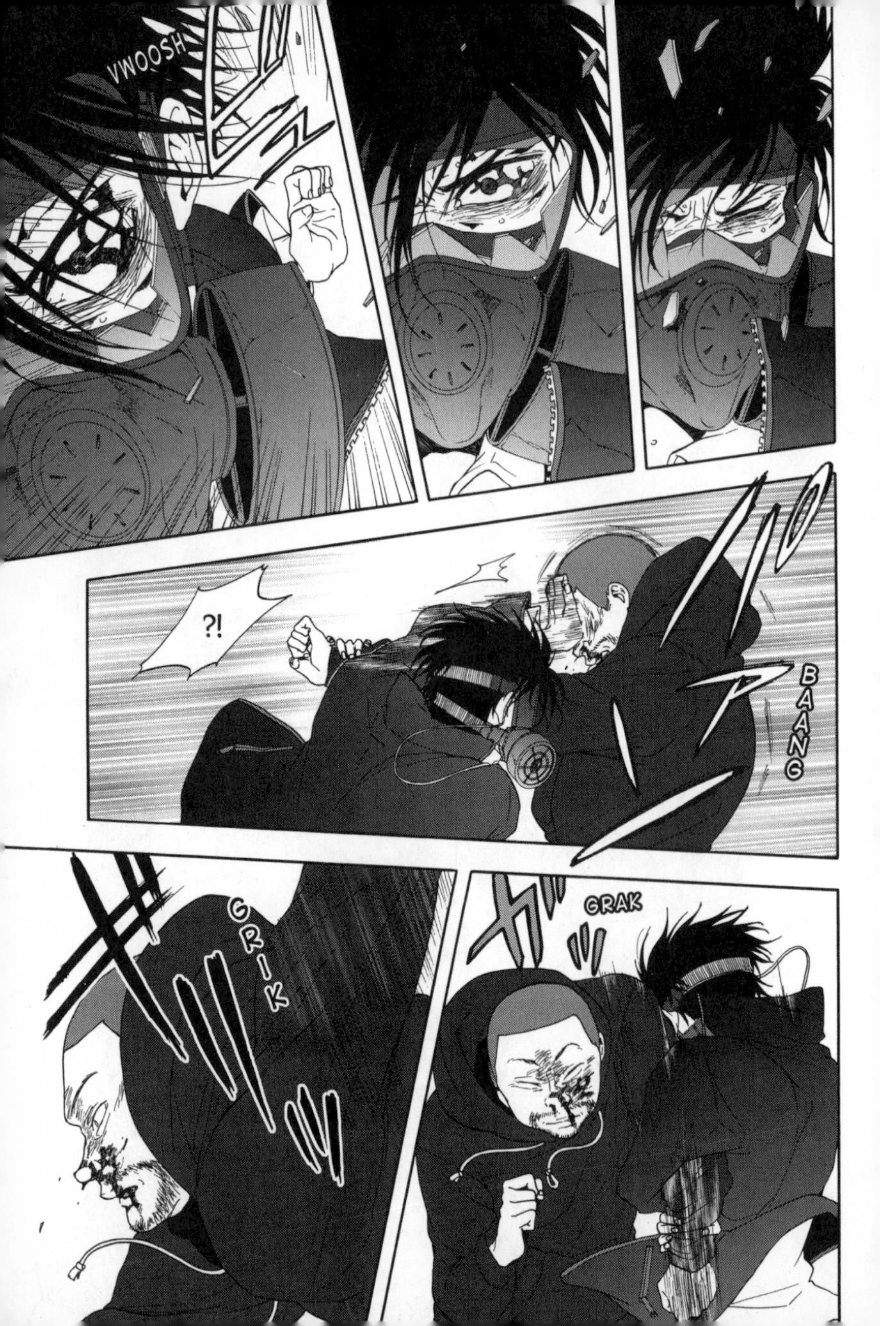
VWOOSH
BAANG
?!
GRAK
GRIK

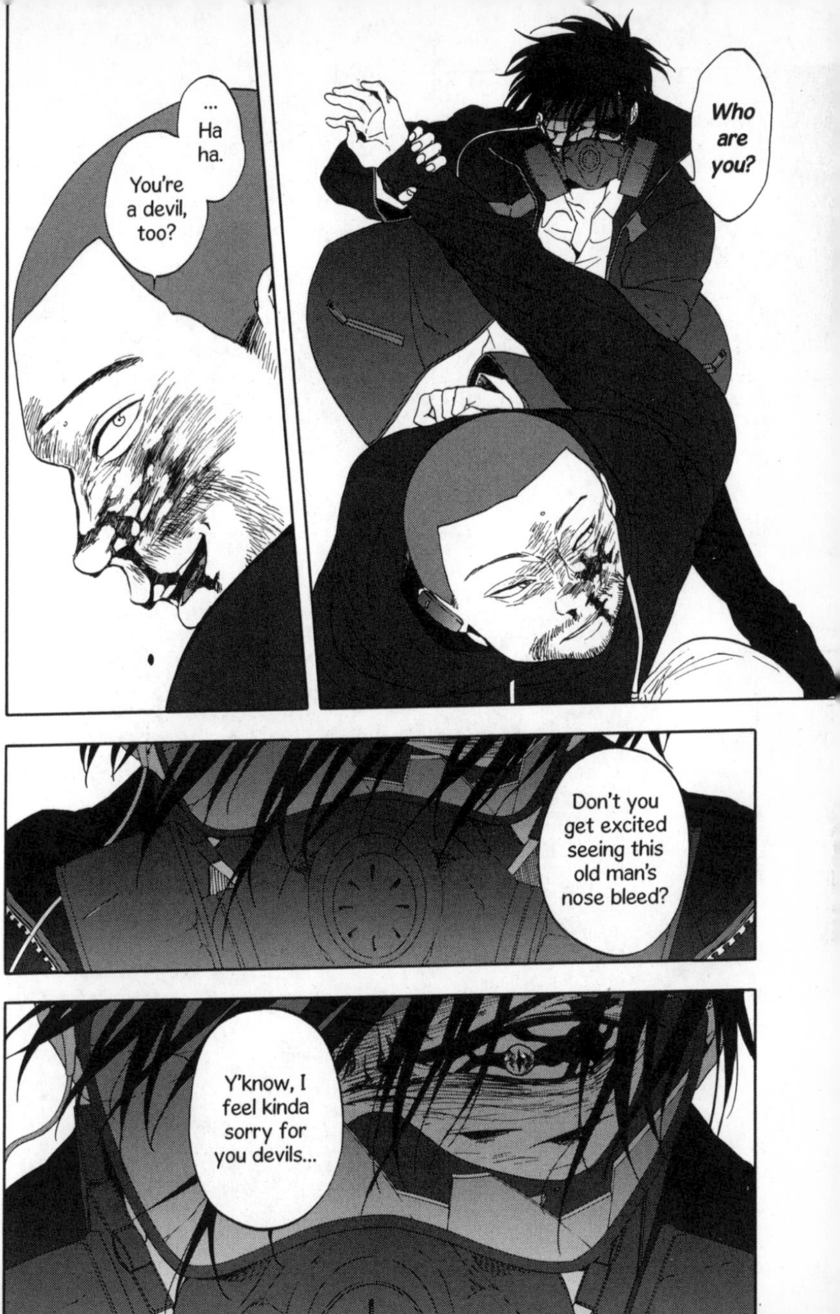

Who are you?
... Ha ha. You're a devil, too?
Don't you get excited seeing this old man's nose bleed?
Y'know, I feel kinda sorry for you devils...

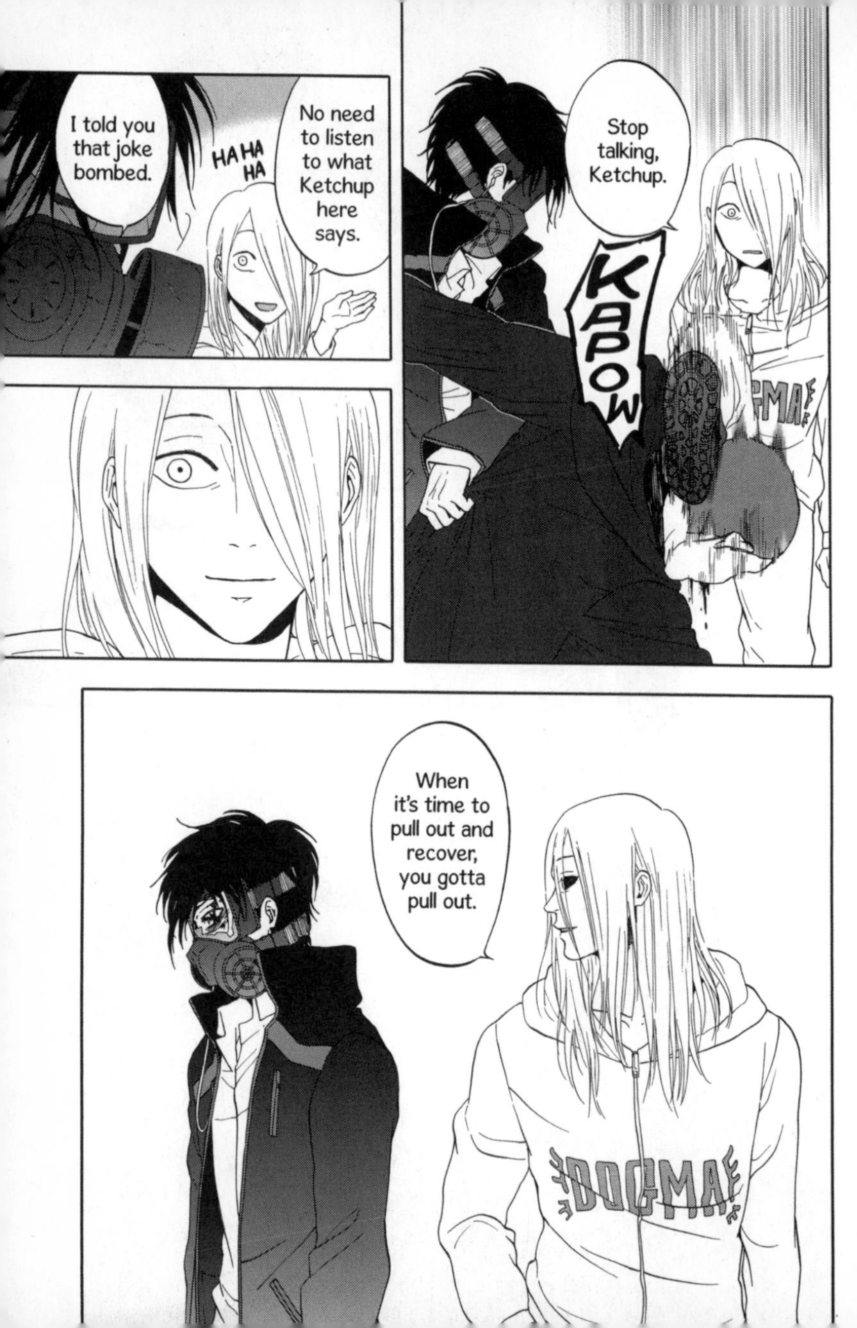
Stop talking, Ketchup.
KAPOW
No need to listen to what Ketchup here says.
HA HA HA
I told you that joke bombed.
When it's time to pull out and recover, you gotta pull out.
DOGMA

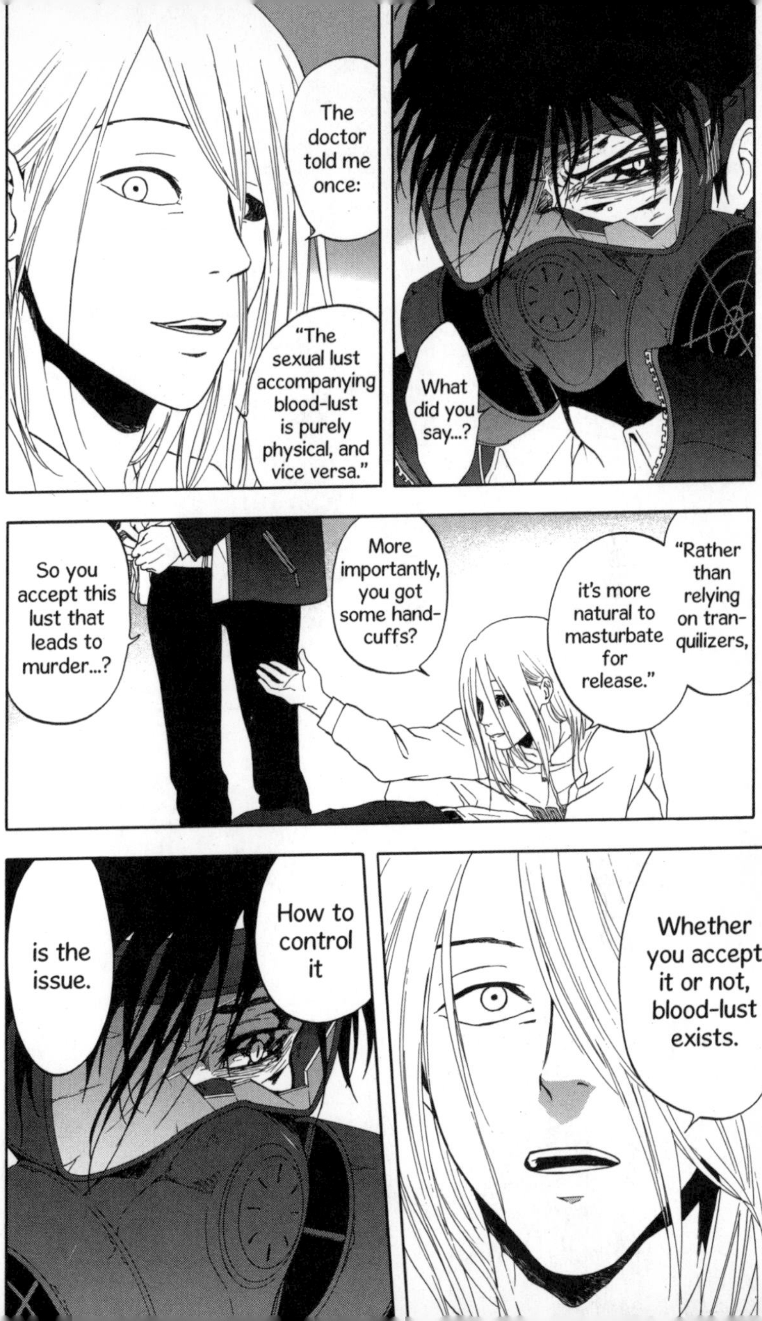
What did you say...?
The doctor told me once:
“The sexual lust accompanying blood-lust is purely physical, and vice versa.”
“Rather than relying on tran-quilizers,
it's more natural to masturbate for release.”
More importantly, you got some hand-cuffs?
So you accept this lust that leads to murder...?
Whether you accept it or not, blood-lust exists.
How to control it
is the issue.

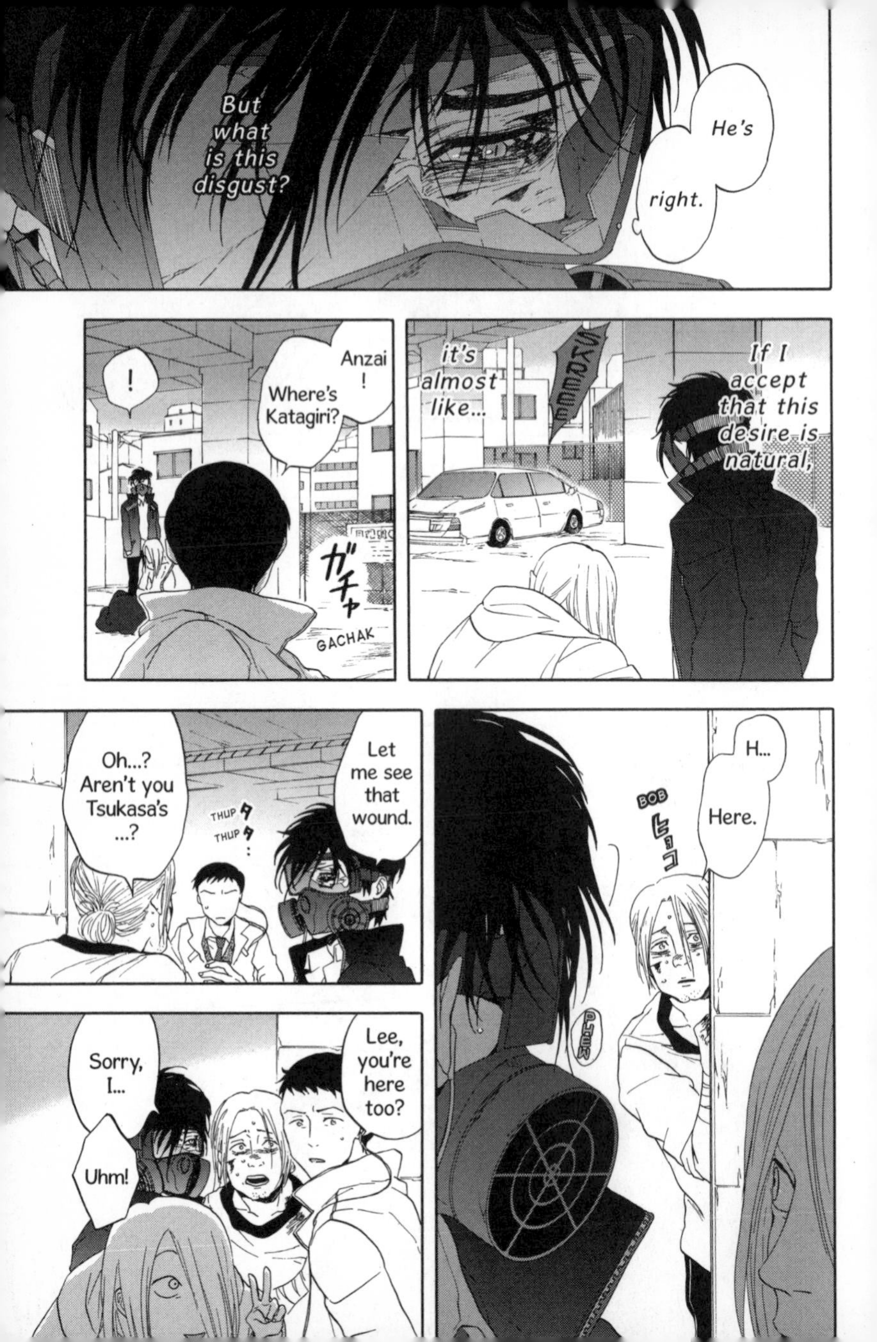
He's right.
But what is this disgust?
If I accept that this desire is natural,
it's almost like...
SKREEE
Anzai!
Where's Katagiri?
!
ガチャ
GACHAK
H... Here.
BOB ヒョコ
Let me see that wound.
THUP タ THUP タ
Oh...? Aren't you Tsukasa's ...?
Lee, you're here too?
Sorry, I...
Uhm!

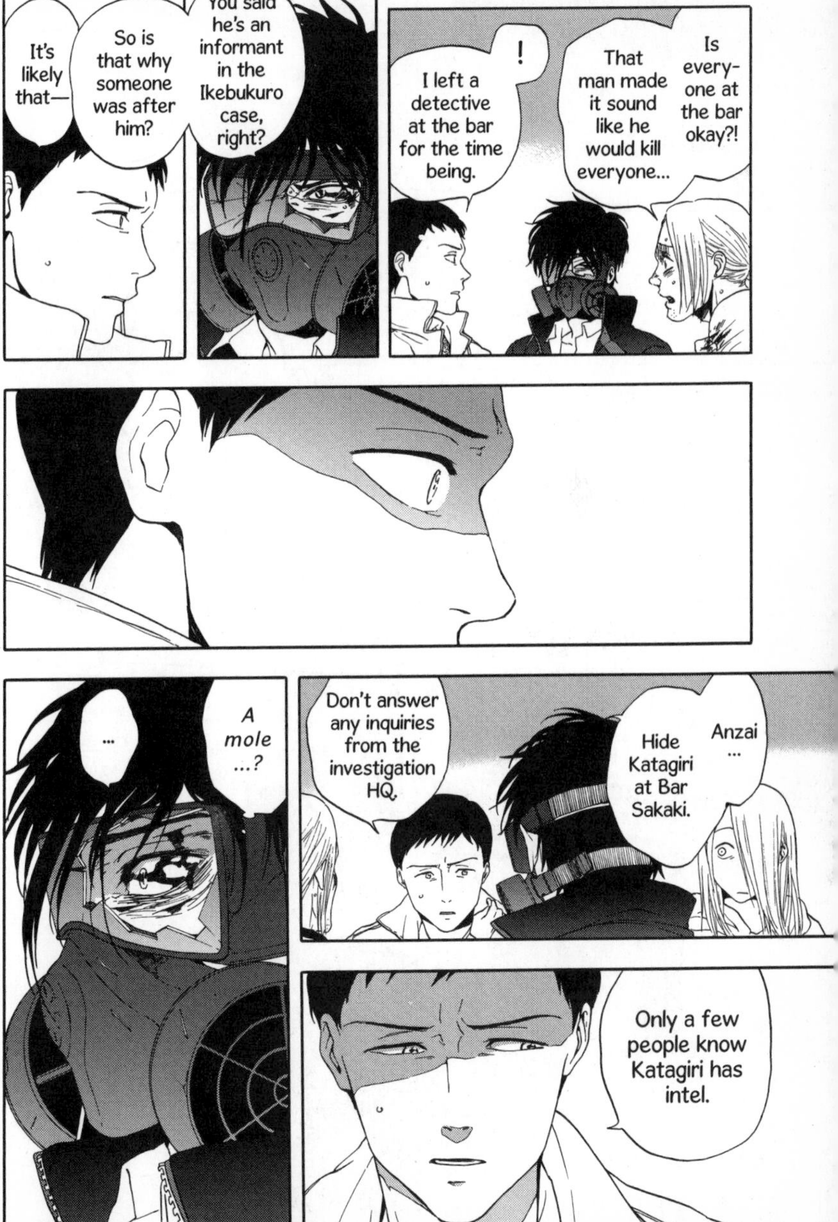
Is everyone at the bar okay?!
That man made it sound like he would kill everyone...
!
I left a detective at the bar for the time being.
You said he's an informant in the Ikebukuro case, right?
So is that why someone was after him?
It's likely that—
Anzai ...
Hide Katagiri at Bar Sakaki.
Don't answer any inquiries from the investigation HQ.
Only a few people know Katagiri has intel.
A mole ...?
...

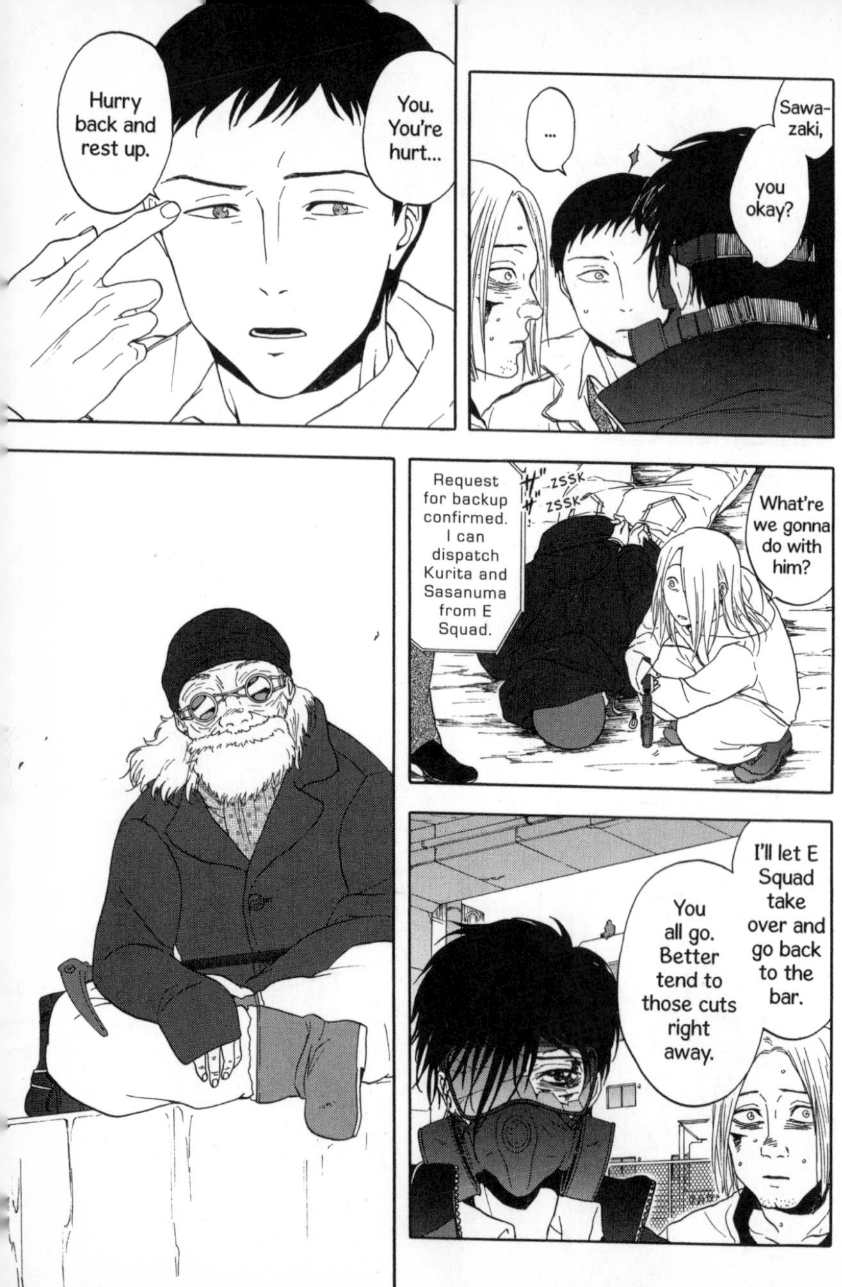
Sawa-zaki, you okay?
...
You. You're hurt...
Hurry back and rest up.
What're we gonna do with him?
ZSSK
ZSSK
Request for backup confirmed. I can dispatch Kurita and Sasanuma from E Squad.
I'll let E Squad take over and go back to the bar.
You all go. Better tend to those cuts right away.

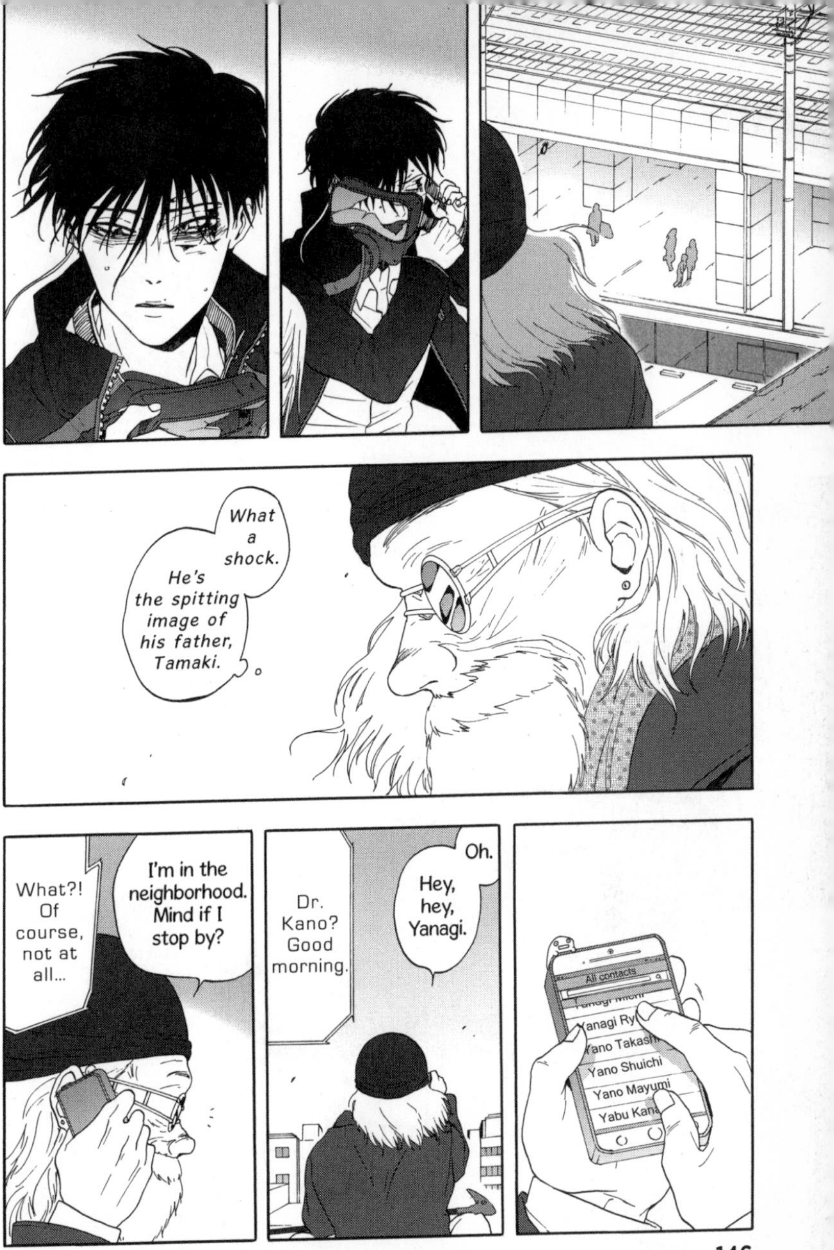
What a shock.
He's the spitting image of his father, Tamaki.
All contacts
Yano Shuichi
Yano Mayumi
Oh.
Hey, hey, Yanagi.
Dr. Kano? Good morning.
I'm in the neighborhood. Mind if I stop by?
What?! Of course, not at all...

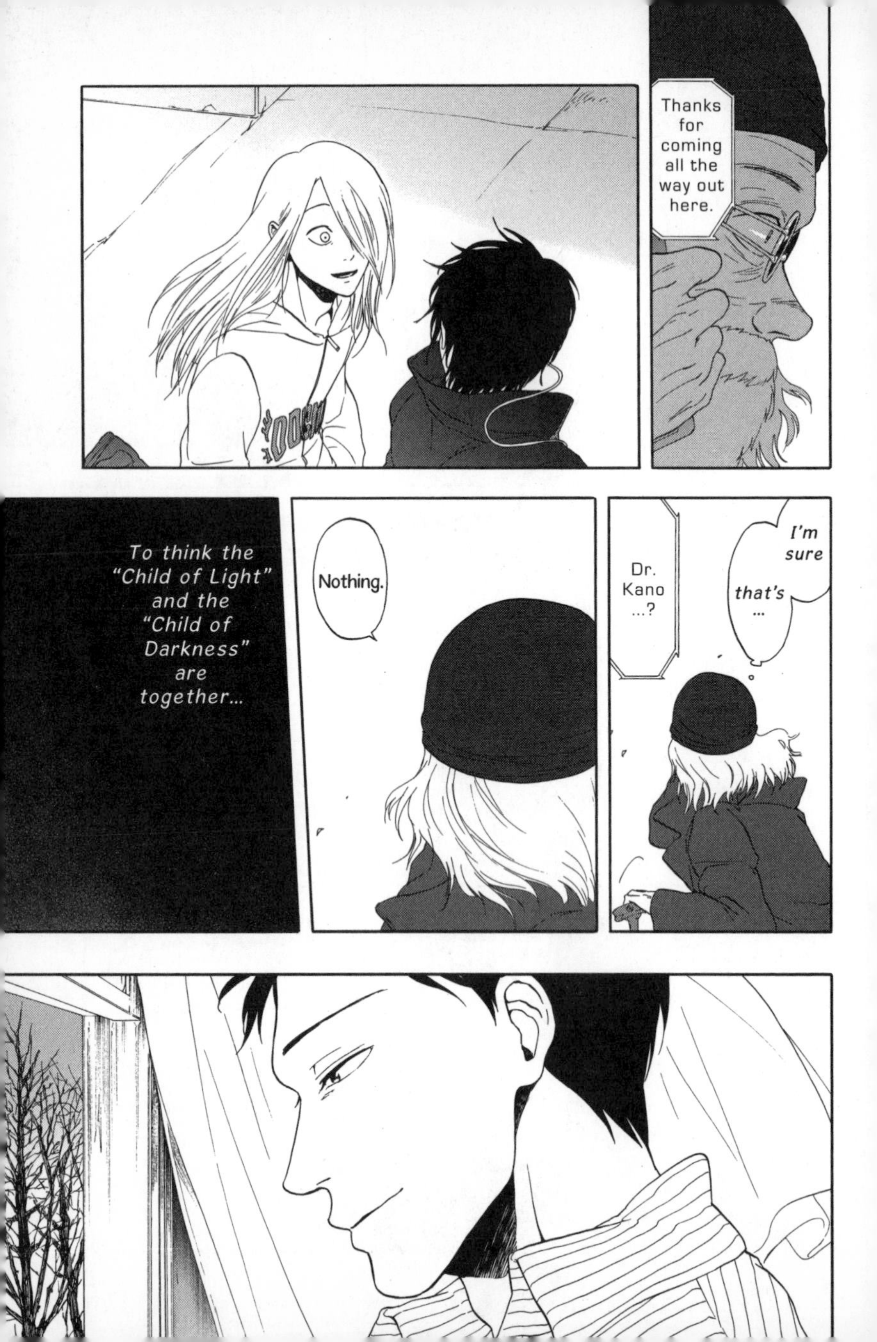
Thanks for coming all the way out here.
I'm sure that's ...
Dr. Kano ...?
Nothing.
To think the "Child of Light" and the "Child of Darkness" are together...

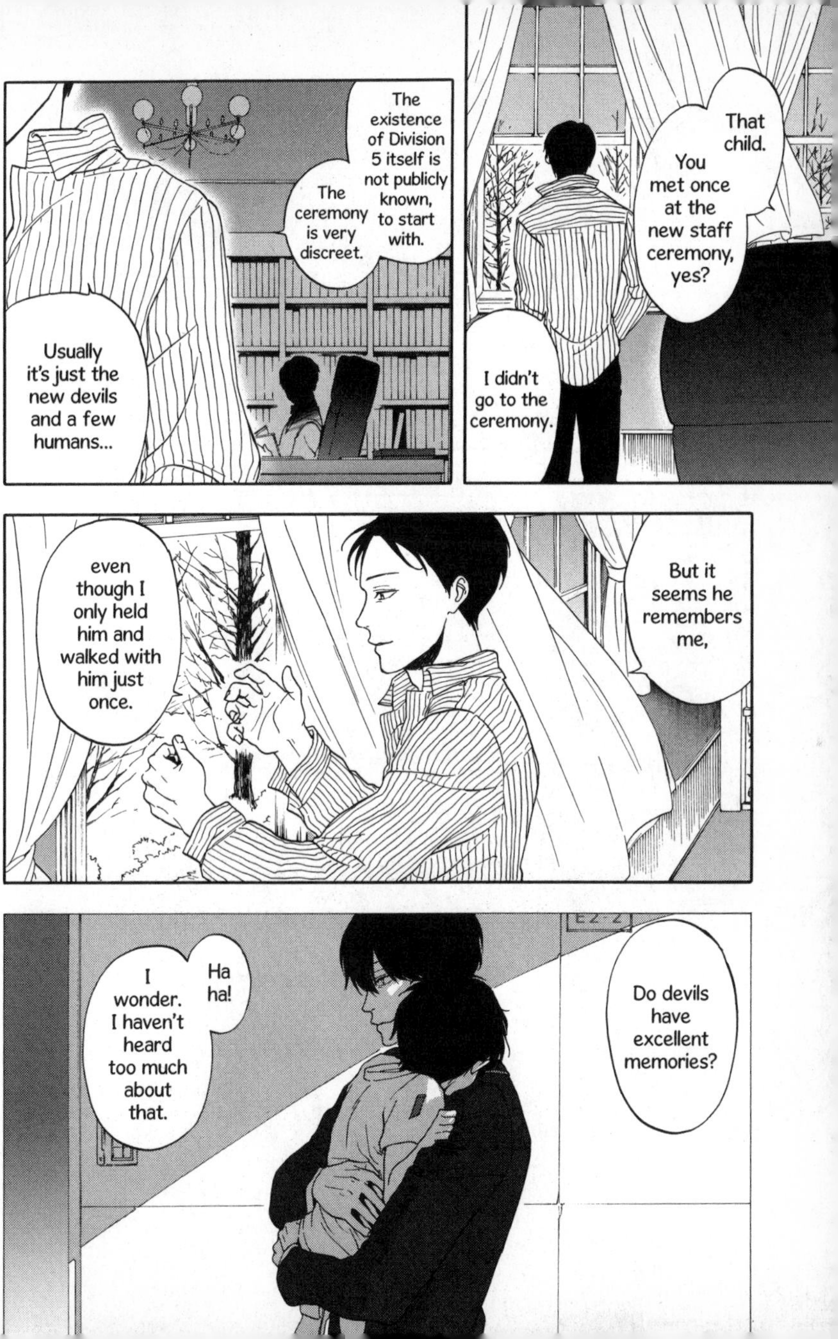
That child.
You met once at the new staff ceremony, yes?
I didn't go to the ceremony.
The existence of Division 5 itself is not publicly known, to start with.
The ceremony is very discreet.
Usually it's just the new devils and a few humans...
But it seems he remembers me,
even though I only held him and walked with him just once.
Do devils have excellent memories?
Ha ha!
I wonder. I haven't heard too much about that.

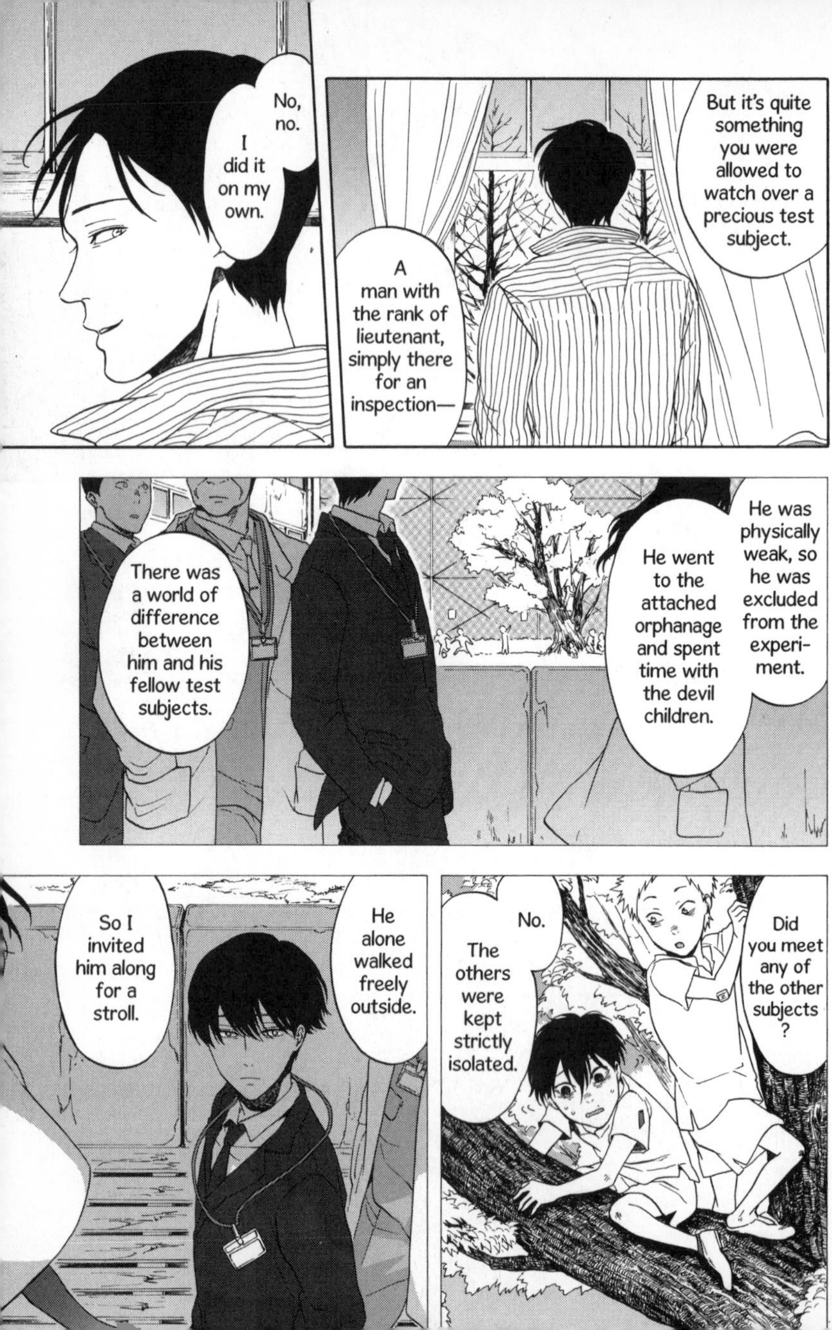
But it's quite something you were allowed to watch over a precious test subject.
A man with the rank of lieutenant, simply there for an inspection—
No, no.
I did it on my own.
He was physically weak, so he was excluded from the experi-ment.
He went to the attached orphanage and spent time with the devil children.
There was a world of difference between him and his fellow test subjects.
Did you meet any of the other subjects?
No.
The others were kept strictly isolated.
He alone walked freely outside.
So I invited him along for a stroll.

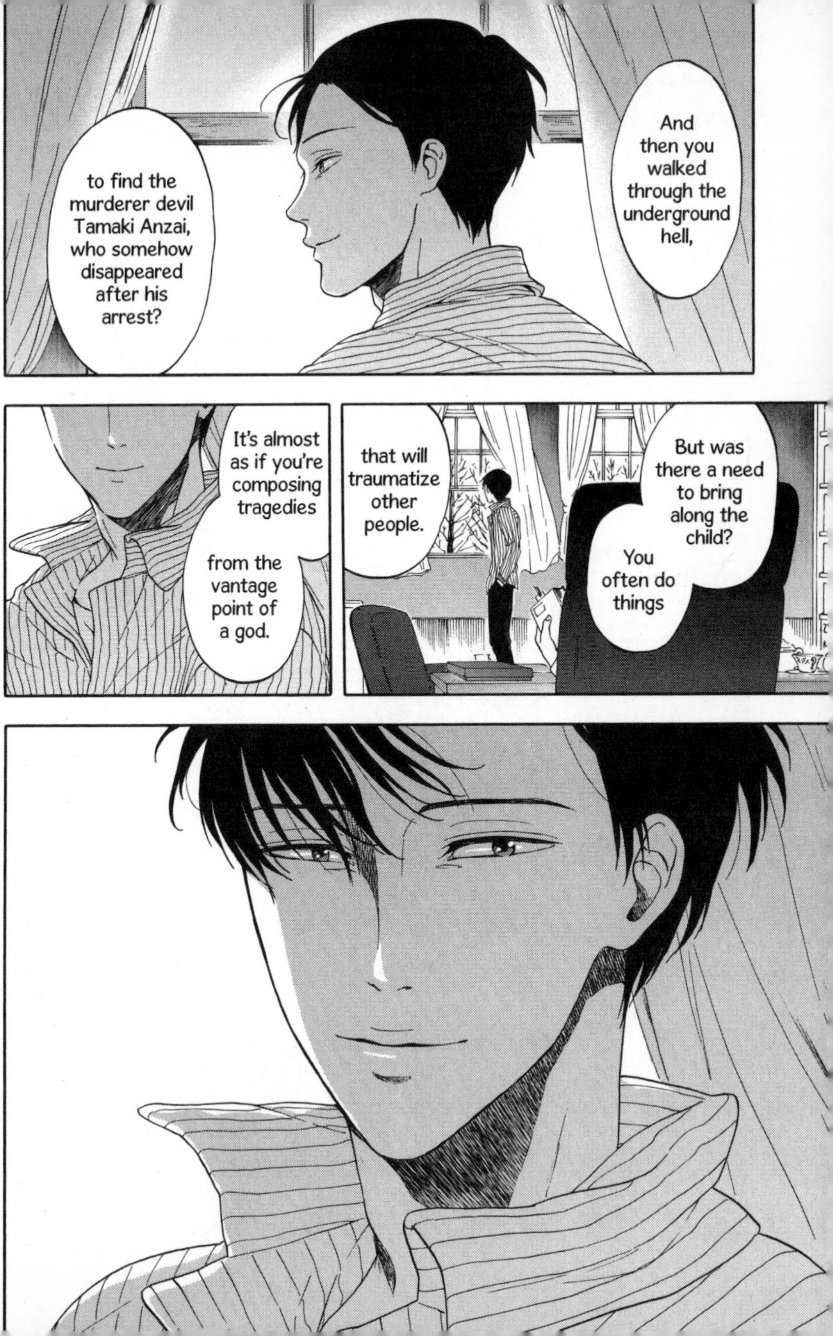
And then you walked through the underground hell,
to find the murderer devil Tamaki Anzai, who somehow disappeared after his arrest?
But was there a need to bring along the child?
You often do things
that will traumatize other people.
It's almost as if you're composing tragedies
from the vantage point of a god.

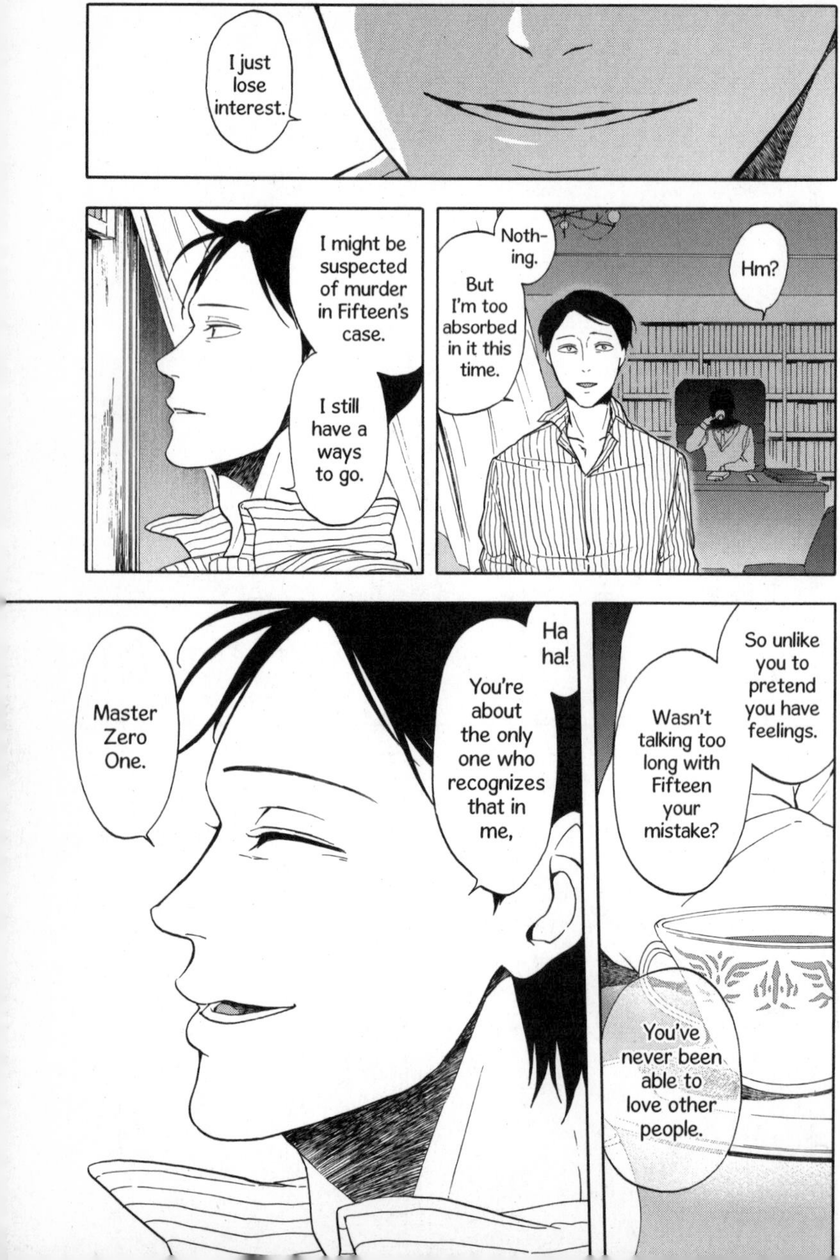
I just lose interest.
Hm?
Noth-ing.
But I'm too absorbed in it this time.
I might be suspected of murder in Fifteen's case.
I still have a ways to go.
So unlike you to pretend you have feelings.
Wasn't talking too long with Fifteen your mistake?
You've never been able to love other people.
Ha ha!
You're about the only one who recognizes that in me,
Master Zero One.

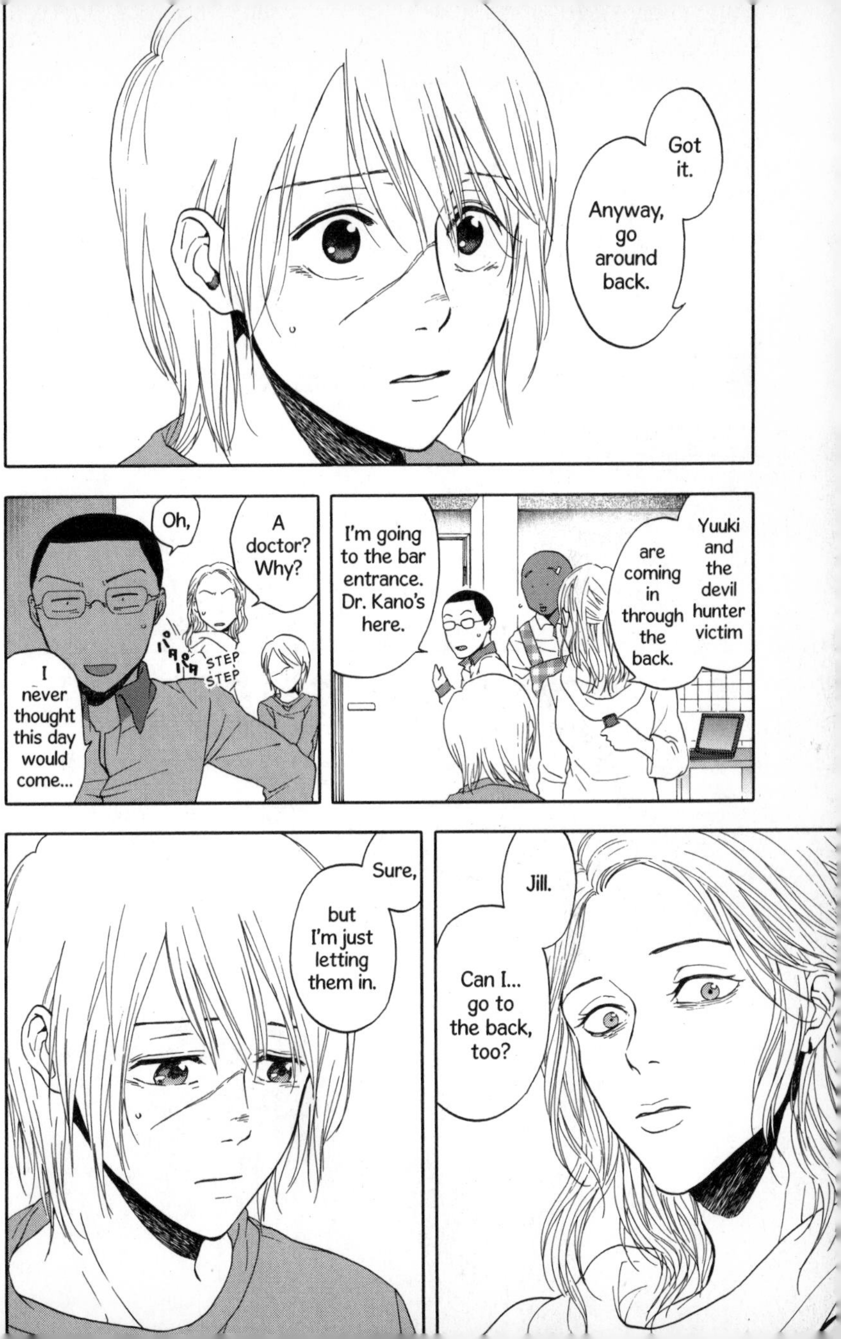
Got it.
Anyway, go around back.
Yuuki and the devil hunter victim
are coming in through the back.
I'm going to the bar entrance. Dr. Kano's here.
A doctor? Why?
Oh,
I never thought this day would come...
STEP STEP
Jill.
Can I... go to the back, too?
Sure,
but I'm just letting them in.

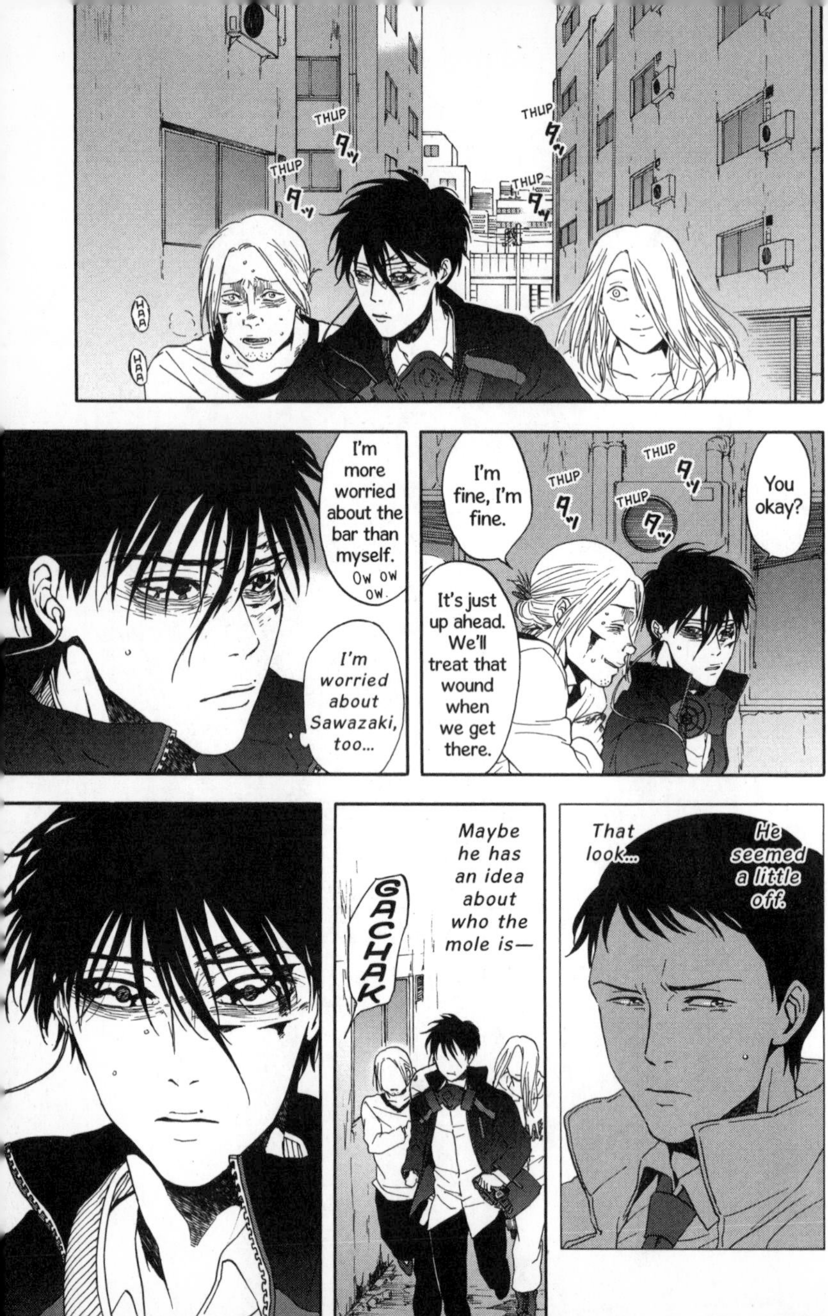
THUP
タッ
THUP
タッ
THUP
タッ
THUP
タッ
HAA
HAA
You okay?
THUP
タッ
THUP
タッ
THUP
タッ
I'm fine, I'm fine.
It's just up ahead. We'll treat that wound when we get there.
I'm more worried about the bar than myself. OW OW OW.
I'm worried about Sawazaki, too...
He seemed a little off.
That look...
Maybe he has an idea about who the mole is—
GACHAK

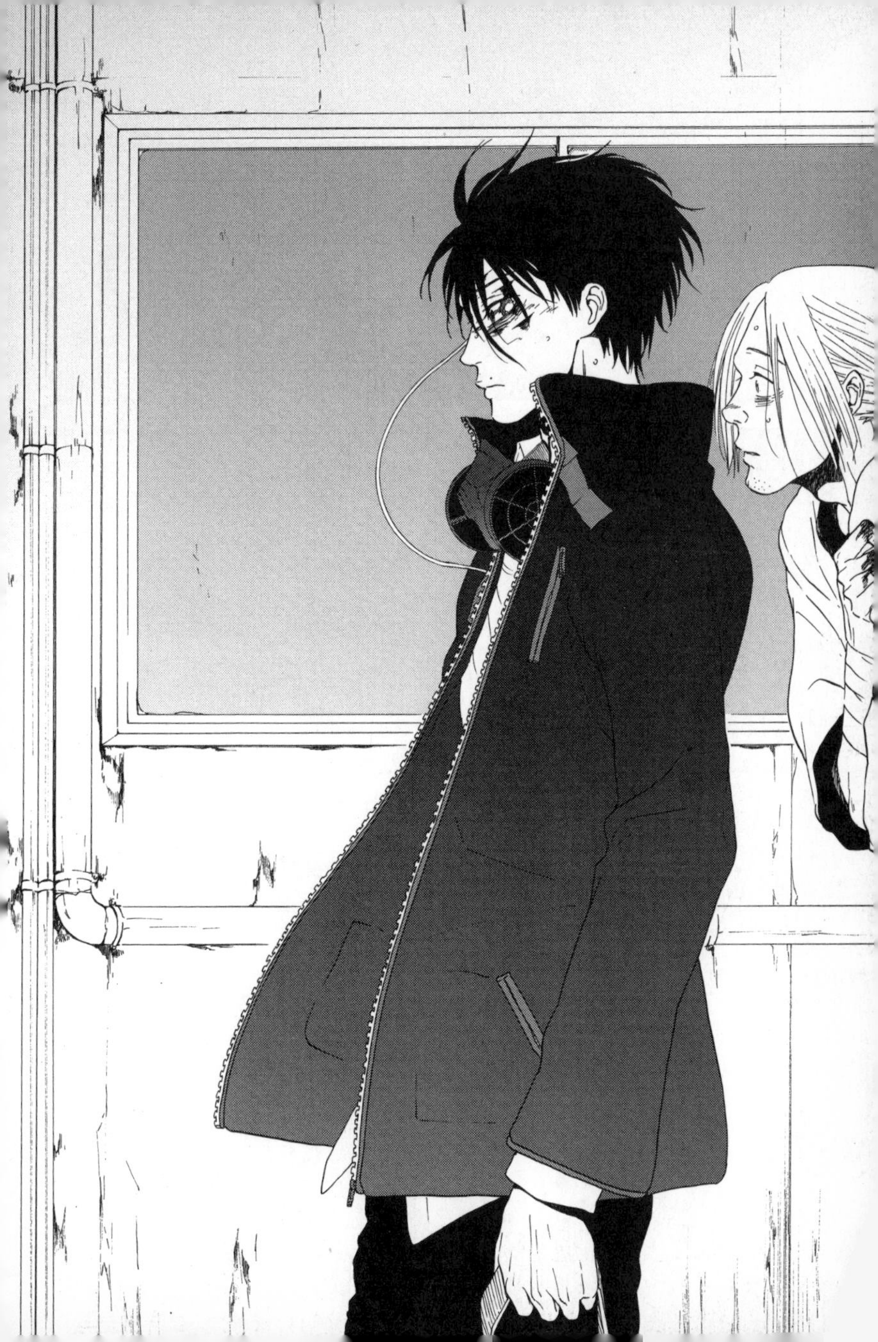

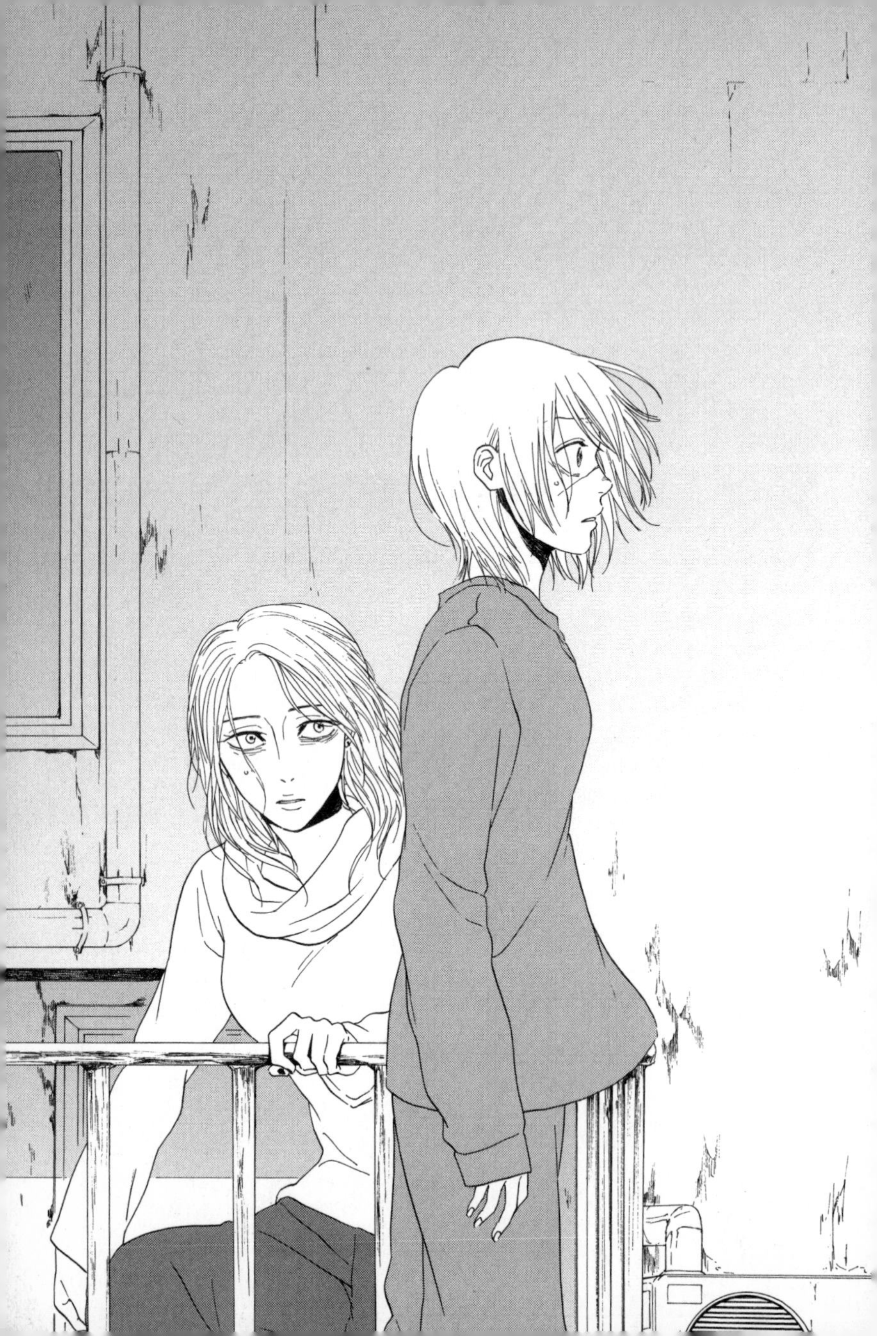

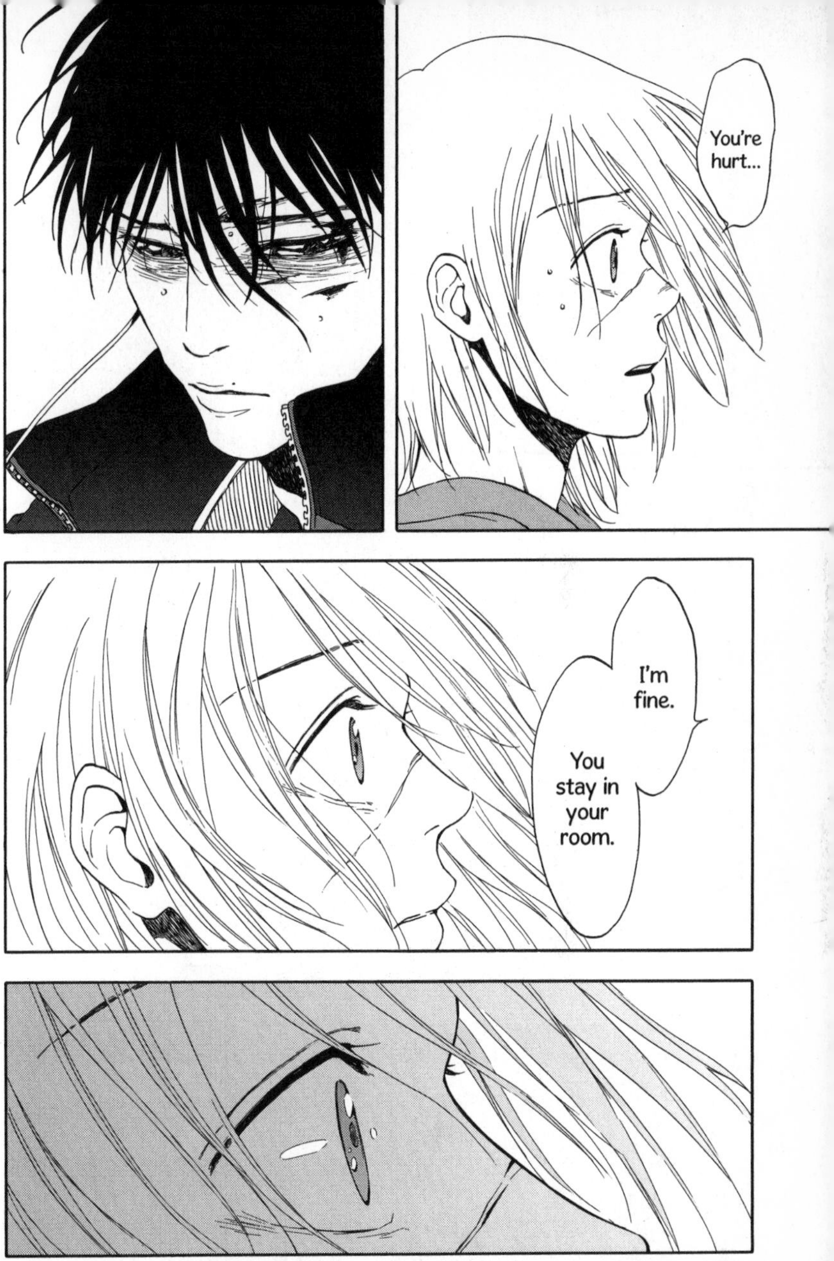
You're hurt...
I'm fine.
You stay in your room.

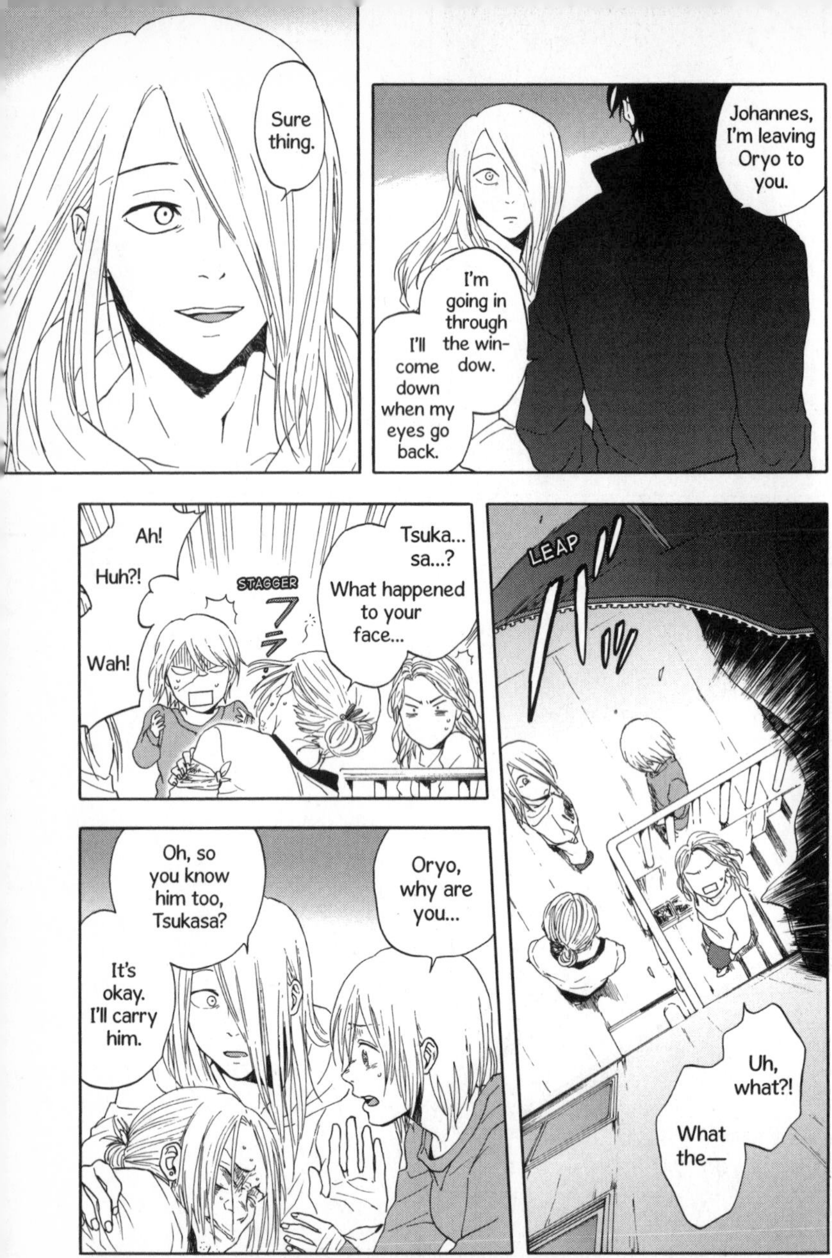
Johannes, I'm leaving Oryo to you.
I'm going in through the win-dow.
I'll come down when my eyes go back.
Sure thing.
LEAP
Uh, what?!
What the—
Tsuka... sa...? What happened to your face...
STAGGER
Ah!
Huh?!
Wah!
Oryo, why are you...
Oh, so you know him too, Tsukasa?
It's okay. I'll carry him.

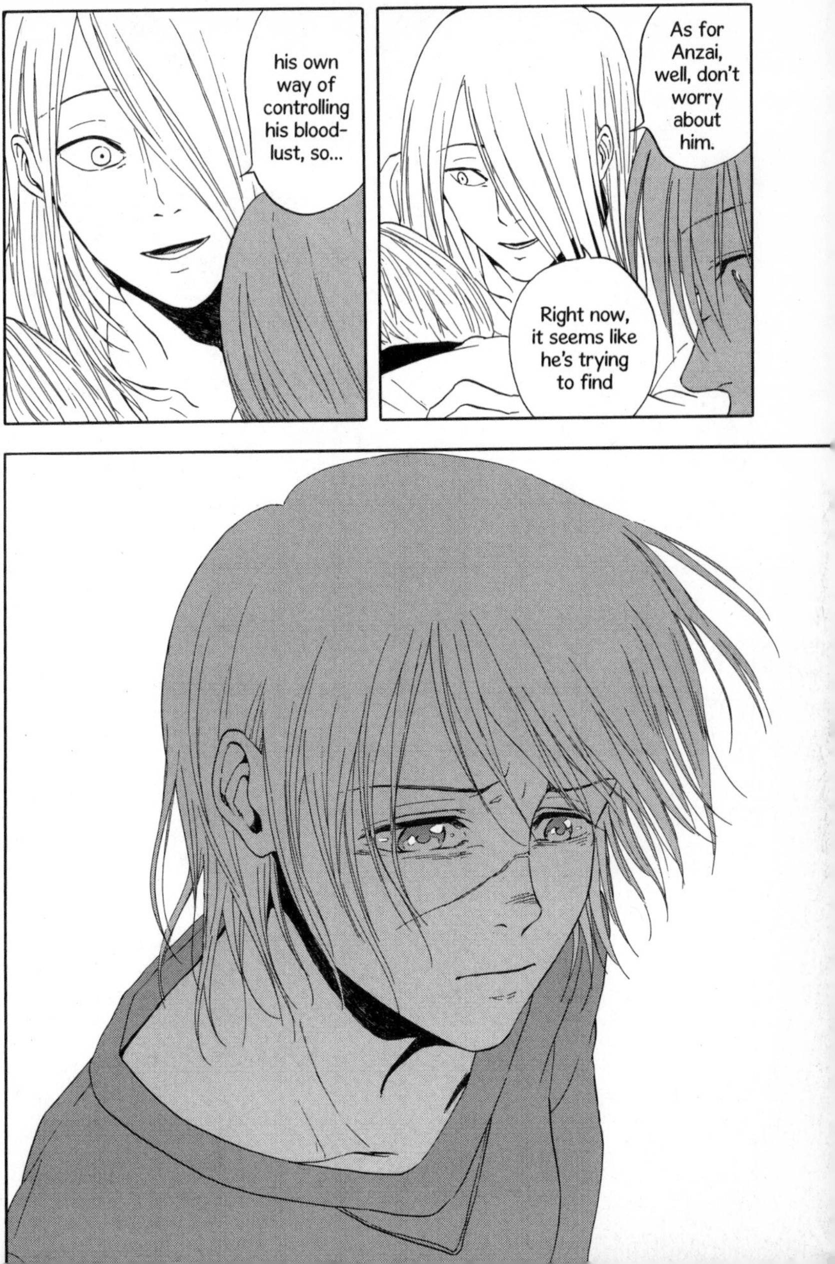
As for Anzai, well, don't worry about him.
Right now, it seems like he's trying to find
his own way of controlling his blood-lust, so...

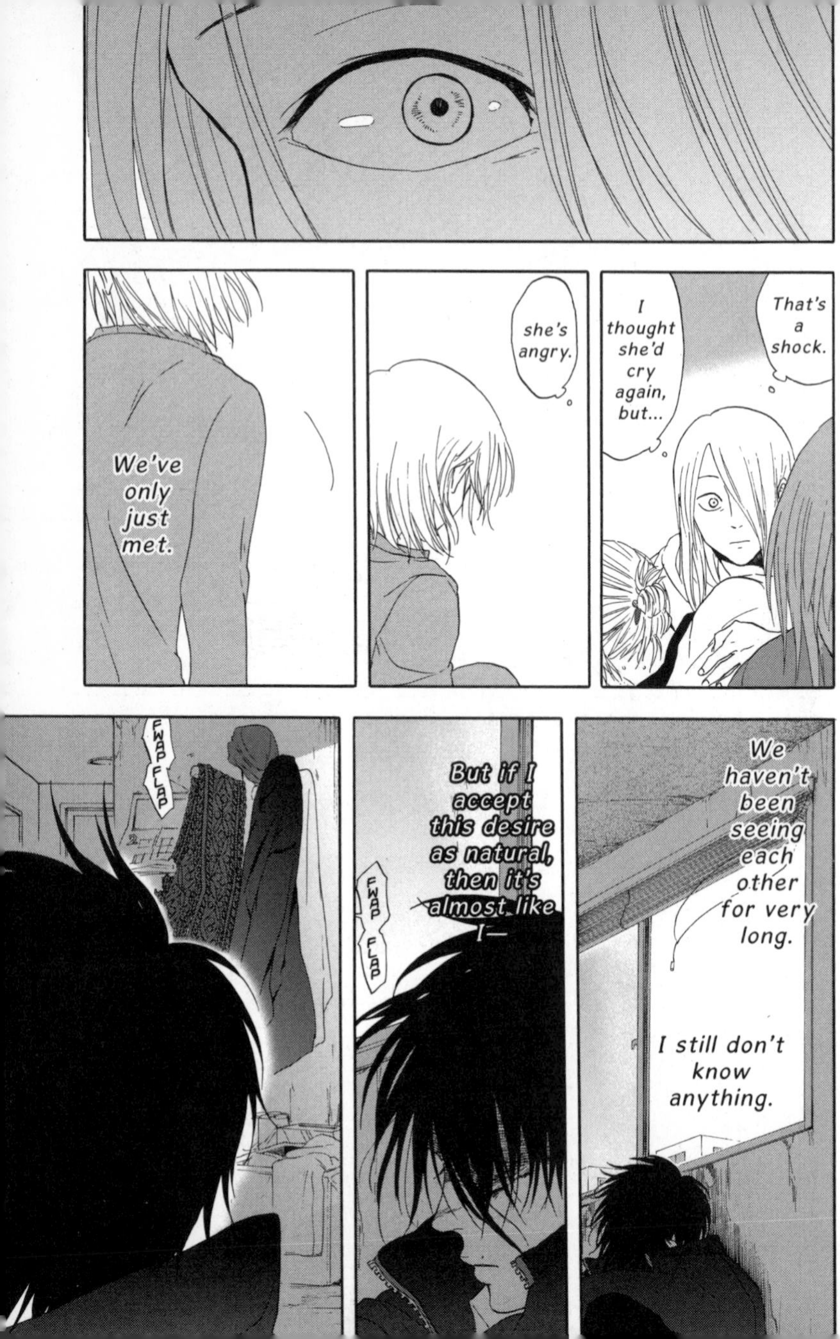
That's a shock.
I thought she'd cry again, but...
she's angry.
We've only just met.
We haven't been seeing each other for very long.
I still don't know anything.
But if I accept this desire as natural, then it's almost like I—
FWAP FLAP
FWAP FLAP

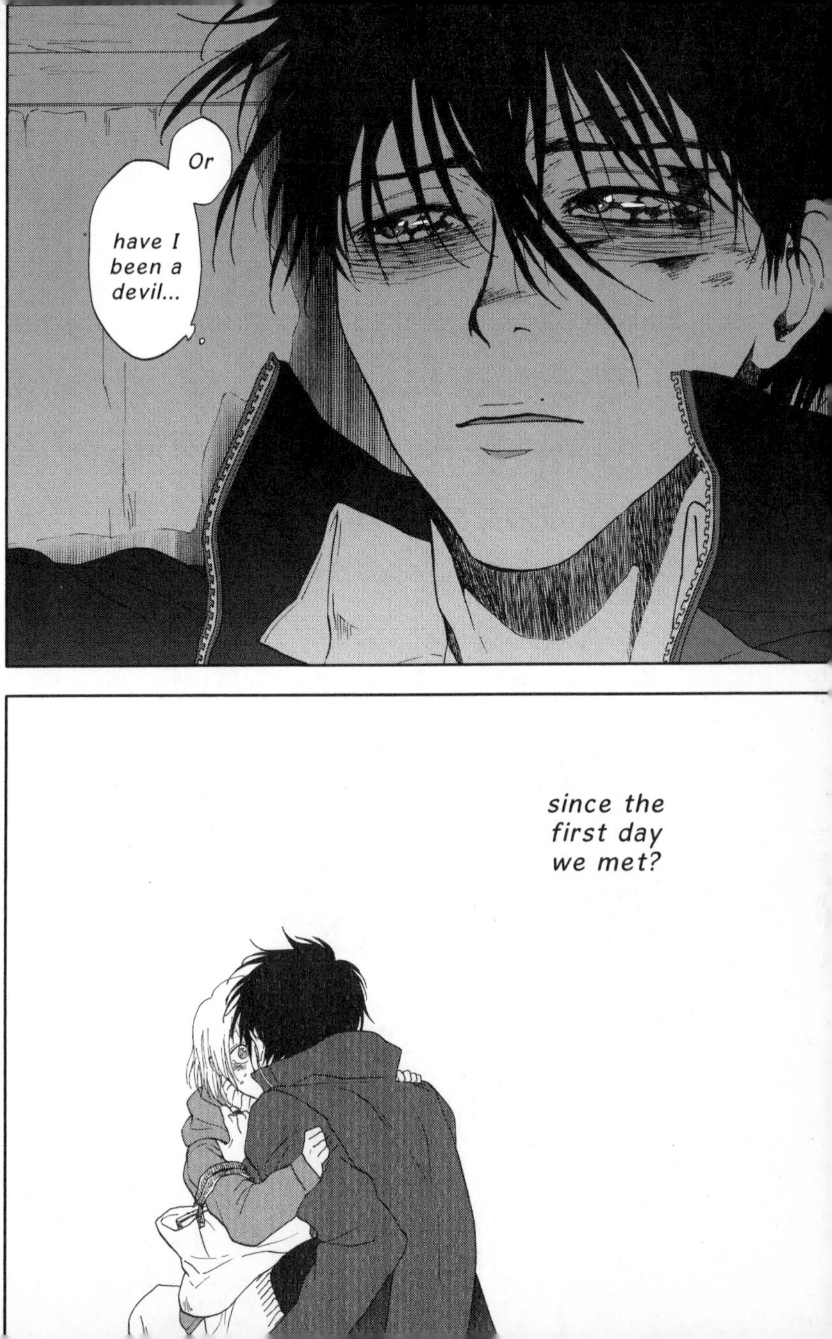
Or
have I been a devil...
since the first day we met?

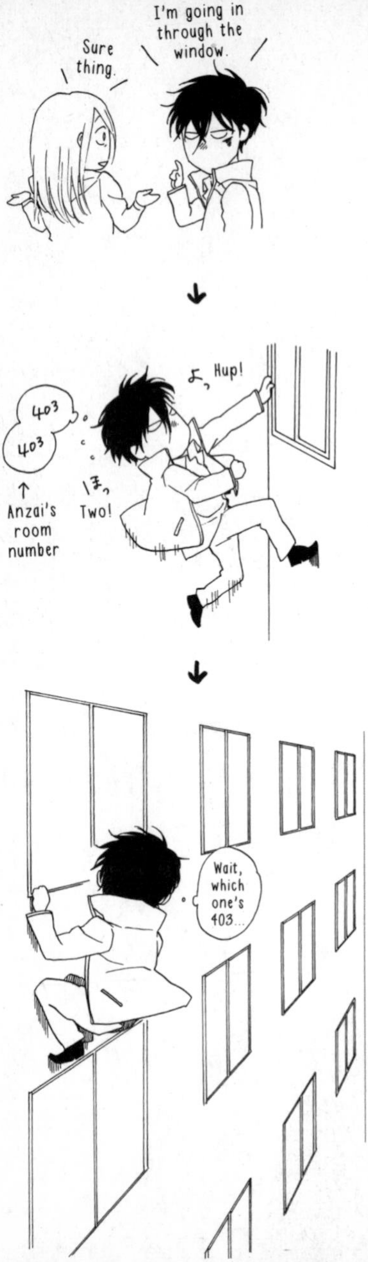
I'm going in through the window.
Sure thing.
よっ Hup!
403
403
Anzai's room number
ほっ Two!
Wait, which one's 403...

DEVILS' LINE SPECIAL
Line of Zero

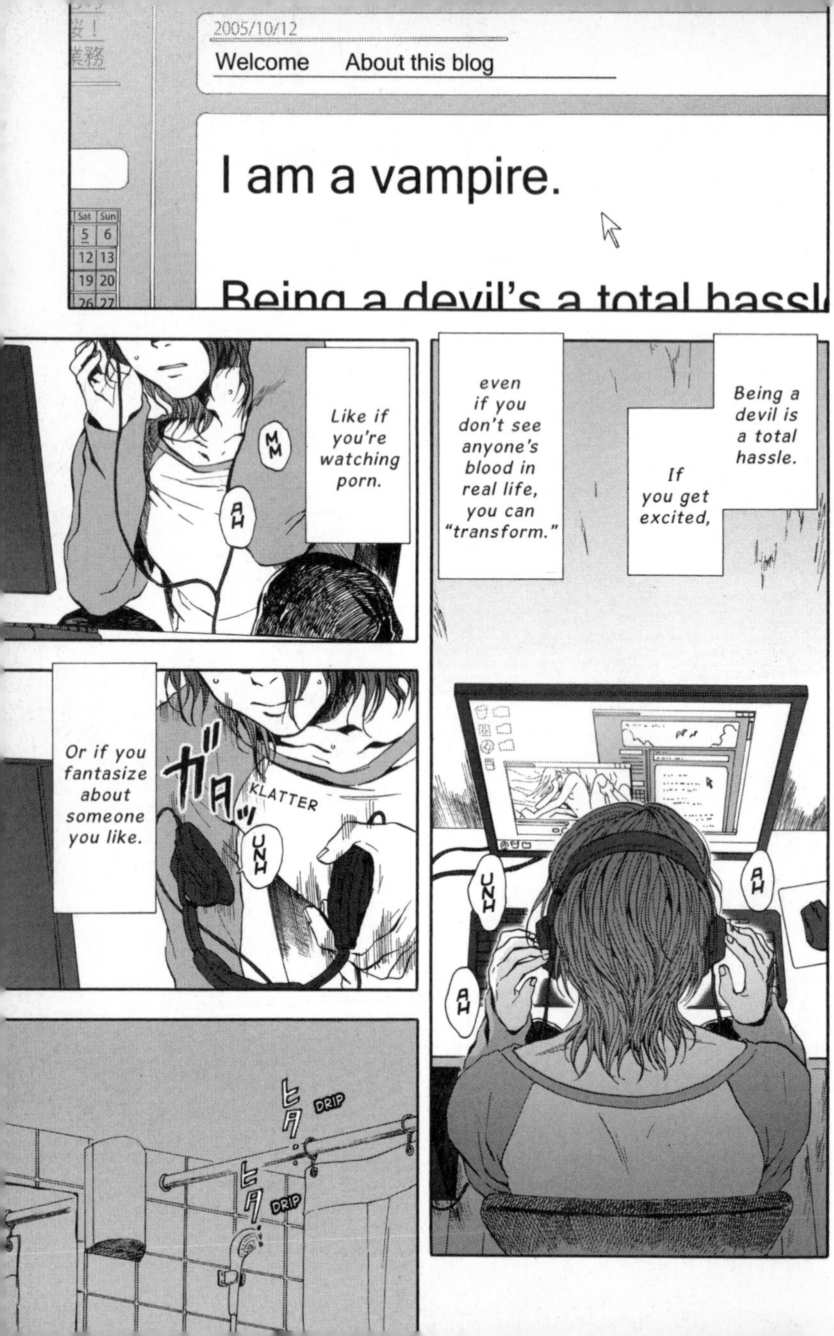

2005/10/12
Welcome About this blog
Sat Sun
5 6
12 13
19 20
26 27
I am a vampire.
Being a devil's a total hassl
Being a devil is a total hassle.
If you get excited,
even if you don't see anyone's blood in real life, you can "transform."
AH
UNH
AH
Like if you're watching porn.
MM
AH
Or if you fantasize about someone you like.
ガタッ
KLATTER
UNH
ヒタ
DRIP
ヒタ
DRIP

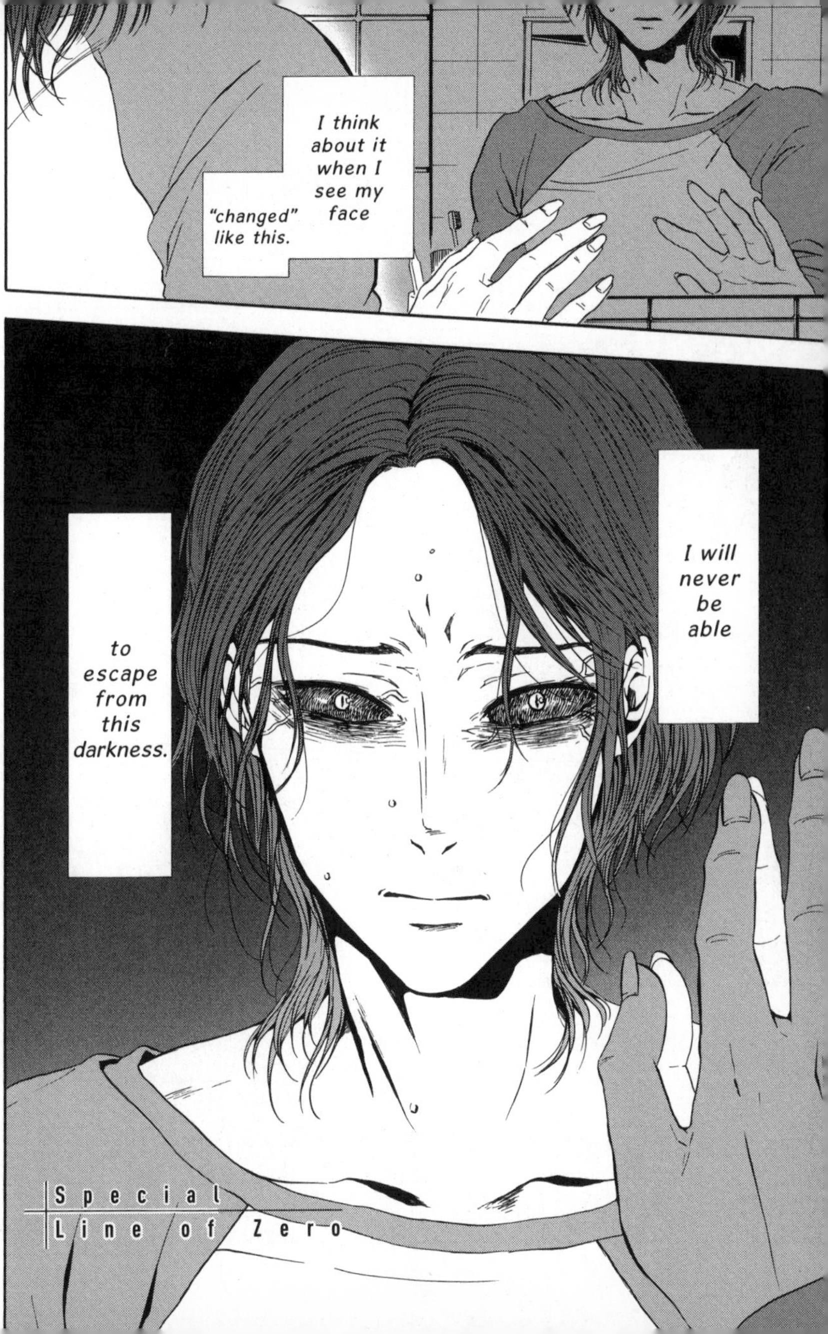
I think about it when I see my face
"changed" like this.
I will never be able
to escape from this darkness.
Special
Line of Zero

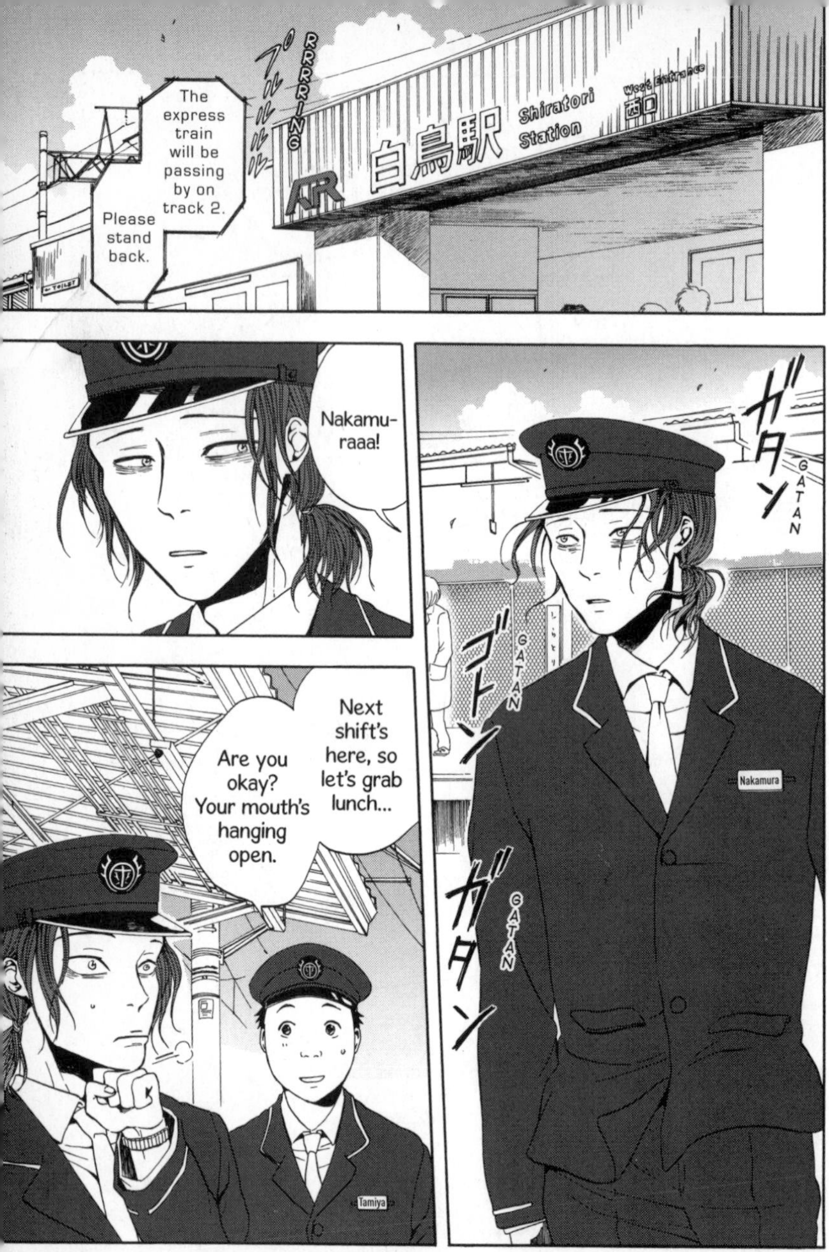
プルル
RRRRING
白鳥駅
Shiratori Station
West Entrance
西口
The express train will be passing by on track 2.
Please stand back.
ガタン
GATAN
ゴトン
GATAN
ガタン
GATAN
Nakamura
Nakamuraaa!
Next shift's here, so let's grab lunch...
Are you okay? Your mouth's hanging open.
Tamiya

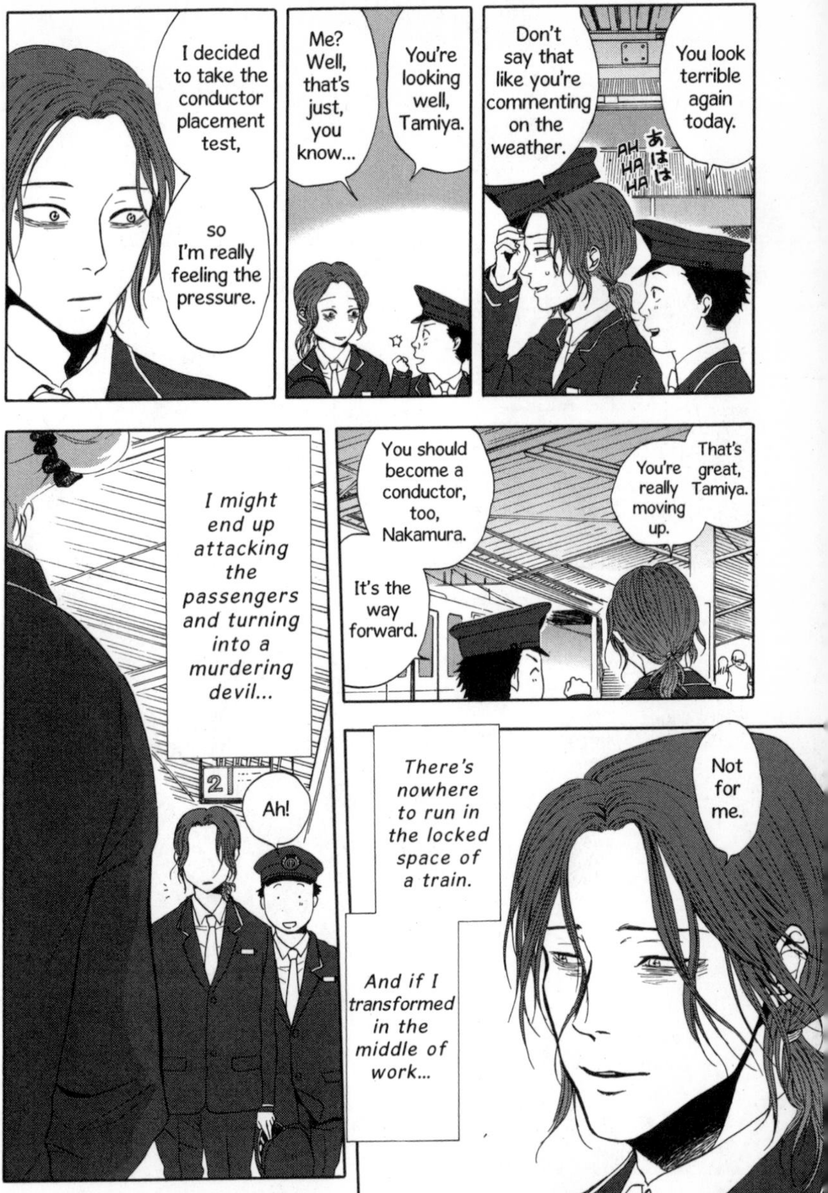
You look terrible again today.
AH HA HA
あはは
Don't say that like you're commenting on the weather.
You're looking well, Tamiya.
Me? Well, that's just, you know...
I decided to take the conductor placement test,
so I'm really feeling the pressure.
That's great, Tamiya.
You're really moving up.
You should become a conductor, too, Nakamura.
It's the way forward.
Not for me.
There's nowhere to run in the locked space of a train.
And if I transformed in the middle of work...
I might end up attacking the passengers and turning into a murdering devil...
Ah!

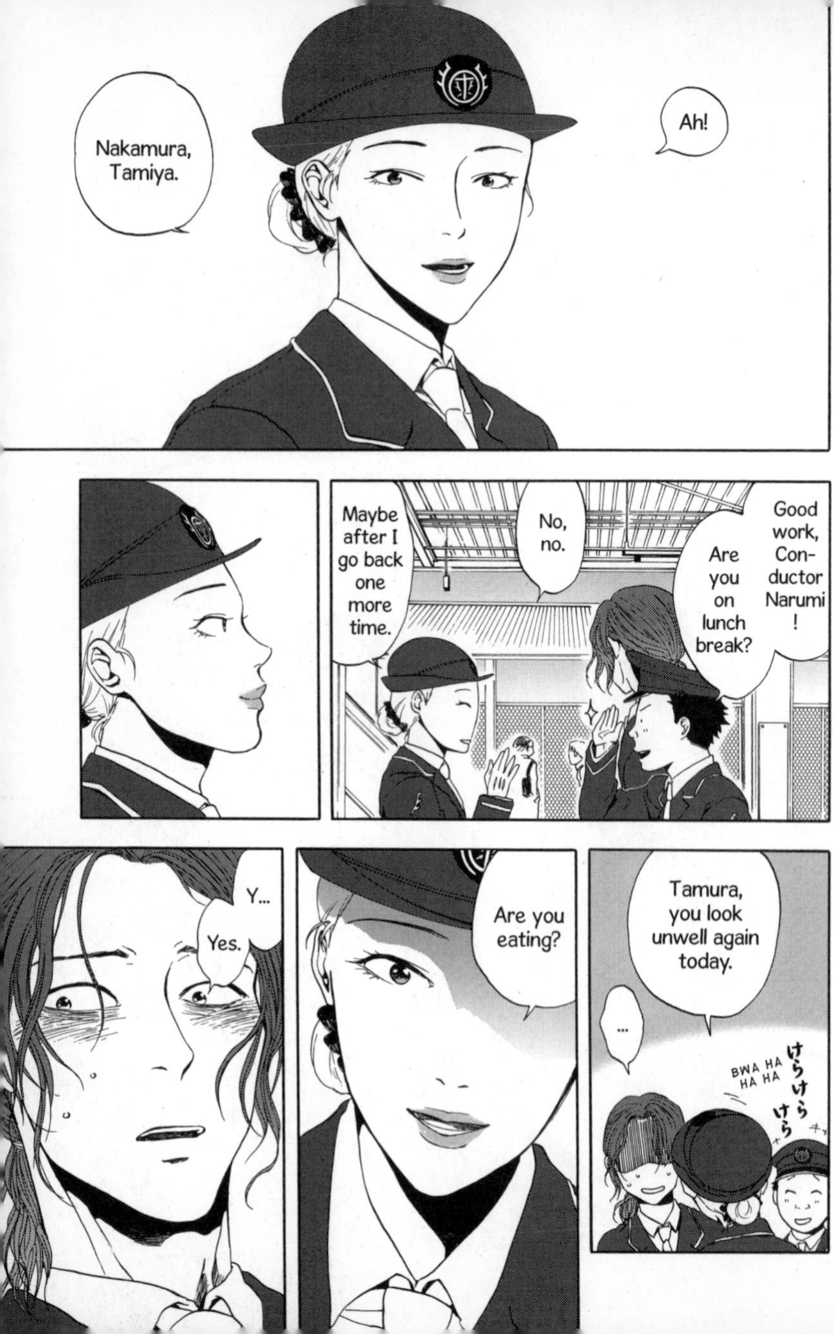
Ah!
Nakamura, Tamiya.
Good work, Conductor Narumi!
Are you on lunch break?
No, no.
Maybe after I go back one more time.
Tamura, you look unwell again today.
...
BWA HA HA HA
けらけらけら
Are you eating?
Y...
Yes.

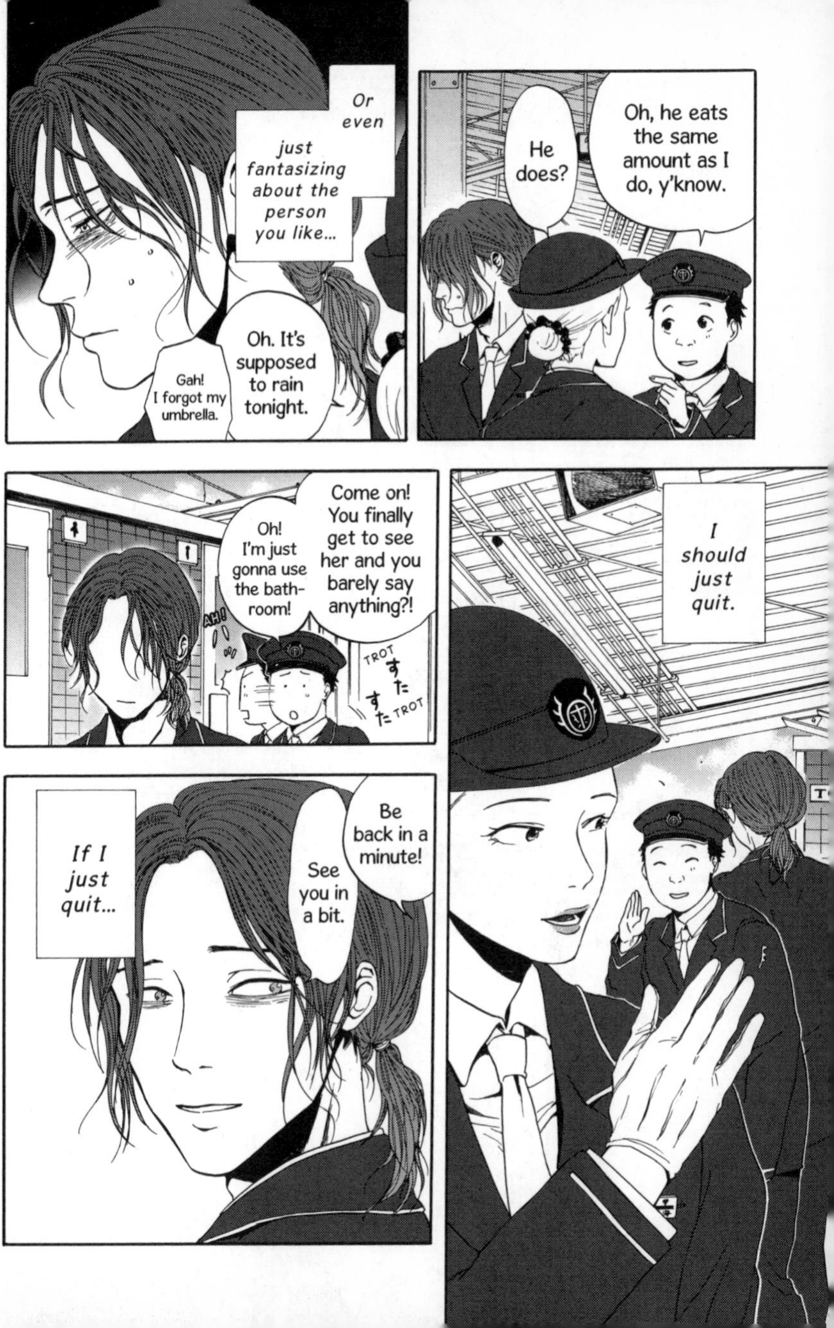
Oh, he eats the same amount as I do, y'know.
He does?
Or even just fantasizing about the person you like...
Oh. It's supposed to rain tonight.
Gah! I forgot my umbrella.
I should just quit.
Come on! You finally get to see her and you barely say anything?!
Oh! I'm just gonna use the bath-room!
AH!
TROT すた
すた TROT
Be back in a minute!
See you in a bit.
If I just quit...

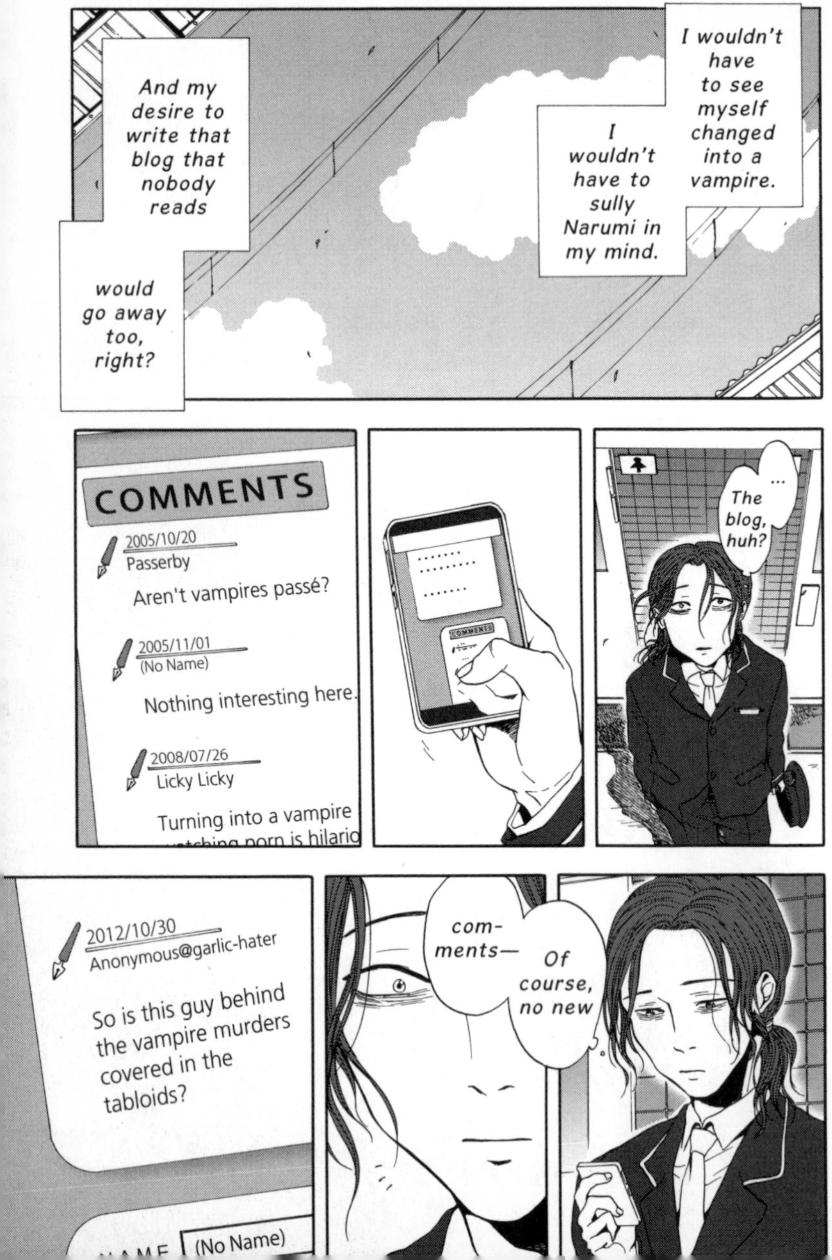
I wouldn't have to see myself changed into a vampire.
I wouldn't have to sully Narumi in my mind.
And my desire to write that blog that nobody reads
would go away too, right?
... The blog, huh?
COMMENTS
2005/10/20
Passerby
Aren't vampires passé?
2005/11/01
(No Name)
Nothing interesting here.
2008/07/26
Licky Licky
Turning into a vampire
Of course, no new
com- ments—
2012/10/30
Anonymous@garlic-hater
So is this guy behind the vampire murders covered in the tabloids?
(No Name)

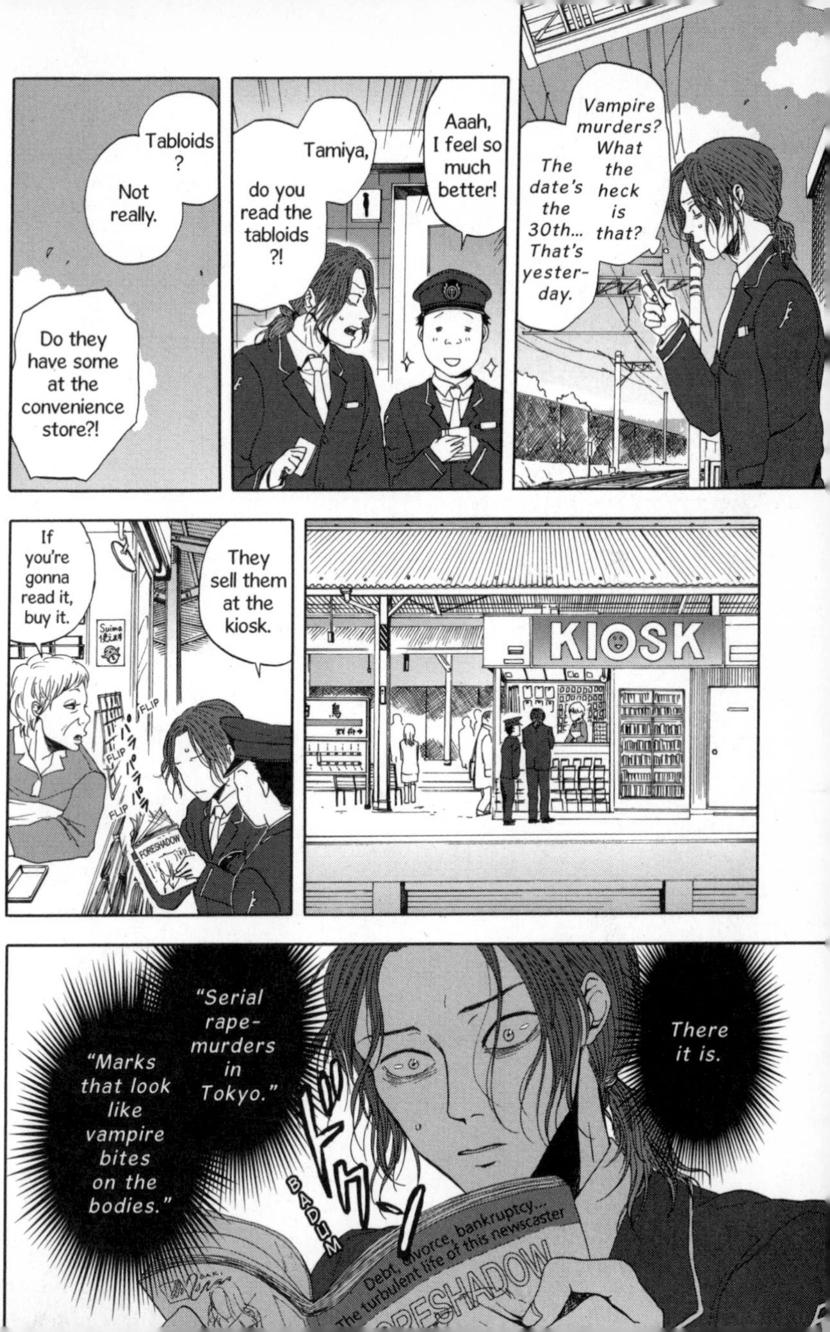
Vampire murders? What the heck is that?
The date's the 30th... That's yesterday.
Aaah, I feel so much better!
Tamiya,
do you read the tabloids?!
Tabloids?
Not really.
Do they have some at the convenience store?!
KIOSK
They sell them at the kiosk.
If you're gonna read it, buy it.
Suima
FLIP
FLIP
FLIP
FORESHADOW
There it is.
"Serial rape-murders in Tokyo."
"Marks that look like vampire bites on the bodies."
BADUM
Debt, divorce, bankruptcy... The turbulent life of this newscaster
FORESHADOW

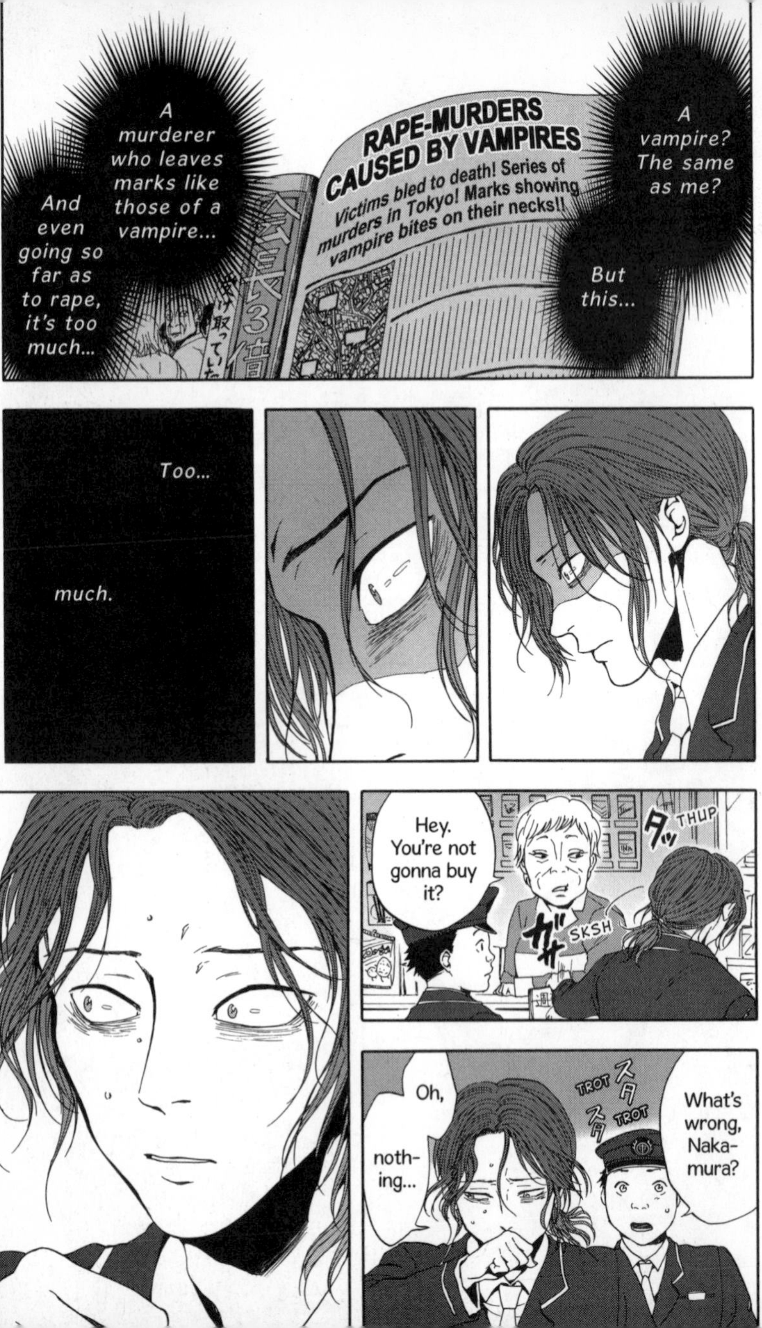
A vampire? The same as me?
But this...
RAPE-MURDERS CAUSED BY VAMPIRES
Victims bled to death! Series of murders in Tokyo! Marks showing vampire bites on their necks!!
A murderer who leaves marks like those of a vampire...
And even going so far as to rape, it's too much...
Too...
much.
THUP
Hey. You're not gonna buy it?
SKSH
What's wrong, Naka-mura?
TROT TROT
Oh, nothing...

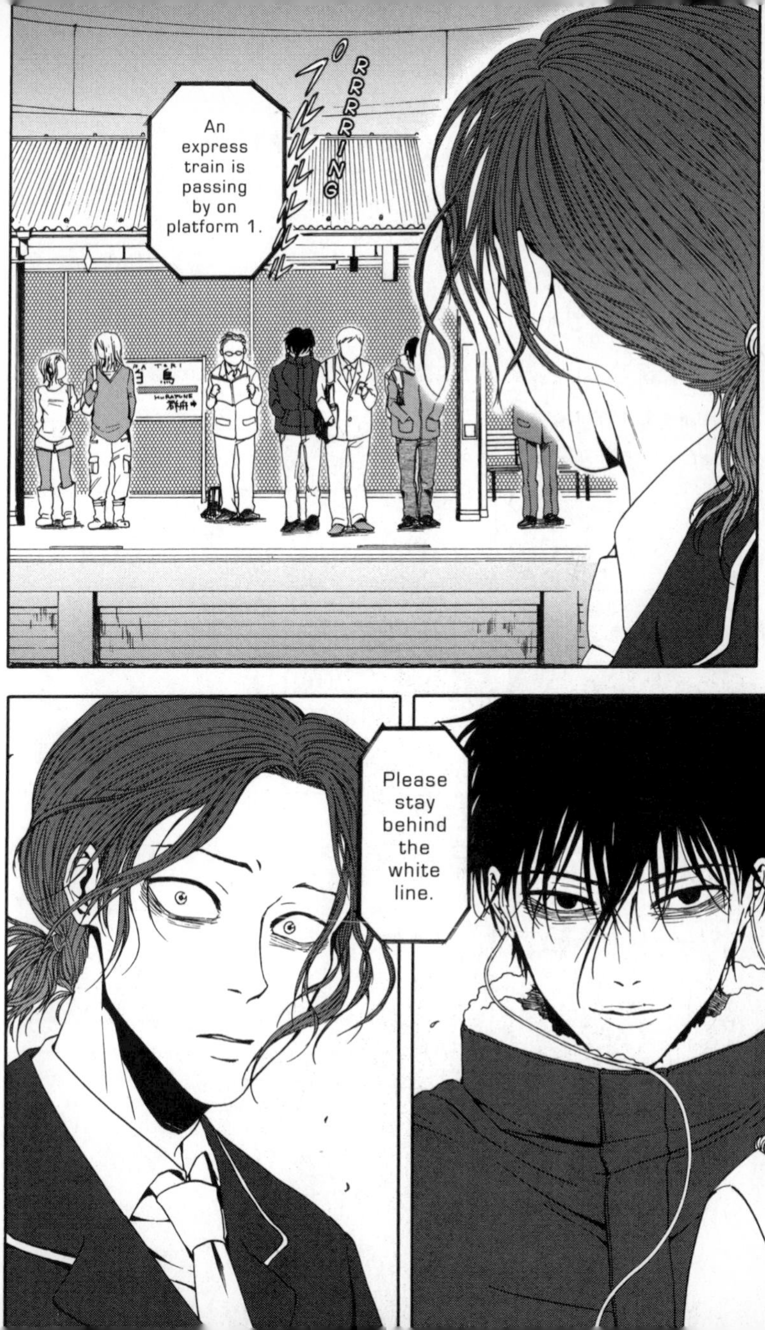
RRRRING
An express train is passing by on platform 1.
Please stay behind the white line.

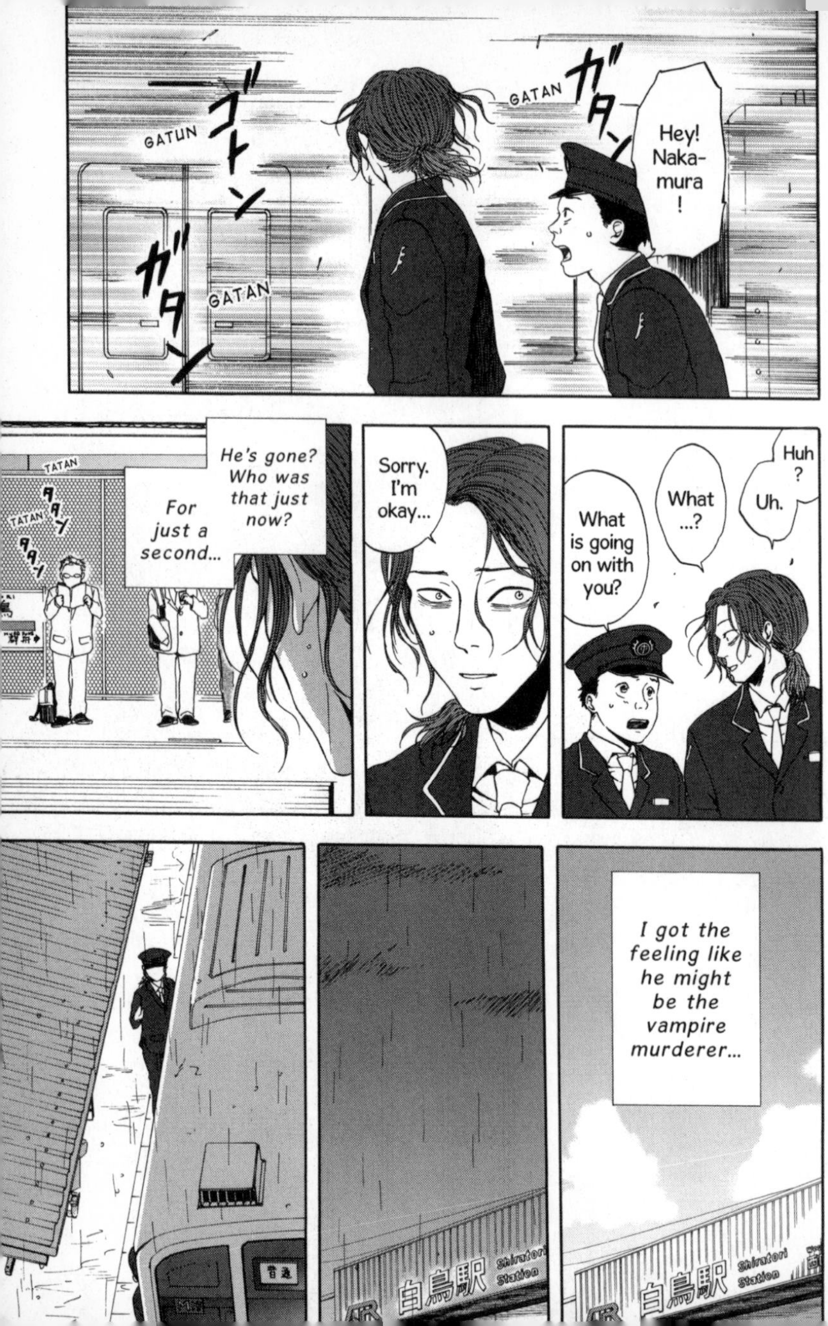
Hey! Nakamura!
GATAN
GATUN
GATAN
Huh?
Uh.
What...?
What is going on with you?
Sorry. I'm okay...
He's gone? Who was that just now?
For just a second...
TATAN
TATAN
I got the feeling like he might be the vampire murderer...
白鳥駅 Shiratori Station
白鳥駅 Shiratori Station

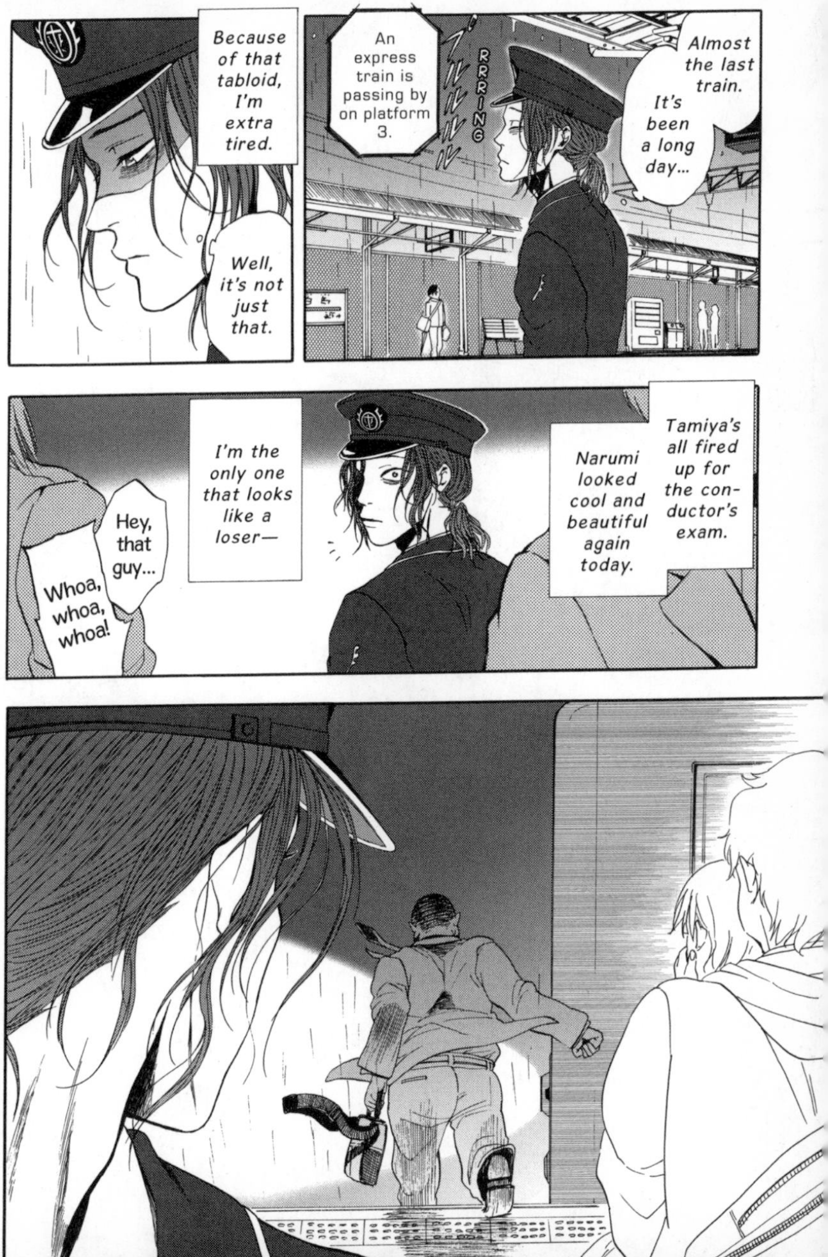
Almost the last train.
It's been a long day...
An express train is passing by on platform 3.
RRRING
Because of that tabloid, I'm extra tired.
Well, it's not just that.
Tamiya's all fired up for the conductor's exam.
Narumi looked cool and beautiful again today.
I'm the only one that looks like a loser—
Hey, that guy...
Whoa, whoa, whoa!